STEINBECK AND HIS CRITICS

STEINBECK
AND HIS
CRITICS

A RECORD OF TWENTY-FIVE YEARS

AN ANTHOLOGY
WITH INTRODUCTION
AND NOTES BY

E. W. TEDLOCK, JR. AND C. V. WICKER

UNIVERSITY OF NEW MEXICO PRESS, ALBUQUERQUE

PREFACE

THIS VOLUME brings together representative reviews and critical essays on the work of John Steinbeck. Thus it relieves the reader of the arduous task of seeking out this material in scattered books and periodicals, some of them difficult to obtain. We have undertaken to include all important attitudes toward Steinbeck and his writing.

We express here our grateful thanks to all the authors, editors, and publishers who have allowed us to reproduce copyrighted material. Specific credit for each of these permissions appears in the note to the appropriate article. Special thanks are due the Viking Press, Mr. Steinbeck's publisher. In addition to granting us the right to reprint Mr. Lewis Gannett's Introduction to The Portable Steinbeck, Viking has given permission for all quotations from Steinbeck's writings that occur in this book and for the quotation from Malcolm Cowley in our introductory essay. It is similarly through the courtesy of Viking that we are able to use the "Timshol symbol" on the binding.

To Mr. Steinbeck we extend special thanks for his interest in the book, for his permission to reprint four of his articles, and for his reading Peter Lisca's "A Literary Biography" and helping with factual details.

Mr. Lisca, now of the English faculty of the University of Washington, wrote his doctoral dissertation on Steinbeck's literary art. By virtue of that fact and of his forthcoming articles on Steinbeck in Publications of the Modern Language Association and Modern Fiction Studies, Mr. Lisca has become an expert on Steinbeck. We are indebted to him for the three hitherto unpublished essays he has supplied as well as for helpful suggestions.

For his editorial skill and for his consideration and care shown in many ways throughout the process of turning our manuscript into a book, we thank Mr. Roland F. Dickey of the University of New Mexico Press.

To many others who have assisted us we are also grateful. These include Donald Boone Smith, graduate student in English at the University of New Mexico, for making available to us the results of his bibliographical study of Steinbeck; Genevieve Porterfield, reference librarian in the University Library, and her assistant, Mrs. Paul Reigstad, for aid in securing material through interlibrary loan; Françoise Gourier of the Department of Modern and Classical Languages for translating the essay by Claude-Edmonde Magny; and Grace Whitlock and Joyce Hemsing for assistance in typing.

The University Faculty Research Committee granted us a sum of money which facilitated our work. We hereby express our gratitude.

E. W. T., Jr.
C. V. W.

Albuquerque
June, 1956

CONTENTS

IV. THE GRAPES OF WRATH

V. THE LATER WORK

A POSTSCRIPT FROM STEINBECK

INTRODUCTION

PERSPECTIVES
IN STEINBECK CRITICISM

A S THE READER of this book explores the divergent views of
John Steinbeck it contains, he may, at times, feel like a sober
late arriver at a cocktail party. If he sometimes feels that the guest of
honor, who is the general topic of conversation, has smilingly and somewhat contemptuously retired to a corner, and is perhaps having more
fun than anyone else, he will share fully the lighter side of the editors'
experience. We remind him now, as we did ourselves in the very midst
of confusion, that the comedy of critical disagreement is not peculiar
to any one author, and that it has the advantage of permitting the
reader to make up his own mind. That, finally, was the kind of book
we tried to create—one that would not be slanted for or against Steinbeck but would present the reader with the most representative, as
well as the best written, views. In this sense, the book can be said to
present almost as much a panorama of critical approaches as a survey
of Steinbeck's works.

Steinbeck's attitude toward critics and various other kinds of inquisi-
tors has a long, complex, and sometimes amusing history. His defenses
are sometimes in the spirit of the practical joke. For celebrity-hunting
editors hoping for a windfall, he keeps on hand a story called "The
Bettencourt" that is so grotesquely indecorous toward the Christmas
season that none of them would dare to print it even though he asks
no fee. In 1951 when the American Humanist Association asked a number of authors it expected to be sympathetic to place themselves among
six categories of humanism, Steinbeck's answer, listed by the Association among those "ambiguous or equivocal," was that he usually approached the question of philosophy "on tiptoe ready to run at the
first growl." He not only hinted thus at bitter experience, but went on
to claim not to have the slightest idea what his philosophy was or even
whether he had one. As a clincher, he cited as his favorite among the
evaluations of his philosophy one in which, he said, an erudite man
had proved that his whole body of thinking was stolen from an eight-
eenth-century Frenchman of whom he had never heard. If he had in
mind Woodburn Ross's "Earth and Stars,"* Steinbeck was mistaken
about the nature of its claims.

* Titles bearing an asterisk are reprinted in the present volume.

Recently, Steinbeck was invited by the editor of *The Colorado Quarterly* to comment on an exchange over the merit of *The Grapes of Wrath* between Bernard Bowron and Warren G. French. Bowron had engaged in a bit of literary assassination that might well have infuriated Steinbeck. He had accounted for the continuing popularity of *The Grapes of Wrath* by what he called Steinbeck's calculated exploitation of perennial formulae of the western story genre. The novel was not great art, but simply a triumph of literary engineering. Against Bowron's rather facetious approach, French had made a serious defense, pointing out that the genre of migration and search for refuge went very far back, and that Steinbeck's refugees are not primitivistic escapists. He concluded that "the whole psychological basis of the book is designed to frustrate the anticipation of the reader geared to smoothly-executed cliches." Steinbeck's reply to the invitation to comment on the controversy, "A Letter on Criticism," * is a masterpiece of refusal to become involved, even on the side of his champion. He engaged in barbed wit at the expense of criticism, and made a dedicated statement of the novelist's "lonely and difficult job," and a sweeping denial that the writer can learn anything at all from criticism.

Steinbeck's attitude toward criticism is further represented by his "Critics, Critics, Burning Bright" * and "Critics—from a Writer's Viewpoint." * The first is a justification of his choice of theme in the play "Burning Bright," which received very rough critical handling; an explanation of the means, both structural and linguistic, he employed to universalize the theme, and of the problems discovered and corrected during testing on the road; and an expression of the hope that the play would be better understood by unfriendly critics after the inevitable time lag between custom and innovation had been overcome. In the second article, published after his reconciliation with *The Saturday Review*, which had attacked him among others for presenting too dark a picture of human nature, and after his assumption of a position as one of the Editors-at-Large, he speaks of the convention that a writer should never answer a critic, cites an example of his own forced abstinence that apparently involved "Burning Bright," and then has his say in general terms by pointing out that the critic is a man interested in his own career and consequently prone to warp things in favor of his own cleverness, and that criticism as well as fiction is an expression of the good or bad nature of the critic.

One thing seems clear. Despite Steinbeck's deep-seated mistrust of the critic and the intellectualism the critic represents, and despite his protestations of modest intentions in his work and of abysmal ignorance of ideas, he is a complex man and a well-read one, and his stories are not merely the simple fables of a naïve, folksy storyteller. This can be illustrated from the history of *East of Eden*, for which he kept a running journal of thoughts and plans on the verso of the sheets of the handwritten draft. As the dedication of the novel to Pascal Covici indicates, Steinbeck had undergone considerable struggle with the problem of good and evil in human experience, as well as "the pleasure of design" and "the indescribable joy of creation." The record of this struggle he placed in a box on the cover of which he had carved the Timshel symbol† that stands at the center of the question of ethical choice in the novel. Interpreted as "Thou mayest," it gave hope to what Steinbeck described as "the permanent war between wisdom and ignorance, light and darkness—good and evil."

I. Man and Career

Steinbeck has been reticent about his life, though occasionally he has written semi-autobiographical sketches having to do with the origins and intentions of his work, like "My Short Novels."* A good deal of early biography, with some inaccuracies, appeared in 1939 in Harry T. Moore's pioneer book, *The Novels of John Steinbeck*. For some time now there has been a need for a detailed account of what may be called "the literary life," the events directly related to the works, as distinct from the private life Steinbeck understandably guards. Peter Lisca's "John Steinbeck: A Literary Biography," written especially for this anthology, surveys the career to 1955, and has been checked for accuracy of fact by Steinbeck and his wife. Of particular interest is the information Lisca gained through his examination of unpublished correspondence with agent and publisher. Those who have sought the key to Steinbeck's world in his combination of biological theory and

---

† Steinbeck's design of the Timshel symbol was adapted for the cover of this book from a photograph courteously supplied by the Viking Press, Mr. Steinbeck's publisher. It consists of the four consonants in the Hebrew word, the vowels being unwritten, as is the Hebrew custom. The carving is well done; the Hebrew characters are quite faithfully rendered. It may be remarked that the word is a symbol only in the sense that Mr. Steinbeck chose to consider it one in the context of *East of Eden*. As has been said above, the "symbol" is central to the meaning of the whole novel, but on pp. 266-72 and 298-309 it is particularly treated.

Writing later ("The Mail I've Seen," *Saturday Review*, August 4, 1956, p. 16), Mr. Steinbeck said, "In 'East of Eden' I made an error in the spelling of Timshol. I spelled it Timshel. I have had over a hundred letters pointing out my mistake, and many of them from profound scholars of Hebrew."

The "misspelled" vowel has the sound of *aw* in the English word *law*; hence *timshawl* would be an even more accurate transliteration than *timshol*.

the philosophy of non-teleological or "is" thinking‡ in *Sea of Cortez*, will be interested in the early beginnings of his experience with marine biology. To some he may well appear as a more intensely dedicated man than they suspected, especially in light of the experience and work that went into *The Grapes of Wrath* and of the meaning of that book to the dispossessed people most intimately involved in its story.

Lewis Gannett's "John Steinbeck's Way of Writing" * traces Steinbeck's personal reactions to the problems of his work and to critical and public response to it in his correspondence with his agency from 1930 to about 1945. Steinbeck's fear of popularity amounted almost to a phobia and is extremely ironic in view of the tendency of some critics to regard him as a sentimental, popular writer. The simultaneous attitude of indifference toward critics seems more assumed than real, especially in the light of his clear, though still masked, sensitivity later. *Tortilla Flat* seems to have been the critical point in the development of Steinbeck's attitudes. The failure of reviewers to see its Arthurian framework was characteristic of their early failure to see that he was more than a "primitive" or a whimsical humorist. His wish to have *In Dubious Battle* printed next seems to have been an effort both to avoid the popularity that had ruined everyone he knew and to prevent the early formation of the myth that he was a humorist. There seems to be a connection between his fear of tags and the versatility that has been both praised and blamed, since the shifts from book to book that result from Steinbeck's way of tackling new artistic problems also have the effect of feinting the enemy out of position. Though it seems certain that Steinbeck distinguishes between critical popularity and the kind that means readers, there is some irony in the fact that at least a certain amount of the latter kind has been a defense for him: he came eventually to answer criticism by pointing to the solid fact of the sale of his books.

A very unfriendly view of Steinbeck's attitude toward publicity is expressed in Margaret Marshall's "Writers in the Wilderness: I. John Steinbeck" in *The Nation*, November 25, 1939. Miss Marshall views his more aggressive protests as signs of immaturity. They exhibit the American artist's inability to cope with an indigenous anti-intellectualism and an emphasis on money success. The result is expatriation or romantic escape, and Steinbeck's escape, she maintains, was manifested

‡ "Is" thinking apparently is Steinbeck's own attempt to make the technical term *non-teleological* more meaningful to his readers. Broadly what Steinbeck means is a way of thinking about life that, by concerning itself with what *is*, not with the questions of why or what *should be*, avoids the false judgments and exclusions of a squeamish and snobbish morality and achieves love of life through acceptance.

in the pellucid, romantic style of the early work. Although *The Grapes of Wrath* represents an advance from this, Steinbeck's facility is still greater than his understanding of social forces and character. Miss Marshall's ambitious socio-critical thesis is more dogmatically and sweepingly applied than are the assumptions of the "social" critics represented in this book, and she does not support it by close scrutiny of the works.

In 1938, T. K. Whipple had questioned Steinbeck's style in "Steinbeck: Through a Glass Though Brightly," an essay collected in *Study Out the Land* in 1943. Writing before *The Grapes of Wrath* was published, Whipple found that only *In Dubious Battle* and the last four stories of *The Long Valley* had escaped an enchantment of style that took the sting out of reality and made it possible for the reader to take an uninvolved and unresponsible view of suffering and violence. For Whipple this probably accounted for Steinbeck's popularity. Both Margaret Marshall's and Whipple's views, though they differ basically in their underlying premises and attitudes, seem to belong to the insistence on social consciousness that was at its height in the Thirties. The involved question of artistic detachment or commitment has become acute again through the events of World War II. The "esthetic" critic, of course, has always argued for a detachment intrinsic to the very nature of art. Gannett's essay shows Steinbeck struggling for an unegotistical view that would raise *The Grapes of Wrath* above the level of easy partisanship.

An elaborate theory that Steinbeck's growth can be measured by his departure from a bookish manner in the early work to a command of common speech that is perfected in *The Grapes of Wrath*, is advanced by Barker Fairley's "John Steinbeck and the Coming Literature," *The Sewanee Review*, April-June, 1942. Since Fairley identifies the use of common speech with sympathy for those who use it, and feels that Steinbeck begins to find himself in a form of socialism, his essay too is in the "social" school of criticism. He seems to achieve a real insight into the nature of Steinbeck's style when he calls it poetic rather than naturalistic, and suited to the development of an epic form of the novel. Yet his conception of the poetic style is clearly determined by his championship of sympathy for the underdog and by his identification of the epic with the folk.

In *The Novels of John Steinbeck* (1939), Harry T. Moore mentions a Steinbeck habit of playing recorded classical music while he is writing, and suggests an influence on the rhythm and structure of his work. Malcolm Cowley's description of Steinbeck's working methods in *The Literary Situation* controverts any notion of careless facility, and points up Steinbeck's concern with a spoken prose, a concern that may be linked to his strong interest in the play or the novel-play.

> John Steinbeck has a complicated method: first he thinks about a novel for months or even a year until it is clear in his head, then early one morning he starts the first chapter in longhand. At the end of the day's work he dictates from the manuscript into a machine, changing as he goes; dictation is an essential part of the process, because what he writes is a spoken prose. His secretary transcribes the record and Steinbeck revises her transcript. At the end of the novel, the whole manuscript is copied and revised once more; sometimes it has to be copied twice before it is ready for the printer.

II.   Artist and Thinker

The majority of Steinbeck's critics are chiefly interested in the philosophy implicit in his fiction and the philosophy explicitly stated in *Sea of Cortez* (1941). Perhaps this was inevitable for a writer who avowed a strong interest in biological naturalism and whose work was at times closely involved in the social crises of the Twenties and Thirties. *In Dubious Battle* dealt with ideologies and the strike among the depressed California agricultural workers, and *The Grapes of Wrath*, as everyone knows, with the dispossessed people of the Dust Bowl and their migration to a Promised Land that did not exactly welcome them wholeheartedly. Treatment of such subjects was bound to tempt a categorizing enmity or friendship from all sides, liberal, humanist, Marxist, Catholic, reactionary and conservative. Once such a pattern of approach was set, it evidently became hard to avoid. The labeling that Steinbeck feared set in with a vengeance. It is interesting to see that he has received relatively little attention from the so-called new criticism, though he has been briefly cited by Blackmur and by Kenneth Burke, the latter of whom in *The Philosophy of Literary Form* noted the function of the turtle in *The Grapes of Wrath* as a kind of "externalizing vessel or 'symbol' " tying together Tom, Casy, and the plot. On the whole, Steinbeck has not received nearly as much attention by explicators of text, symbol, and structure as Faulkner and Hemingway have. Despite Steinbeck's feeling that such approaches are rather like taxonomy, the work of Peter Lisca and of other young critics may augur well for more detached appreciation of Steinbeck and the complex facets of his art.

Nevertheless, the essays reprinted here do, on the whole, tend to evaluate Steinbeck by the extent to which his philosophy is compatible with the beliefs of the critics. In a sense, most of them have ideological axes to grind, though this does not mean that some do not permit Steinbeck deviations without utterly condemning him. And after all there is something to be said for a criticism that tries to hold writers responsible to the best the critic knows; the writer does have a responsibility to society. On the other hand, his whole individuality depends to a large extent on the freedom that society allows him. Some of the critics seem much too dogmatic, even to the extent at times of not being able to distinguish between art and propaganda, as Steinbeck certainly tried to do.

In 1942, Maxwell Geismar could predicate a whole book, *Writers in Crisis*, on the thesis that social consciousness was essential to good literature. Geismar's chapter on Steinbeck stretches the career on a framework of developing awareness of social problems and involvement in them. He takes the ironic view that Steinbeck arrived at awareness just as the bubble of the Twenties broke, so that his success depended on social failure. Surprisingly he regards *The Pastures of Heaven* (1932) as perhaps Steinbeck's finest novel and reads it as concerned with a tragic curse which the later novels seek to define and escape. In 1929, *Cup of Gold* had contained a premature attempt to answer the question of the curse with a veiled form of the American success myth. *To a God Unknown*, Geismar says, retrogressed from this individualistic, piratical answer to the fallacious primitive thinking of such writers as D. H. Lawrence, Jean Giono, and Sherwood Anderson. Yet Steinbeck had also gained by discarding egocentric individualism for even this odd identification of the individual with his world. In *Tortilla Flat* the paisanos had lacked all the marks of "American progress," and Steinbeck had come close to an illuminating comparison of social values when he had related the subtle but quite formalized code of the paisanos to the ethics of the "power age." Though trapped by a sentimental concept of poverty, he had begun to introduce himself to a new world in which he would "assume the responsibilities of his craft in an age of crisis."

Geismar sees *Of Mice and Men* as flawed by the earlier tendencies to sentimentality and sadism, but also as measuring the inadequacy of American civilization and creating in the simple, "bourgeois," and even banal concept of the outcasts' home a poignant reality that must be accepted. *In Dubious Battle* also reveals Steinbeck's "popularizing gift," or, as Geismar puts it elsewhere, "an urbanity of psyche bought a little easily"; yet there is a final uneasiness and sense of bleak misery that gives the novel its strength. Steinbeck's "repressed realism" has triumphed over his "romantic serenity." As for *The Grapes of Wrath*, "the Joads emerge as idealized in their own way as those smooth personages who dwell in the pages of *The Saturday Evening Post*," and the novel often represents "the dubious nuptials of *Tobacco Road* with *The Ladies' Home Journal*"; yet force and sincerity break through these moulds of presentation. The extent of Geismar's praise can perhaps be measured by his pointless paradox: " 'The Grapes of Wrath' is not at all Steinbeck's best novel. But it is, all in all, his biggest."

It is clear that Geismar's criticism is extremely limited by its central criterion that an author's social concern must be compatible with his own. Social consciousness means roughly having the same enemies as the liberal, and even radical, intelligentsia of the times. Geismar concludes that Steinbeck came to realize that "our true happiness must derive, not through any mystical and mythical freedom from society, but through making our society genuinely free." He sees Steinbeck as closer to his audience than any other comparable writer because he applies typical American sentiment to the relatively fresh field of social welfare. The traits in him which "fluster the critics are those which endear him to mankind." Geismar is so consistently facetious about Steinbeck's popularity that it is hard to tell just how qualified his praise is. He ends by saying that if *The Grapes of Wrath* evolves a new American success story, "it is not inconceivable that in the end the United States will bring about its great sweeping social changes as a new sort of popular fashion." In the latter part of this statement there is the possibility of a shrewd hit, since some sociologists, for example David Riesman in *The Lonely Crowd*, think this is what has happened in the 1950's.

At the time of *In Dubious Battle* (1936), Steinbeck remarked in a letter to his agents that Burton Rascoe was one of only two reviewers who had discovered that the book was a novel, not a tract. Much of Rascoe's essay, "John Steinbeck," * is devoted to the success of *Of Mice and Men* as a play. Unlike a good many critics, he treats the play in terms of the writing problems that had to be solved and finds it comparable in manner and stature to Sophoclean tragedy. In preferring Steinbeck to the hard-boiled writers who imitate Hemingway, he raises the question of sentimentality that has haunted a good deal of Steinbeck criticism. What to one critic has been true compassion and a much-needed affirmation of man's dignity has to another been evidence of lack of theological soundness, as in Kennedy's "John Steinbeck: Life Affirmed and Dissolved," * and to still another evidence of capitulation to popular demands.

Perhaps the most interesting part of Rascoe's essay is his use of conversations with Steinbeck to try to get at the writer's philosophy. Whether or not Steinbeck abhors the tag "mystic," such critics as

Woodburn Ross argue cogently for a mystic vein in his work. As for his deep concern with the problem of Good and Evil and with the possibility of treating them as phenomena in life rather than conventionally, the essays in this book are ranged for and against Steinbeck's moral sense. The puzzlement over Steinbeck's metaphysics and ethics was compounded by the publication of Sea of Cortez (1941) with its emphasis on the value of "is" thinking as a lesson learned from biology. While the explicit statements of his philosophy gave the critics more frame of reference than they had before, the resultant reinterpretations of his fiction were not at all in agreement. Sometimes they found Steinbeck lacking in the profound concern with Good and Evil that Rascoe was sure of. If human life merely reflected the amoral drives studied by biology, Good and Evil were either beside the point or Steinbeck had involved himself in a confusion of ideas and a rather desperate personal struggle as the events leading to World War II demanded moral action of him. For this problem we have brought together here the essays by Hyman, Bracher, Ross, and Nevius, the first of these being particularly concerned with the crisis of the war.

Apparently no critic has followed up very thoroughly Rascoe's suggestion of Steinbeck's belief in will, thought, and emotion as immediate, dynamic, and kinetic—effective without the employment of physical means. The sin of hubris and its consequences may be related to the need of human understanding that is implied in The Grapes of Wrath to the point of constituting a warning. Rascoe's idea that in Of Mice and Men Steinbeck was expounding "the complete nonmorality of Nature in her physical aspects and of the morality of expediency that must necessarily arise from Nature's blundering," seems to touch on the influence of scientific objectivity on Steinbeck's thinking.

In "John Steinbeck: Journeyman Artist"* Joseph Warren Beach, like other critics, notes the versatility of Steinbeck's talent, but instead of being baffled into accusations of immaturity or inconsistency, as some critics have been, he discusses the fiction up to The Grapes of Wrath in terms of Steinbeck's intentions and special subjects. He is not disturbed to find Steinbeck something more than an objective realist. And Steinbeck's style suggests to him no mellifluous evasion of responsibility, as at least one critic has thought, but is remarkable for its feeling for rhythm and right English idiom. Altogether his method is to compare Steinbeck's characteristics with those of a broad range of literary accomplishments and to grant him a place when he measures up, rather than to judge the correctness of his position regarding contemporary urgencies and controversies. Beach regards Steinbeck as the artist that Steinbeck has felt it necessary to insist he is. At the same time, Beach suggests that Steinbeck himself confuses art and life in his vehement post-publication defense of the people of *Tortilla Flat*. Obviously the whole question of the involvement of the novel with life has been particularly thorny for both Steinbeck and his critics.

Another sympathetic approach through literary tradition is George Snell's chapter on Steinbeck in *The Shapers of American Fiction: 1798-1947*. Snell sees Steinbeck's strengths and weaknesses as paralleling those of Dickens: an enormous gift of story-telling, catholicity of sympathy and a "common touch," ease of character creation through types rather than individuals, love of exaggeration and a resulting humor, and a basic sentimentalism which results in the gravest weakness of both Dickens and Steinbeck. Like Beach, Snell has much good to say of the early books. Particularly acute is his remarking that it was clear from the first that Steinbeck would never be a literary naturalist despite his interest in biology. Snell's judgments on *The Moon Is Down* and *Cannery Row* are interesting. The first novel has all the faults imputed to Steinbeck—sentimentalism, exaggeration, too neat plotting. The latter is a return to Steinbeck's most satisfactory manner, the great distinction and real value of which "lie in the warm humanity suffusing it, and the humor—Dickensian, but with twentieth-century frankness." In 1947 Snell thought that Steinbeck still gave promise of being "our most gifted all-round novelist." The danger for him lay in pushing the technique of whimsy so far that it would please neither the whimsical nor the tough-minded.

Frederic Ives Carpenter's "John Steinbeck: American Dreamer," * which places Steinbeck in a native American social tradition, should be read with his "The Philosophical Joads," * which places *The Grapes of Wrath* in the tradition of Emerson, Whitman, and William James. The debate over the nature and origin of Steinbeck's social views has been as various as that over his morality and his philosophy in general. Marxist critics have viewed him with mixed feelings, as Edwin Burgum does in "The Sensibility of John Steinbeck"* or as Harry Slochower does in his chapter on Steinbeck in *No Voice is Wholly Lost*. Defenders of the *status quo* in Oklahoma and California were particularly virulent in their attacks on *The Grapes of Wrath*, as reported in Shockley's "The Reception of *The Grapes of Wrath* in Oklahoma" * and as recorded in the press at the time.

Carpenter finds in Steinbeck's first eight books a consistent and developing concern with an American dream that has evolved through stages of conquest, of escape, and of settlement and ownership—all vitiated by some possessive egotism—to a modern reinterpretation of the dream. A new freedom of opportunity is gained by integrating the traditional democratic dream with reality. In this essay Carpenter does not make as clear as he does in "The Philosophical Joads" his conception of the American tradition used by Steinbeck; but his reading of Steinbeck's handling of the Communist dream in *In Dubious Battle* as imperfect because it is a product of partial vision and of hate makes it clear that his social interpretation of the novels does not follow the Marxist pattern. His emphasis can be seen as part of the upsurge of social consciousness among intellectuals during the Thirties. But it was during another kind of crisis, political rather than economic, during the Forties, that intellectuals turned once more to American history for a usable past.

Another discovery of liberal American tradition in Steinbeck is Floyd Stovall's discussion of him in *American Idealism* (1943). Stovall finds Steinbeck's social philosophy to be essentially that of Whitman, Emerson, and Jefferson. Though the latter, he says, would place more emphasis on the individual as compared with the group, and would stress moral values more than Steinbeck seems to do, Steinbeck and they are "all at one in their faith in man's power to rise above circumstances and advance towards the ideal." It is interesting to note that Stovall, unlike most critics, regards *The Moon Is Down* as Steinbeck's most brilliant achievement, "a further proof of his ability to adapt his genius to the mood of the moment without sacrificing the permanent values of his art." Its emphasis on spiritual qualities, rather than social and economic problems, is, to Stovall, an affirmation of Steinbeck's faith in the dignity and worth of human nature.

Lincoln Gibbs' "John Steinbeck: Moralist" * is one of the few essays to handle the question of the morality of Steinbeck's fiction without finally revealing that the critic has some institutional axe to grind. That is, he does not approach the problem with rigid ideological criteria, either religious or social. If his approach can be labeled at all, it is apparently that of the eclectic humanist equipped with considerable knowledge of the theory and history of the relationship of literature to life. Gibbs' treatment of *Tortilla Flat* recognizes the problem that troubles Beach and others—that Steinbeck's angry preface to the second edition forced the critics to take seriously a book they would otherwise have treated as a gay satire on respectability. His sweeping defense of the paisanos placed Steinbeck in the category of moralist. Gibbs' comments on the naturalism Steinbeck brought to the defense of the paisanos may be compared with the essays devoted to the effects of Steinbeck's interest in biology on his philosophy. Gibbs is one of the first Steinbeck critics to argue that successful adaptation to environment, or mere survival value, is not enough for human beings. Nor is an ethic of impulsive kindness. Gibbs' misgivings about the range of Steinbeck's philosophy are broadly representative of the least prejudiced and least condemnatory of the critics who share them. There may be a shrewd hit at the *épater le bourgeois* tendency in modern literature in Gibbs' saying that Steinbeck's revulsion against prudery and hypocrisy carries him to violent extremes. He anticipates critics who had the advantage of Steinbeck's naturalistic speculations in *Sea of Cortez* in saying that sexual license in Steinbeck's work is supported by a nature mysticism and a fantastic humanism so that his immoralities are not merely incidental or merely the extreme product of revulsion but are grounded in a comprehensive philosophy, or perhaps in two philosophies. Gibbs is not the last critic to call this philosophy confused and immature. Yet, taking his stand on a distinction between a writer's philosophy and his art, he concludes that Steinbeck's human sympathies and artist's perception are different from and superior to his philosophic confusion. Steinbeck's interest in the human worth of the underdog or the obscure person has been a real service to a democracy worshiping at the shrine of a plutocratic, slick image of efficiency. While Gibbs occasionally uses such terms as *communism* and *class conflict*, he is free of ideological bias and jargon. In substantiating the importance of a sense of fraternity stemming from a non-Marxist tradition, he refers to Tolstoi and quotes Howells. His humanistic conclusion is that Steinbeck's writing extends our knowledge of men beyond the expedient range of experience and makes for a fuller realization of democracy.

A sharp attack on Steinbeck's morality is to be found in Donald Weeks' "Steinbeck Against Steinbeck" in *The Pacific Spectator*, Autumn, 1947. For Weeks there is not much difference between Steinbeck's defense of the paisanos in the preface to the second edition of *Tortilla Flat* and "denying that grandmother is a drunkard because she's so nice to the kids." His association with Dr. Edward Ricketts, the biologist, may have produced the philosophy of *Sea of Cortez*, a philosophy which encouraged Steinbeck to rationalize his sentimentality, that is, to derive from the idea that a "thing is because it is" justification for a sentimental handling of the incompetent and the maladjusted. For Weeks, this is the philosophy of the *wino*, for a writer "can get just as tight with a typewriter as with alcohol," and when Steinbeck gets sentimental, "life becomes warm, beautiful, satisfying." Since the sentimentalist tends to limit his range of expression to absolutes, Steinbeck turns for contrast to cruelty and dirt. His alternation of blacks and whites is like the flicker of a primitive movie. The trouble may lie in the fact that "there is now no critic intimate with Steinbeck, no one to challenge the writer's best." As for Steinbeck's handling of sex, he is, in using it to criticize middle-class morality, "fighting a battle already won and endangering the victory by confusing the issue." Here Weeks may be speaking of a battle won for the sophisticated reader but not yet won in our culture at large.

Ten years before Weeks' attack, Edmund C. Richards had found it possible to take exactly the opposite view in his "The Challenge of John Steinbeck" in *The North American Review*, Summer, 1937. For Richards, not to appreciate *Tortilla Flat* was to be an incurable barbarian. Since Steinbeck was primarily a masculine writer in a contemporary culture in which the cultivated mind was undoubtedly feminine, he had stimulated the masculine mind by "his fearless grappling with ideas and human passions as well as sacred taboos." His books were distinguished by a maturity that went counter to the romantic adolescence of much American thinking and many American books. Yet his revolt against puritanism was not without religion, "a kind of mysticism which is not the less impressive because it is as naturalistic as his ethics." Richards' encomium ranged from saying that *Tortilla Flat, In Dubious Battle,* and *Of Mice and Men* had made "an enviable place for themselves among the few imaginative pieces today," to pointing out that, contrary to the impression that might be given by some of Steinbeck's books, his culture was not negligible, and he had gone deeply into philosophy as well as science. *Of Mice and Men* was a work of art so nearly perfect that it was "a work of supererogation to heap up adjectives about it." Since a woman was the destructive force in it, it was a "daring affront to America's pet piety—the sanctity of woman"—that only a great prose artist could have carried off. It is ironic that ten years later, Richards' great enemies—Victorianism, gentility, or puritanism—could seem dead to Weeks.

Edwin Berry Burgum's approach in "The Sensibility of John Steinbeck" * is apparently Marxist—that is, it seems to represent a fairly systematic application of Marxist criteria of the proper attitude toward economic and moral problems. Here in a different perspective are the familiar Steinbeck problems: the technical versatility with its changes of tone and genre, the apparent sanction of moral decadence, the breadth of sympathy that goes so far as to seem at times sentimental or perverse, *The Grapes of Wrath* as the peak of achievement, and the failure of *The Moon Is Down*.

Here the middle class is under attack from a new angle. To Burgum, Steinbeck himself reflects the hesitancies and confusions of the petty bourgeoisie in its new interest in the proletariat. The development of his fiction is not a matter of interest in technique, as Steinbeck would sometimes have it, of an evolving American dream as Carpenter would have it, of a combination of nature mysticism and fantastic humanism as Gibbs would have it, or of a confusion of scientific "is" thinking with compassion and values as some of the essayists on Steinbeck's interest in biology would have it. The reason for Steinbeck's oscillations from one book to another is a personal confusion reflecting, and by implication resulting from, the instability of our society.

For Burgum, Steinbeck's career is essentially a succession of achievements of and lapses from the right social concerns and attitudes. In the controversy over *Tortilla Flat*, he takes the view that Steinbeck's amused tolerance of ignorance, poverty, and depravity represents a decadence that he recovered from in the social novels, though even in them the elements composing the decadence are present. The question of the sociological meaning in *Of Mice and Men* and the possibility of sympathy for the half-wit Lennie receives a strict dichotomizing. While the tensions of the novel, Burgum says, are set up by the nature of capitalism, to find Lennie a symbol of the proletariat would render confidence in the working class absurd.

Only *The Grapes of Wrath* merges Steinbeck's extremes in such a way as to remove the taint of degeneration. Burgum tends to view it pragmatically, in terms of its making the sophisticated reader more tolerant of a broader social conception of the novel and making the man in the street improve his esthetic insight while satisfying his practical demands. Its social enlightenment should serve as a pattern for world movements for independence. After this peak, Steinbeck failed in *The Moon Is Down* to achieve a still more comprehensive social awareness because he set up a vague kind of aristocratic government and tended to idealize the Junker general. Afterward, in *Cannery Row*, he lapsed into an amiable superficiality like that of *Tortilla Flat*.

The question of Steinbeck's ideological alignment arose primarily in connection with *In Dubious Battle, Of Mice and Men*, and *The Grapes of Wrath*. Besides the journalistic debate surrounding them, part of which is recorded in Martin Shockley's "The Reception of *The Grapes of Wrath* in Oklahoma," * there are more formal essays.

In 1939, the year of publication of *The Grapes of Wrath*, V. F. Calverton made an estimate of the comparative worth of Steinbeck, Hemingway, and Faulkner for the *Modern Quarterly: A Journal of Radical Opinion* (Fall, 1939). Somewhat like Burgum, he finds *Of Mice and Men* indefensible except as a "pot-boiler, a side-show trick, a clever stunt." This failure is redeemed by *The Grapes of Wrath*, in which the farmers are not "the eternal farmers of poetic legend" but "people of today, suffering from the economic crucifixions of our present environment." Hemingway is written off as a "primevalite" more concerned with action than reasons for action. Steinbeck is preferable to Faulkner for much the same reason Burgum preferred *The Grapes of Wrath* to *Of Mice and Men*. While Faulkner's conception of life is futilitarian, since his characters have nothing to live for, "Steinbeck, on the other hand, who has seen poverty, disease, and disaster, is optimistic about the future." Unlike Faulkner's, his characters represent not "the corruption of the earth, but the unfulfilled promise of it."

In *No Voice Is Wholly Lost* (1946), Harry Slochower has treated Steinbeck under the thematic heading "Toward the Communal Personality." Slochower is interested in "attempts at reintegrating the extremes of the individual and the communal, freedom and determinism, process and substance, culminating in the effort to synthesize 'Marx' and 'Freud.'" Unlike Burgum, he finds the "cheer and humour" in Steinbeck's fiction one aspect of a faith that though man is determined by his work, he grows beyond it and helps to make his history. Through this faith Steinbeck can love his people and believe in their coming liberation. Steinbeck does not regard collectivism as only stultifying, but pictures "the creative effects of group co-operation." Much of Slochower's material had appeared in 1939 as a lecture, "John Dos Passos and John Steinbeck," published in *Byrdcliffe Afternoons*. There he said that the difference between the two writers is that in Dos Passos determinism is "broken through by spectacular single acts that peter out in futile gestures"; whereas in Steinbeck the individual reaction takes place within the confines of the social, and "non-acceptance of surplus production, of the law of wages, of the enemy's invincibility, is the *note of freedom*."

In Dubious Battle and *The Grapes of Wrath* are accepted as "proletarian literature" by Samuel Levenson in "The Compassion of John Steinbeck," *Canadian Forum*, September, 1940. They may not escape the defects of this genre, since the characters are "free of the prejudices and bigotries that afflict workers as well as plutocrats." But in the latter novel Steinbeck's "socialist ideas have resolved themselves into little more than a profound awareness of the bad effects of an imbalance of property and means." Of Karl Marx's ideology he represents the "simple but flaming" idea that "every man is entitled to comfort and social security, that poverty is something that must be, and will be abolished."

The tendency to classify Steinbeck as a proletarian writer is challenged by Claude E. Jones in "Proletarian Writing and John Steinbeck,"*Sewanee Review*, October-December, 1940. After making a careful definition of the proletarian novel as a genre having Marxist criteria, and after illustrating how many English and American novelists work instead within a native tradition of the reform novel, he places Steinbeck in the latter group. The only link between *The Cup of Gold* and proletarian writing is "an unsympathetic, in some places excoriating, treatment of middle-class morality and ideals." *To A God Unknown* has not even this connection. *Tortilla Flat* was only incidentally, in a reception that angered Steinbeck, "gathered to the bosoms of the socially indignant." If *Of Mice and Men* was to the socially conscious a study of proletarian conditions, it was "to almost everyone else . . . simply a swift moving tale of psychopathic phenomena . . . , of horror and sudden deaths, of man's love for man." While *In Dubious Battle* aroused conservatives and radicals alike to name-calling, it was not "a study of labor movements in the abstract, of proletarian universals, but of a specific sore spot in one particular place." Its problem (and that of *The Grapes of Wrath*) was a California problem that had to be solved by Californians. The theme of *The Grapes of Wrath*, Jones said, is not "Workers of the World, Unite" but "Help these new-comers to find a home, let them live as human beings, as worthy citizens of a state to which God has been good, and in time they will be a blessing where now they seem a curse."

John S. Kennedy's "John Steinbeck: Life Affirmed and Dissolved" * represents broadly the application of Catholic criteria to Steinbeck. When one recalls the early attacks of T. S. Eliot on the humanism of Babbitt and More as omitting religion, it seems likely that Kennedy's conclusion resembles the one that would also be reached by critics approaching Steinbeck from a conservative or neo-Protestant point of view, though the issue would not be so much the new humanists' omission of God as the omission of reason and moral choice Kennedy assumes in Steinbeck. Kennedy's opening paragraphs exhibit a pattern that often characterizes both approving and disapproving Steinbeck critics. He pays tribute to Steinbeck's versatility, and for a time seems to accept the philosophy by praising him for not fitting into the prevalent negativism of modern fiction. Not only this, he finds it impossible to pigeonhole Steinbeck's assertion of life, and defends him from charges of pro-Communism and crypto-Nazism. Steinbeck's seeming approval of a popularly chosen and controlled socialism is not to be dismissed as absurd or pernicious. The trouble, and here Kennedy gets to his main point, is that Steinbeck places the fullness of life in the group rather than in the individual, and that his tendency to "animalize" his characters robs his books of human meaning. Kennedy's citation of Edmund Wilson on this point is somewhat ironic, since Wilson's *The Boys in the Back Room: Notes on California Novelists* (1941) had praised Steinbeck's tendency to present human life in animal terms, preferring it to Aldous Huxley's mystic distinction of a fundamental moral difference in man. Huxley had been frightened back into a synthetic cult; whereas Steinbeck, while his philosophy was obviously not satisfactory because he had nothing to oppose to man's destructiveness except faith in life, maintained an unpanicky scrutiny of life Wilson felt was most likely to lead to something of value for the ennoblement of life. Kennedy also cites Alfred Kazin, who, in *On Native Ground* (1942), had also begun by praising Steinbeck's promise of a realism "not submissive to the spiritual stupor of the time" and equal, "if only in its aspiration, to the humanity, the gaiety, the wholeness, of realism in a more stable period." Kazin had gone on to say that despite Steinbeck's moral serenity and sympathetic understanding, his people are "always on the verge of becoming human, but never do." Steinbeck's simplicity and naturalness were gains, but he was unable to rise above simplicity and primitivism and establish his truths in human character; and Kazin had ended by suggesting that slickness and trickiness were the outcome of this inability.

Kennedy's view has the considerably sharper focus of orthodox theology. Turning to *Sea of Cortez* (1941), so often used as evidence by Steinbeck's later critics, he begins an extended attack on what he reads as Steinbeck's adoption in fiction of the biological notion of the amorality of nature. *Burning Bright* (1950), with its theme of renunciation of the egotism of personal fatherhood and—for Kennedy—consequent tacit condonement of adultery and even murder, is the center of his attack. In handling the problem of true Christian faith, he places Steinbeck among a large group of contemporary novelists who, in rejecting a "peculiar, diluted blend of Calvinism and Lutheranism," think they are refuting authentic Christianity. He recognizes "crude" intimations in Steinbeck of something beyond the biological terms of man's being. These should be subjected by Steinbeck to the rigorous examination from which alone can come avoidance of the sophistry and the sentimentality inevitable in a view of humanity through feeling rather than reason.

Another Catholic estimate of Steinbeck is Michael F. Moloney's "Half-Faiths in Modern Fiction" in *The Catholic World*, August, 1950. Fitzgerald, Hemingway, and Steinbeck are found wanting, while, as one might expect, praise goes to Eliot, Thomas Merton, Evelyn Waugh, and Graham Greene. Modern half-faith originates for Moloney in what he calls the three leading atheistic humanists of the nineteenth century—Ludwig Feuerbach, Friedrich Nietzsche, and Auguste Comte. Unlike Fitzgerald and Hemingway, Steinbeck has been deeply motivated by humanitarian impulses, and thus has "after a fashion at least fused the teaching of Comte with the heritage of Feuerbach and

Nietzsche." Because he loves the dispossessed, he writes with power and conviction; but since his love lacks the "intimacy of the creational relationship which God himself cannot deny," and since the weakness of his people lacks a heart-subduing kinship with the absolute, he smiles at them "in scarcely concealed condescension." The defect is no fault of Steinbeck's; he has simply used the materials available to him in an era of great disillusionment. For Moloney his work is testimony that on the literary as on the political level "banishing God does not make man God-like" and exalting disordered human nature dramatizes "the insufficiency of man unto himself."

As the opening pages of Freeman Champney's essay "John Steinbeck, Californian"* suggest, it was written after several months' experience in what is called the Steinbeck country and is the most ambitious effort to assess Steinbeck in terms of the geographical, cultural, and economic influences on him. In discussing the limitations of economic and political understanding imposed on Steinbeck by his region, Champney makes assumptions about Steinbeck's direction in the Thirties that are challenged by other critics—especially the assumption that Steinbeck accepted Marxism or the semblance of Marxism. There may well have been, as Champney says, a great difference between economic and political conditions in California and in other parts of the country, but the suggestion that Steinbeck overlooked the dynamic of American democracy that somehow avoids the extremes of civil war and revolution, is debatable. On the other hand, his thesis that Steinbeck is still belaboring enemies either dead or transformed is a challenging one supported by such sociological studies as David Riesman's *The Lonely Crowd*. Besides a possible failure to distinguish between universality on the political and on the emotional and philosophic level, Champney may be prone to the error of reading on only one level of meaning. Like many other critics, he makes Steinbeck a one-book man—only in *The Grapes of Wrath* did his tensions and conflicts reach an 'affirmative equilibrium."

Champney's view of Steinbeck's later development as a rejection of "Man as Reformer or Revolutionary" and a turning to "Man as Animal" places his essay in the cluster of those that, beginning with Edmund Wilson's suggestion in 1941 in *The Boys in the Back Room*, concentrate their search for the essential Steinbeck in the philosophy arising from the writer's long-standing interest in biology and stated in *Sea of Cortez*. Driven back by the war to the tough-minded nihilism of "is" thinking, Steinbeck went to his usual extreme and jettisoned "not only hope and progress but cause and effect as well." Champney is acute on the resemblance of this emphasis on physical reality in a time sick of abstractions and ideologies to Hemingway's after World War I. A new and important idea in Steinbeck criticism is Champney's belief that Steinbeck's greatest contribution may turn out to be "the exploration and colonization of the no-man's-land between intellectual and non-intellectual, rational and subrational," a problem in human isolation less apparent in the West than in other areas. This isolation, one recalls, troubled an older culture in E. M. Forster's *Howards End*, which rather hopelessly and bloodlessly attempts to bridge it from the top down, and agitated the fiction of D. H. Lawrence. Champney's discussion of *The Wayward Bus* is an illuminating synopsis of the personal problems it presented to the critics, some of whom it baffled because as intellectuals they had in their frame of reference no vital counterparts for the characters; some of whom it stimulated to overpraise as a reaction to their own lack of vitality.

As early as 1942, Stanley Edgar Hyman's "Some Notes on John Steinbeck" * began the intensive interpretation of Steinbeck through a possible conflict between his scientifically derived "is" thinking and the value judgments needed in a human world. While Hyman's essay focuses on *The Moon Is Down*—rated by many reviewers and critics as one of Steinbeck's least successful books, and, contradictorily, by a very few as one of his best—it uses the play to construct an elaborate hypothesis about Steinbeck's philosophic and technical development. For Hyman, Steinbeck was increasingly driven to the dialogue form of his plays by the pro-and-con-demanding necessity of conflicting views of man and society. A part of Hyman's hypothesis is his reading of Steinbeck's moon symbolism. Once a symbol of hope and realization, the moon that is down in the play is Steinbeck's personal moon, the moon of a whole past nexus of preoccupations. In *Sea of Cortez* he had killed off his remaining social compulsion and emerged into a perfect scientific vacuum. His view of war had been that of the completely objective observer; and his view of human nature, accepting on biological grounds the survival of the strongest, had not been far from justification of Nazism. Then, disturbed by the war, Steinbeck lost his scientist's isolation. In the play his conquered people express his own need of a new sociality; but his Nazis, with their disinterest in people and with their ecological good sense, are his scientists in disguise. Thus what Edmund Wilson had suggested rather approvingly in 1941 as Steinbeck's emphasis on man as animal is developed by Hyman into a full critique of the man and the career.

Four years after Hyman, Woodburn Ross in "John Steinbeck: Earth and Stars," * made a friendly and detailed analysis of the conflict he saw between Steinbeck's expressed preference for non-teleological

thinking and his tendency to be intuitive and even mystical. Using, as
do most of the later critics, *Sea of Cortez* as his central illuminant, he
finds that Steinbeck accepts the scientific method of thinking, which
seeks to avoid all metaphysical considerations, but that at the same
time he reveals an unusual affection for the objective world which seriously compromises his rational, scientific position. Thus the basic
problem of Steinbeck's novels is how to decide between the equally
powerful but sometimes contradictory claims of reason and intuition.
Ross uses this conception of Steinbeck to defend him from charges of
being a "slick" writer, one who has, as James T. Farrell once said, "all
the mannerism and none of the substance of genuine realism." As a
believer in the scientific method, Steinbeck must write realistically, but
"as a man of powerful affections and intuitions he must reflect irrational attitudes . . . justifiable only in terms of the desire of the human spirit." That is why he is both brutal and tender, rational and
irrational, concrete and abstract. The last part of Ross's essay makes
an elaborate comparison of Steinbeck's thought with that of Auguste
Comte, regarded by the Catholic critic Michael F. Moloney as one
of the fathers of the modern half-faith he finds to be a defect in Steinbeck and most other modern writers. Without denigration, he finds
Steinbeck, like D. H. Lawrence and Aldous Huxley, basically an
irrationalist.

Frederick Bracher's "Steinbeck and the Biological View of Man" *
emphasizes the extended influence of biological study on Steinbeck
from his Stanford undergraduate days through his late association with
the marine biologist Edward F. Ricketts. Citing not only *Sea of Cortez*,
the book on which Ricketts and Steinbeck collaborated, but the evidence in "John Steinbeck and the Non-Teleological Bus" by Toni
Ricketts (Antonia Seixas), that the fiction reflects Steinbeck's scientific
views, Bracher is able to make extensive parallels between Steinbeck's
characters and his thinking. For Bracher, Steinbeck is neither a humanistic writer nor a coldly objective naturalistic one. Edward Ricketts had
once argued that an inability to take sides is not a necessary corollary
of non-telelogical thinking—an inability that is the crux of Stanley
Hyman's "Some Notes on John Steinbeck." But Bracher, like Hyman
and Ross, believes that Steinbeck "never really resolves some of the
paradoxes involved in a non-teleological approach."

Bracher makes extensive application of the theory of biological influence. Thus he finds that the true Steinbeckian sin is to become "so
sunk in the social organism as to lose one's biological individuality."
Steinbeck's attack on the middle class, as in *Cannery Row*, is partly on
its loss of adaptability and power to survive. The poison he puts into

his cream puff of readability is a glorification of the biological virtues. Bracher concludes by saying, somewhat as Ross does, that "when Steinbeck goes beyond the simple biological virtues, it is to a set of values equally nonhumanistic: the mystical." The saving grace is "to be aware of the whole thing and to accept one's part in it."

Blake Nevius in "Steinbeck: One Aspect"* indicts Steinbeck for evasion of moral responsibility by combining the relatively recent view that his non-teleological thinking has seriously affected his fiction with the literary historian's view that American fiction has developed in terms of a shifting attitude toward the conflict of illusion and reality. For the generation of Hawthorne, Howells, and James, disillusionment was likely to be the prelude to regeneration. For their successors— Hemingway, Fitzgerald, and Dos Passos—disillusionment was an inescapable fact of existence, though for them too illusion was an obstacle to the liberation of mind and personality. Steinbeck, on the other hand, argues that "there is a saving grace in illusion because without it, life may be unsupportable." Nevius locates the source of the trouble in Steinbeck's "is" thinking which, when applied to the problem of evil, becomes a means of begging the question by simply saying that evil *is* and avoiding the question *why*. Evil arises spontaneously and unpredictably and has no source in illusion as it had for the inheritors of the puritan tradition. Nevius also locates a moral impasse for Steinbeck in the modern idea of cultural relativity. While this idea has served a good purpose in widening the ground of tolerance, it has resulted in the applying of the term *good* "only to those motives which appear in common at the most primitive level," which is what Steinbeck does.

In 1949, Woodburn Ross returned to the problem of Steinbeck's values in "John Steinbeck: Naturalism's Priest."* Like Nevius, he is concerned about the tendency of ethics to become purely relative in modern times. Unlike Nevius, he sees Steinbeck as the first significant writer to build a mystical religion upon a naturalistic base, a compromise that can to some extent support principles of conduct. Ross feels that though it is impossible to know how influential this combination will be, the significance of Steinbeck may prove to lie in it. His work "accepts the intuitive, non-rational method of dealing with man's relation to the universe—the method of the contemporary mystics. But, unlike them, it accepts as the universe to which man must relate himself the modern, scientifically described cosmos." Thus to Ross what to other critics has been sheer contradiction, or the ultimate outcome of nineteenth century skepticism, has become the possibility of a new synthesis.

Claude-Edmonde Magny's "Steinbeck, or the Limits of the Impersonal Novel" * provides an interesting coda to considerations of Steinbeck as artist and thinker because of its international point of view and because of its fresh, cogent development of a somewhat familiar theory about Steinbeck. At the center of her argument lies the idea that Steinbeck characteristically portrays the sub-human and the animal. On the side of strength, Steinbeck has "an extraordinary power to catch and paint man in his most elementary terms, terms that also seem bound to be the most essential, those that bring him closer to other men, or even to other beings." But on the side of weakness, he fails "whenever he tries to paint more complex individualities such as, after all, we have to meet in modern civilization."

In her critique of *East of Eden* that appeared in *Perspectives U.S.A.*, Fall, 1955, Magny applied something of the same view, though she had much to say in praise. She spoke of Steinbeck's constant propensity —and that of his characters—"to take refuge in Innocence as their shield and alibi. . . . The mythical patterning of characters and situations is used to endorse a fictitious Edenism. . . . The effect is not so much to justify the Edenism as to absolve it from all need for justification." Steinbeck is not alone in this. Indeed, one is tempted by American fiction to believe that the whole country is "refusing to achieve a full consciousness of good and evil."

A fascinating account of Steinbeck's reputation in France is contained in *Trans-Atlantic Migration: The Contemporary American Novel in France* by Thelma M. Smith and Ward L. Miner, 1955. Of the Big Five—Dos Passos, Hemingway, Faulkner, Caldwell, and Steinbeck, who was the last to arrive—André Malraux has said that Steinbeck has given him "the greatest satisfaction." It will surprise intellectuals who rate Steinbeck low to learn that one of their heroes, André Gide, thought very highly of some of Steinbeck's work, particularly *In Dubious Battle*, which he called a beautiful and cruel book, and the stories in *The Long Valley*, which he thought equalled or surpassed the most moving stories of Chekhov. It would be incorrect, however, to suggest here that French criticism is much more unanimous than American criticism in its attitude toward Steinbeck.

III.   The Grapes of Wrath

If the success of *Tortilla Flat* frightened Steinbeck with the prospect of a popularity that, he felt, had ruined everyone he knew, the novel that really made him a celebrity and that has brought upon his later work the charge of anti-climax was *The Grapes of Wrath*. The story of its success, both popular and critical, is largely the story of the economic and political concerns of the depression era of the Thirties.

Martin Shockley's "The Reception of *The Grapes of Wrath* in Oklahoma" * gives the fullest single account of what might be called "the vested interest" reaction to the novel, which ranged from irony through angry threats and book burnings to plain slapstick comedy. There was a great deal of wind over Capitol Hill from Oklahoma senators; and in the land of the Okies all kinds of skirmishes occurred between parochial chauvinists and liberal readers. Perhaps the greatest irony Shockley reveals is the perennial one that people often take violent attitudes toward a novel they have not read. His conclusion, outlining the two main bodies of opinion, tries to distinguish between the universal problems the novel treats, and the problem of a disintegrating regional culture it also raises.

Naturally such a novel challenged the critics' ability to distinguish between a soundly native and a dangerously foreign program of reform or even revolution, and between art and propaganda. Frederic Ives Carpenter's "The Philosophical Joads" * finds in Nineteenth Century American thought the roots of the novel's challenge to the *status quo*. Steinbeck brought together for the first time the "three great skeins of American thought." One is represented by Emerson's oversoul, faith in the common man, and Protestant self-reliance; the second by Whitman's religion of the love of all men and his mass democracy; and the third by William James' emphasis on action. With this combination the novel develops a new kind of Christianity that is not "otherworldly and passive, but earthly and active." Unlike many critics, Carpenter defends the inter-chapters that more or less explicitly develop mystical ideas and moralizing interpretations. Novels that become classics offer a criticism of life, and *The Grapes of Wrath* is a novel of ideas, though these of course do not reside only in the inter-chapters.

Chester E. Eisinger's "Jeffersonian Agrarianism in *The Grapes of Wrath*," published in the Winter, 1947, *University of Kansas City Review*, adds an older American tradition to Carpenter's list. After a thrust at one wing of "the new criticism" for what he calls their feudal, aristocratic agrarianism as outlined in 1930 in *I'll Take My Stand*, and soon abandoned for authoritarian esthetics, he traces in *The Grapes of Wrath* the Jeffersonian view that the farmer is the productive, healthy member of society, drawing spiritual strength as well as sustenance from the soil, and that the city and the machine, essentially inhuman and unproductive, are to be mistrusted. Eisinger finds that the role of the Okies in a revolutionary social action is "as American as Jefferson's successful efforts to abolish entail and primogeniture." After granting

Steinbeck this protective American orthodoxy, Eisinger questions the efficacy of the agrarian ideal in solving contemporary economic and social problems. World War II has, he says, seen the triumph of American capitalism and industry, and Louis Bromfield is now almost the only voice calling men back to the land. The road to the independence and dignity expected from democracy must take some other direction. Eisinger draws no conclusion about the universality and lasting power of a novel which contains for him an unfeasible solution.

Joseph Warren Beach's "John Steinbeck: Art and Propaganda" * examines the question of the possibility of art in a novel so closely and idealistically bound up with contemporary problems. Accepting the label of proletarian novel, which he defines as one dealing "primarily with the life of the working classes or with any social or industrial problem from the point of view of labor," he calls Steinbeck's book the finest example of that genre in the United States to date (c. 1940). Like other critics, he notes the resemblance of this theme and, at times, the manner of its celebration to Carl Sandburg's The People, Yes; but unlike some he does not sweepingly accuse Steinbeck of a vague, rhetorical sentimentality. While he feels that the passages of prophetic tone concerning Manself are a trifle stiff, abstract, "talky," and magniloquent, he thinks that on the whole Steinbeck's technical virtuosity has been neglected because of the homeliness of the subject matter.

Much of Beach's essay is devoted to the accusation of sentimentality that has plagued Steinbeck more than any other charge. He defends the use of the ideal in fiction as a legitimate pole of the imagination along with the real. On esthetic grounds, Steinbeck can be considered superior to such a realist as James T. Farrell because "we are more aware of the principle of selection, a merit making for definition and appeal."

In his final defense of the novel from the charge of being propaganda, Beach again resorts, as do many critics, to assertion of its essential truth rather than to a theoretical distinction between art and propaganda like that outlined by Wellek and Warren in The Theory of Literature—unlike propaganda, art does not prompt the reader to naïve or premature action. The Grapes of Wrath is an effective means of making people aware of "the social problems which remain to be solved within the system which is so good to so many of us."

The question of the enduring value of The Grapes of Wrath is, of course, as yet unanswered. Steinbeck's tendency to point more or less mutely to its sales is perhaps as good an answer as any, for the book's continuing popularity is at least as likely to be based on something universally appealing as on any unintentional or deliberate exploitation of a peculiarly American sentimentality. It may even be that as prosperity and gadgets increasingly cushion our struggle for life and a comfortable, middle-class existence becomes universal, as David Riesman predicts in *The Lonely Crowd*, the novel's earthy experience will become even more essentially appealing. The critics who approach literature with the concept of "myth" ought to have something to say about this.

Martin Shockley's "Christian Symbolism in *The Grapes of Wrath*" * points partially in this direction. His explication is satisfyingly attentive to what the writer is implicitly saying. While the universality of a Christian frame of reference may be limited pretty much to Western culture and while it may have been diminished by contemporary skepticism and even ignorance, it goes much deeper into the conscious mind, and perhaps the unconscious, than a concept of Steinbeck's pilgrim's progress that is couched in contemporary political and sociological jargon.

IV. The Later Work

Whatever the critical success or travail of his work, Steinbeck has not stopped producing. Since 1939 and *The Grapes of Wrath* he has published *Sea of Cortez* (1941), *The Moon Is Down* both as a play and a novel (1942), *Cannery Row* and the periodical form of *The Pearl* (1945), *The Wayward Bus* (1947), *Burning Bright* (1950), *East of Eden* (1952), and *Sweet Thursday* (1954). Currently he is at work on another long novel.

"John Steinbeck and the Non-teleological Bus" * by Toni Ricketts (Antonia Seixas) can be regarded as something of an *apologia* by a member of the inner circle who knows Steinbeck's literary intentions intimately. In lieu of a serious statement from him, which he tends to avoid making despite invitation or provocation, this is probably the next-best thing.

According to her, Steinbeck purposely writes on several levels of meaning, and critical evaluations of him are seldom based on understanding of all these levels. First, there is the obvious story level. Second, there is a "social protest" level, to which most readers are particularly susceptible, representing Steinbeck the reformer. Third, there is a symbolic level, apprehended by readers who are more thoughtful or more inclined to read in their own vision of the truth, and one on which the interpretations are limited only by the ingenuity of the reader. And fourth, most likely to be missed or misunderstood by the reader, there is a philosophical level explicitly and frequently stated in *Sea of Cortez*. On this level the artist attempts the difficult feat of avoiding teleological thinking in order to create a pattern of reality; that is, he considers events as outgrowths and expressions of an existing pattern, rather than as results of specific causes. He is not concerned with what could be, or should be, or might be, but with what actually is. He attempts to answer the already sufficiently difficult questions *what* or *how*, but not the question *why*.

Antonia Seixas does not discuss the possibility of an inherent philosophic contradiction between the social protest and symbolic levels and the non-teleological level that troubles the criticism of Hyman, Bracher, Nevius, Ross, and others. She tends to view it as a governor of technique, determining such things as tone and selectivity. The author is "like an entomologist describing the antics of a group of insects," understanding and even loving, but not praising or blaming.

She seems to indicate the nature of a "saving grace" in Steinbeck's fiction, though she probably would not use such a theological term, when she talks of our dependence on unsentimental realists for our rescue.

Peter Lisca in "The Wayward Bus—A Modern Pilgrimage" reads the novel closely in terms of such a grace and its effects on character and structure. The "saved" characters, those whom Ricketts might have described as specimens by which the entomologist was more charmed, have four important traits in common: "honesty with themselves and others, an ecological view of things, ability in their respective fields, and sexual attractiveness." Despite Lisca's understandable dislike of "the old bogie of Steinbeck's 'animality,'" these traits point up Steinbeck's emphasis on what might be called the virtue of man's being a good animal, as at least a fundamental starting point for honesty and strength.

In his discussion of "The Pearl," Lisca demonstrates again the value of close reading. He shows how Steinbeck decided to give the story the quality of folklore because the strongly parabolic nature of the story demanded it. His explanation of the allegory is welcome after the tendency of many reviewers to dismiss the story with little if any understanding. He argues that Steinbeck's philosophy and technique achieve aesthetic distance and that his emphasis on the natural scene has been allowed to obscure the human significance of his stories. He recognizes Steinbeck's tendency to think of groups as unit animals and the tendency of his non-teleological thinking to be accompanied by an unwillingness to assign blame. But beyond this, Lisca says, there is in Steinbeck's work an interest in man's mytheopoeic heritage. His great accomplishment is that he has been able to interfuse a materialistic level of meaning with archetypal, mythic reference. In arguing this, Lisca uses an approach pretty well neglected by other Steinbeck critics.

Steinbeck did not attempt another novel on the scale of *The Grapes of Wrath* until *East of Eden*, published some fourteen years later, in 1952. This was a Sunday punch, an all-out effort to do something really big again. Whether such a marshaling of forces was the natural climax of a long period of incubation or a response to adverse criticism, or both, it is impossible to say. It is not likely that Steinbeck was unaware of what was being said about him, particularly about the lack of adequate basis for moral action in his biologically-grounded philosophy. One possibility for second-guessers is the presence in *East of Eden* of a strong, at times explicit, affirmation of man's freedom of moral choice which does not sound quite like the former emphasis on what *is* that Antonia Seixas regarded as his highest level of meaning.

Joseph Wood Krutch's review* of the novel is distinguished by a careful and fair-minded account of the intention he sees in it. Here Steinbeck cannot be dismissed as "merely a routine manipulator of the tough-tender, hardboiled-softboiled school." Krutch regards Steinbeck as going beyond the embodiment of myth in the history of a modern family to pronounce the thesis that "Good and Evil are absolute not relative things" and that "in making a choice between them man is a free agent, not the victim of his heredity, his environment, or of anything else." In affirming this, Steinbeck rejects the tenets of the hardboiled school with which he has sometimes been loosely associated and plainly announces that he wants to be taken as a moralist. Krutch does not commit himself on the merits of the novel as art. On the esthetic side he only predicts that the verdict will not depend upon the validity of the moral thesis but upon the question of whether or not the fable really carries the thesis, the moral is implicit in the story, and the author has recreated a myth rather than merely moralized a tale.

Mark Schorer in the *New York Times*, September 21, 1952, praised *East of Eden* as probably Steinbeck's best. His approach, emphasizing technique, excludes the thesis of moral freedom that Krutch emphasizes. The novel is different from the earlier ones in being less intent on singleness of theme and effect, and in being devoid of the earlier regional, sociological, or political emphases. Steinbeck has achieved a strange, original work by weaving in and around the central story a fantasia of history and myth. His technical virtuosity does not result in merely an eclectic resolution of view but constitutes a wide-ranging, imaginative freedom. There are defects in Steinbeck's imagination— a tendency "to be fascinated by depravities that he seems helpless to account for," and inversely a "gap between speculative statement and novelistic presentation" that can be called sentimentalism since Steinbeck has always accepted "certain noble abstractions about human nature that his melodrama is hardly designed to demonstrate"—but on the whole Steinbeck's handling of point of view and tone holds the book together and gives it originality. Schorer's praise goes to what he calls "the audaciousness with which the novelist asserts his temperament through his material, and the temperamental means by which he defines that material for us."

In many other reviews praise tended to be overwhelmingly qualified by what to the student of Steinbeck criticism have become its clichés, and condemnation tended to be sweeping. Critics aligned with religious institutions talked of an impact that was on the side of cruelty, lust, and evil no matter what Steinbeck's intention was. Those who saw his wrestling with a moral theme as the first instance of this in his career, felt that it might be a hopeful sign of the times but concluded that in this book any beauty and understanding were almost extinguished by an obsession with animality, violence, and wickedness. For somewhat more sophisticated reviewers the novel progressively betrayed improbabilities, sentimentality, and intellectual naïveté. While Steinbeck might be a highly gifted virtuoso, he was constitutionally incapable of seeing the true significance of life. At least one reviewer seized upon the appearance of The Old Man and the Sea to make a comparison of Steinbeck and Hemingway. Granting Steinbeck a shift away from an earlier theme of social justice to a moral one, he felt that this novel, apparently like his others, exhibited a writer "more concerned with the generalities of social and moral truth than with the play and intensity that make for exciting fiction"; Hemingway, of course, showed the opposite weakness, "a narrow, somewhat immature sense of the world."

If East of Eden raised in some quarters recognition of, or merely hopes for, a new Steinbeck, the next novel, Sweet Thursday (1954), seems to have impressed most reviewers as a disappointing reversion to the vein of Tortilla Flat and Cannery Row. Though it might contain an enjoyable gusto, it was an indubitable best seller instead of the novel one had hoped for. The trouble could lie in an oscillation between good and bad work because Steinbeck was constituted that way or because he had lost the power of self-criticism through easy success. While Steinbeck fans who liked Cannery Row might be eager to read such a delightfully inconsequential book, more critical readers could regard it as further evidence that Steinbeck was no longer an author to be taken seriously. Even a reviewer who was willing to acknowledge that Steinbeck knew the people he was writing about and had a gift for low comedy, talked of a romantic streak that was perilously close to being cute and that was saved only by the rowdy humor and the satire. Despite the rather general dissatisfaction, at least one reviewer was able to see in the book a clear statement of the Steinbeck theme of the common bonds of humanity and the goodness and happiness they make possible.

If Steinbeck received any satisfaction from one segment of the reception of *East of Eden*, he must now have felt himself thoroughly back in the same old rut of relationship with his critics. Apparently he was not at all abashed by it, or by Carlos Baker's remark that *Sweet Thursday* was so gaily inconsequential that it might serve as the working script for a musical comedy, for not long afterward he was pleasurably involved in collaborating on just that project with Rodgers and Hammerstein.

Steinbeck has not fared well in the hands of the historians of contemporary literature. Frederick J. Hoffman in *The Modern Novel in America: 1900-1950* concluded that with the exception of *In Dubious Battle* Steinbeck's novels reveal "the deficiencies of a homespun philosophy, in which the suggestions made are vitiated and confused by a 'hausfrau sentimentality' and a naïve mysticism." His interest in biology is a source of confusion in his interpretation of the human scene. He is "unable to give us a convincing definition of his people because, having once reduced the scale of definition to their animal nature, he has subsequently shifted his ground of interpretation and with a desperate earnestness grasped at the most superficial but convenient ideational strategy available to him in the 1930's." Even *The Grapes of Wrath* receives rough handling from Hoffman on this score. Its philosophical strategy "involves what are perhaps some of the most wretched violations of aesthetic taste observable in modern American fiction," and it reveals an intellectual poverty that is a common failure among naturalistic writers. Hoffman's praise is reserved for *In Dubious Battle*, in which he sees a major modern theme—the facts of "ideological death" which have been treated also in André Malraux's *Man's Fate* and in the poetry of Randall Jarrell. Here Steinbeck made a starkly simple literary examination of the kind of strategic, self-effacing sacrifice, "quite thoroughly dissociated from leftist strategies as such," which characterize the cyanide capsule episode in Malraux and the deaths of the aviators in Jarrell. Hoffman writes off Steinbeck's later fiction—*The Moon Is Down, Cannery Row,* and *The Wayward Bus*— as clearly showing "the poverty of conception which had in greater or less degree hurt his earlier work."

Steinbeck's short fiction received somewhat kinder treatment from Ray B. West, Jr., in *The Short Story in America: 1900-1950*. Though these stories are dominated by the "pseudopastoral, folksy manner" of such a novel as *Tortilla Flat*, in the best ones "the underlying symbols achieve a control which, combined with his strongly emphasized themes, proves more satisfying than the loosely constructed histories of Dreiser and Farrell." West singles out "The Red Pony," "The Chrysanthemums," "The Harness," and "Johnny Bear" as "not among the best stories of the century," but serious attempts to celebrate "the natural instincts of man and to suggest agrarian values more satisfying than those in most of the regional writing during the same period." While Steinbeck's reputation has declined since *The Grapes of Wrath*, he has not suffered the neglect accorded Willa Cather, Ruth Suckow, and Sherwood Anderson. On the whole West treats Steinbeck as a good but minor and regional writer.

Conclusions

The editors of this anthology, as they came to the end of the long, rather twisting, somewhat bumpy trail of Steinbeck criticism, found themselves a bit weary and confused. If we may repeat the metaphor of the cocktail party with which this introduction began, we came home late at night not entirely sure what all the talk was about but determined to think clearly about it some other and soberer day. Supposing that day to have come, here are our findings.

One of our beliefs is that a good many of the reviewers and critics have made serious blunders. Steinbeck is right in accusing them of having no table of constants, a lack that is most apparent when they deal with his so-called philosophy. They start from assumptions of what a correct philosophy is and judge Steinbeck's fiction to be faulty because he does not agree with them. They show themselves unable or unwilling to follow the old, sane, fundamental rule which obligates critics to try to understand the author's intention and to judge his success or failure in realizing it before they shift ground to more universal and—wry thought in an eclectic age—controversial considerations. Their procedure requires him to be all things to all men in order to be universally praised. Other inconsistencies can be pointed out. For example, there is a tendency to call him a realist and then to condemn him because he is not the critic's particular brand of realist—and this despite the fact that even in his early work it ought to have been apparent that Steinbeck characteristically worked through symbol and myth as well as some sort of verisimilitude and that to read him on only one level, that of mere story, was to miss the point.

Another of our beliefs is that some critics take their own craft too seriously. They seem not only to lack a sense of humor but even the common awareness that readers can delight in a story without feeling that the author must settle world or cosmic affairs as they themselves would. Some critics even lack the respect that discursive, logical men ought to have for the imaginative man who provides them with their fodder. They seem unaware of the difference and difficulty of his problems. It is probably on this ground that much of Steinbeck's disgust with critics is based. He may justly feel that to become involved with their personal concepts of higher truth would be to abandon art for polemics or appeasement. To say this is neither to eulogize Steinbeck nor to deny that much helpful and perceptive criticism has appeared.

On the other hand, it may be said that Steinbeck's attitude towards critics, and intellectuals in general, shows an antagonism more suited to the Bohemian rebellions of the Twenties than to the responsibility-demanding Fifties. There are signs that the present drift in our society is toward a reconciliation of artist and intellectual from which each can learn. Steinbeck is, of course, right in insisting that during the creative act the writer must depend on his own resources. But in the interval between, he can and should develop like any other man. Whatever growth he makes is bound to be reflected in his work. Steinbeck's friendship with Edward Ricketts is proof of the possibility of such interpenetration of men in different occupations. It may even be that not to have many such relationships is impoverishing. It is one thing for a writer to be angered by the injustices and falsenesses in his society and quite another to be so alienated that he damns and rejects indiscriminately.

If there is a lesson here, it is for the critic also. Those who accuse Steinbeck of sentimentality ought to take another look at the necessity of an either-or attitude. Such an attitude is ingrained in our culture and language; yet there are respectable thinkers, even modern ones, who have found nothing disreputable about combining in a single vision of life an objective attitude and affection. The reports are that Edward Ricketts displayed such a combination and that it made him a singularly likeable man.

As for Steinbeck's stature, we can say that our respect for his art has increased as we have looked at it and the problems rising from it. We find him deserving of further critical attention and think he is quite likely to receive it. Clearly there is much still to be said about him, particularly by those willing to read him closely and patiently before attempting general statement and synthesis. We think that future critics will find him to be an artist with an artist's intentions, methods, and stature.

I. MAN AND CAREER

Peter Lisca

JOHN STEINBECK:
A LITERARY BIOGRAPHY

> *I really like the biographical method used by my dictionary. It would say, John Steinbeck, writer, born 1902, died (?). There is method. There is finish. There is even suspense.*—JOHN STEINBECK.

PERHAPS the most important biographical link between John Steinbeck and his writings is that he was born and came to maturity in the Salinas Valley. In this area of California, bounded on the north and south by the Pajaro and Jolon valleys and on the west and east by the Pacific Ocean and the Gabilan Mountains, Steinbeck found the materials of his fiction. There he came to know and admire the paisanos and bums of *Tortilla Flat*, *Cannery Row*, and *Sweet Thursday*; there he met and worked with the migrant laborers of *In Dubious Battle*, *Of Mice and Men*, and *The Grapes of Wrath*; there also he came to know the people of *The Long Valley*, *The Pastures of Heaven*, *The Red Pony*, *The Wayward Bus*, and *East of Eden*. From his California valleys Steinbeck gained that intimate knowledge and love of nature which plays so large a role in his works. From the Pacific Ocean he obtained that biological view of life (made explicit in *Sea of Cortez*) which informs his observation of man and society.

John Ernst Steinbeck was born in the town of Salinas on February 27, 1902, the son of John Ernst Steinbeck, Sr.; his mother's maiden

---

PETER LISCA has taught English at the Woman's College of the University of North Carolina, and in the fall of 1956, he will join the English faculty of the University of Washington. He received his doctor's degree from the University of Wisconsin in 1955. His dissertation, The Art of John Steinbeck: An Analysis and Interpretation of Its Development, is probably the most thorough study of Steinbeck's work so far attempted and constitutes a critical reappraisal. Mr. Lisca plans publication of a book on Steinbeck in the near future. He has published two articles on William Faulkner and one on Chaucer. Besides the essay appearing here, two others by Mr. Lisca may be found elsewhere in this volume. All three essays were written specially for this book.

In writing "John Steinbeck: A Literary Biography" Mr. Lisca has tried to avoid duplicating material covered by Lewis Gannett in "John Steinbeck's

name was Olive Hamilton. Like John Whiteside in *The Pastures of Heaven*, Joseph in *To A God Unknown*, and Adam Trask in *East of Eden*, Steinbeck Sr. came to California shortly after the Civil War; and like Elizabeth in *To A God Unknown*, Molly Morgan in *The Pastures of Heaven*, and Olive Hamilton in *East of Eden* (an authentic portrait), Steinbeck's mother taught for many years in the public schools of the Salinas Valley area. John Steinbeck Sr. was for many years treasurer of Monterey County, and his son's early novels and stories are written in the pages of abandoned double-entry ledgers.

Steinbeck's childhood must have been much like that of the boy Jody in *The Red Pony*, whose love for the Gabilan Mountains to the east and fear of the Santa Lucia range toward the ocean Steinbeck acknowledged as a personal childhood experience on the opening page of *East of Eden*. Like the Jody who made a death symbol out of the black cypress trees under which the pigs were scalded and a life symbol out of the mossy tub which caught the spring water, Steinbeck was a sensitive boy. Replying to a publisher's request for early biographical information, Steinbeck wrote back that the most important things in his childhood would be of no meaning to others— ". . . the way the sparrows hopped about on the mud street early in the morning when I was little . . . . the most tremendous morning in the world when my pony had a colt." This sensitivity to the experiences of childhood is also revealed in some remarks Steinbeck made early in 1936, when he was thinking about *The Red Pony*: "I want to recreate a child's world, not of fairies and giants but of colors more clear than they are to adults, of tastes more sharp and of queer heart breaking feelings that overwhelm children in a moment. [Jody's feelings at the end of "The Great Mountains," for example.] I want to put down the way 'afternoon felt'—and the feeling about a bird that sang in a tree in the evening." This acute consciousness of the way "afternoon felt" remained in the man who wrote *The Red Pony*.

Another important factor in Steinbeck's early years was undoubtedly his mother's former position as a school teacher. There must have been books around the household to interest a young boy. In *The Pastures*

Way of Writing"; the two essays complement each other and should be read together. For this biographical essay as well as for his doctoral study Mr. Lisca had the great advantage of access to manuscripts and correspondence in the files of both Steinbeck's agents and his publishers. Besides this, Mr. Steinbeck and Mrs. Steinbeck have both been generous enough to read Mr. Lisca's essay in typescript and to check the accuracy of its facts and to supply additional information.

of Heaven Steinbeck represents Molly Morgan as reading to her pupils from the novels of Scott, Zane Grey, James Oliver Curwood, and Jack London. Junius Maltby reads to the boys from Stevenson's *Treasure Island* and carries a copy of *Kidnapped* in his pocket. But a teacher's library (in those days) was expected to be a bit more solid. Commenting on his early reading, Steinbeck once wrote that he remembered "certain books that were realer than experience—*Crime and Punishment* was like that and *Madame Bovary* and parts of *Paradise Lost* and things of George Eliot and *The Return of the Native*. I read all of these when I was very young and I remember them not at all as books but as things that happened to me."

Speaking of his later reading interests, Steinbeck admitted falling under the influence of James Branch Cabell and Donn Byrne. "These men," he said, "were specialists in sound—and that's what I was after." It is possible to see some influence of Cabell in his first novel, *Cup of Gold*, but beginning with *To A God Unknown* in 1933 there can be no doubt that the greatest influence on his prose was that of Hemingway, of whom Steinbeck wrote in 1938, "I am convinced that in many ways he is the finest writer of our time." Other authors whom he has at various times admired include D. H. Lawrence, Willa Cather, Sherwood Anderson, and Thackeray. But Steinbeck is not an avid reader of fiction, and his most steady interest has been in the "Great Books": the Bible and Apocrypha, the literatures of ancient India, Goethe, Dante, the church fathers, and the Greeks—especially the historians Herodotus, Xenephon, and Thucydides.[1] Steinbeck particularly avoids reading fiction when working. When he was deep into *The Grapes of Wrath* he apologized for not reading the book a friend had sent him by saying, "I can't seem to read anything at all except very dry treatises when working. Just now it's Hallam's Middle Ages."

Steinbeck must have been a pretty well-read boy when he entered high school. His being president of his senior class, however, was due more to his position on the track and basketball teams than his scholarship or literary efforts for *El Gabilan*, the school paper. During his high school years he extended his experience of the California countryside and its people by spending many of his holidays as a hired hand on nearby ranches. In the year's interval between graduation and entering Stanford he took employment as assistant chemist in a sugar-beet factory nearby.

Steinbeck's career at Stanford was sporadic.[2] Although he registered as an English major and was in attendance over a period of five years, he did not take a degree. During this period he contributed two stories to *The Stanford Spectator* and three poems to the *Stanford Lit*. One story, called "Fingers of Cloud: A Satire on College Protervity," is an account of a sub-normal girl who marries a Filipino laborer but leaves him because he insists on keeping horse heads in the rain barrel. This odd mixture of the realistic and the fantastic is even more pronounced in the other story, "Adventures in Arcademy: A Journey into the Ridiculous," an obscure and satirical allegory of college life at Stanford. Various fruit trees seem to symbolize courses of study, and penguins, pigeons, buffaloes, and other animals seem to represent the faculty. The three poems published in the *Stanford Lit* are in the same vein of comic satire, as the titles indicate: "If Eddie Guest Had Written the Book of Job: HAPPY BIRTHDAY," "If John A. Weaver Had Written Keats' Sonnet in the American Language: ON LOOKING AT A NEW BOOK BY HAROLD BELL WRIGHT," and "Atropos: Study of a Very Feminine Obituary Editor." This interest in burlesque and satire is carried into some of Steinbeck's mature work—*Cannery Row*, *The Grapes of Wrath* (the Joads' encounter with flush toilets), *The Wayward Bus*, *Sweet Thursday*, and especially "St. Katy the Virgin"; but it becomes a strategic humor, devoid of undergraduate preciosity and developed in terms of earthy realism or symbolic reference. During this period Steinbeck also wrote a short story called "A Lady in Infra-Red," which was to grow into his first published novel—*Cup of Gold*. He had apparently settled on a career as writer, and although he was not admitted into the play-writing class, he did manage to take many courses in writing.

During those periods when he was not in attendance at Stanford, Steinbeck worked on ranches and on a road gang. These were experiences from which he profited, gaining an intimate knowledge of the working man—his attitudes, habits, and language. It is this knowledge which gives *In Dubious Battle*, *Of Mice and Men*, and *The Grapes of Wrath* that solidity of observation conspicuously absent from the majority of ideological parlor-proletarian novels of the thirties. That Steinbeck was a keen observer is evident from a letter he wrote his agents years later justifying the language of *In Dubious Battle*: "The use of the final g in *ing* is tricky, too. The g is put on for emphasis and often to finish a short hard sentence. It is sometimes used for purpose of elision but not always. Certain words like *something* rarely lose the final g or if they do, the word becomes *somepin* or *sompm*. . . . I tell you these things so you will understand why, in one sentence having two present participles, one g will be there and the other left off."

Another of Steinbeck's jobs during his college career was as night chemist in the sugar-beet factory where he had worked earlier. This too provided him with materials for his later writings. While finishing the final draft of *In Dubious Battle* and thinking about his next novel, Steinbeck wrote his agents that there were "some fine little things that happened in a big sugar mill where I was assistant chief chemist and majordomo of about sixty Mexicans and Yaquis taken from the jails of northern Mexico." Two of these "fine little things" (the story of the ex-corporal and the story of old man Ravanno), became episodes in *Tortilla Flat*.

In 1926 Steinbeck left Stanford, and in November of that year he went to New York to become a writer. The unfortunate circumstances of his first stay in New York he has recorded in a recent piece of auto-biography[3]—his jobs as laborer and reporter, his unsuccessful attempts to publish some short stories, and his ignominious retreat to California as a deck-hand via the Panama Canal. The experience was so bitter that fifteen years later, even when he was a celebrity, he came to New York "as a St. Anthony to temptations" and as soon as possible he "fled the whore of Babylon with relief and virtuous satisfaction."

Back in California, Steinbeck took a job as caretaker of an estate on Lake Tahoe, and later, after being fired for allowing a huge tree to crash through the roof, he worked in a nearby fish hatchery. It was during the two winters he spent in the high Sierras that he completed *Cup of Gold*, which appeared two months after the stock market crash in 1929. Seven years later, after the successes of *Tortilla Flat* and *In Dubious Battle*, Steinbeck said he was "not particularly proud" of his first novel, and that "outside of a certain lyric quality" there wasn't much to it. He believed then that *Cup of Gold* was the only book of his that could be filmed.

Despite the relative unsuccess of his first novel, Steinbeck was still determined to be a writer. In 1930 he married and went to live in Pacific Grove, where his father provided him with $25 a month and a small house. Here he continued to work on a 30,000 word manuscript called "Dissonant Symphony" and, to pay for groceries, a deliberately cheap thriller called "Murder at Full Moon." Steinbeck considered both of these failures and withdrew them from his agents. Concerning "Murder at Full Moon" he wrote, ". . . the quicker I can forget the damn thing the happier I'll be." Also at this time, Steinbeck began revising *To A God Unknown*. An earlier version called "The Green Lady" had been rejected by several publishers. This version had for its protagonist a character who fell in love with a forest, somehow identified in his mind with his daughter, and who killed himself by walking sacrificially into that forest while it was ablaze. A second version called "To An Unknown God" was in his agents' hands before he started work on *The Pastures of Heaven* early in 1931. When this version, too, failed to find a publisher, Steinbeck wrote his agents that "To An Unknown God should have been a play. It was conceived as a play and thought of and talked of as such for several years. . . . It is out of proportion because it was thought of as two books. I should like to write it again." By this time, however, he was deep into his next book and was not able to begin a thorough revision of "To An Unknown God" until January of 1932, after completing *The Pastures of Heaven,* which was published in the autumn of that year.

In addition to his two published novels, none of which made money, and the two manuscripts he withdrew, Steinbeck was also writing short stories. He had submitted a volume of these to McBride and Company as early as 1926, when he was in New York, but they were not accepted. The first magazine to print his stories was the *North American Review,* which published the first two parts of *The Red Pony* in November and December of 1933, "The Murder" and "The Raid" in April and October of 1934, and "The White Quail" in March of the following year.

In the summer of 1932 Steinbeck moved to the Eagle Rock area of Los Angeles and tried unsuccessfully to free lance a series of short articles of local interest. Also, he wrote to the Mexican government and received permission to make a four-hundred-mile horseback trip in Mexico for the purpose of doing a series of little stories utilizing local color. He was planning to leave for Mexico near the end of November, but these plans did not materialize. His agents were anxious for him to finish *To A God Unknown,* and in November Steinbeck wrote that "the necessity for making a living" had forced him to take a job again. Not until the successes of *Tortilla Flat* and *Of Mice and Men* was Steinbeck able to stop looking for odd jobs.

Probably the most important thing that happened to Steinbeck in the early thirties was his making the acquaintance, in Pacific Grove, of Edward F. Ricketts, who ran a small commercial laboratory specializing in marine invertebrates. Ricketts' influence can be seen in the succession of characters which Steinbeck patterned after him—Dr. Phillips of "The Snake," Doc Burton of *In Dubious Battle,* Doc of *Cannery Row,* and Doc of *Sweet Thursday.* Even more, this influence is evident in that biological view of life which underlies all of Steinbeck's mature works. Steinbeck had had a scientific bent since his high school days and had continued this interest by taking several science courses while at Stanford, but through Ricketts this interest was guided and developed to its explicit expression in *Sea of Cortez,* the "journal" of their scientific expedition to the Gulf of California. In his memorial sketch "About Ed Ricketts" Steinbeck has paid real homage to his friend's remarkable personality and the fifteen years of comradeship which were ended by Ricketts' accidental death in 1948.

Steinbeck returned to Pacific Grove from Los Angeles that winter and, after completing his final version of *To A God Unknown*, began work on *Tortilla Flat*, some of whose incidents he had planned to write as short stories. In addition to those incidents he had observed while working in the sugar-beet factory, others were told to him by Susan Gregory, a long-time resident of Monterey to whom the book is dedicated. Robert M. Ballou, then Steinbeck's publisher, was unenthusiastic about the new novel, and the story goes that as many as eleven publishers turned down *Tortilla Flat*. The rejection for Knopf was written by Louis Kronenberger, who added that while he could not have the confidence in that book necessary in those hard times he would like to see the next book—"I think the man has a future." That the book was published at all was the result of a happy accident. Pascal Covici visited Ben Abramson's book shop in Chicago and was pressed to read *The Pastures of Heaven* and *To A God Unknown*, which Abramson felt to be the works of a very promising writer. When Covici got back to New York he telephoned McIntosh and Otis, who passed on to him the manuscript for *Tortilla Flat*. It was published by Covici-Friede in 1935, a year and a half after it was completed.

Ironically, it was the first Steinbeck book to make money. It appeared on best-seller lists for several months, received the California Commonwealth Club's annual gold medal for the best novel by a Californian, was produced as a stage play (unsuccessfully, however), and made into a motion picture. Also, it was banned in Ireland and attacked by the Monterey Chamber of Commerce, who, fearing for its tourist trade, announced the book was a lie. Its success surprised Steinbeck. "I do not see," he wrote his agents, "what even Hollywood can make of *Tortilla Flat* with its episodic treatment."

The money from *Tortilla Flat* made possible at last Steinbeck's trip to Mexico and, urged by the "considerable nuisance" of publicity, he left for Mexico that autumn in a battered second-hand car. He was back before the year's end, and when asked about his trip he replied, "Mexico fades very quickly. I can't remember it very well. I think possibly the people there live on a mental level about equal in depth to our dream level. The contacts I made there are all dreamlike."

Although *In Dubious Battle* was published in January of 1936, just before the outbreak of a lettuce strike in Salinas, Steinbeck had actually completed that novel a year earlier, three months before the publication of *Tortilla Flat* in May of 1935. This delay in publication, like that of the previous novel, was caused by his publisher's anxiety about the

book's salability. None of the strike novels of the last two or three years
had succeeded, and in addition there was some concern about the
book's language, which Steinbeck refused to change. "A working man
bereft of his profanity is a silent man," Steinbeck wrote. "I've used only
those expressions that are commonly used. I hope it won't be necessary
to remove them. To try to reproduce the speech of these people and to
clean it up is to make it sound stiff, unnatural and emasculated. I think
it is vulgar only in the Latin sense."

Steinbeck was suspicious that his strike novel would be "jumped on
by both sides." "Communists will hate it," he remarked, "and the other
side will too." He said he had tried to write *In Dubious Battle* "without
looking through the narrow glass of political or economic preconcep-
tion" and that he was not concerned with his protagonists as communists or capitalists but rather as humans "subject to the weaknesses
of humans and to the greatnesses of humans." But *In Dubious Battle*
was a critical success and Steinbeck again received the California Commonwealth Club's gold medal. It remains today the finest strike novel
written in America. In addition to his own general knowledge of working men and conditions, Steinbeck used some firsthand information
provided by a person called Tom Collins, who was director of a mobile
camp unit under the Farm Security Administration. This is the same
"Tom who lived it" to whom *The Grapes of Wrath* is dedicated. About
the time Steinbeck was working on *Tortilla Flat*, he had begun a realistic biographical sketch in the first person based on information given
him by a communist district organizer; this work was not completed
and some of the material went into *In Dubious Battle*. Steinbeck's
"grass-roots" information from organizers "in the field" had unforeseen
repercussions. After he had sent the manuscript of *In Dubious Battle*
to Covici-Friede, he received a three-page closely typed letter from one
of the publisher's readers criticizing the ideology and practice of the
party organizers in the book and suggesting various ways in which these
technical deviations could be corrected. Steinbeck refused to consider
these changes and asked that the manuscript be returned. The agents
then submitted the manuscript to Bobbs-Merrill, who was willing to
publish it and claimed it by default. Macmillan also was interested.
But Pascal Covici found out what had happened and asked Steinbeck
to disregard the reader's letter; he would bring the book out after all
if Steinbeck really wanted it published though the firm was still worried
because its protagonists were communists. There ensued a wrangle over
publishing rights which was settled only upon Miss Otis' return from
abroad in the summer of 1935. The book was finally issued by Covici-
Friede.

Although *Of Mice and Men* appeared in January of 1937, exactly one year after *In Dubious Battle*, two years had elapsed since the strike novel had been completed. Steinbeck had hardly finished the final draft of *In Dubious Battle* when he wrote his agents, "I'm doing a play now. I don't know what will come of it. If I can do it well enough it will be a good play. I mean the theme is swell." Another time he wrote that *Of Mice and Men* was "a study of the dreams and pleasures of everyone." But Steinbeck was doing so many other things during this time that attention to the new work must have been sporadic. For one thing, he was deeply involved in the wrangle over the publication of *In Dubious Battle*. For another, his father was very ill that spring and died in June. He was also occupied with his Mexican trip, which was made possible that September.

Steinbeck completed the novel version of *Of Mice and Men* in late August of 1936 and found that *In Dubious Battle* had given him some status as an expert on California's labor problem. He went into the field to collect material for an article commissioned by *Nation* ("Dubious Battle in California," Sept. 12, 1936) and a series of eight articles by the *San Francisco News* ("The Harvest Gypsies," Oct. 5-12, 1936). Back in Los Gatos, where he had built a house that year, Steinbeck wrote, "I just returned yesterday from the strike area of Salinas and from my migrants in Bakersfield. This thing is very dangerous. Maybe it will be patched up for a while but I look for the lid to blow off in a few weeks. Issues are very sharp here now."

Of Mice and Men was published in January of 1937 and was an immediate success. For the first time, really, Steinbeck found himself in the spotlight of nation-wide publicity. The novel appeared on best-seller lists, was a Book-of-the-Month selection, and was sold to Hollywood, where one producer irked Steinbeck by suggesting that in the motion picture someone else should kill the girl and Lennie should get the blame. This would keep the audience's sympathy with Lennie.

The public attention focused on Steinbeck as a result of *Of Mice and Men* made him uncomfortable, but it also made it easier for his agents to place some of his short stories, though there was still no great competition for them. "St. Katy the Virgin" had been in the hands of his agents since 1932 and was finally issued by Covici-Friede as a monograph in 1936. "The Snake" could find no publisher and in 1935 Steinbeck wrote that he had given it to a magazine "run in conjunction with a stable" (the *Monterey Beacon*) in return for six months' use of a big bay hunter. (In January of that year Steinbeck, under the pseudonym of Amnesia Glasscock, had published eight poems in this periodical, all of which were in the same vein as his Stanford pieces nine years earlier.)

Referring to "The Snake," Steinbeck humorously suggested that the agents could get their 10%, but would have to come out to California to do the riding. In 1937 this story was rejected by both *Atlantic* and *Harper's*. One of Steinbeck's best short stories, "Flight," was rejected by *Saturday Evening Post* and *Scribner's* in 1937 and didn't appear until it was collected in *The Long Valley* (1938). Things were changing, however. "The Chrysanthemums" and a third part of *The Red Pony* ("The Promise") were published by Harper's in August and October of 1937. *Esquire* accepted "The Ears of Johnny Bear" in September of the same year, and in June of 1938 *Atlantic* printed "The Harness." "The Leader of the People" first appeared in *The Long Valley* and, while included in the 1945 edition of *The Red Pony*, was not a part of the 1937 edition, although it had probably been written by then. One version called "Grandfather" is found in the same manuscript book with *Tortilla Flat*, "The Murder," and "The Chrysanthemums."

The selection of *Of Mice and Men* by the Book-of-the-Month Club made it possible for Steinbeck to do some traveling, and in the spring of 1937 he left San Francisco for New York, traveling his favorite way by freighter via the Panama Canal. Steinbeck stayed briefly in New York to see his agents and publishers, reluctantly attended a dinner for Thomas Mann (in a borrowed suit), and in the middle of May sailed for England on a Swedish freighter. (It was on board this ship that he wrote the special Foreword to the Modern Library edition of *Tortilla Flat*.) He traveled to his mother's homeplace in Ireland, over to Sweden, and then to Russia, which country he found as bewildering in its own way as Mexico had been.

Before leaving on this trip Steinbeck had been working on a dramatization of *Of Mice and Men*, and on his return to New York early in August (aboard another freighter) he stayed at George Kaufman's farm in Bucks County, Pennsylvania, and with some advice from Kaufman, who was to direct it, finished the final version of the play. *Of Mice and Men* opened November 23, 1937, on the stage of the Music Box theatre in New York and won great critical and popular acclaim. It brought Steinbeck the Drama Critics' Circle award in a season which saw the production of *Our Town*, *The Cradle Will Rock*, *Golden Boy*, and *Prologue to Glory*. On the very first ballot, *Of Mice and Men* received nine votes to a total of seven for the others.

But Steinbeck did not stay for the laurels. Upon completing the stage version, not even waiting for the play to be produced, he went to Detroit, bought a car, and, after visiting Ben Abramson in Chicago, drove to Oklahoma. There he joined a band of migrant workers, lived with them in their Hoovervilles, and worked with them when they got to California. He was already writing *The Grapes of Wrath*. During one period that autumn Steinbeck lived in one of the federal migrant camps in central California and wrote to Lawrence Clark Powell, "I have to write this sitting in a ditch. I'm out working—may go south to pick a little cotton. Migrants are going south now and I'll probably go along." At another time that autumn, he was planning to accept a Hollywood contract of $1000 a week for six weeks' work on *Of Mice and Men* so he could give two dollars apiece to three thousand migrants. Pascal Covici flew to the coast to talk him out of it. When *Life* offered to send him into the field with a photographer to write about the migrants, Steinbeck informed his agents that he would accept no money other than expenses—"I'm sorry but I simply can't make money on these people . . . the suffering is too great for me to cash in on it."

Steinbeck was absorbing the materials of his great novel at first hand, and he went into the field with no ready-made theory to substantiate. When the editors of *Occident* asked him for an article of a political nature, he refused, saying, "Generalities seem to solidify so quickly into stupidities. A writer can only honestly say—'This is the way it seems to me at this moment.' " He didn't think he knew enough about the situation and didn't wish to retire into some "terminology"—fascism or communism, for example. He was "simply listening to men talk and watching them act, hoping that the projection of the microcosm will define the outlines of the macrocosm." And it is just this conjunction of the microcosm and the macrocosm, the concrete and the universal, which makes *The Grapes of Wrath* a great novel.

The Grapes of Wrath was a phenomenon on the scale of a national event. It was publicly banned and burned by citizens; it was debated on national radio hook-ups; but above all it was read.[4] Those who didn't read it saw it as a motion picture. It brought Steinbeck the Pulitzer prize and got him elected to the National Institute of Arts and Letters. He was also accused of being Jewish, to which he replied, "I'm sorry for a time when one must know a man's race before his work can be approved or disapproved. I cannot see how *The Grapes of Wrath* can be Jewish propaganda, but then I have heard it called communist propaganda also." One bit of attention, however, Steinbeck did welcome. A group of migrant laborers sent him a patchwork dog sewn from pieces of their shirt-tails and dresses and bearing around its neck a tag with the inscription "Migrant John."

In addition to being plagued by public demands, Steinbeck was increasingly concerned about the war. On New Year's Eve, 1940, he wrote to Pascal Covici, "So we go into this happy new year, knowing that our species has learned nothing, can as a race learn nothing—that the experience of ten thousand years has made no impression on the instincts of the million years that preceded."

It was in such a frame of mind that Steinbeck was preparing for a scientific expedition to the Gulf of California with his friend Ed Ricketts, the marine biologist. The object of this expedition or "trip," as they preferred to call it, was "to collect and preserve the marine invertebrates of the littoral." Steinbeck's association with Ed Ricketts had done much to stimulate and expand his scientific interests. Late in 1939 he had accompanied Ricketts on a similar expedition to the littoral north of San Francisco, and in that year Ricketts published his book on marine invertebrates, *Between Pacific Tides*, which was reissued in 1948 with an introduction by Steinbeck. In March of 1940 the Mexican government granted the two men permits for their expedition along the Mexican coasts, and on the eleventh of that month they lifted anchor for the Gulf of California, which the two men preferred to call by its older name—Sea of Cortez.

Steinbeck returned to Monterey about the middle of April and immediately set off again for Mexico to work on the motion picture *The Forgotten Village*, which also appeared in the form of a book of pictures accompanied by Steinbeck's script. It is a simple and moving account of one Mexican community in its fight against disease, a fight hindered by its own superstitions and ignorance. This he completed in January of 1941, and he immediately began work on the manuscript for *Sea of Cortez*, which occupied him until August of that year.

Although the material for the narrative and speculative portion of the book came in part from two journals, one kept by Ricketts and the other by Steinbeck, it is clear from constant references in the letters to "my part" that the narrative was actually composed by Steinbeck, while Ricketts was working on the highly technical biological sections. Steinbeck was very excited about the book; he wanted to do a "good job" and refused to be rushed. He was planning the book very carefully and found "a great poetry in scientific thinking." Another time he wrote of the book, "It will only outrage the second rate scientists who are ready to yell mysticism the moment anything gets dangerously close to careful thinking and a little bit out of their range."

Sea of Cortez had a mixed reception. But whether the book has value as philosophy or science, it is an important document for understanding Steinbeck and his work. As he himself noted while writing it, "When this work is done, I will have finished a cycle of work that has been biting me for many years and it is simply the careful statement of the thesis of work to be done in the future." The book is far more than a journal of travel. It is a record of Steinbeck's basic attitudes and beliefs, and stands to his work as *Death in the Afternoon* and *Green Hills of Africa* stand to that of Hemingway.

Sea of Cortez was published the same month that the United States entered the war, and although Steinbeck was shocked at this new evidence that wars are a biological trait of man, he was also eager to participate in the struggle. One of his efforts grew directly out of his knowledge of marine biology. Together with Ed Ricketts, Steinbeck compiled a list of papers written by Japanese zoologists, papers which gave minute information about "depth, tide, currents, reefs, nature of coast, etc." pertaining to Japanese-held islands of the Pacific—"all the information needed if we were to make beach landings." But the Military was suspicious of this information and apparently nothing came of the suggestion. Another of these schemes was actually approved by President Roosevelt. Early in the war Steinbeck suggested that counterfeit money, properly "aged," be dropped behind enemy lines to cause inflation and disrupt financial traffic. According to Steinbeck, this idea was rejected by Secretary Morgenthau and Lord Halifax. It is interesting that this "secret weapon" was used with great effectiveness by the Germans.

Less spectacular, but perhaps more efficient, was Steinbeck's work on *Bombs Away*. The idea for this book grew out of a series of suggestions made by General "Hap" Arnold of the Army Air Force. The purpose of the book was frankly propagandistic. In Steinbeck's words, ". . . mostly this book intends to tell the whole people of the kind and quality of our Air Force, of the caliber of its men and of the excellence of its equipment." Accompanied by the photographer and flier John Swope, Steinbeck traveled from one training base to another gathering material for the new book. *Bombs Away* had a wide sale and was bought by Hollywood for $250,000, but Steinbeck turned over all royalties to the Air Forces Aid Society Trust Fund. Even in such a piece of journalism as this, Steinbeck refused to compromise his integrity. He was asked to write a final chapter depicting the climax of that rigorous training which the book describes by giving an account of an actual bombing run. Steinbeck refused to write such a chapter because he had never been on a bombing run and was afraid his description might be false.

Although most of Steinbeck's writing during the war was frankly journalistic, he did produce during this period his second play-novelette, *The Moon Is Down*. Even this book, however, had its roots in Steinbeck's war effort. It was the result of several conversations he had with Colonel William J. Donovan of the OSS on ways of aiding resistance movements in Nazi-occupied countries. Steinbeck began work on the book in the late summer of 1941, right after completing *Sea of Cortez*, and it was published in March of 1942.

Its publication was followed by a deluge of pro and con criticism which continued through the whole period of its career on the Broadway stage and motion picture screen. As three years earlier Steinbeck had been called a communist, so now he was labeled a fascist, and for the same reason—his insistence on seeing the conflict in human rather than political terms. Steinbeck was concerned with dramatizing, in the abstract, the nature of a clash between democratic and "herd" men. His motion picture of this period, *Lifeboat*, had the same theme. But however much *The Moon Is Down* was attacked at home, it was published by a French underground press, translated into many languages, and became very popular among resistance movements throughout Nazi-occupied Europe. The king of Norway thought enough of its effectiveness to decorate Steinbeck for it.

Not content with these contributions to the war effort, Steinbeck took a position as foreign correspondent for the *New York Herald Tribune* and in the spring of 1943 he left for Europe aboard a troopship. He stayed abroad until October of that year. At first Steinbeck was stationed with a Flying Fortress unit in England. In August his reports came from Algiers, and in early September, after two weeks of silence, his communiques came from the Italian front. Steinbeck had gone on the beaches with the American assault force. In his communiques Steinbeck wisely left general military comment and analysis to more qualified observers. Instead he stresses what is called "human interest"—the hopes, fears, and activities of G.I. Joes under the various conditions of war. Occasionally, these communiques are in the form of a short story, such as the ones about "Big Train Mulligan." At other times they describe the horrors of war—"a small Italian girl in the street with her stomach blown out." Steinbeck's ability to mix with the common man, an ability he had put to good use with the migrants, is everywhere evident in his dispatches. In his review of *Cannery Row* in the *New York Times Book Review*, F. O. Mathiessen has remarked on the "freshness of observation" which some of these pieces have. They reveal the same intimate, casual, yet shrewd observation that is apparent in the cartoons of Bill Mauldin.

Shortly after Steinbeck returned from his overseas assignment in October of 1943 he had ready for publication a book about his experiences, but he was too disheartened by what he had seen of the war to prolong the experience in any way and decided not to publish it. Instead he set himself to work on a new novel, and in six weeks produced *Cannery Row*. Although the book was not published until December of 1944, it is certain that it was finished eight months earlier, in March of that year, just four months after his return from Europe.

Although many critics saw a great similarity, *Cannery Row* was in no sense a repetition of *Tortilla Flat*. In the intervening ten years Steinbeck had written *In Dubious Battle*, *Of Mice and Men*, *The Grapes of Wrath*, *Sea of Cortez*, *The Moon Is Down*, and had spent six months as a war correspondent. The experience of these years is in *Cannery Row* and accounts for the difference in tone between the two books. The detached, amused acceptance of the paisanos of *Tortilla Flat* gives way in *Cannery Row* to an active championing of Mac and the boys, who are "the Virtues, the Graces, the Beauties" of a mangled world ruled by "tigers with ulcers, rutted by strictured bulls and scavenged by blind jackals. . . ." About the book's instant popularity, Steinbeck remarked, ". . . people are rushing to send it overseas to soldiers. Apparently they think of it as a relief from war." And upon hearing that on second reading Malcolm Cowley had called *Cannery Row* a "poisoned cream puff," Steinbeck replied that if Cowley had read it yet again he would have discovered how very poisoned it was.

By the time *Cannery Row* appeared in December of 1944, eight months after it was completed, Steinbeck was well into a novelette which while still in progress was called "The Pearl of La Paz." Although the story was finished by early February of 1945, it did not appear until ten months later in the December issue of *Woman's Home Companion* under the title of "The Pearl of the World." It was first published in book form two years later to coincide with the RKO release of the motion picture Steinbeck had adapted from it, and was called simply *The Pearl*. The essential story had been in Steinbeck's mind since before the war. The germ can be found in a paragraph in *Sea of Cortez* relating an incident "which happened at La Paz in recent years." When Steinbeck came to write "The Pearl of the World" four years later, he kept the basic pattern of this incident—the discovery of the pearl, the persecution, and the renunciation—but he fleshed out this pattern with greater human context, making of it a parable of man's soul. Five years after its publication, he said of *The Pearl*, "I tried to write it as folklore, to give it that set-aside, raised-up feeling that all folk stories have."

The next book of this postwar period, *The Wayward Bus*, appeared early in 1947, two years after "The Pearl of the World" was written, but almost a whole year before that story was published in book form as *The Pearl*. It too had been in Steinbeck's mind for a long time, possibly since his trip to Mexico in 1940. By July of 1945 he had sketched out the book's structure and theme, and as originally conceived it was to have a Mexican background. *The Wayward Bus* was not actually

written until the summer of 1946. Like the other two books Steinbeck
had written after the war, *The Wayward Bus* was dedicated to an
examination of the assumptions underlying modern civilization. But
whereas *Cannery Row* seemed to suggest a retreat from the world, and
The Pearl a tragic resignation, *The Wayward Bus* holds out a positive
hope. Steinbeck seems to be saying that despite the deluded Normas,
the cynical Van Brunts, the self-centered Alices, and the vulgar Louies
there are also realistic and objective people like Juan Chicoy, without
whom the world would founder, who always return to dig it out of the
mud. Steinbeck conceived of Juan Chicoy, the driver of the wayward
bus, as "all the God the Fathers you ever saw driving a six cylinder,
broken down world through time and space."

Burning Bright, Steinbeck's next book of fiction, did not appear until
1950, almost four years after the affirmation of *The Wayward Bus*. But
these intervening years were busy ones. In the summer of 1947, just a
few months after the publication of *The Wayward Bus*, Steinbeck
went to Russia with Robert Capa, the photographer. On his return
he published *A Russian Journal* (April, 1948), parts of which had appeared in the *New York Herald Tribune*. *A Russian Journal* was an
interesting piece of reporting and, despite its controversial subject, was
well received by reviewers. Anyone who had followed Steinbeck's career
up to this time was not surprised to learn that while Steinbeck found
the common people of Russia as human as people anywhere, he was
depressed by the regimentation, bureaucracy, and lack of individual
freedom. What he saw in Russia seemed to confirm the suspicions
about a highly cooperative society which he had expressed in *Sea of
Cortez* seven years earlier.

During this period he also wrote a motion picture script from *The
Red Pony* (Republic, 1948), and from the fall of 1948 until May of
1950 he was writing both the story and script for *Viva Zapata* (Twentieth Century Fox, 1952). Both these Hollywood ventures turned out
well. Steinbeck was pleased that Hollywood followed his script for *The
Red Pony* carefully, and he worked conscientiously on *Viva Zapata*.
He even wrote a special, long introduction to the shooting script so
that the producer, director, and camera man would understand what it
was about, and he went on location with Twentieth Century Fox to
supervise the actual filming. Steinbeck has at various times expressed
his distrust of Hollywood, but with the exception of *Tortilla Flat* and
A Medal for Benny, the first of which he had nothing to do with and
the second of which departed very much from his script, all his motion
pictures have been first-rate.

Two short stories also date from this period: "The Miracle of

Tepayac" (Dec., 1948), and "His Father" (Sept., 1949). It was during this period, too, that he suffered the loss of his great friend, Ed Ricketts, and wrote his memorial sketch, "About Ed Ricketts," which introduced *The Log from Sea of Cortez* (1951). Also, Steinbeck was doing research in the files of Salinas Valley newspapers, particularly the *Salinas Index*, and wrote a good part of the material which went into *East of Eden*, at that time called "Salinas Valley."

The new emphasis of Steinbeck's work indicated by *The Wayward Bus* was sustained in his next two books of fiction, *Burning Bright* and *East of Eden*. *Burning Bright* was Steinbeck's third attempt in the play-novelette form, and from late in 1949 until its completion in the summer of 1950 the book underwent several thorough revisions and changes of title. It was variously called "In the Forests of the Night," "Tiger, Tiger," and finally *Burning Bright*. This title was decided upon after Steinbeck had read the proof sheets, which bear the title "In the Forests of the Night." The fact that all of these titles are from Blake's poem testifies to the affinity Steinbeck must have felt between that poem and his play-novelette.

Unlike his previous experiments in this form, *Burning Bright* was put on Broadway before being published in novelette form, one month later. Also unlike his previous two experiments, *Burning Bright* was a miserable failure, running less than two weeks. Critics seemed to vie with one another in heaping abuse upon the play. But although at first Steinbeck was puzzled by the failure of *Burning Bright*, he came to see the book's deficiencies, and it was not included in *The Short Novels of John Steinbeck* (1953). Four years after the book's publication he admitted in a private conversation that the play was a failure in writing, that it was too abstract, that it preached too much, and that the audience was always a step ahead of it.

Steinbeck's original plan for *East of Eden* was "to set down in story form for his two small sons the full record of their ancestors from the time they moved westward to Salinas Valley just after the Civil War." The first draft began with an address to his two sons: "Dear Tom and John: You are little boys now, when I am writing this. . . ." To Pascal Covici, Steinbeck wrote that "Salinas Valley" would be "two books— the story of my country, and the story of me." He began this work in 1947, and as late as March of 1949, he was still thinking of it in terms of "Salinas Valley." It was not until two years later that the book's new theme, the Cain and Abel myth, was acknowledged by a change in the proposed title—*East of Eden*.

Steinbeck was moving around a great deal during this period, from New York to California to the Virgin Islands. Pascal Covici was kept busy sending Steinbeck materials, especially translations of the Bible and commentaries. The new theme resulted in several complete revisions of the manuscript, in which Steinbeck substantially reduced the story of his own family and struck out all the special passages addressed to his sons.

Steinbeck finished *East of Eden* early in 1952 and it left him exhausted. While writing the manuscript he had to get his first pair of glasses, and for two months after finishing, his correspondence was done in printing rather than his usual longhand. That spring Steinbeck left for Europe. While in Italy he found himself under specific and personal attack by the communists as an American who countenanced war crimes and bacteriological warfare. Steinbeck did not let the charge go unchallenged. He wrote a long open letter to the communists and it was first printed in the red *L'Unita* (where it was cut) and then in *Il Tempo*, which published it in its entirety. As a consequence of this exchange Steinbeck's stay in Italy was attended by much publicity. In Ireland, he visited the ancestral home of his mother's people, the Hamiltons, and found everything very depressing. The people were humorless, unfriendly, and suspicious; they did not seem to remember his family.

In September, Steinbeck returned to New York, which he had made his home since 1950, and began work on *Sweet Thursday*, which appeared in June, 1954, just a year and a half after *East of Eden*. Critics were confounded by this sudden change of pace, but *Sweet Thursday* had been in Steinbeck's plans while he was still within a year of completing *East of Eden*, when he wrote to Pascal Covici that he wanted to do a comedy next, possibly in play form. In an interview shortly after the publication of *East of Eden* Steinbeck remarked, "I'm just determined I'm going to learn something about the theatre. Last time out [*Burning Bright*] we were kicked around like dogs but I still want to do it. . . . I'm so fascinated by everything about the theatre I don't really care if the show's a flop." A year later it was reported that Steinbeck was well into a new short novel which would be converted into a musical for the sponsors of "Guys and Dolls." The origin of *Sweet Thursday* as a musical comedy is also attested by the fact that the title was decided upon after Pascal Covici informed the author that Rodgers and Hammerstein were already writing a song by that name for Fauna. Earlier the book had been announced variously as "The Palace Flophouse" and "The Bear Flag Cafe," two institutions made famous by *Cannery Row*. The Rodgers and Hammerstein adaptation of *Sweet Thursday*, called *Pipe Dream*, opened at the Sam S. Shubert Theatre on December 19, 1955, and was an instant popular success.

Coming after the moral affirmations of *Burning Bright* and *East of Eden*, *Sweet Thursday* was a great disappointment to critics and reviewers. Several even prophesied Steinbeck's demise as a writer who should be taken seriously. Actually, this kind of change of pace has been one of Steinbeck's most consistent traits as a writer—*In Dubious Battle* after *Tortilla Flat*, *The Moon Is Down* after *The Grapes of Wrath*, *The Wayward Bus* after *The Pearl*, and *Burning Bright* after *The Wayward Bus*. As Steinbeck has summed it up, "My experience in writing has followed an almost invariable pattern. Since by the process of writing a book I have outgrown that book, and since I like to write, I have not written two books alike. . . . If a writer likes to write he will find satisfaction in endless experimentation with his medium . . . techniques, arrangement of scenes, rhythms of words, rhythms of thought."

Steinbeck has never belonged to nor has he founded a "school" of writing, and what his next book will be like it is impossible to say, but he has never repeated himself. Since moving to New York he has been doing a great deal of nonfiction in the form of essays on such assorted topics as travel, Model T's, juvenile delinquency, and McCarthyism. He has also taken an active interest in television, which has produced some stories from *The Pastures of Heaven*. As early as 1948 he set up an organization called World Video with Robert Capa, Henry S. White, and Phil Reisman, the object being to provide literate shows and films for television. There is no doubt that this kind of activity, so different from his interests in the thirties and forties, will have some effect on his art. It is equally certain that Steinbeck will not depart from the moral position he made explicit in the journal he kept while working on *East of Eden*:

> The writers of today, even I, have a tendency to celebrate the destruction of the spirit and God knows it is destroyed often enough. It is the duty of the writer to lift up, to extend, to encourage. If the written word has contributed anything at all to our developing species and our half developed culture, it is this—great writing has been a staff to lean on, a mother to consult, a wisdom to pick up stumbling folly, a strength in weakness and a courage to support weak cowardice. And how any despairing or negative approach can pretend to be literature I do not know. It is true that we are weak and sick and ugly and quarrelsome but if that is all we ever were, we would, milleniums ago have disappeared from the face of the earth and a few remnants of fossilized jaw bones, a few teeth in a strata of limestone would be the only mark our species would have left on the earth.

1. For a fuller account of Steinbeck's reading and literary references see the biographical sketch in Harry Thornton Moore's *The Novels of John Steinbeck* (Chicago: Nor-

mandie House, 1939), pp. 73-96. The present writer is indebted to Mr. Moore for several details.

2. Moore (op. cit., pp. 76, 77, 78) states that Steinbeck graduated from Salinas high school in 1918, entered Stanford in 1919, left in the spring of 1920, returned briefly in the autumn of 1921, attended during 1922-23, and left for good in 1925. Lewis Gannett [see below, p. 23] states that Steinbeck was a high school senior in 1919. Seeking to solve this problem the present writer asked directly of the registrar at Stanford and received the following cryptic reply: "I can tell you that Mr. Steinbeck attended Stanford during three quarters during the academic year 1920-21, during the academic year 1922-23, 1923-24, and during the year 1924-25."

3. John Steinbeck, "Making of a New Yorker," New York Times Magazine, February 1, 1953, Part II, pp. 26-27.

4. For a good sampling of the reaction to The Grapes of Wrath, see Martin Staples Shockley, "The Reception of The Grapes of Wrath in Oklahoma." [See p. 231, below.]

Lewis Gannett

JOHN STEINBECK'S
WAY OF WRITING

CRITICS have had a holiday detecting exotic symbolisms in John Steinbeck's work. Maybe they are there. He would be the last man to affirm or to deny it. To inquirers for biographical data he has been known to reply: "Please feel free to make up your own facts about me as you need them. I can't remember how much of me really happened and how much I invented. . . . Biography by its very nature must be half-fiction." Nonetheless, in John Steinbeck's letters to his literary agents, McIntosh and Otis, covering almost fifteen years of a unique partnership in creative writing, appears a singularly honest and revealing record of what John Steinbeck himself thought about what he was writing, when he was writing it. Out of those letters emerges as much of an autobiography as John Steinbeck is likely ever to write.

Steinbeck has been interested in writing as long as he can remember. When he was four, he discovered, to his flabbergasted delight, that "high" rhymed with "fly," and from that day to this the permutations and combinations of words have charmed and fascinated him. He wrote for the Salinas, California, high school paper, *El Gabilan*, in 1919, when he was president of the senior class and on the basketball and track teams. He wrote during his intermittent sessions at Stanford University. In the early 1920's he functioned briefly as a reporter for the New York American, but he didn't like that; he wanted to do his own kind of writing. He wrote hard for almost fifteen years before he had his first success. He has always written more than he has published. Indeed, he wrote three full-length novels, two of which he destroyed

---

LEWIS GANNETT, *well-known critic and author, has been a member of the editorial staff of* The New York Herald Tribune *since 1928 and editor of its daily book review column from 1931 to 1956. Before that he was for nine years on the staff of* The Nation. *He has traveled widely in Europe and has visited Russia and the Orient. He lives in New York City and at Cream Hill, his Connecticut place, about which he has written a delightful book. He is a friend of Steinbeck. The essay that appears here is from* The Portable Steinbeck, *copyright 1946 by the Viking Press, Inc., and is reprinted here by permission of the Viking Press and of the author.*

before anyone else saw them, before *Cup of Gold*, his first published novel, made its public appearance.

Cup of Gold appeared in 1929. Steinbeck had sent it to Stuart Rose, editor for Robert M. McBride and Company, and Rose had been enthusiastic about it. But Rose and McBride had a controversy; Rose left the firm just before *Cup of Gold* appeared, and the book was neglected. Seven years later, when Steinbeck's name had become known, another publisher suggested reissuing *Cup of Gold*. "I'm not particularly proud of *Cup of Gold*," Steinbeck wrote to McIntosh and Otis, who had become his agents. "Outside of a certain lyric quality there isn't much to it. I rather wish it had never been published. But as long as it has, it can't be recalled, and further printings can do no harm."

It was in 1930 that Steinbeck began his long association with the literary agency. It was a new firm then, consisting of Mavis McIntosh and Elizabeth Otis, with Annie Laurie Williams as associated theatrical agent. Mary Squire Abbott joined the firm in 1931, Mildred Lyman several years later; in the 1940's Miss McIntosh left. The firm's office became John Steinbeck's office and home whenever he was in New York. In his early years he consulted its partners for literary advice and sometimes for literary consolation. In later years the firm became his bookkeepers, his guards against an intrusive public, and, most important of all, his friends. His letters, at first shyly impersonal, grow increasingly warm; eventually they become comfortable, casual, intimate, family letters. The agents believed in Steinbeck from the first; they tried, mostly in vain, to market his early stories and for some time had little to report except a discouraging series of rejections. But Steinbeck no more lost faith in them than they in him; in fact, at times he seems to have had more faith in his agents than in himself.

"I think I told you that the imperfections of *The Unknown God* [an earlier version of *To a God Unkown*] had bothered me ever since I first submitted the book for publication," the young author wrote in August 1931, before his agents had succeeded in marketing any book of his. "Your announcement of the book's failure to find a public is neither unwelcome nor unpleasant to me. . . . I shall rewrite it. Whether my idea of excellence coincides with editors' ideas remains to be seen. Certainly I shall make no effort to 'popularize' the story. . . . Thank you for your help. I am an unprofitable client."

Times changed. Six years later, when the tide had turned, Steinbeck wrote a brief note to the same agents: "Dear All: Acknowledging another check. Since I took your course I have sold. Do you want a testimonial?" Many authors, when success comes to them, shift restlessly from one agent and from one publisher to another. Steinbeck has never left a publisher who remained interested in his work; he has never had any agent but McIntosh and Otis.

The Pastures of Heaven, Steinbeck's second published book, had a rather bewildering publishing history because of an epidemic of upsets in the New York book world. Robert Ballou, editor for Cape and Smith when he first saw the manuscript—later for Brewer, Warren and Putnam, still later in business under his own name and now (1945) associated with the Viking Press—recognized the quality of the book on first reading and accepted it with enthusiasm. Even before it had appeared in America, he wrote Martin Secker of London that it was "one of the most distinguished novels I have ever read in manuscript."

Before The Pastures of Heaven appeared Steinbeck had written several drafts of To a God Unknown, which no publisher then wanted. He had also finished a book called Dissonant Symphony, which was equally unmarketable; this he later withdrew, saying that, on re-reading, he was ashamed of it. He had even written a murder mystery which he thought "might help pay for coffee." He had been groping, experimenting, finding his way. In Pastures he first struck what was to become known as the Steinbeck vein.

He announced his theme early in 1931. "There is, about twelve miles from Monterey, a valley in the hills called Corral de Tierra," he wrote. "Because I am using some of its people I am calling it Las Pasturas del Cielo. The valley was for years known as the happy valley because of the unique harmony which existed among its twenty families. They were ordinary people, ill educated but honest, and as kindly as any. In fact, in their whole history I cannot find that they have committed a really malicious act or an act which was not dictated by humble expediency or out-and-out altruism. There have been two murders, a suicide, many quarrels and a great deal of unhappiness in the Pastures of Heaven, and all of these things can be traced to the influence of the A——s. So much is true. I am using the following method. The manuscript is made up of stories, each one complete in itself, having its rise, climax and ending. Each story deals with a family or an individual. They are tied together only by the common locality and the common contact with the A——s. I am trying to show this peculiar evil cloud which follows the A——s. Some of the stories are very short and some as long as 15,000 words. . . . I wonder whether you think this is a good plan."

McIntosh and Otis didn't keep carbons in those days, and there is no record to show whether they thought it a good plan. The book of course turned out a little differently; everything Steinbeck has ever written has grown and changed in the process of coming to birth; he is not the type of writer who maps every detail of his book, like a mail-order catalogue, before he begins writing, and sticks to his plan. He learns a good deal about his stories, and his characters, in the process of writing.

The Pastures of Heaven appeared in 1932; it had a friendly critical reception, but sold few copies. *To a God Unknown* appeared in 1933; it sold even less well. Robert Ballou had to "remainder" the unsold copies of both books, and neither sold even as well as *Cup of Gold*. When, after the success of *Tortilla Flat* in 1935, Pascal Covici bought the remaining unbound sheets and took over rights to the two books, he discovered to his amazement that the sales had not paid for even the pitifully small advances made to Steinbeck. With three published books, Steinbeck's total sales were fewer than three thousand!

Steinbeck never expected large sales; all his later successes surprised him. When he sent the final version of *To a God Unknown* to his agents, in February 1933, he explained: "The book was hellish hard to write. I had been making notes for it for about five years. It will probably be a hard book to sell. Its characters are not 'home folks.' They make no more attempt at being human than the people in the *Iliad*. Boileau insisted that only gods, kings and heroes are worth writing about. I firmly believe that. The detailed accounts of the lives of clerks don't interest me much unless, of course, the clerk breaks into heroism. But I have no intention of trying to explain my book. It has to do that for itself. I would be sure of its effect if it could be stipulated that the reader read to an obbligato of Bach."

At that time Steinbeck was so poor that he could not even afford a dog. He had had a big dog named Omar as a companion when, as a hermit in the High Sierras, he wrote *Cup of Gold*. The first letter from him in the McIntosh and Otis files, after explaining the project for *The Pastures of Heaven*, continued to report that "Tillie Eulenspiegel the Airedale has puppies, as sinful a crew as ever ruined rugs. Four of them found your letter and ate all of it but the address. I should imagine they were awed by the address if I had not learned that they hold nothing in reverence. At present they are out eating each other."

But in 1933 he needed a dog. That was the year he reread his manuscript of *Dissonant Symphony* and hastened to advise New York that he wanted it killed. "I reread my copy and was ashamed of it," he wrote. "The Murder I thought might be sold to a pulp if it were cut down. Even a little money would be better than a bundle of paper. We are very happy. I need a dog pretty badly. I dreamed of great numbers of dogs last night. They sat in a circle and looked at me and I wanted all of them. Apparently we are headed for the rocks. The light company is going to turn off the power in a few days but we don't care much. The rent is up pretty soon and then we shall move, I don't know where."

He was writing *Tortilla Flat* then, and, strange as that seems today, *Tortilla Flat* also proved hard to market. There is a tradition in the office of Steinbeck's agents that eleven publishers rejected it, but the files preserve copies of only two turndowns. Robert Ballou said, "There is not a bad page in it. . . . You have created a fine set of characters and an excellent background against which they may live, and then given them no life which justifies a novel." He felt that Steinbeck ought to withdraw the manuscript. Louis Kronenberger, writing for the house of Alfred A. Knopf, said, "We cannot have the confidence in *Tortilla Flat* that I think a publisher should have nowadays when he backs a book against hard times." Finally Pascal Covici, then in business as Covici-Friede but since 1938 associated with the Viking Press, accepted *Tortilla Flat*.

Steinbeck was puzzled, both before and after publication of *Tortilla Flat*, at the failure of critics and readers to distinguish his theme. "I want to write something about *Tortilla Flat*," he told his agents in March 1934. "The book has a very definite theme. I thought it was clear enough. I had expected that the plan of the Arthurian cycle would be recognized. Even the incident of the Sangreal in the search of the forest is not clear enough, I guess. The form is that of the Malory version—the coming of Arthur, and the mystic quality of owning a house, the forming of the Round Table, the adventures of the knights and finally, the mystic translation of Danny. The main issue was to present a little known and to me delightful people.

"Is not this cycle or story or theme enough? Perhaps it is not enough because I have not made it clear enough. Then I must make it clearer. What do you think of putting in an interlocutor, who between each incident interprets the incident, morally, aesthetically, historically, but in the manner of the paisanos themselves? This would give the book much the appeal of the Gesta Romanorum, those outrageous tales with monkish morals appended, or of the Song of Solomon in the King James Version, with the delightful chapter headings which go to prove that the Shulamite is in reality Christ's Church. It would not be as sharp as this, of course. But the little dialogue would at least make clear the form of the book, its tragi-comic theme, and the strong but different philosophic-moral system of these people.

"A cycle is there. You will remember that the association forms, flowers and dies. Far from having a hard theme running through the book, one of the intents is to show that rarely does anything in the lives of these people survive the night."

Obviously, John Steinbeck as a writer was never quite the naïve primitive discovered by some of his hoity-toity critics.

Fortunately, Steinbeck gave up the plan for an interlocutor; and readers of *Tortilla Flat* took it to their hearts, with or without the Arthurian cycle. It was Steinbeck's first experience of success, and that bothered him. He had written *Tortilla Flat* more rapidly and easily than some of its predecessors, and he remarked to his agents, "Curious that this second-rate book, written for relaxation, should cause this fuss. People are actually taking it seriously."

He added, in a vein that ran like a motif through his letters of those years, "I am scared to death of popularity. It has ruined everyone I know. That's one of the reasons I should like *In Dubious Battle* printed next. Myths form early, and I want no tag of humorist pinned on me, nor any other kind."

He was leery of the conventional publishers' publicity. "I am never photographed," he told his agents. "This is not temperament on my part, nor is it self-consciousness. I do not believe in mixing personality with work. It is customary, I guess, but I should like to break the custom. A public nauseated with personal detail would probably be more grateful than otherwise. . . . Please get this point over with enough force to make it stick for some time."

Steinbeck may have been wrong about the public's nausea with personal detail, but he stuck to his point. He was so convinced of it that, living out in California, he thought that even Alexander Woollcott must agree with him. After the Book-of-the-Month Club had taken *Of Mice and Men* and made Steinbeck a national figure, Woollcott asked for material he could use in a broadcast. The agents passed on the request to Steinbeck.

"I think you know my hatred of personal matter," he replied. "I hope you will get some of that impression over to Mr. Woollcott. On the other hand I should like to have him talk about the work. Factual material doesn't matter, but tell him, please no personalities. I simply can't write books if a consciousness of self is thrust on me. Must have my anonymity. . . . Unless I can stand in a crowd without self-consciousness and watch things from an uneditorialized point of view, I'm going to have a hell of a hard time. I'm sure Mr. Woollcott will understand this. I'm sure that of his own experience he will know the pressures exerted by publicity are unendurable."

Mr. Woollcott knew far more than Steinbeck about the pressures exerted by publicity, but he was not the man to find any of them unendurable; he lived for limelight. Steinbeck, unhappy about the ballyhoo over *Mice* in 1937, could not then dream what pressures would be

exerted on him after *The Grapes of Wrath*. But he was right in his attitude; the writer who becomes a public personality inevitably loses something of his normal attitude to his fellow-men. He becomes an Author
with a capital A, set apart from common men. It seldom helps.

Still, the royalties from *Tortilla Flat* and the later and much larger
returns from *Of Mice and Men* changed the material conditions of
Steinbeck's life. "Life has become very beautiful since I got a kerosene
heater for my workroom," he wrote. "Completely changed attitude
toward all kinds of things. Warm hands are fine."

Tortilla Flat was sold to the movies for $4,000, which seemed big
money to Steinbeck in those days, and on conventional terms which he
later regretted—they gave him no control over changes made in the
script. But in 1935 Steinbeck had not yet developed that passionate
interest in dramatic forms and in the mass audience of the movies
which was so powerfully to affect his career for the next decade. When
a possible dramatization of *Tortilla Flat* was suggested in October
1935, he instructed his agents to do as they thought best about it; he
knew, he said, nothing of the process. When a movie contract was suggested, he again expressed indifference. "On an average," he wrote, "I
go to about one movie a year."

"My stuff isn't picture material," he was still insisting in January
1936. "If it is bought it is because of some attendant publicity. *Tortilla
Flat* was the exception. There won't be a nibble on *In Dubious Battle*
and if there were the producers would not use the story, and it is a con-
scientious piece of work. But there won't be anything lost. I'm not a
popular writer in spite of the recent fluke."

In Dubious Battle was the first of three very different Steinbeck
books dealing with the migratory farm laborers on the California fruit
farms, and it was the bitterest of the three. "I guess it is a brutal book,"
he wrote when he was still at work on it, in February 1935, "more
brutal because there is no author's moral point of view. The speech of
workingmen may seem a little bit racy to ladies' clubs, but since ladies'
clubs won't believe that such things go on anyway, it doesn't matter.
I know this speech and I'm sick of workingmen being gelded of their
natural expression until they talk with a fine Oxonian flavor. . . . A
workingman bereft of his profanity is a silent man."

A New York editor in Pascal Covici's office read the manuscript of
In Dubious Battle conscientiously and wrote a three-page single-space
report indicating points at which Steinbeck's Communist organizer
diverged from the orthodox party line as expressed by the ideologists of
New York. Steinbeck took this letter as a rejection and almost went to
another publisher, but when Mr. Covici discovered what his assistant

had written he hastily assured Steinbeck that he was willing to publish the book if Steinbeck wished, though he was obviously somewhat alarmed at its violence.

"I would rather stay with Covici-Friede than with anyone I know," Steinbeck informed his agents. "I like the way they worked on *Tortilla Flat* and I like their make-up and everything about them. This letter this morning from them offers to publish *In Dubious Battle* if I wish it. Of course I wish it. It is a good book. I believe in it." As to the Communist ideology, he explained, "My information for this book came mostly from Irish and Italian Communists whose training was in the field, not in the drawing-room. They don't believe in ideologies and ideal tactics. They do what they can under the circumstances."

The book was published as Steinbeck wrote it. Critics, not unnaturally, tended to discuss its politics. Steinbeck was irked. "So far," he complained to McIntosh and Otis, "Burton Rascoe and Ben Abramson are the only two reviewers who have discovered that *In Dubious Battle* is a novel and not a tract. Perhaps more will later."

Of Mice and Men was Steinbeck's first big success, and Steinbeck had had various troubles in writing it. "The microcosm is rather difficult to handle and apparently I did not get it over," he remarked when the book was in process: "the earth longings of a Lennie who was not to represent insanity at all but the inarticulate and powerful yearning of all men." Another time he spoke of the book as "an experiment in making a play that can be read or a novel that can be played . . . to find a new form that will take some of the techniques of both." This was a problem that was to concern him for years.

By this time, of course, Steinbeck again had a dog, Toby, "a very serious dog who doesn't care for jokes," and Toby made trouble for *Mice*. "Minor tragedy stalked," he wrote on May 27, 1936. "My setter pup, left alone one night, made confetti of about half of my manuscript book. Two months' work to do over again. It sets me back. There was no other draft. I was pretty mad, but the poor little fellow may have been acting critically. I didn't want to ruin a good dog for a manuscript I'm not sure is good at all. He only got an ordinary spanking." After the Book-of-the-Month Club had accepted *Mice*, and critical enthusiasm began to boil, Steinbeck still felt that Toby might have been right. "I'm not sure Toby didn't know what he was doing when he ate the first draft," he wrote. "I have promoted Toby-dog to be lieutenant-colonel in charge of literature. But as for the unpredictable literary enthusiasms of this country, I have little faith in them."

He was already mulling over *The Grapes of Wrath*, and it was hard going. "Having the devil's own time with this new book, but I am enjoying it," he wrote in January 1937. "The new book has struck a bad snag," he said two weeks later. "Heaven knows how long it will take me to write. The subject is so large that it scares me. And I'm not going to rush it. It must be worked out with care. That's one thing this selection will do. It will let me work without a starvation scare going on all the time. This may or may not be a good thing."

The success of *Of Mice and Men* made possible Steinbeck's first trip to Europe. He sailed on a Swedish ship. He had always been interested in the Scandinavian countries. Scandinavian translations of *Tortilla Flat* were the only ones he had asked to see, explaining that perhaps his interest was because of his fondness for Selma Lagerlöf's *Gösta Berling*. But on that Swedish ship his heart turned to the Norway of which he would write so memorably, in *The Moon Is Down*, five years later.

"This is a fine ship," he reported cheerfully from shipboard in May 1937. His agents had sent him a "lovely bottle" as a bon voyage gift, and he thanked them for it. "The day after we sailed we were invited to a party in honor of the king and queen of Sweden. At least two-thirds of the people on board were Swedes. Well, we toasted the king and queen in punch. We listened to stuffy speeches and gave a few half-hearted guttural cheers and we went to bed. Now there are only two Norwegians on board. One at our table. He told us that the seventeenth of May was the Norwegian Fourth of July, the day of independence. Immediately we felt a surge of patriotism. Spiritually we felt Norwegian. And your bottle was the nucleus. With only two Norwegians, and we two as a kind of auxiliary Norwegians, we turned the ship into a fury. We made speeches. Wine, beer and brandy ran like water. All evening we toasted everything we could think of. Gradually the Swedes began to feel a certain love for Norway. At two this morning the riot was still going on. The Swedes are jealous but admiring. Even the two Norwegians don't know just how it happened. And your bottle of wine started it. I know you will be glad that your gift was the node of a new international brotherhood. I know you will. And I bet you never heard forty Scandinavians rise with their glasses in their hands and solemnly sing

'Sent Looisss Voomans, vit you diment errings
Chessed det men aroun de apon strings.'

It was unique in international feelings. It was very beautiful."

The Steinbecks visited Russia, but came out sooner than they had planned. They returned from Europe sooner than planned. On September 12 Steinbeck wrote from Los Gatos, "So very glad to be home." He went back to work on *The Grapes of Wrath*.

He had written a series of articles on the migrant workers for the San Francisco *News* in October 1936, before *Of Mice and Men* was published. He had worked on the farms of his long valley long ago in his school vacations. He knew the work; he knew the people. He knew the bitternesses. He felt them in the marrow of his bones. He also had a deep affectionate sense of identification with the fruit-pickers; and he was a Californian, and he felt a responsibility.

"I must go over into the interior valleys," he wrote Elizabeth Otis in the midst of reports on work in progress. "There are five thousand families starving to death over there, not just hungry but actually starving. The government is trying to feed them and get medical attention to them, with the Fascist group of utilities and banks and huge growers sabotaging the thing all along the line, and yelling for a balanced budget. In one tent there are twenty people quarantined for smallpox and two of the women are to have babies in that tent this week. I've tied into the thing from the first and I must get down there and see it and see if I can do something to knock these murderers on the heads.

"Do you know what they're afraid of? They think that if these people are allowed to live in camps with proper sanitary facilities they will organize, and that is the bugbear of the large landowner and the corporation farmer. The states and counties will give them nothing because they are outsiders. But the crops of any part of this state could not be harvested without them. . . . Talk about Spanish children. The death of children by starvation in our valleys is simply staggering. . . . I'll do what I can. . . . Funny how mean and how little books become in the face of such tragedies."

He did what he could, and returned home to dash off a book that was once announced under the title *L'Affaire Lettuceburg*. And when it was done he sat down and wrote a joint letter to his agent and his publisher, a letter beautifully and painfully illustrative of Steinbeck's attitude toward his own work:

"Dear Elizabeth and Pat," he began. "This is going to be a hard letter to write. I feel badly about it. You see this book is finished and it is a bad book and I must get rid of it. It can't be printed. It is bad because it isn't honest. Oh! the incidents all happened but—I'm not telling as much of the truth about them as I know. In satire you have to restrict the picture and I just can't do satire. I've written three books now that were dishonest because they were less than the best I could do. One you never saw because I burned it the day I finished it. The second was the murder novel and this is the third. The first two were written under rather frantic financial pressure, and this last one from an obligation pressure I felt. I know, you could sell possibly 30,000 copies. I know that a great many people would think they liked this book. I, myself, have built up a holeproof argument on how and why I liked it. I can't beat the argument, but I don't like the book. And I would be doing Pat a greater injury in letting him print it than I would by destroying it. Not once in the writing of it have I felt the curious warm pleasure that comes when work is going well. My whole work drive has been aimed at making people understand each other and then I deliberately write this book, the aim of which is to cause hatred through partial understanding. My father would have called it a smart-alec book. It was full of tricks to make people ridiculous. If I can't do better I have slipped badly. And that I won't admit—yet.

"See, Pat—the danger is very great now. A short time ago I had a hostile line of publishers to keep me up, and after them a hostile line of critics. You would print this book now and most critics would praise it. I have only myself to keep me in line. It is the overtone that is bad. It is sloppily written because I never cared about it. I know I promised this book to you, and that I am breaking a promise in withholding it. But I had got smart and cagey you see. I had forgotten that I hadn't learned to write books, that I will never learn to write them. A book must be a life that lives all of itself and this one doesn't do that. You can't write a book. It isn't that simple. The process is more painful than that. And this book is fairly clever, has skillful passages, but tricks and jokes. Sometimes, I, the writer, seem a hell of a smart guy—just twisting this people out of shape. But the hell with it. I beat poverty for a good many years and I'll be damned if I'll go down at the first little whiff of success. I hope you, Pat, won't think I've double-crossed you. In the long run to let this book out would be to doublecross you. But to let the bars down is like a first theft. It's hard to do, but the second time it isn't so hard and pretty soon it is easy. If I should write three books like this and let them out, I would forget there were any other kinds. For criticism is confusing. Once a book is out there's no knowing by the writer, what it is about. And don't forget that criticism of my work now is not aimed at the thing in itself, but is conditioned by the others. Mice was a thin, brittle book, and an experiment but at least it was an honest experiment. This one is an experiment in trickery and trickery in a book is treachery.

"I think this book will be a good lesson for me. I think I got to believing critics—thought I could write easily and that anything I touched would be good simply because I did it. Well any such idea conscious or unconscious is exploded for some time to come. I'm in little danger now of believing my own publicity.

"I can almost hear Pat say, 'How do you know it is bad? Let me see it. Writers don't know when their work is good or bad.' But you see, Pat, if I know it is bad, it is bad. And I know more about my book than anyone else because I know what went into it and I know that a book is only the sum of what went into it.

"I'm sorry you announced it. If I had known you were going to, I should have advised against it. I guess it will have to be the short stories this year. I'll go back to work, but I can't get the other one ready for fall. In fact I'm never going to promise again when I'll have any book done because I don't know.

"Again I'm sorry. But I'm not ready to be a hack yet.

"John."

So he went back to the grind, plodding his way through *The Grapes of Wrath*. For a long time the book had no title. In September 1938 the title went to New York on a postcard, followed by a letter saying that Steinbeck liked the title "because it is a march, because it is in our own revolutionary tradition and because in reference to this book it has a large meaning. And I like it because people know the Battle Hymn who don't know the Stars and Stripes."

That autumn he was on the home stretch. "I am desperately tired," he wrote, "but I want to finish. And mean. I feel as though shrapnel were bursting about my head. I only hope the book is some good. Can't tell yet at all. And I can't tell whether it is balanced. It is a slow plodding book but I don't think that it is dull." He also didn't think it would be a popular book.

It wasn't dull and it was popular. It made history in the publishing world and it changed history in the migrant camps of California. It was wildly praised and even more wildly denounced; what mattered was that it was read. But it left Steinbeck exhausted; it took months for him to recover from the long process of gestation. It was utterly impossible for him to do as he had often done before: to start work on a new book before the last was published. And the success of the book did to him some of the things he had feared success might do. "I'm so busy being a writer that I haven't time to write," he complained. "Ten thousand people have apparently put aside all other affairs to devote themselves to getting me to speak. And I'm so increasingly afraid in crowds that I do not talk comfortably to a pair of dice any more."

Moreover the war was looming on Steinbeck's, as on the world's, horizon, changing his course as it changed the world's. He tried for a time to escape in Mexico, first on the collecting expedition with Edward F. Ricketts which later bore fruit in *Sea of Cortez*, and subsequently in writing the script for the Mexican movie, *The Forgotten Village*. He took flying lessons, and was amazed to discover that "far from giving one a sense of power it gives one a sense of humility." He helped make pictures in Hollywood and out of Hollywood. But all this seemed secondary. "There's an immanence in the air as though anything not having to do with the war must be quickly done," he wrote in February 1942. "If there is a London, I want to be in London this summer."

He liked writing *Sea of Cortez*. He had always been something of a biologist at heart, and very much of a craftsman. He had enjoyed the techniques of collecting; he enjoyed applying some of the technique of novel writing to a book about science. "Perhaps it is a little crazy," he explained, "but it is a good clearing-out of a lot of ideas that have been working on me for a long time and they do fit into the loose framework and design of such a book. . . . Pat is getting a darned fine book and one that he probably can't sell at all. It will be fun to read but not by the take-a-book-to-bed public. . . . The more I consider it the less very wide appeal it seems to me to have. The general public is not given to playful speculation. The rage and contempt of the critics will be amusing and like old times. It will be kind of good too because the work is pretty good. I know it is. It certainly is the most difficult work I've ever undertaken."

The war loomed ever larger. Steinbeck wanted to help, and various agencies of the government asked him to help. He responded eagerly to every opportunity—and was constantly frustrated, as so many others were, by the wide gap between enthusiasm at the top and the ruts of bureaucratic routine. *The Moon Is Down* actually grew out of a serious discussion with Colonel William J. Donovan of the Office of Strategic Services on techniques for aiding resistance movements in the occupied countries of German-held Europe. *Bombs Away* was the outgrowth of a series of suggestions made by General "Hap" Arnold of the Army Air Force. But chasing about the United States of America in pursuit of material usable in wartime about the Army Air Force was an occupation which involved very considerable psychic frustrations.

Steinbeck felt more at home when, early in 1943, he crossed to Europe in a convoy packed with G.I.'s to do war reporting for the New York *Herald Tribune*. That was his own idea; he had shyly inquired whether the *Herald Tribune* would be interested in having him as a correspondent. He worked hard, and at first happily. The restraints of censorship eventually gnawed him, as they gnawed every correspondent. He did a good steady daily job; but when he came home, in October 1943, he knew that his daily stories were not a book. For him a book was not just a collection of journalistic pieces; it had to have a life of its own; it took time to grow.

Yet so long as the war was on it was impossible for John Steinbeck to settle down to sustained work on anything not connected with the war. His wartime letters are full of unfinished projects—war and non-war. All through the years, indeed, odd projects had been appearing in them, then disappearing, and usually reappearing. *Cannery Row*, however, came suddenly, late in 1944, without preparation in the letters—a nostalgic return to the moods of *Tortilla Flat* days, a "mixed-up book," as Steinbeck himself described it, with a "pretty general ribbing" in it.

A play referred to as *The Pipes* turns up in the letters occasionally, then fades away; various movie projects and temporary government jobs receive passing mention; there is a long saga of excitements and postponements concerned with the moving picture, *The Pearl of the World*, produced in Mexico in 1945, for which Steinbeck wrote a script that became a magazine story and may some day become a book—"a strange piece of work," according to its author, "full of curious methods and figures. A folktale, I hope. A black-and-white story like a parable." Perhaps that job ended Steinbeck's long absorption with cinematic techniques—and perhaps not. "I don't think I shall ever do another shooting script," he wrote in July 1945. "It isn't my kind of work—this moving a camera around from place to place."

For a time Steinbeck turned aside to work on a "wizard" tale which, he assured his agents, was "not meant for publication," though almost inevitably some day, in some transformation, it will reach print. And in the letters appears at first casual, then increasingly excited, talk of a book to be called *The Wayward Bus*—"It might be quite a book," Steinbeck thought in mid-1945, adding, "There is no hurry." There are also, of course, always references in the Steinbeck letters to the Steinbeck dogs—after 1943 to a huge blue-eyed English shepherd dog, Willie, and later, to Steinbeck's son, Tom, whose advent changed Willie's nature. Willie, like his master, had been a bit of a rover, which sometimes complicated the pattern of Steinbeck family life. But after Tom appeared, when Willie could have had complete freedom, he didn't want it. Willie just wanted to stay at home and take care of the baby.

So there, in fifteen years of letters to an agent's office that became an author's permanent home, is the story of a creative writer at work. Certain patterns are recurrent: the restless wandering, when a story is in gestation; the false starts; then the utter absorption in creation, when the letters become sparser and the work is everything; finally, fatigue, uncertainty of the product, and a few wisps of anger at critics' misunderstanding. The war interrupts, but merely interrupts, the recurrent pattern; and now the war is over. The rest of the autobiography is for John Steinbeck—aided, of course, by Willie and by Tom and by Gwyn —to write, and it would be presumptuous for a critic to attempt to anticipate it. But there is a suggestive footnote which occurs in a letter written in the spring of 1945:

"Ed Ricketts says that when he was little he was in trouble all the time until he suddenly realized that adults were crazy. Then, when he knew that, everything was all right and he could be nice to them. He says he has never found occasion to revise that opinion. Tom will probably be going through the same evaluation. And if he doesn't discover it for himself I will try to help him."

John Steinbeck

MY SHORT NOVELS

I HAVE never written a preface to one of my books before, believing that the work should stand on its own feet, even if the ankles were slightly wobbly. When I was asked to comment on the six short novels of this volume, my first impulse was to refuse. And then, thinking over the things that have happened to these stories since they were written, I was taken with the idea that what happens to a book is very like what happens to a man.

These stories cover a long period of my life. As each was finished, that part of me was finished. It is true that while a work is in progress, the writer and his book are one. When a book is finished, it is a kind of death, a matter of pain and sorrow to the writer. Then he starts a new book, and a new life, and if he is growing and changing, a whole new life starts. The writer, like a fickle lover, forgets his old love. It is no longer his own: the intimacy and the surprise are gone. So much I knew, but I had not thought of the little stories thrust out into an unfriendly world to make their way. They have experiences, too—they grow and change or wane and die, just as everyone does. They make friends or enemies, and sometimes they waste away from neglect.

The Red Pony was written a long time ago, when there was desolation in my family. The first death had occurred. And the family, which every child believes to be immortal, was shattered. Perhaps this is the first adulthood of any man or woman. The first tortured question "Why?" and then acceptance, and then the child becomes a man. *The Red Pony* was an attempt, an experiment if you wish, to set down this loss and acceptance and growth. At that time I had had three books published and none of them had come anywhere near selling their first editions. *The Red Pony* could not find a publisher. It came back over and over again, until at last a brave editor bought it for *The North American Review* and paid ninety dollars for it, more money than I thought the world contained. What a great party we had in celebration!

It takes only the tiniest pinch of encouragement to keep a writer

MY SHORT NOVELS appeared originally in the Literary Guild Review Wings, October, 1953. It is reprinted here by permission of the Literary Guild, of Mr. Steinbeck's publishers the Viking Press, Inc., and of Mr. Steinbeck.

going, and if he gets none, he sometimes learns to feed even on the acid of failure.

Tortilla Flat grew out of my study of the Arthurian cycle. I wanted to take the stories of my town of Monterey and cast them into a kind of folklore. The result was *Tortilla Flat*. It followed the usual pattern. Publisher after publisher rejected it, until finally Pascal Covici published it. But it did have one distinction the others had not: it was not ignored. Indeed, the Chamber of Commerce of Monterey, fearing for its tourist business, issued a statement that the book was a lie and that certainly no such disreputable people lived in that neighborhood. But perhaps the Chamber of Commerce did me a good service, for the book sold two editions, and this was almost more encouragement than I could stand. I was afraid that I might get used to such profligacy on the part of the public, and I knew it couldn't last. A moving-picture company bought *Tortilla Flat* and paid four thousand dollars for it. Thirty-six hundred came to me. It was a fortune. And when, a few years later, the same company fired its editor, one of the reasons was that he had bought *Tortilla Flat*. So he bought it from the company for the original four thousand dollars and several years later sold it to M-G-M for ninety thousand dollars. A kind of justification for me, and a triumph for the editor.

Of Mice and Men was an attempt to write a novel in three acts to be played from the lines. I had nearly finished it when my setter pup ate it one night, literally made confetti of it! I don't know how close the first and second versions would prove to be. This book had some success, but as usual it found its enemies. With rewriting, however, it did become a play and had some success.

There were long books between these little novels. I think the little ones were exercises for the long ones. The war came on, and I wrote *The Moon Is Down* as a kind of celebration of the durability of democracy. I couldn't conceive that the book would be denounced. I had written of Germans as men, not supermen, and this was considered a very weak attitude to take. I couldn't make much sense out of this, and it seems absurd now that we know the Germans were men, and thus fallible, even defeatable. It was said that I didn't know anything about war, and this was perfectly true, though how Park Avenue commandos found me out I can't conceive.

Subsequently I saw a piece of war as a correspondent, and following that wrote *Cannery Row*. This was a kind of nostalgic thing, written for a group of soldiers who had said to me, "Write something funny that isn't about the war. Write something for us to read—we're sick of war." When *Cannery Row* came out, it got the usual critical treatment.

I was wasting my time in flippancy when I should be writing about the war. But half a million copies were distributed to troops, and they didn't complain. We had some very warlike critics then, much more bellicose than the soldiers.

In Mexico I heard a story and made a long jump back to the *Tortilla Flat* time. I tried to write it as folklore, to give it that set-aside, raised-up feeling that all folk stories have. I called it *The Pearl*. It didn't do so well at first either, but it seems to be gathering some friends, or at least acquaintances. And that's the list in this volume. It is strange to me that I have lived so many lives. Thinking back, it seems an endless time and yet only a moment.

II. STEINBECK ON CRITICISM

John Steinbeck

CRITICS, CRITICS,
BURNING BRIGHT

THE WRITING, production, and reception of the play-novelette "Burning Bright" have been extremely interesting to me. I had anticipated some opposition to both theme and method but I did not expect such violent critical reaction.

I can find no play, poem, essay, or novel which uses sterility as its theme. There may be examples of the use of this theme but I have not heard of them. The fear of sterility is one of the most powerful human emotions and has been so from most primitive times. Ancient and medieval law takes strong cognizance of sterility. Until recent times it was always attributed to the woman and in nearly all law it is one of the basic causes for dissolution of marriage, equal indeed to adultery. In our own experience nearly all of us have known marriages strained and broken by it. It is strange that it is not mentioned in literature. Impotence has its many references but not sterility. Oddly, once "Burning Bright" was finished I found that many people thought impotence and sterility the same thing.

In working with this theme I began to fear that if the subject had not been used, it might be that it was too terrible and secret a thing to be brought into discussion. And yet I cannot believe any basic human problem not a fit subject for literature.

This matter of subject, however, was only one of the hazards of the play.

In an attempt to indicate a universality of experience I placed the story in the hands of three professions which have long and continuing traditions, namely the Circus, the Farm, and the Sea. The story continues unbroken through the three sections. This method was bound to appear a kind of contraption to many who do not care for innovations.

Third in the list of hazards was the use of a kind of universal language not geared to the individual actors or their supposed crafts but rather the best I was able to produce. While I had eminent authority

CRITICS, CRITICS, BURNING BRIGHT *is reprinted here by permission of Mr. Steinbeck and of the editors of* The Saturday Review, *where the article originally appeared, November 11, 1950.*

for this method from Aeschylus down through O'Neill, it was still problematical whether audiences used to the modern realistic theatre would accept such expression. This language did not intend to sound like ordinary speech, but rather by rhythm, sound, and image to give the clearest and best expression of what I wanted to say. The attempt was to lift the story to the parable expression of the morality plays. It is a method not without its great exponents. The test is whether it can be found acceptable in a modern book or play or whether an archaicness in its sound cuts it off. A number of critics both of book and play have become so enraged by the method that they have not looked beyond it at the subject matter.

When the book and the play were finished and rehearsals over we took the play on the road to test it with audiences and to make those changes which only audiences can suggest. And from the first I was fascinated by the audiences: we found that to the average audience the whole subject of sex is funny if the audience is permitted to find it so. Sentences which had seemed clean were dirty to an audience although on test the same sentences were clean to an individual. We found that pregnancy was a matter for laughter and in some cases for great distaste. The group mind of an audience is very different from the minds of the individuals who compose the audience. We found that we could not use the slightest image indicating the act of sex without drawing a curious self-conscious laughter. Perhaps not oddly, the individuals most likely to react to a sexual image were women of a certain age who usually came in groups and who were obviously not often subject to sex as an active principle.

It seemed to us that perhaps because of taboos, censorships both public and private, from the convention of the dirty whispered joke, and perhaps from a not-too-healthy sexual background, many people could only conceive of the procreative process as a kind of self-conscious joke. The individuals most likely to react in this way were those who held prudish standards socially.

The reaction of audiences to the change of background and to the method of language was equally interesting. Young people, as one would expect, were much more likely to go along with the innovations than older people. Since we made it our practice to listen to comments during the intermissions we were able to arrive at some conclusions.

A LARGE number of people in the age group forty-five and upward were not able to follow the background changes although they were clearly stated. They simply did not listen very closely. Again and again we heard that circus people live on a farm part of the year. This group also resented the language. The statement of a middle-aged woman that "circus people don't talk that way" is a perfect example of this resentment.

There is no doubt whatever that circus people do not talk that way —although how a New Haven housewife knew that is in question. As a matter of fact, no one talks that way; but that is only a matter of degree. No one talks as the characters do in any play or movie: to put real speech on stage would be to subject an audience to gibberish. It just sounds like speech. And in this case and to this woman it did not. She could take the speech of fourteen-year-old Juliet as real because it happened long ago.

The younger people in the theatre, particularly the student groups, seemed to find no difficulty either with the method or the speech. Sometimes they disagreed vociferously with the ideas but not from failure to listen nor to understand.

All in all, however, it was good to see how quickly audiences did accept the convention of language and method. Some there were, of course, who simply closed their minds, but they were not many. Mostly they accepted as soon as they grew used to it.

This reminds me of a remark of Richard Rodgers to the effect that when one buys a ticket to the theatre he makes a contract to try to leap a gulf of unreality and to join the company in creating a greater reality. For some people I suppose we made the leap too long, but it was gratifying to see how very many did make the leap into participation.

ON THE ROAD we made many changes in the play, the shifts and rearrangements which seem to be necessary even with the plays of tried playwrights and which are even more necessary when one is little experienced in the theatre, as I am. In Rodgers and Hammerstein and Guthrie McClintic I had, of course, the ultimate in experience and knowledge of the theatre.

On the road some critics came back several times to see the changes made and to verify or to change an opinion or an impression. Harold Bone of Variety came back four times and afterward discussed with me the play and its method. Elliot Norton of the Boston Post returned a second time and wrote a second review revising and elaborating on some of his first conclusions. His comments were constructive and interesting.

We came into New York knowing we were going to have some difficulty but we did not know quite the extent of the difficulty. The play was running smoothly and seemed to hold its audiences.

The reaction of the New York drama critics surprised and dismayed us. We had favorable notices from two critics, a mixed review from one, and the rest gave the play a series of negatives—from a decisive no through a contemptuous no to an hysterical and emotional no, no, no. Indeed, most of the criticism seemed emotional beyond the importance and the danger of the play. The critical impulse seemed to be to kill it quickly and get it buried before it contaminated any more audiences. And this in spite of every indication that the audiences liked the play. It is a matter of wonder to me.

This is in no way a criticism of the critics. They are the custodians of the public interest and if their judgments were not usually accurate they would have neither the following nor the power they possess. I simply wonder at their vehemence. I wonder what bothered them so much. With one exception they did not denounce the production nor the acting nor the sets. They went out of their way to admire these if only to show how reprehensible the play was. And in denouncing the play they did not touch on what the play said but on its method. This seemed to enrage them. One critic was aroused to such an enthusiasm of rage that he wrote a notice which is incomprehensible to everyone to whom I have shown it. If the play were obscure or illiterate or in bad taste this would be understandable. But it was the kind of method and the kind of language which fulminated them. They did not investigate the theme. I wonder why they were so angry. It was not that important.

My experience in writing has followed an almost invariable pattern. Since by the process of writing a book I have outgrown that book, and since I like to write, I have not written two books alike. Where would be the interest in that? The result has been (and I can prove it with old reviews) that every book has been attacked by a large section of the critical family. I can also prove by old notices that the preceding book is compared favorably over the current one and the one before over the preceding one. To a sensitive reader this would indicate that starting nowhere I have consistently gone down. Or perhaps, having made up their minds what the next book would be like, the critics experienced anger when it was different. But there is one advantage in the book over the play to the writer. A book can wait around and perhaps gradually pick up its adherents and defenders while a play cannot. A play goes or dies very quickly. If my books, almost without exception, could have been killed by initial criticism, as a play is, they would have been killed and my work would be very largely unknown.

AGAIN I am not criticizing critics. They must translate to their audiences, and to do this they must think as their audiences do. But a book can wait until any frightening innovations have ceased to be objects of fear or derision. If my work had been exclusively for the theatre I believe that it would be unknown—and perhaps rightly so—for the theatre cannot wait.

If a writer likes to write, he will find satisfaction in endless experiment with his medium. He will improvise techniques, arrangements of scenes, rhythms of words, and rhythms of thought. He will constantly investigate and try combinations new to him, sometimes utilizing an old method for a new idea and vice versa. Some of his experiments will inevitably be unsuccessful but he must try them anyway if his interest be alive. This experimentation is not criminal. Perhaps it is not even important, but it is necessary if the writer be not moribund.

And sometimes the experiment, which at first seems outrageous to the critic and the reader who have not been through the process of its development, may become interesting and valid when it is inspected a second and third time. The structure of literature is not endangered thereby in any case and the growth of literature springs from no other source.

I have had fun with my work and I shall insist on continuing to have fun with it. And it has been my great good fortune in the past, as I hope it will be in the future, to find enough people to go along with me to the extent of buying books, so that I may eat and continue to have fun. I do not believe that I can much endanger or embellish the great structure of English literature.

I had a wise uncle who, coming upon me in my teens, with my chin down and shoulders bulging as I fought viciously for a highly problematical literary immortality, said as follows: "You know, if you succeed perfectly in doing what you are trying to do, the most you can hope to gain is the undying hatred of a few generations of undergraduates." Even at that age I was so impressed with his logic that I never put on the gloves with Maupassant or Proust again.

I just like to have fun with whatever equipment I have.

John Steinbeck

CRITICS——
FROM A WRITER'S VIEWPOINT

RECENTLY my publisher, with the best intention in the world, gave me a scrapbook of all or nearly all the criticisms of a volume of mine. On first reading this compendium was confusing. In many cases one critic canceled out another; while the exponents of the new criticism wrote a parochial language which was completely obscure to me. I became depressed after first looking into this scrapbook, for it seemed to me that there were no laws of criticism. Read all together one had an appalling sense of anarchy.

It is the convention that a writer should never answer a critic, no matter how violent or seemingly unfair the review. For example, when a *New Yorker* critic attacked a play of mine on the basis of parts and lines which had been removed in rehearsal I knew that he had not looked very carefully at the play and had refreshed his memory from a script which had been abandoned during production. It did not occur to me to protest. This piece is not a protest. It is rather an attempt to scrutinize and perhaps understand present-day American criticism as it is seen by a writer.

One thing we are prone to forget is that the critic is primarily a writer himself and that his first interest lies in his own career. This being so, is it surprising that he is prone to warp his piece in favor of his own cleverness. The critic is nearly always a creative writer or wants to be. Thus, we find him invariably with a novel or play in process or in mind and the critical process can by no means carry over into the creative process. A reviewer who hates dulness is quite capable of writing a dull book. A drama critic of inexorable standards can write, and within our memory has, a play which violated every standard his critical pattern set up.

We are likely also to forget that critics are people with all of the frailties and attitudes of people. One critic explained to me after the fact that he had given me a ferocious beating because he had a hangover.

CRITICS—FROM A WRITER'S VIEWPOINT appeared first in The Saturday Review of August 27, 1955. It appears here through the courtesy of the editors of The Saturday Review and of Mr. Steinbeck.

Another, with a reputation for blistering anything he touched, suddenly went enthusiastically appreciative of almost everything. The explanation was not hard to find. He had published three novels which failed and his fourth was well received and his whole approach changed. Another reviewer uses a neurosis stemming from his birth under unusual circumstances and from unusual parents as the gall in which he dips his pen. Still another critic of personal indecision, reviewing a novel with a homosexual theme, attacked it hysterically on points of grammar.

Here is a thing we are most likely to forget. A man's writing is himself. A kind man writes kindly. A mean man writes meanly. A sick man writes sickly. And a wise man writes wisely. There is no reason to suppose that this rule does not apply to critics as well as to other writers.

One might go farther into the effects of personal life on criticism. It is reasonable to suppose that the reviewer privately unloved will take a dim view of love; that the childless critic will be intolerant of children; that the failure will hate success; a bachelor be cynical of marriage; the tired and old find youth and enthusiasm intolerable; and the conservative be outraged by experiment.

In inspecting present-day American reviewers, one should also take into consideration the fact that the critic very rarely intended criticism as his career. It is in many cases a means of surviving until he can become novelist, playwright, or poet and if, in the course of years, he should become none of these he must, no matter how much he may resist, develop an anger against those who do.

ANOTHER thought that comes to me is that people get tired of their jobs, no matter what they are. I can well imagine that a man who is compelled for his living to read book after book after book might well grow to detest books; that a drama critic forced to go to plays, when he might rather have some private evening social life, could develop a fierce animosity towards the theatre. This is more than a conjecture.

But let us consider success within criticism itself. It consists in building up a large body of readers, as large as possible. To do this the critic must attract attention, just as people are more interested in violence than in quiet, in murder and in accidents than in uneventfulness, in divorce than in marriage, so they read destructive attack with greater avidity than praise. Indeed, one critic made his whole reputation by denouncing Dante, Goethe, and Shakespeare as literary hacks. He lived on that one for years. He was considered original.

There are generalized tendencies which emerge after much reading of notices.

A reviewer is prone to like the previous book or play of a writer better than the present one, but the previous one he didn't like as well as the one previous to that. Reading a course of reviews of a critic over a period gives a writer the idea that he started with nothing and got nowhere. In fact, is in a continual state of slipping back. Drama critics have apparently great power in determining whether a play shall survive or not. Book critics, on the other hand, seem to have little to do with the success or failure of a book. Some years ago a publisher placed a self-addressed postcard with checkboxes in every book sent out. The response indicated that 3 per cent bought the book because of advertising, 2 per cent because of reviews, and 95 per cent because of word-of-mouth. A national magazine review section has, over a period of ten years or more, torn into every book of mine with a vehemence far beyond the call of duty or even of hatred. This magazine has enormous circulation, yet its campaign has had no appreciable effect on the sale of my books.

I HAVE spoken to some extent of unfavorable reviews. I think a writer squirms much more at a favorable notice if the reviewer has missed the point. I remember some overwhelmingly flattering reviews which gave me great sadness because the critic had not understood one thing I was talking about.

What, from a writer's standpoint, is the function of a critic? Some critics seem to feel that they are the directors of writers. They show them the path they should take and punish them if they fail to take it. This has little value to a writer since he is not likely to repeat the book in question.

Should the critic, then, be a kind of intermediary between writer and reader? I don't know, but I suspect that if a writer cannot make himself clear to a reader a critic has little chance of making him clearer. Is the critic a kind of traffic-cop of literature? Is he a separator of sheep from goats? Is he an interpreter? Perhaps different reviewers assume different roles. One dramatic critic who apparently must have had a fine time in Germany before the turn of the century has found no pleasure since. Another reviewer for a magazine prefers anything first written in French.

It is amusing to me how many critics are deeply involved with immortality. They threaten the writer with mortality. They have even convinced some of our best living authors that the immortality of their work is important so that they quarrel like children over the billing on a tombstone. A sad state for otherwise brilliant men who should know that literary immortality is a relative matter subject to unforeseen futures. It has occurred in the past too often not to be possible in the future, that the writer most read fifty years after his death was unknown or unacceptable during his life. Our immortal of the future may be someone the present critics do not know about or do not consider important.

It would be very interesting for a good and intelligent critic to exercise his craft on a body of work of his fellow critics. If this should happen I think it would be found that the product of a reviewer is not objective at all, but subject to all of the virtues and vices of other writers in other fields. I don't think critics should change; only our attitude toward them. Poor things, nobody reviews them.

John Steinbeck

A LETTER ON CRITICISM

Feb. 5, 1955

Dear Editors:

Thank you for your very kind letter and your offer to make space available for my comment on the two recent articles on the *Grapes of Wrath* which have appeared in the *Quarterly*. I wish I could so comment but I have no opinions nor ideas on the subject. Indeed, both pieces seem to me to be nearer to taxonomy than to criticism. Much of the new criticism with its special terms and parochial approach is interesting to me, although I confess I don't understand it very well, but I cannot see that it has very much to do with the writing of novels good or bad. And since the new critics fight each other even more fiercely than they do the strapped down and laid open subjects of their study, it would seem to me that they do not have a table of constants. In less criticismal terms, I think it is a bunch of crap. As such I am not against it so long as it is understood that the process is a kind of ill tempered parlour game in which nobody gets kissed. What such an approach would do to a student beyond confusing him and perhaps making him shy away from reading, I have no idea. I do not read much criticism of my work any more. In the first place it is valueless as advice or castigation since the criticised piece is finished and I am not likely to repeat it. And in the second place, the intrafrontal disagreements only succeed in puzzling me. Recently a critic proved by parallel passages that I had taken my whole philosophy from a 17th century Frenchman of whom

JOHN STEINBECK wrote "A Letter on Criticism" in response to the invitation of the editor of The Colorado Quarterly to comment on two essays which had appeared in the pages of that periodical. The first of these essays, "The Grapes of Wrath: a 'Wagons West' Romance," by Bernard Bowron, appeared in the Summer, 1954 issue. The quite inadequate, if not wholly mistaken view expressed in this article was partly corrected by the second piece, "Another Look at The Grapes of Wrath," by Warren G. French, which appeared in the Winter, 1955 issue. Mr. Steinbeck's response to the editorial invitation was printed in the Autumn, 1955 issue.

Permission to reprint "A Letter on Criticism" here has been granted by the editor of The Colorado Quarterly and by Mr. Steinbeck.

I had never heard. I usually know what I want to say and hope I have the technique to say it clearly and effectively. As Tennessee Williams once said, "I put it down that a way and that's the only way I know to put it down."

I don't think the Grapes of Wrath is obscure in what it tries to say. As to its classification and pickling, I have neither opinion nor interest. It's just a book, interesting I hope, instructive in the same way the writing instructed me. Its structure is very carefully worked out and it is no more intended to be inspected than is the skeletal structure of a pretty girl. Just read it, don't count it!

Please believe me when I say I have nothing against the scholarly or critical approach. It does seem to me to have very little to do with the writing or reading of books.

The writing of books is a lonely and difficult job, and it takes all the time I have. Remember the negro boy in Texas who when asked by a priest whether he was a catholic, replied, "Hell no, father, I'm having enough trouble just being a nigger." Well I'm having enough—just being a writer.

I am working now on a long novel, trying to get it straight and clear —trying to fit method to subject and tone to surround the whole—trying to fit the thousand details and people into the pattern. Imagine, if you will, the confusion if criticism should come now. No book would ever get written if the critic could get at the mind of a writer rather than his work. Afterwards, critics are hardly more destructive than silver fish.

Yours,

John Steinbeck

III. ARTIST AND THINKER

Burton Rascoe

JOHN STEINBECK

O N THE EVENING of November 23, 1937, an aesthetic miracle was performed on the stage of the Music Box Theatre in New York City. It was the occasion of the first presentation of John Steinbeck's play *Of Mice and Men*. The more literate portion of the reading public had become familiar with the story or theme of the play because *Of Mice and Men* had first appeared in book form as a novel and had met with great critical acclaim, and, fortunately, this critical acclaim had been followed by purchases of the book in large quantities.

Although I have long practiced the profession of book-reviewing myself, I am not one to count much upon the verdict of reviewers as determining the sales of a book. I have known books to receive universally enthusiastic praise from reviewers and yet to be failures commercially. It is my guess that the public's interest in a new Steinbeck novel was largely a carry-over from the enjoyment they had taken in *Tortilla Flat*, once they had been induced, almost as if by social pressure, to read it.

Tortilla Flat was gay, irresponsible, charming. It was a yarn about *paisanos*. *Paisanos* are mixed-breed Mexicans. That is to say, a people who may have flowing in their veins the blood of Spanish conquistadors, Mayan chieftains, Inca artisans, Mongol Manchus, Ute Indians, and descendants of Cotton or Increase Mather, collateral or direct.

BURTON RASCOE has had a very distinguished career in American letters as journalist, critic, and author. His chief associations have been with The Chicago Tribune, The New York World-Telegram, The New York Tribune, American Mercury, Newsweek, Esquire, and Ken, as well as with the publishing firm Doubleday Doran. His autobiography, Before I Forget, appeared in 1937 and was very popular. Other books by Mr. Rascoe include the equally popular Titans of Literature and Prometheans. His career spanned the decades in which Steinbeck developed as a writer and in which he achieved his fame. Writing in 1938, before the appearance of The Grapes of Wrath, Burton Rascoe was one of the earliest to give serious critical consideration to the work of Steinbeck.

The essay reprinted here first appeared in the March, 1938 issue of The English Journal and is reprinted here by permission of the National Council of Teachers of English, publishers of The English Journal.

In a *paisano* there may be the blood of Ghengis Khan, Montezuma, and Pizarro; stout Cortez may have contributed to him some of his sinew; but your true *paisano* is also a true aristocrat: he is drained by years and centuries of frantic striving so he is utterly lacking in the highly acquisitive, possessive instincts. He may steal a chicken when he is hungry (and, indeed, he is quite likely to, if a chicken practically comes up to him and asks to be stolen), but he does this stealing either because he is hungry or because he wants to provide for a friend; and he is rather careful to inquire of the bird if its owner is in such circumstances that he can afford to lose a chicken.

The *paisano*, in fact, is your better self; and, if you wish and expect to fare well in a highly acquisitive society and if you wish to be well thought of by your worst possible neighbors, it is better to keep this better self hidden or in abeyance. The better self is always there, however, and so many people recognized this part of themselves in the characters of Danny, Pilon, Mrs. Morales, Pablo, Mrs. Torrelli, Jesus Maria, Gracie Montez, and Cornelia Ruiz that the book was a popular success.

Quite a few, it appears, had so successfully concealed the *paisano* in them beneath the stiff shirts and visages, creamed and mantled like a standing pond, or beneath the rouge, mascara, and the throaty-voiced ineptitudes of the well-heeled socially, that they became a source of sorrow and regret to Mr. Steinbeck. In the Preface to the Modern Library edition of *Tortilla Flat*, he said:

> I wrote these stories because they were true stories and because I liked them. But literary slummers have taken these people up with the vulgarity of duchesses who are amused and sorry for a peasantry. These stories are out, and I cannot recall them. But I shall never again subject to the vulgar touch of the *decent* these good people of laughter and kindness, of honest lusts and direct eyes, of courtesy beyond politeness. If I have done them harm by telling a few of their stories, I am sorry. It will not happen again.

Mr. Steinbeck had identified his *paisanos* by place. They were those happy, shiftless nondescripts who live in shacks in the hills above Monterey, California. Monterey and Santa Barbara are asylums for the rich. They are towns set in such natural beauty as to seem unnatural. From the far end of the pier at Santa Barbara you survey the semicircle of the hills which cup the bay, and all seems splendor, for in this amphitheater elaborate white castles, clothed luxuriously with every imaginable kind and color of flower, occupy the seats, and beyond and above them are the purple and yellow mountains merging almost imperceptibly with a purplish and yellow sky which lightens into rich blue and then into azure. Then you walk the length of the pier into the main street of the town, and you find yourself faced with the most horrible anomalies, sordid catch-penny commercial devices—badly outfitted chain stores, unclean barrooms, cheap restaurants, newsstands displaying most conspicuously all the infinite variety of sexy magazines—juxtaposed with the elegance the very rich can support—gown and trinket shops on the windowpanes of which are the gold-lettered advices that the proprietors have similar shops in Paris, London, New York, Palm Beach, Southampton, Bar Harbor, Aiken, and White Sulphur Springs, elaborate cocktail bars, and casinos.

Monterey, with its pebble beach and incomparable golf course, set in a scene of dismal, wild beauty like something imagined by William Blake and color-toned by Goya, is also a heaven-spot haven for the privileged, with its much publicized seventeen-mile drive over which roll sight-seeing buses filled with long-frustrated elderly people and eager young honeymoon couples, and with its harsh contrast of the privileged with those who wish, or hope, to be privileged. The *paisanos* belong to neither of these classes: when Rosa and Maria, the daughters of old Guiermo Lopez (see *The Pastures of Heaven*, pp. 141 ff.), found they could no longer grow vegetables on the soil they inherited and decided to turn their talent for making the thinnest tortillas and the tastiest enchiladas and tamales into commercial account, they held four cents spent for a candy bar for themselves to be almost a sinful indulgence, and, when a "rich" man was so reckless with his money as to buy and pay for *three* enchiladas, Maria gave herself to the extravagant customer out of sheer gratitude—but hastened to kneel, as soon as the customer was gone, before the little virgin on her bedroom wall to ask forgiveness for her breach of chastity.

Mr. Steinbeck was aggrieved to learn, after the success of *Tortilla Flat*, that people of the Babbitry of Monterey and tourists in California were looking up and pestering the *paisanos* and invading their privacy because they had discovered, in a book, that the *paisanos* were "quaint." Mr. Steinbeck began to feel sorry he had written the book.

I am very glad Mr. Steinbeck did not attend the opening performance of *Of Mice and Men* in New York and that he has not, as yet, seen a performance of the play. For, although the play was an instantaneous hit and although it drew from the drama critics the most gravely and warmly worded notices of praise that have been accorded any native drama since *Tobacco Road* (and hence is likely to enjoy a run as extended as the Erskine Caldwell drama), a distressingly large part of the audience on the opening night took the tragic, heart-breaking lines of George and Lennie to be comedy. They laughed outrageously when tears should have been streaming down their faces. They appeared to think that the lumbering, dimwitted, pathetic Lennie was supposed to be funny. Village idiots laughing at the village idiot all over again. I am told that this laughter at the wrong places occurs during at least part of the first act at every performance.

But the consummate art of Steinbeck conquers every time even the more insensitive elements of a New York theater audience before the first act is over. Compassion for the misfits of life, for those who are handicapped by the imponderables of heredity and environment and for those who are warped physically and emotionally, is so deeply and so understandingly felt and expressed by Steinbeck that, before the curtain comes down on the first act, the light, superficially cynical mood of the less sensitive members of the audience has changed, and pity and wonder has taken possession of them.

This is the miracle I referred to in the opening sentence of this discourse.

It seemed to me after my first reading, subsequent re-readings, and careful analysis of the novel, *Of Mice and Men*, that Steinbeck as a literary artist had deliberately posed for himself the most difficult problem conceivable to a writer of fiction and that he had resolved it in a Sophoclean manner, that is, without poetic or rhetorical fault. He had even done a braver thing than Sophocles had done (though, please, let no one be so silly and so supercilious as to imagine that, in my saying this, I am comparing Sophocles and Steinbeck to the disadvantage of Sophocles or even that I am ranking Steinbeck as remotely in the class of Sophocles: he may be, before he is finished, a greater poetic dramatist than Sophocles, for he strives to learn the most delicate nuances and the most meaningful emphases of—in the Aristotelian sense— the arts of poetry and rhetoric; but he is thirty-eight years old, and Sophocles was only twenty-eight when he triumphed over the long preeminent tragic poet, Aeschylus, by writing *Antigone*; so, in order to be classed with Sophocles, Steinbeck has much ground, in little time, to cover). I am talking about a writing problem. Sophocles chose to treat in poetic and dramatic form the legends[1] already familiar to the Athenian audiences who had witnessed tragic dramas since the days before Aeschylus. Steinbeck, on the other hand, chose as the most important character of his novel, and of his play, *Of Mice and Men*, a believable contemporary figure—a man who would be described on any police docket or in a detective's dossier as a sexual pervert or degenerate and in almost any psychiatrist's case history as, probably, a man afflicted with gigantism, with an abnormally low I.Q., unusual thyroid deficiency, excessive pituitary secretion with resulting imbalance, a tactile fetish, psychic and/or physical impotence, and with improperly functioning adrenals which caused him in moments of fear to act destructively without intention—and Steinbeck chose to, and did, make this monstrosity a sympathetic figure, one whom you, if you had heart in you, would regard with all the despair but also with all the affection with which the giant Lennie is regarded by his bindle-stiff guardian and companion, the more astute and intelligent George.

In the novel and in the play the relationship between George and Lennie is a paradigm of all the nonphysical, nonsexual (let us use the so tritely inadequate and now almost meaningless word "spiritual" to help out in indicating the meaning) emotions, concerns, and aspirations in the world. George has toward Lennie the tenderness and the protective instinct which some of even the most hard-bitten and most hard-boiled have toward the helpless, the maimed, the dependent. A lonely, itinerant bindle-stiff, a migratory ranch hand, barley bucker, mule skinner, fruit picker, and general handy man, without a home or family, George has encountered and embraced a responsibility, a social responsibility, a humanitarian responsibility. It is to take care of, protect, save from hurt, the dim-witted, loyal, and devoted Lennie.

George nags and rags Lennie at times like a distracted, exasperated harridan wife; scolds him like a long-suffering mother whose child is a constant worry and trial. He gives way at times to eloquent fancies as to how much more enjoyable, unconstrained, and livable life would be if he were only free—if he didn't have Lennie as a burden, a yoke, a ball and chain to hamper him. But as George speaks and as his character becomes plain, you know that life would be wholly meaningless and empty for him without Lennie to take care of. And he has his emotional recompense in Lennie's pathetic and doglike devotion to him, a loyalty so great and so intense that Lennie's weak brain scarcely comes alive except where George is concerned—when George is angry with him, when George is planning a future for them wherein they will have a little farm of their own and won't be subject to the whims of bosses or to the seasonal variations in employment, or when harm seems to threaten George.

The never-quite-realized, too often tragically shattered dreams of men toward an ideal future of security, tranquillity, ease, and contentment runs like a Greek choral chant throughout the novel and the play, infecting, enlivening, and ennobling not only George and Lennie but the crippled, broken-down ranch hand, Candy, and the twisted-back Negro stable buck, Crooks, who begs to come in on the plan George has to buy a little farm. Lennie is so enthralled by the prospect that he begs George to tell the story over and over again:

LENNIE (pleading): Come on, George. . . . . Tell me! Please! Like you done before.

. . . .

GEORGE: Guys like us that work on ranches is the loneliest guys in the world. They ain't got no family. They don't belong no place. They come to a ranch and then they go into town and blow their stake. And then the first thing you know they're poundin' their tail on some other ranch. They ain't got nothin' to look ahead to.

LENNIE (delightedly): That's it, that's it! Now tell how it is with us.

GEORGE (still almost chanting): With us it ain't like that. We got a future. We got somebody to talk to that gives a damn about us. We don't have to sit in no barroom blowin' our jack, just because we got no place else to go. If them other guys gets in jail, they can rot for all anybody gives a damn.

LENNIE (who cannot restrain himself any longer; bursts into speech): But not us! And why? Because . . . . because I got you to look after me . . . . and you got me to look after you. . . . . And that's why! (He laughs.) Go on, George!

GEORGE: You got it by heart. You can do it yourself.

LENNIE: No, no. I forget some of the stuff. Tell about how it's gonna be.

GEORGE: Some other time.

LENNIE: No, tell how it's gonna be!

GEORGE: Okay. Some day we're gonna get the jack together and we're gonna have a little house and a couple of acres and a cow and some pigs and. . . . .

LENNIE (shouting): And live off the fat of the land! And have rabbits. Go on, George! Tell about what we're gonna have in the garden. And about the rabbits in the cages. Tell about the rain in the winter . . . . and about the stove and how thick the cream is on the milk, you can hardly cut it. Tell about that, George!

GEORGE: Why don't you do it yourself—you know all of it!

LENNIE: It ain't the same if I tell it. Go on now. How I get to tend the rabbits.

(GEORGE continues to elaborate the story of the dream place.)

And now you must observe that Steinbeck has compassion without maudlinity, sentiment without sentimentality, a stern, realistic, very observant and deductive sense about the realities and about the consequences in a chain of causes. Anyone with any deductive sense at all needs to read only five pages of the novel Of Mice and Men to discover the "plot," to know what is going to happen. The intelligent reader knows that poor Lennie is going to "do a bad thing again" as he did before when he wanted to stroke a girl's dress (and that was all he wanted to do), and the girl got frightened and screamed because she thought she was being attacked, and Lennie and George had to run away and hide in a swamp in water up to their necks to escape the mob that was going to lynch Lennie.

You know that *this* time Lennie, who likes to stroke soft things and who has killed a pet mouse because his hands are so strong and he is so dumb, is going to kill a girl, unintentionally, because of all the things wrong in his disordered brain. The impatient, plot-minded reader doesn't have to turn to the back of the book to see how it comes out. Steinbeck tells you, in effect, in the first five pages just about how it is "going to come out."

And that is his terrific moral. Also it is his gambit to the reader to prove his power as a convincing and enthralling narrator. The reader who, having read that far, fails to go on, is a reader whose mentality is equal only to, and has been conditioned by, very bad, tricky, detective stories, which have no true relation to literature any more than have crossword puzzles, or, indeed, any more than crossword puzzles have (as they are alleged to have) to the increase of the vocabulary you would ordinarily, or potentially, use.

You see, Steinbeck not only indicates to the sentient reader in those first five pages that Lennie is going "to do a bad thing" unintentionally: he also indicates to the sentient reader that Lennie will have to die for it this time and, also, that it is highly necessary and just that Lennie should die. For Lennie's condition is an inimical and destructive force. It is a condition he is not responsible for. It is something he cannot help. One can have all the feeling for him in the world—but Candy in the second act of the play has an old, rheumatic, blind, crippled dog, smelly with age and disease, of whom Candy is very fond because this old dog is the only thing left to Candy on which, or on whom, to lavish human affection, warmth, and care; and Candy has to carry the old dog around in his arms until the dog's disintegrating smell so permeates the bunkhouse that the other ranch hands can no longer stand it, and they have to persuade Candy, with the utmost kindness and consideration, to let them put the old dog out of his misery.

Therein, truly, is a displayed sense of the *lacrimae rerum* of which John Steinbeck is a master. For, when the posse is seeking poor Lennie to string him up and "blow his guts out," as the egoistically inflamed and sadistic leader of the posse demands, George humors Lennie by telling him again about the place they are going to have. He tells it all over, word for word, with promptings by Lennie, who knows it all but wants to hear it from George. He tells it to keep Lennie in ecstasy until the shouts and other noises disclose that the posse is near upon them. Then:

GEORGE: And you get to tend the rabbits!
LENNIE (*giggling with happiness*): And live on the fat o' the land!
GEORGE. Yes. (LENNIE *turns his head. Quickly*): Look over there, Lennie. Like you can really see it.
(GEORGE *pulls* CARLSON's *Luger from his side pocket and fires at the base of* LENNIE's *brain, to put him out of his misery, just as* CARLSON *had told* CANDY *he could put* CANDY's *old dog out of his misery and the dog wouldn't know or feel it, because the bullet would go right into the base of the brain.*)

After that, it seems to me that many of the "hard-boiled" writers who imitate Hemingway's hard-boilism (and including Hemingway who now imitates himself) are like just so many Lennies parroting what George has said, except that their George was about as unimaginative in the brainpan as Lennie and even much more undeveloped, however facile and neat were the hard-boiled word patterns their George was able to patter out. The George of Steinbeck's novel and play was hard-bitten and hard-boiled; but he had imagination, a sense of reality, true compassion, and the dream of life.

Steinbeck abhors and abjures the tag "mystic" which some critics have used in describing him. He is deeply concerned with the problem of Good and Evil, not in any conventional, moral, or philosophical sense but as phenomena in life and as animating principles in life. I have heard him use no word indicating the nature of his beliefs and intimations; but I should vaguely describe them as comprising a curious, very modern Manicheanism, derived perhaps in part from the Indians of the West Coast he has known since boyhood, from acute observation of cause and effect operating among primitive or untutored men, and from a frank facing of the evidence of his own hidden resources of mind and will. Although I have not heard him mention the late Mary Austin or give any evidence of having read her studies of the mind and will, it occurred to me that his psychic beliefs and convictions are probably akin to those of Mrs. Austin. Mrs. Austin believed that will, thought, and emotion are forces that are immediate, dynamic, and kinetic and that they can bring about definite ends, for good or evil, without the employment of any physical means whatever.

It would appear from a long conversation at my house which followed upon Steinbeck's bland, resolute affirmation that what is commonly called witchcraft and the "hexing" of one person by another person is not a superstition but a fairly common and attestable fact. It is, he says, merely the operation of the kinetic and highly destructive emotion of hate. This is, he says, a disturbing and terrible fact. He says that he knew of a man who had reason to hate another man greatly and did so hate him with such concentrated emotion that he was able to say to that man, "You are going to die next Tuesday. At 2:15 next Tuesday you are going to step in front of a truck." And the man did step in front of a truck at 2:15 the following Tuesday and was killed. Steinbeck denied that this was hypnotism, although he believes that all of us daily perform hypnotism and are subjects of hypnotism almost daily in degrees depending upon the force unconsciously exercised upon us, our resistance to it, and upon the strength of our own will and purpose.

He said that he was mortally afraid of hate and that he never wanted to hate anyone or have anyone hate him—very much. The only defense against concentrated hate, he said, was immediate surrender, capitulation; and this must take the form of humility, benevolence, friendliness. The only way to combat hate is to remove from within yourself the reasons for this hate; only thus can you disarm the one who hates you; only thus can you render the terrible force of his hate impotent. "If I knew a man hated me a great deal," he said, "I would try to make friends with him; if I had done him harm I would try to undo that harm quickly. I wouldn't try to hate him back, no, no, because then the only reason I would have for hating him was because he hated me, and that isn't reason enough to generate any strong, counteracting emotion. This would only intensify his hate and he might take it into his head to will disaster or death upon me."

Presently I perceived that Steinbeck's metaphysics was having to do, in a language and ratiocination of his own, with what in the Greek consciousness was the high sin of *hubris* or arrogance or insolence and its consequences. In Greek tragedy there are degrees and kinds of *hubris* each with degrees and kinds of punishment extending up to dire suffering and disaster, the reasons for which the victim in his *hubris* or unwarranted and exaggerated self-conceit cannot figure out; he does not know why he has offended the gods; but the audience knows; he thought too well of himself and so aroused hatred by insolence without even knowing he was insolent and so brought punishment upon himself.

In *Of Mice and Men* Steinbeck's thematic intention, not wholly obvious, was, in a way, to expound the complete nonmorality of Nature in her physical aspects and of the morality of expediency that must necessarily arise from Nature's blundering. The giant imbecile was certainly not responsible for being what he was, and nothing could right the bungling of Nature, and yet this giant imbecile, fully meriting our pity, sympathy, and tenderness, must be killed; for society cannot permit, out of pity, the dumb, destructive force of bungling, nonmoral Nature to operate.

In her critical survey of the sources of contemporary literature, *From These Roots*, Mary M. Colum despairingly states: "The widespread development of an uninspired and decadent realism and a flat, impoverished materialist philosophy has brought about a concentration on exterior life, and the routine of exterior life, to the discrediting of all forms of interior literature."

It occurs to me that, in making this statement, Mrs. Colum makes the mistake she attributes to all her confreres in criticism—that of paying the utmost attention to the works of the contemporary writers who command the most publicity through advertising contracts or otherwise from fortuitous circumstances and of paying very little attention to the work of the genuine artists of our time. It is easy enough, after all these years, for Mrs. Colum to admit, with almost terrifying insistence, now, that James Joyce and Marcel Proust are very, very good, in the light of the general critical consensus, even if for a long time, when she was olympiating for the *New Freeman* and elsewhere, that neither Proust nor Joyce had any particular merit. Mrs. Colum devotes considerable space to the literary merits of Thomas Wolfe, a disgorger of every single detail of every single squint-eyed view of every single experience he has had in life (or imagined), and yet she laments the concern of the contemporary writers with the things of the mind, soul, the spirit, of selective writers who make significance out of small things that matter in the everyday life of man. She appears never to have heard of John Steinbeck. She wins her point; for her contention is that criticism was never at so low a point as it now is in America and England and the western European countries; and her further contention is that she is the only remaining one to keep alive the tradition of criticism of Lessing, Herder, and Sainte-Beuve. I'd say: "To hell with Lessing, Herder, Sainte-Beuve, and Mary M. Colum!" Read *Of Mice and Men*, *In Dubious Battle*, *Tortilla Flat*, and (by all means, because it is a rich, overflowing first novel, containing the genes and germs of so much of his later work), *The Pastures of Heaven*. Then you might read, not merely for enchantment but for a more personal reason, *The Cup of Gold* and *To a God Unknown*, for they are novels which, like *The Pastures of Heaven*, were such complete failures that not only did Mary M. Colum not notice them, and not many functioning critics (sic) noticed them, but the books themselves did not sell in enough quantities to pay for the typesetting. While one of the best of these was being brought out, Steinbeck, with the timorous author's expectancy of reward for his labors, happily worked to earn his keep as a hod carrier in the building of the new Madison Square Garden in New York.

1. See my *Titans of Literature* (p. 55): "The favorite source of tragic plots and the one made use of by nearly all the (Greek) dramatists was the legend of the descendants of Laius. The legends concerning this family corresponded very closely to the legends built up by 'scientific investigators' about the notorious Jukes family so dear to American eugenists. The Jukeses, as you may remember, were supposed to be a notoriously incestuous family in northern New York, whose descendants turned out very badly, according to the 'reports,' becoming parricides, murderers, imbeciles, epileptics, common criminals and prostitutes. This was also the Greek story of the incestuous descendants of Laius: they were parricides like Oedipus and Orestes, adulterous murderers like Clytemnestra, epileptics like Orestes, common criminals like Eteocles."

It was long the favorite "scientific" stunt of the ardent eugenists to contrast the more morbid careers in the vague family history of the Jukeses with the allegedly much healthier descendants of Jonathan Edwards, whom the eugenists sought to display as conspicuous examples of the benefits of proper breeding in that (from the case histories they chose) it would appear that the descendants of Jonathan Edwards were all men and women of probity, character, and consequence, eminent in statesmanship, the clergy, jurisprudence, and finance. More disinterested investigators set to work and found that among the Jukes' descendants there were a number of men and women possessing all the virtues attributed to the Edwards's, whereas there were descendants of Jonathan Edwards who were very like the degenerate Jeeters family of southern poor whites portrayed by Erskine Caldwell in *Tobacco Road* and who had been variously embroiled with the law on charges of rape and other sex crimes, manslaughter, vagrancy, petty thievery, and like crimes and misdemeanors. This comment is merely to dissipate a faulty and pernicious legend and to keep the record reasonably straight.

68

Frederic I. Carpenter

JOHN STEINBECK:
AMERICAN DREAMER

JOHN STEINBECK has published eight volumes of fiction, each as different from the others as all are different from the writings of most novelists. He has employed a variety of techniques to describe an assortment of characters; pirates, farmers, storekeepers, *paisanos*, Communists, half-wits, children, and migrants have appeared successively in romantic, realistic, mystical, mock-heroic, dramatic, psychological, and sociological novels. His readers have come to expect the unexpected; his critics have taken refuge in enthusiasm or despair.

But beneath this apparent variety, Steinbeck has been astonishingly consistent. A single purpose has directed his experimentation, a single idea has guided his literary thought. Always his fiction has described the interplay of dream and reality; his thought has followed the development of the American dream. The significance of dream in the motivation of Steinbeck's stories is often explicit, and may be described in detail. Most of his titles have been symbolic: *Cup of Gold, The Pastures of Heaven, To a God Unknown, In Dubious Battle, Of Mice and Men, The Grapes of Wrath.* Only *Tortilla Flat* and *The Long Valley* seem literal. And in all these tales the dramatic conflict springs from the opposition between the "Golden West" of the imagination, and the actual California of the farmers' associations and the migrants. The real name of the valley called "the Pastures of Heaven" was, significantly, "the Corral of Earth."

Besides this unity, Steinbeck's writing shows a steady progression of subject, of thought, and of technique. Chronologically, his stories describe the pageant of the American West. From *Cup of Gold*, which dealt with the early pirates of Panama, to the contemporary epic of the

FREDERIC IVES CARPENTER has taught American literature and philosophy at the University of Chicago, Harvard University, and at present is at the University of California at Berkeley. He is the author of Emerson and Asia. "John Steinbeck, American Dreamer" is reprinted here by Mr. Carpenter's permission and that of The Southwest Review, in the July, 1941 issue of which it first appeared. The present volume contains "The Philosophical Joads," also by Carpenter.

Okies, they have their background in history. First the Spaniards and Indians, then the American homesteaders, then the *paisano* descendants of the Spaniards and Indians, then the Communist agitators, and now the depression migrants—all have lived, actually.

But beyond history, these novels illustrate the logical development of an idea: they describe successive phases of the American dream. First the dream of conquest, then of escape, then of settlement and ownership. But something was lacking in all these early dreams—some possessive egotism vitiated them. The novels of Steinbeck's second period describe more unselfish types of Americans, who fail for other reasons: irresponsibility, or fanaticism, or defective mentality. Most recently, *The Long Valley* and *The Grapes of Wrath* have suggested the possible realization of the American dream through courage and active intelligence.

Finally, Steinbeck has gradually developed an artistic technique for describing dreamers. His first three novels failed through lack of objective reality: the earliest described pirates as if they were dreamers; the second described dreamers without explaining their motivation; the third mystically merged characters and author in a confused symbolism. But his mature novels succeeded because they described dreamers objectively, and made clear their motivation; the creator separated himself from his creatures. These characters remained insignificant in so far as they remained dreamers, merely. In his later short stories and in *The Grapes of Wrath* Steinbeck's characters have integrated dream with action and have lived on both levels, independently of their author.

Let us follow the dream.

I

In Steinbeck's first published novel, the American dream appears most obviously and least successfully. The story is subtitled: *A Life of Sir Henry Morgan, Buccaneer, with Occasional References to History.* These "occasional references" are not very important.

Historically, Henry Morgan preyed upon Spanish shipping and settlements in America, conquered Panama, and helped open the way for the English colonization of the Western world: he was a man of action and, indirectly, an empire builder. But *Cup of Gold* converts this Morgan into the first American dreamer. So, when the young hero's patron seeks to persuade him to settle down, Henry replies: "Sir, I must be off a-buccaneering. Why, in all my years it has been the one aim. I must go, sir." And later the author explains: "There was a power of dream in him. Out of his mob of ragamuffin heroes he wanted to make a strong, durable nation, a new, aggressive nation in America.

As more and more of the buccaneers flocked to his command, his dream solidified." And this fictional Henry Morgan partially realized his American dream: in the moment before his death, "Henry was conscious of the deep, mellow pulsation of the Tone."

Clearly, *Cup of Gold* offers an extreme example of the romantic idealization of history. It would seem as though Gilbert and Sullivan had mocked it before it was written: "It is, it is a glorious thing to be a pirate king!" Upon sober second thought, the whole motivation appears absurd: pirates are not apt to be dreamers; and even the most inspired Elizabethan dreamers hardly thought of making a new, independent nation in America. To read back the modern American dream into the conscious mind of an English pirate is to falsify both history and psychology. But the idea is suggestive. In the later novels this dream constantly recurs and with increasing realism motivates the action.

From *Cup of Gold* to *The Grapes of Wrath* seems a far cry. But the crude artistic pattern of the first novel finds perfection in the latter: young Henry Morgan, the criminal leader of ragamuffin heroes, followed the strange advice of the bard Merlin, much as Tom Joad follows the counsel of the mystical preacher Jim Casy. In each case a dreamer prophesies the future actions of a rebellious leader of the people. But where Merlin was mythical, Jim Casy is real; where Merlin miraculously imparted his dream to the self-conscious Henry Morgan, Jim Casy teaches Tom Joad by slow suggestion and example, remaining realistically a man of flesh and blood. And where Merlin's American dream was impossibly prophetic, Jim Casy's develops naturally from the historic events of his time and place. The dream-technique of the first novel was naïve and artificial, while that of *The Grapes of Wrath* has become skilful and realistic. But the dream persists.

And the dream develops. Even though *Cup of Gold* romanticized Henry Morgan, it offered some valid criticism of his motives. It did not romanticize the blind violence of this first phase of the American dream. For this Henry Morgan "wanted the moon," selfishly:

> "I think I understand," said Merlin to him. "You want the moon to drink from as a golden cup; and so it is very likely that you will become a great man. . . . All the world's great have been little boys who wanted the moon."

But the world's great who have dreamed only of personal power, and have sought to achieve it only through violence, have always failed ultimately. So this Henry Morgan failed in love and in happiness:

although he achieved his dream of power through violence, it did him little good. He embodied the first logical stage of the American dream: success in action, but failure in imagination. This first "American dreamer" remained narrowly egotistical.

Thus, in spite of the artistic failure of his first book, Steinbeck did foreshadow in it his future literary development. Through the father of Henry Morgan, he prophesied the dream-life he was to describe:

> "I say to you, without pleasure, that this son of ours will be a great man, because—well—because he is not very intelligent. He can see only one desire at a time. I said he tested his dreams; he will murder every dream with the implacable arrows of his will. This boy will win to every goal of his aiming; for he can realize no thought, no reason, but his own. And I am sorry for his coming greatness."

Ultimately, Steinbeck suggests, a man's "intelligence" is more important than his individual success. And so Tom Joad will never become as "great" (successful) as this Henry Morgan; but he will dream more greatly, because he will see life whole. And the greatness of his dream will raise him above his more successful fellows.

II

The prologue to Steinbeck's second novel, *The Pastures of Heaven*, describes the discovery of a beautiful California valley by a Spanish conquistador, and the man's failure to find happiness there. Then come the stories of a succession of later settlers, with their ill-fated attempts to possess the ideal beauty of the valley. The book ends with the exclamations of a group of tourists who dream of the lives that they also would live there if they could. But through all these stories runs the theme of romantic idealization, possession, and frustration. The self-righteous spirit of the conquistadors leaves its curse upon the valley. And this abstract spirit of place gives unity to an otherwise disconnected series of stories. T. B. Allen, the storekeeper, suggests it at the beginning: "Maybe there'll be a lot of baby curses crawling around the Pastures the first thing we know."

The historic pattern of conquest, idealization, and frustration gives purpose to this book. But within this general outline live a group of characters who suggest the rich variety of the later novels. In detail their stories are realistic. But even this realism contributes to the development of the idea: the different characters illustrate the ways in which the American dream may fail. Thus the book is dual in technique: as a whole it repeats the self-conscious dream-motivation of *Cup of Gold;* but in its particular stories it makes the dream implicit and unconscious, as it is in actual life.

Within the "Pastures of Heaven" four types of American dreamers live. The first seek to realize a false ideal, and fail because of their lust for possession. So the Spanish conqueror fails. And so the mad religious fanatic, who attacks a rattlesnake as a symbol of the devil, is killed. And "Shark" Wicks, who dreams of paper profits and of keeping his daughter "pure," is disgraced. And so Helen Van Deventer, who in her possessive lust finally becomes insane, commits murder. But these dreamers are psychopaths, and their dreams nightmares.

A second group of American dreamers seek to realize different ideals, valid historically but now outworn. So Richard Whiteside came to California in 1850, not to plunder the earth of gold, but to set up a new dynasty. "In his mind there was the definite intention of founding a house for children not yet born and for their children." He built an ideal house; but his children moved away, the house burned, and the dynasty failed. And so Pat Humbert, the hard-working settler from Vermont, furnished an ideal Colonial room for his love, copying it perfectly out of *House Beautiful,* only to have his love marry another and the room remain empty. And the hero of *To a God Unknown* was to learn that the old ideal cannot be transplanted. The American dream must grow from the soil.

The third group of dreamers who live in the Pastures are natives, half-breed descendants of the Spanish conquerors and the Indians, *paisanos,* and "children of nature." What destroys them is neither a lust for possession nor an alien idealism, but their own irresponsibility. So the amoral Lopez sisters find themselves dispossessed, like the later *paisanos* of *Tortilla Flat.* And so the imbecile Tularecito is judged criminally insane, like the later Lennie in *Of Mice and Men.* These children of nature must also become children of civilization. In *Cup of Gold* Henry Morgan had remarked, "Civilization will split up a character, and he who refuses to split goes under." The first groups of American dreamers, who were exclusively agents of the old "civilization," ignored "nature." Now these native *paisanos* ignore "civilization." And both go under.

Who, then, shall be saved? Only one citizen of *The Pastures of Heaven* seems wholly admirable, and even he is forced to leave the valley at last. But Junius Maltby, born there, will return again to become a leader of the people. For he is child both of nature and of civilization, whom ease will not make irresponsible, nor the world corrupt. In *The Long Valley* he will reappear as Jody Tiflin, son of a

rancher, grandson of a pioneer, and inheritor of the American dream.
And in *The Grapes of Wrath* this child will grow up. Meanwhile, many
dreamers fail in many ways.

III

Steinbeck's third novel, *To a God Unknown*, seems almost to have
been written in a dream. On the surface it tells the story of Joseph
Wayne, who emigrated from Vermont to California about the turn
of the century and took a homestead on the marginal land of an interior valley. It tells of his marriage, his struggle with drought and
defeat, and his death. But the true novel lies below this surface in the
symbolism by which Joseph Wayne becomes the type of Western
Man, and his death the sacrifice of a man for his country. Historically,
Joseph Wayne is the pioneer settler. Symbolically, he is the Man of
Nature.

Artistically, then, Steinbeck's third novel attempts a new kind of
symbolic realism. The dream-motive, which had been external in *Cup
of Gold* and had appeared as bare framework in *The Pastures of
Heaven*, becomes integral with the plot. Every reality is a symbol:
Joseph's journey through the pass is real, yet suggests the passage of the
soul to maturity; Joseph's union with Rama is real, yet suggests the
communion of man with humanity; and his sacrificial death is real,
yet symbolizes the relation of man to nature. The general theme is
pointed by the recurrent refrain quoted from the Rig-Veda: "Who
is the God to whom we shall offer sacrifice?" But the novel fails: as
realism it becomes incredible; and as symbolism it lacks the visionary
grandeur which, for instance, gives life to the poetry of Robinson Jeffers. Either dreams must be described objectively, or they must be
transmuted into poetry.

But if this books fails, it fails greatly. It attempts through symbol
to prophesy, and through prophecy to create the future. It seeks to go
beyond the despair of most modern literature to a new affirmation.
Where Jeffers had described dreams as nightmares of possessive lust
and introversion, and considered even the self-sacrifice of Christ as
motivated by a desire for spiritual power, Steinbeck seeks to imagine
a new savior who will sacrifice himself for the Western land, freed of
the lust of power. So, at the end of the book, a Catholic priest exclaims
of Joseph Wayne: "Thank God this man has no message. Thank God
he has no will to be remembered, to be believed in . . . else there might
be a new Christ here in the West." *To a God Unknown* describes in
symbolic language a third phase of the American dream—the religious

ideal of self-sacrifice, through the union of the human individual with the "Unknown God" of nature.

Stated thus abstractly, this dream-idea sounds silly. The early novel was unsuccessful. But in modified terms the idea dominates all of Steinbeck's later work. And the novel remains important because it marks the end of his apprenticeship. His later stories all describe the dream objectively. And all describe it as successful (that is, as contributing to the happiness of the individual and of society) in so far as it is selfless. The *paisanos* of *Tortilla Flat*, the Communists of *In Dubious Battle*, the ranch hands in *Of Mice and Men*, and the Okies of *The Grapes of Wrath* all dream of something beyond themselves, and all achieve happiness to the degree that they sacrifice themselves for that dream. This becomes their greatness.

IV

I have given considerable attention to Steinbeck's first three novels because their very imperfections suggest the key to his work. The self-conscious use of dream and symbol disappears in his successful fiction, but continues subconsciously as part of its structure.

So *Tortilla Flat* describes the indolent *paisano* descendants of the Spanish conquerors with a mock-heroic humor which sympathizes even while it laughs. It tells how "love came to Big Joe Portagee" and of how his friends "succored the poor Pirate." Within the pseudo-pattern of heroic legend, it describes the misadventures of a group of ragamuffins who are not heroes. The contrast between the dreams of these primitive Californians and the mechanisms of modern society gives the book its unique flavor. Where *Cup of Gold* had failed through lack of a sense of humor, *Tortilla Flat* succeeds through possession of this quality. The common denominator remains the dream.

Where the dream of Henry Morgan and his pirates had been one of possession and conquest, the *paisanos* imagine a kind of primitive communism. The book's chapter headings suggest the new values: "How Pilon was lured by greed of position . . ." "How the poison of possessions wrought with Pilon . . ." "How Danny's Friends swore comradeship," "Of the good life at Danny's House . . ." and "How through sacrifice Danny's Friends gave a party." On the primitive level, the ideal of these ragamuffins is social, unselfish, and fundamentally good. Clearly, the author sympathizes with it, even while he recognizes its impossibility in this naïve form.

But this primitive ideal of communal life fails for other reasons than its primitiveness. Danny has inherited from an uncle a fortune almost sufficient to his needs. And his friends have contributed to the support of their fellowship. Together they have almost achieved social security. But nevertheless they are bored. Living only for pleasure, they crave action and even self-sacrifice. The communal ideal, Steinbeck seems to say, must go beyond sociability and security to include purposeful and responsible action.

These *paisanos* are children of nature. Civilization punishes them because they ignore its laws. But their natural community fails finally through its own lack of purpose. To the values of nature must also be added the values of civilization. Where these "heroes" dream only of tortillas on the flatland, the American dream includes the ideal of progress and of a struggle to the heights.

Therefore the foil of *Tortilla Flat* is *In Dubious Battle*. Where the one was mock-heroic, the other is heroic. Where the *paisanos* dreamed of pleasure, the Communists dream of the new society. Where the first were survivors of a primitive era, the second imagine themselves citizens of the future. But both seek "the good life" through group action, unselfishly. At the end of the "battle" one Communist declaims over his dead comrade: "This guy didn't want nothing for himself." At bottom both novels seek to answer the age-old question: "Who is the God to whom we shall offer sacrifice?"

But because these novels are fundamentally opposite, they use contrasting techniques. Where the mock-heroic suggested the abyss between dream and reality, the heroic describes the attempt to make the dream real. *In Dubious Battle*, therefore, becomes exclusively realistic. The very existence of the dream is denied by its dreamers. Dr. Burton says to Jim:

> "You're living the good life, whatever you want to call it."
> "I'm happy," said Jim. "And happy for the first time. I'm full-up."
> "I know. Don't let it die. It's the vision of Heaven."
> "I don't believe in Heaven," Jim said.

So the Communists live wholly on the realistic level, as men of action should. Steinbeck's earlier artificialities of dream-framework and symbolism have been abandoned. Only Dr. Burton remains as seer and interpreter, and even he is necessary to the action. The dream has become naturalized.

And the dream has grown. The possessive egotism of *Cup of Gold* has become altruism. The utopianism of *The Pastures of Heaven* has become practical. The mysticism of *To a God Unknown* has become active. And the primitivism of *Tortilla Flat* has become civilized.

But two imperfections remain: this communistic dream is partial, and it is violent. It is a product of imperfect vision, and of hate. So the doctor explains: "I want to see the whole picture, as nearly as I can. I don't want to put on the blinders of 'good' and 'bad,' and limit my vision." And later he continues: "The other side is made of men, Jim, men like you. Man hates himself. . . . Damn it, Jim, you can only build a violent thing with violence." But this doctor remains solitary. Not until *The Grapes of Wrath* will the idealist act without hatred, striving as a part to realize the purpose of the whole.

Meanwhile, *Of Mice and Men* describes the individualistic survival of the old American dream. Constantly repeated, because it is common to all Americans, this dream gives significance to a story of outcasts and failures: "Just like heaven. Ever'body wants a little piece of lan'. . . . Nobody never gets to heaven, and nobody gets no land. It's just in their head. They're all the time talkin' about it, but it's jus' in their head." Security, independence, a piece of land, the pioneer's dream and once almost the American reality; but now it's "just in their head." This is the American tragedy.

But why an imbecile for a hero? Why a nigger, a cripple, and a moron for supporting cast? It has been said that this story is not tragic, because its characters lack significance. But I think the story is tragic, although it is not primarily a tragedy of character. It is a tragedy of idea. These "heroes" achieve significance because they give expression to the American dream in its simplest form. They become heroic, because they refuse to deny their dream. George says, "Guys like us got no fambly. They make a little stake an' then they blow it in. They ain't got nobody in the worl' that gives a hoot in hell about 'em—." They refute the despair of Vachel Lindsay:

> Not that they starve, but starve so dreamlessly,
> Not that they sow, but that they seldom reap,
> Not that they serve, but have no gods to serve,
> Not that they die, but that they die like sheep.

Serving an unknown God, they do not die like sheep:

> George was quiet for a moment. "But not us," he said.
> "Because—"
> "Because I got you an'—"
> "An' I got you. We got each other, that's what, that gives a hoot in hell about us," Lennie cried in triumph.

And so they die in triumph with their dream.

In this novel the dream which has dominated Steinbeck's thought from the beginning reaches its final phase. George and Lennie express what is best in it. Unlike Henry Morgan, who was "not very intelligent" because he was utterly selfish, these poor men see beyond themselves. Like the Joad family, these native Americans seek unselfishly to band together. George becomes a responsible leader, and the others share. If they are doomed, it is not because of what is false within—they have achieved inner integrity. They lack only the pragmatic "intelligence" necessary to bring the dream to realization. Because they lack that, they remain dreamers merely: at the end George gets drunk and tries to forget. But Tom Joad will remember, and will go on. The dream lives.

V

Steinbeck's first three novels told of dreamers subjectively, with imperfect realism; and described dreams which were selfish and distorted. His next three novels told of dreamers objectively, with increasing realism; but described dreams which, for one reason or another, were doomed to defeat. His last two books have described characters whose dreams are valid, and who have (to some degree) realized them.

After To a God Unknown, Steinbeck wrote two brilliant short stories which were later combined as "The Red Pony." After Of Mice and Men he wrote two more about Jody Tiflin, the young owner of the red pony. These stories he collected in The Long Valley. They announced the literary maturity of the author. In them Steinbeck finally achieved complete realism, and carried his literary thought through to its logical consequences.

The story of the red pony, of his death, and of the birth of his successor is so real that no symbolism seems intended. But the dream-motivation of the earlier novels and a few hints in these stories suggest that the red pony is also the physical symbol of the old American dream. Owning him, Jody becomes the man on horseback: his schoolmates "knew instinctively that a man on a horse is spiritually as well as physically bigger than a man on foot." And so Jody's rides became "a strange time and a mysterious journey—an extension of a dream." And Jody became a leader among his schoolmates. The last story in the group, entitled "The Leader of the People," suggests that he will succeed his pioneer grandfather as a leader among men also.

These stories describe the death of Jody's red pony, his sorrow over it, and finally the birth of his new colt. They suggest how these experiences lead him to maturity. For the red pony was the plaything of a child, bought by an indulgent father for an irresponsible son. But the colt is the reward of Jody's own work. And its birth teaches him the tragic cost of life.

The red pony is physically real. But he also suggests the old American ideal of life—the "genteel tradition" of the past. He is beautiful and lovable, but not suited to the hardships of ranch life nor strong enough to survive the neglect of his masters. Like the great house which Richard Whiteside built for his children, and the perfect room which Pat Humbert furnished for his love, he is a lovely anachronism. The ideal of the new America must be born of the experience of the younger generation with the land. And the birth of the new colt is not easy. Jody's grandfather has given up hope for the future. But Jody has not. He has brought the new life to birth.

Jody's grandfather despaired of America because, he said, "Westering isn't a hunger any more." In the early days he had led men West, but now "there's a line of old men along the shore hating the ocean because it stopped them . . . there's no place to go." To this fundamental American problem Steinbeck addressed himself in The Grapes of Wrath. Tom Joad leads a new westward migration. He rediscovers America, and recognizes that its land is not being used nor its opportunities kept open. He becomes a leader of the new pioneers, spiritually as well as physically.

The Grapes of Wrath is too large a novel to be described briefly.[1] In it the many skeins of Steinbeck's thought are woven into new patterns. But primarily it is a novel of the American dream. In the strange character of Jim Casy the old dream finds new expression. For this ex-preacher, who has abandoned the old forms in order to see the desires of men as they are, dominates the story. In him the magic prophecies of the early Merlin find mature expression, and the earthy mysticism of the unknown God, and the self-sacrifice of In Dubious Battle. Jim Casy reinterprets the American dream.

But he also transforms it, and (with Tom Joad) helps to realize it. Unlike Merlin who prophesied mysteriously on the mountain-top, and unlike Joseph Wayne who acted without realistic motive, and unlike the Communist doctor who merely observed, Jim Casy shares in the experiences of his people, and develops from them. And unlike the earlier idealists, he acts with his people. From him Tom Joad learns, both through words and through deeds. When Casy dies, Tom gives expression to his dream, and continues to act upon it.

And if Tom Joad dies, it will not matter, for the dream will live. His soul will become the soul of America, struggling for freedom. "—They might kill ya," Ma Joad had objected. But Tom replied:

"It don' matter. Then I'll be all aroun' in the dark. I'll be ever'where —wherever you look. Wherever they's a fight so hungry people can eat,

I'll be there. Wherever they's a cop beatin' up a guy, I'll be there. If Casy knowed, why, I'll be in the way guys yell when they're mad an'— I'll be in the way kids laugh when they're hungry an' they know supper's ready. An' when our folks eat the stuff they raise an' live in the houses they build—why, I'll be there. See?"

His soul goes marching on. The dream continues.

1. See "The Philosophical Joads," by Frederic I. Carpenter. [P. 241, below.]

Joseph Warren Beach

JOHN STEINBECK:
JOURNEYMAN ARTIST

IT WAS in the late thirties that Steinbeck's reputation came to a head and was crowned with the international fame of *The Grapes of Wrath.* That is certainly a very fine book; but its tremendous vogue was founded partly on what we call an accident—that it concerned itself with one of the major economic problems of its day, the problem of seasonal labor in California, and with the largest scale agricultural catastrophe of American history in our century, the catastrophe of the dustbowl. It is, we might say, an accident that so great a talent as John Steinbeck's should have come upon so great and so topical a theme. But that so great a talent should have come to flower in our time is not in the same sense an accident. It is, let us say, the bounty of nature; and it is, moreover, what we have all been looking for, the fruit of long cultivation—the ripening of American literary culture in our day.

And the first thing we should take note of in Steinbeck is the sheer literary genius with which he is endowed. The dustbowl might never have thrown its dreary blight over the vast empire of the cattle lands; the state of California might never have been faced with this terrible labor problem. But the connoisseurs in the written word would have known—and they did know—that an American writer had appeared with a sure and subtle sense for literary effect, a storyteller worthy to be compared with Chekhov or Anatole France for his skill in shaping up the stuff of human lives in forms that delight the mind and imagina-

JOSEPH WARREN BEACH, Professor of English, Emeritus, University of Minnesota, retired from active teaching in 1941 after a very distinguished career. He is the author of many books and articles on nineteenth and twentieth century literature. Among his many achievements, Mr. Beach is generally regarded as having pioneered in the criticism of the modern novel. His book American Fiction: 1920-1940 *was published by Macmillan in 1941.*

The essay that appears here, "John Steinbeck: Journeyman Artist," as well as "John Steinbeck: Art and Propaganda," which appears elsewhere in this collection, are chapters from that book. Both essays have been slightly revised by Mr. Beach for appearance here and are reprinted by his permission as holder of the copyright.

tion. This is a rare event in our day or any day. It is like what we mean when we speak of a born musician—having reference to a composer—a finder of melodies, a natural shaper of harmonies—a Schubert or a Brahms. And *The Grapes of Wrath* was simply to demonstrate, what was already apparent to the discerning, that this was an unusually versatile talent, capable of being turned to themes of various sorts, and suiting itself to the theme like hand and glove.

Let me illustrate what I mean by his versatility. I have spoken of Chekhov. In our day the most distinguished writers have a disposition to feature characters like those in *The Grapes of Wrath*, who live on the barest subsistence level, and whose besetting concern is therefore with the primary needs of the animal organism. Or if the people are not so depressed economically, the disposition is still to represent them largely in terms of sensations and urges but one remove from the animal level, with small regard for the refinements of thought and sentiment which, we pride ourselves, are the distinguishing mark of our more civilized manner of life. They seem not to have "souls," or spiritual personalities, in the sense that we feel ourselves and our friends to have them. Now, the characters of this Russian storyteller, whatever their economic status, seem invariably to have "souls." There is a depth, a feeling quality, a diversification to their personal experience which makes them seem important—important individually for what they are in themselves over and above what they are as members of the tribe of men, as hungering and sex-ridden gregarious animals with the gift of speech. Chekhov is not a sentimental writer. He is objective and realistic enough and sets down what he has observed without any shrinking. But his people are so interesting for their individual quality, their inner world is so rich and diversified, his report on human nature so fresh, direct and authentic, that one always comes away from one of his stories moved and diverted and with a heightened sense of the interest of living. These people are suffused with the feeling which we attach to the living experience, as if bathed in the atmosphere of sensibility and aspiration which makes up our sense of life.

Well, there are many of Steinbeck's short stories that remind one of the Russian writer. There is the opening story of the volume entitled *The Long Valley* (1938). It is called "Chrysanthemums." It gives us the picture of a wholesome and attractive woman of thirty-five, wife of a rancher in that enchanting Salinas Valley where Steinbeck lived as a boy. This woman has what are called planter's hands, so that whatever she touches grows and flourishes. She is shown on a soft winter morning working in her garden, cutting down the old year's chrysanthemum stalks, while her husband stands by the tractor shed talking with two

men in business suits. Nothing is said about the relationship of this
married pair, but everything shows that it is one of confidence and mutual respect. He refers with simple pleasure to the size of her chrysanthemums. She applauds his success in selling his three-year-old steers at
nearly his own price. And she welcomes his suggestion that, since it is
Saturday afternoon, they go into town for dinner and then to a picture
show. But she wouldn't care to go to the fights. The feminine note is
sounded in the unaffected shrinking of the refined woman from the
brutality of a sport which men enjoy. "Oh, no," she said breathlessly,
"I wouldn't like fights." And he hastens to assure her he was just fool-
ing; they'll go to a movie. It is not the author who tells us that he is
making a sacrifice, and that he is glad to do so, for he likes his wife better thus than if she wanted to go to the fights. The beauty of this kind
of storytelling is that the author does not waste words and insult his
reader with that sort of explanation. He gets his effects with an elegant
economy of words, and leaves some scope for the reader's imagination.

And now is introduced a third character, picturesque and individual,
and a new balance of forces in human relations. The new character is
an itinerant tinker who comes driving up in his queer covered wagon
from the country road that runs along the bank of the river. He is a big
stubble-bearded man, in a greasy black suit, graying but not old-looking,
with dark eyes "full of the brooding that gets in the eyes of teamsters
and of sailors." He is a shrewd, dynamic personality. And there ensues
between him and Eliza Allen a combat of wits in which she shows herself a person of right feeling, one who doesn't let her charitable instincts run away with her, but who has at the same time a soft side
where you can get round her. That is her love of flowers, and the pride
she takes in her way with chrysanthemums. The author says nothing
of this tug-of-war, nor of the shrewdness of the tinker, nor of the quality
in Eliza Allen that makes her a victim. All these things he shows us in
the brief dialogue—again with a richness of reference which makes us
feel the whole quality of these two by no means commonplace lives.
Among other things he makes us feel how, beneath her brisk and con-
tented exterior, this woman harbors an unsatisfied longing for some
way of life less settled than that of the rancher's wife, something typified by the shabby tinker camping nightly in his wagon underneath the
stars.

Eliza Allen has nothing that needs mending, but the tinker does not
want to leave without something to feed his hungry frame. He has the
inspiration to take an interest in her chrysanthemums; he begs her for
some of the shoots to take to a lady down the road who has asked him
to bring her some. The upshot of it is that she finds some old pans for

him to mend and he goes away with fifty cents in his pocket and a pot of chrysanthemum shoots. She watches him go down the road by the river, and is filled, as the author manages to make us know, with a kind of troubled joy at the thought of him on his vagabond trail.

And now she turns to the bustle of washing up and dressing for the trip to town. I wish I knew how the author manages here to convey the sense he does of the energy and well-being of this rancher's wife moved by thoughts unnamed and perhaps not brought above the level of consciousness. Her husband observes how "strong" she seems, but has no notion of the special occasion for it.

But Eliza Allen has a grief in store, and we have still the pleasure of seeing how mad and hurt she can be when she realizes that she has been outwitted by the man who means so much to her in the obscure places of her imagination. As she drives along to town with her husband she discovers a dark spot on the pavement where the tinker had thrown her chrysanthemums the moment he was out of sight of the ranch. The pot he kept. The thing remains a secret with her. She says nothing of it to her husband. We know it only by the tone she takes in asking him again about the fights. She asks him if the fighters do not hurt each other very much. "I've read how they break noses, and blood runs down their chests. I've read how the fighting gloves get heavy and soggy with blood." He is surprised and rather shocked that she should ever have thought of things like that; but he is willing to take her to the fights if she really wants it. "She relaxed limply in the seat. 'Oh, no. No. I don't want to go. I'm sure I don't.' Her face was turned away from him. 'It will be enough if we can have wine. It will be plenty.' She turned up her coat collar so that he could not see that she was crying weakly—like an old woman."

This is no tragic grief. But it does assure us that Eliza Allen is very much of a woman, and of the same flesh and blood with ourselves—that she shares with us our sensitive pride, our reluctance to let someone get the best of us, and more than that, our secret romantic longing for something more than "human nature's daily food." She is one of the most delicious characters ever transferred from life to the pages of a book. There is no doubt that she has a "soul." And she is much less simple than she seems.

The most famous story in The Long Valley is "The Red Pony." This is dedicated to a boy's passion for animal pets, and is quite in a class with Mrs. Rawlings' Yearling. It represents a more privileged level of human living than that, and aspects of nature more benign and lovely. It has its own splendor and pathos. I mention it here as another case of human types and relationships as fine and subtle as any in Chekhov.

There is the opening enchantment of a boy's world in touch with the primitive joys of wild life. And there is the boy's shyness and secretiveness—the sternness of responsibilities laid on him as a member of a serious farming community—the ticklish balance of his relation to a stern but just and loving father—and the suffering inflicted on him by the indifferent cruelties of nature. The finest thing of all is the relation between the boy Jody and Billy the hired man, whose pride of skill as well as his affection for the boy is involved in his effort to save the lives, first of the red pony, and then of the mare who is chosen to be the mother of Jody's colt.

There is in Steinbeck much of the romantic poet and of the mystic, at least the love of themes embodying mystical attitudes. I will say little of his first experiment in psychological romance—*Cup of Gold* (1929) —which has for its subject the life of the buccaneer, Sir Henry Morgan. It opens with a glimpse of his hero as a boy at home in a Welsh manor house, and starts his adventures with an interview on a mountain-top with the sage magician Merlin. Altogether it is a very interesting performance and is another illustration of Steinbeck's versatility. But he did not know quite what he was after. There are echoes of many different manners, including, I think, that of the author of *Jurgen*. But he had not quite found himself in any of the several distinct genres in which he later became a master.

Very much more successful, and altogether delightful as imaginative evocation, is *To a God Unknown* (1933). This is the story of a man devoted to the land, who left his New England farm to establish himself as a pioneer in the fertile secluded valley of Nuestra Señora, not far from the sea in California. He was followed there by his brothers and their families, and they made altogether a highly prosperous and idyllic colony of ranchers while the good years lasted. But the main interest of the story lies in the mystical feeling of Joseph Wayne in regard to the land and his relation to it. He was the one of the brothers to receive the patriarchal blessing of their father. He has a nature poetic and aloof, regarding himself as a sort of priest, whose paramount concern is to promote the fertility of the earth and of the men and cattle who live upon its surface. He has great sympathy with the pagan superstitions and rituals which survive among the Indians and the Mexican half-breeds; and has notions and practices of his own which are sinful and blasphemous in the eyes of his Christian brother, while to the other brother they come to seem the infliction of madness. He believes that the spirit of his dead father has followed him West and is lodged in the great live-oak tree that shades the farmyard. He is possessed by the pagan theory of sacrifice, and in the end he makes a sacrifice of himself to bring back the rain upon a country made barren with drought. His favorite resort in times of joy and sorrow is a great moss-covered rock, which stands in a temple-like grove of pines, and beneath which in a mysterious cave is the source of a spring regarded by the Indians as sacred. It was there that his wife met her death by accident, herself a sacrifice to the unknown god of the earth.

Steinbeck's subject here is one suggested in part by his deep feeling for the land, especially in its virgin phase, and for the life of the early settlers in this lovely wilderness, partly by the more intellectual interest in primitive psychology and religion. It is a theme of utmost delicacy, hard to carry through in the right key, without sentimentality or self-consciousness in the handling of the fantastic and uncanny. Steinbeck has brought to his task a most unusual literary tact and a sympathetic imagination capable of fusing the diverse elements into a consistent and plausible whole. He has brought a style remarkable for its expressiveness without loudness or eccentricity, and a sense for rhythm and for right English idiom most unusual among contemporary writers; a manner of expression in which a strong reflective bent is felt beneath the surface of simple sentences shaped by the sensuous imagination and the proprieties of narrative. The style is strictly of today, but without the slightest suggestion of what is bizarre in the Hemingway manner, the Faulkner manner or the Wolfe manner. With a theme broadly suggestive of Arthur Machen, there is no hint of that romantic effusiveness, à la De Quincey, which repels the fastidious reader in The Hill of Dreams. Steinbeck's style in this book is the nearest to what we mean by "classical" of almost anything in contemporary fiction, but without dryness or coldness.

To a God Unknown belongs to the world of dreams rather than that of urgent realities. It has not the strength of Steinbeck's later work. It has not the emotional power of Hudson's Green Mansions, to name perhaps the greatest of novels of fantasy. But it has much of the charm of Hudson, and an intriguing quality of its own in the treatment of a local American subject. There is not the remotest suggestion of the proletarian themes which came to the fore in Steinbeck's later work. It is another reminder of his extraordinary versatility.

But it is time we were coming to what will be our special subject, which is Steinbeck's dealing with children of the earth. By this I mean human beings more lowly than prosperous ranchers—I mean those helpless children of earth who can never raise themselves more than a few feet from its surface, and for whom the question of the next meal remains a major obsession.

But here again I must distinguish types and dwell once more on the versatility of this author, who has a different manner for each class of subject matter which he treats. Before the publication of *The Grapes of Wrath* (1939) Steinbeck had already produced two books which were widely read and hailed by critics as masterpieces. The first of these was *Tortilla Flat* (1935) and the second was *Of Mice and Men* (1937).

Tortilla Flat is, I believe, the favorite with academic readers, and this for the obvious reason that it is most unmistakably among his books a literary feat. It is a very skillful blend of several varieties of comic writing; it recalls *Don Quixote* and *Gil Blas* and Anatole France and Charles Lamb. And in addition it recalls the simple heroic manner of Malory's *Morte d'Arthur* and the sweet simplicity of the *Little Flowers of Saint Francis*. So that any lover of these classic masterpieces is bound to have his palate titillated by its grave and playful cadences. Steinbeck was for several years, off and on, a student at Stanford University, where he followed only such courses as pleased his fancy and quite neglected to take a degree. And it is clear that he used his time to as great advantage as the average faithful student who comes away with a B.S. in Education or a B.A. in Sociology.

Steinbeck's subject in *Tortilla Flat* is the paisano of Monterey. The paisano is, as he tells us, "a mixture of Spanish, Indian, Mexican, and assorted Caucasian bloods. His ancestors have lived in California for a hundred or two years. He speaks English with a paisano accent and Spanish with a paisano accent. When questioned concerning his race, he indignantly claims pure Spanish blood and rolls up his sleeve to show that the soft inside of his arm is nearly white." The paisano lives in a special district in Monterey where town and pine forest intermingle. He has little property and is little subject to the civic and financial worries of other citizens. Steinbeck's particular subject is one Danny and his friends Pilon and Pablo and Portagee Jo, Jesus Maria Corcoran, and a certain ragamuffin called the Pirate. For the most part these men have no occupation, but work occasionally on ranches or cutting squids in a canning factory. Most of them were enlisted in the war with Germany. On his return from the army, Danny, who had preferred as a boy to sleep in the woods, finds that his grandfather, a man of exceptional wealth in this community, has died and left him two small unpainted houses in Tortilla Flat. So for the first time in his life he is a man with a roof over his head and burdened with the cares of property. Unable to support this condition alone, he invites his friends to join him. They rent his second house, but never pay him any rent except an occasional purloined chicken or gallon jug of red wine. When the Virgin Mary gently admonishes them for their careless life by burning down their rented house, they move in with Danny, who welcomes them to his small room on condition that no one occupy his bed but himself. When the Pirate is added to the group with his five mangy dogs, a special corner is assigned to the dogs, and they all live happily together.

They lead an eventful life. These are true stories, Steinbeck assures us, though sometimes elaborated by the people of Tortilla Flat in oral narration. "It is well," he says, "that this cycle be put down on paper so that in future time scholars, hearing the legends, may not say as they say of Arthur and of Roland and of Robin Hood—'There was no Danny nor any group of Danny's friends, nor any house. Danny is a nature god and his friends primitive symbols of the wind, the sky, the sun.' This history is designed now and ever to keep the sneers from the lips of sour scholars."

The first reviewers of the book perceived that these people were curious or quaint, dispossessed or underdoggish. Steinbeck's feelings were hurt, so he tells us. He had never thought that they were anything of the sort. They were friends of his, people whom he liked, and if he had thought they were quaint he would never have written of them. This disclaimer it is impossible to take at its face value. He liked these people and they were his friends. Well and good. That we can heartily believe. It is clear throughout his writing that Steinbeck is fond of the underdog; and that for good and sufficient reasons. Because he is the underdog, and because of his many virtues. And then, because in him the primary human impulses are less overlaid with disguise, and stand out in stark simplicity. But this last, observe, is an artistic reason, a literary reason. The likings of an artist are always open to suspicion; and we have to distinguish between his liking for people themselves and his liking for his *subject*. The paisanos are doubtless likable in themselves; but they are still more likable as subject for the literary artist. And they are all the more likable, it may be, for traits of which the artist could not well approve. Danny and his friends were frank and courtly in manner, fond of wine and women, full of charity, piety and good nature, ingenious and enterprising in odd ways of securing food and drink; and these may well be regarded as virtues as well as subjects for artistic representation. But they were also shiftless and lazy; they were inveterate if petty thieves; they were ignorant and superstitious; they were something very like drunkards; and these are hardly traits which their author could regard as moral virtues.

He likes them, he says, because they are people who merge successfully with their habitat. Well, that may be argued. On his showing they do make shift to live with satisfaction according to their notions; perhaps they have adapted themselves instinctively to the conditions imposed on them by race and the social set-up. But I doubt whether any jury of sociologists would rate them high as members of the body politic, or would give a clean bill of health to the social set-up which calls for this sort of adjustment.

The fact is, of course, that Steinbeck is not thinking primarily in sociological terms. The blending of these people with their background is an artistic circumstance, like that of Millet's peasants in the Angelus and the Man with the Hoe. We'll not call it quaint if that hurts his feelings, but he can hardly stop us from calling it picturesque. And the proof that he himself regards these people as at least curious is that he has written an essentially comic history of them. If he doesn't know that this is funny, then he doesn't know what he has done; and that is quite obviously contrary to fact.

It is certainly funny when Danny, in pursuit of amorous designs on Sweets Ramirez, presents her with a vacuum cleaner though it is well known that there is no electrical power in Tortilla Flat to run it. It is funnier still that she should daily pass this vacuum cleaner over the floor "on the theory that of course it would clean better with electricity, but one could not have everything"; that her stock should rise so much in her community because of the possession of a machine that would not work; so that she grew puffed up with pride and dragged her sweeping-machine into the conversation on every occasion. It was funniest of all when, Danny growing tired of this lady, his loving friends took back the vacuum cleaner by stealth and sold it to Torelli the bootlegger for two gallons of wine, and when on their departure Torelli looked into the machine and found it had no motor—it had never had a motor.

The story of the Pirate is funny too in a way—this ragamuffin who lives in a chicken house with his five dogs, and every day in a secret place buries the quarter of a dollar he earns from the sale of firewood. Danny's friends conclude by some process of paisano logic that he must have a buried treasure; and with a view to making it theirs, they treat him with a friendliness that he has never known. They bring him to their house and install him there with his five mangy dogs. They use on him every wile they know to worm out of him his secret. What is their surprise when he finally brings to them his treasure of two hundred dollars and puts it under their special protection! He has dedicated this treasure to the Virgin, promising her a gold candlestick for the favor she had done him in saving the life of a sick dog. These scalawags have their honor and piety, and much as they crave this money for their own uses, they guard it sacredly for the Virgin Mary.

On the day when the candlestick was dedicated, the dogs were ad-

monished not to enter the church. They did break into the church in
their enthusiasm and interrupted the sermon on Saint Francis of Assisi
and his love for dumb beasts. But Father Ramon was indulgent. He
could not help laughing. "Take the dogs outside," he said, "let them
wait until we are through." The Pirate took them out and gave them a
good scolding. "He left them stricken with grief and repentance and
went back into the church. The people, still laughing, turned and
looked at him, until he sank into his seat and tried to efface himself.
'Do not be ashamed,' Father Ramon said. 'It is no sin to be loved by
your dogs, and no sin to love them. See how Saint Francis loved the
beasts.' Then he told more stories of that good saint."

This anecdote ends with the Pirate's taking the dogs out into the
woods, ranging them as an audience, and telling them the story of Saint
Francis. And then a miracle occurred.

> The dogs sat patiently, their eyes on the Pirate's lips. He told every-
> thing the priest had told, all the stories, all the observations. Hardly a
> word was out of its place.
> When he was done, he regarded the dogs solemnly. "Saint Francis
> did all that," he said.
> The trees hushed their whispering. The forest was silent and
> enchanted.
> Suddenly there was a tiny sound behind the Pirate. All the dogs
> looked up. The Pirate was afraid to turn his head. A long moment
> passed.
> And then the moment was over. The dogs lowered their eyes. The
> tree-tops stirred to life again and the sunlight patterns moved
> bewilderingly.
> The Pirate was so happy that his heart pained him. "Did you see
> him?" he cried. "Was it San Francisco? Oh! What good dogs you must
> be to see a vision."
> The dogs leaped up at his tone. Their mouths opened and their tails
> threshed joyfully.

There is much more than humor here, and the book shows throughout a genuine love for the charm and virtue of these childlike paisanos.
I will not quarrel with Mr. Steinbeck over terms to characterize his people. Let them not be quaint or dispossessed. The point I wish to make
is that his artistic sensibility has led him to choose for his subject here
a manner of living and feeling which is not much in evidence in contemporary America, which reminds us more of rural Mexico today or
of Italy of the Middle Ages. He has invested his tale with the tender
pathos of distance that attaches to Saint Francis and Robin Hood and

Shakespeare's Forest of Arden. And this he has colored with the quaint humor—oh, excuse me—the delicious humor of Don Quixote, Sancho Panza and Dulcinea Del Toboso. I refuse to quarrel with Mr. Steinbeck. I am trying to praise him. I am trying to say that the author of *The Grapes of Wrath* and *Of Mice and Men* is one who can bring to his representation of American life today the subtle skills of the great tradition in European writing.

Steinbeck's next major literary venture was in a very different vein, as far as possible from the gentle comedy of *Tortilla Flat*. *Of Mice and Men* is a tragic story of friendship among migratory laborers. And it is told with the directness and severe economy of a tale of Maupassant. The economy is that of drama as well as short story. We are told that Steinbeck's aim was to see how near he could come in narrative to the form of a stage play. And the story was no sooner written than it was turned into a successful drama.

It is the tale of two men whose custom it is to move from ranch to ranch, spending their little stake in town as soon as they have made it and passing on to another place where work may be had. But as with the Okies in *The Grapes of Wrath*, the secret dream of these two men is to save up enough money to buy a little farm and live in peaceful and settled independence. One of them is the mentally defective Lennie, a huge man of colossal strength, but simple as a child and helplessly dependent on the care of his friend George. George had taken him after the death of Lennie's aunt. Lennie is a millstone round his neck, standing between him and everything he would like to do. But George is deeply attached to his backward friend, knowing that without him he would lapse himself into the dreary state of a friendless wanderer. The huge Lennie has a child's passion for small animals, which he loves to hold in his hands and stroke; but the strength of his hands is so great that the frail creatures are likely to be broken and killed without his meaning any harm. He wishes earnestly to keep from doing anything bad, so as not to incur the wrath of George, but with the best of intentions he is forever getting them into trouble. And when it is a woman and not a puppy who becomes the victim of his ill-directed force, there is nothing left for his friend but to put an end to Lennie. That is the only way to save him from lynching.

One who has not read the book can hardly be made to appreciate the tone of humanity and beauty with which Steinbeck invests this tragic episode. The almost paternal affection of George for his blundering witless pal, and the sore grief he suffers over the necessity of putting him away—all this you are made to feel without the use of sentimental phrase or direct statement. Back of this lies the life of the bunkhouse—

the essential decency and pathos of these rough homeless men whom circumstance has condemned to a life of physical and moral squalor. There is no touching on the industrial and social problems involved, as in *The Grapes of Wrath*, though the tale may have its bearing on the treatment of certain types of mental defectives. In this as in the earlier books, Steinbeck was content with the imaginative, the basically human, factors in the drama.

I think I have said enough to indicate that, by the time Steinbeck came to *The Grapes of Wrath*, he had served his artistic apprenticeship. If in this greatest of his fictions he has shown himself a social propagandist of unusual power, it is not because he lacked the literary skills required for pure imaginative writing, or the disposition to regard the art of fiction as primarily a matter of esthetics. It remains to see whether he left his artistry behind when he dealt directly with a sociological theme.

Lincoln R. Gibbs

JOHN STEINBECK: MORALIST

THREE OBSTACLES confront the writer of fiction who advocates social reform. First and least important, there is a small number of readers of a metaphysical or aesthetic bent, who dislike literature that deals realistically with contemporary life. They distrust it as partisan and tendentious; they demand that the artist rise above his world or go beyond it and treat life *sub specie aeternitatis*. Second, opponents of the novelist-reformer have an easy weapon at hand. This is the retort that all his facts are products of his imagination. Third, he must, since he is an artist, supply concrete detail, and much of this detail must needs be sordid, some of it vulgar and uncouth, much of it ribald, immoral, and blasphemous. Graphic pictures of vice and degradation alienate not only the prudish but also thousands of respectable persons, most of whom read fiction solely for entertainment and do not wish to be disgusted, offended, or distressed.

Steinbeck meets all these obstacles in exceptional force, plus a powerful and vocal contingent of business magnates and their minions, who have vested interests in the existing state of things.

The demand that literature concern itself solely wtih absolute truth and absolute beauty is a voice from the ivory tower, which is not a spacious structure and accommodates few dwellers. This demand may be ignored.

The charge that Steinbeck has invented or distorted his facts takes the case beyond the court of literary criticism into sociology. Most fortunately, the novelist's facts and findings, so far as California is concerned, are verified in the writings of Carey McWilliams and others. Mr. McWilliams' books and articles are widely read. They constitute a documentation of *Grapes of Wrath* and *In Dubious Battle*. Incidentally, it is well worth noting that, although there has been no collaboration, the parallel between Steinbeck and McWilliams is a striking

LINCOLN R. GIBBS was professor of English at Antioch College from 1928 till his death in 1943. Before that he had taught also at the University of Pittsburgh, Wells College, Mount Union College, University of Miami, and Boston University. He was a member of the original editorial board of The Antioch Review, where "John Steinbeck: Moralist" first appeared in June, 1942. It is reprinted by permission of The Antioch Review.

example of the division of labor between art and social science. It is a happy augury of the integration of our national culture. If Steinbeck needs a defense on the score of veracity, well-informed persons are ready to give him support.

The third complaint—of indecency—is, at the moment, the most important. It comes honestly from the very persons who most need to learn what Steinbeck has to impart, the responsible, "middle-class," well-intentioned citizens of America. This charge the artist himself must refute or forestall, within the compass of his creative writings (with such modest aid as friendly critics can render).

The facts must be admitted. There are in Steinbeck's books hundreds of unsavory incidents, ribald speeches, scores of perverts, thieves, lechers, bullies and prostitutes, a few horrible tales of sex perversion[1] and one irreverent parody of a saint's legend.[2] For the reading of Steinbeck one needs a good heart and a strong stomach—like the person (in *Tortilla Flat*) who rescues from the ditch a drunken friend who had lain there several days. The rescuer probably held his nose and Steinbeck's readers are often moved to do the same.

There is no adequate defense (though there is mitigation) in the fact that many of the revered classics of literature are open to the same charge. There is abundant pornography in Boccaccio, Chaucer, Rabelais, Shakespeare, Herrick, Fielding, Sterne, Balzac, Samuel Butler, Daudet, and Walt Whitman—not to mention scores of authors who have written since the recent repeal of reticence. There are touches of it even in Robert Browning (a mid-Victorian by date, if not wholly in temper). Some of these authors are used mainly in expurgated versions (notably Shakespeare). In other cases the smut can be isolated, printed in an appendix or omitted, kept off the juvenile shelves, and wholly disregarded by persons whom it offends. But in many works it is an organic element of the pattern (e.g., Shakespeare's *Othello*), as in Steinbeck. If pornography is a cardinal sin, it is matter for penitence in these masters of literature, no less than in smaller writers, since it is part of their total product and an indication of the spirit that was in them. (In fact, Chaucer disavowed his scurrilous tales and Herrick repented of his "unbaptized rhymes," with how much sincerity one is at a loss to say.)

To repeat, the example of great literary masters is no adequate defense. But it is a mitigation and it helps to narrow the issue. It indicates a recognition, by great minds, of animal appetites and physiological facts. Earth is an obscene planet, if you choose. The philosopher must make the best of its obscenity, among other factors in his problem. The question is that of the author's attitude and purpose. Does he wallow in filth because he loves it? Does he throw it at his readers because he has a mischievous delight in shocking the middle-class puritan? Or perhaps he tells smutty stories by way of an innocent discharge of animal impulses which must otherwise be inhibited? May he not be concerned, as an honest realist, to make a full report of the deeds, talk, and nature of his characters?

Applying these tests to Steinbeck I wholly absolve him from the charge that he loves bestiality for its own sake. Perhaps it fascinates him, as even anguish and horror may fascinate the most innocent and especially the artist, who must have acute sensibility. Steinbeck's senses are delicate and wonderfully perceptive, as evidenced by the California landscapes one finds on his pages—lovely small farms, trim homesteads and gardens, wooded cañons with a little stream at the bottom, mountain ranges and peaks, cliffs bordering the Pacific, rich flat lands in the valleys and at the mouths of rivers. All these he describes in short graphic phrases, with accurately shaded color, with chiaroscuro, outline, and motion. His human sympathies are equally acute, and he has the priceless grace of discovering the redeeming trait in the most degraded person—the prostitute, the jail-bird, the drunkard that neglects his family, even the hard prosperous person who is correct and presentable, but inhumanly cold. He has a special interest in fanatics, eccentrics, half-wits, the insane, the lonely, the ugly, the ridiculous. His treatment of these is sometimes exaggerative and melodramatic—but there is no question of the genuineness of his sympathy.

Now acute perception and lively wide-ranging sympathy are a large part of the artist's equipment. They often betray him into sentimentalism and melodrama; there are instances of this in Steinbeck. But, more to the point in hand, they cause him to see filth and vice, as well as charm, purity, and grace. He wishes to do justice to every fact, like the realist Fra Lippo Lippi, in Browning's poem. We applaud Walt Whitman for ability to feel in his own mind and flesh the terror of the hunted slave as he hears the baying of bloodhounds and to sense the sting of the lash and the drip of mingled blood and sweat; yet many of us (the writer among them) look askance at "Children of Adam." But a poet or novelist cannot have sensibility for one class of experiences without applying it to all. He may, indeed, refrain from writing poems, plays, or novels about obscene subjects and from isolating horrible and disgusting facts by selective attention. But he cannot, if he wishes to create a comprehensive picture of life, exclude offensive facts.

One suspects that Steinbeck would cheerfully plead guilty to the charge of deliberately shocking the respectables. Convinced as he is that many of them are Pharisees, and deeply impressed by the graces and virtues and wrongs of the proletarians, he would be somewhat less than human if he did not now and then delight in ruffling the composure of prudes and making them squirm. In the preface of *Tortilla Flat* he complains of having suffered long from the oppression of decency. "The unco guid and the rigidly righteous" are a sore trial to generous, sympathetic souls, especially to artists. Their quarrel is not new to begin. One is confident that Shakespeare himself speaks in the voices of Sir Toby and the Clown:

> Sir Toby. Dost thou think, because thou art virtuous, there shall be no more cakes and ale?
> Clown. Yes, by Saint Anne! and ginger shall be hot i' the mouth too.[3]

Steinbeck overdoes this matter, but his license of speech does not spring from a vile mind; it springs from the heart of a rebel who hates cant and injustice. Many years ago Dr. Holmes, apostle of decorum and consummate flower of the genteel tradition, told us that there are many swearing saints and praying devils in the world. At the very worst, Steinbeck's indecencies should be condoned for the sake of the art and understanding he provides. Probably they are most strongly resented by the very persons who ought most to listen to what he has to say.

II

Tortilla Flat, the first of Steinbeck's books to be widely read, provides illustration. It is an extravaganza, with a good deal of slapstick comedy, a touch of parody (of the *Morte d'Arthur*), and many examples of the author's innuendo. One enthusiastic admirer has set up the enjoyment of *Tortilla Flat* as a criterion of literary taste: if one doesn't like the book, let him not profane the temple of literature, let him be in outer darkness. This is an uncatholic shibboleth; there are persons who dislike even Shakespeare who yet have a lively appreciation of literature.

The book is a gay trifle. One would not treat it seriously if the author had not invited such treatment. It is a late addition to picaresque fiction; instead of a single thief, it represents a fraternity of rascals and a slum community, in which women of easy virtue bear a shocking ratio to the total population. With a few exceptions the characters are *paisanos*, of Mexican and Indian blood, who live in squalid poverty in the outskirts of Monterey. Their pursuits are fighting, drinking, and making love. The chief persons in the comedy—Danny and his mates— live by minor thefts from their neighbors, merchants in Monterey, and one another. Occasionally—when the emergency is desperate—they reluctantly and shamefacedly do a day's work cutting squids for a Chinese on the wharves. Of a lively Latin temperament, they scorn and evade most that the Anglo-Saxon tradition prescribes, especially the rigorous discipline of Puritanism and industrialism.

They do this with charm, gaiety, and abandon. The result is amusing; and one would be content to let it go at that if the author had not invited us to take these rascals seriously. In the preface to the second edition he deplores the fact that his book has excited the pity of literary slummers for his *paisanos*; he denies that he regards them as underprivileged or underdoggish; he almost repudiates the book. He told the stories because they were true and he loved the characters. He credits them with "honest lusts" and a successful adaptation to their environment, "which is philosophy." These comments place Steinbeck in the category of moralists.

Successful adaptation to environment is indeed an indispensable element of morality. But for human beings it is not enough—or rather, the environment must be broadly conceived. All that a wholly naturalistic philosophy can provide is survival value; man and woman aspire to something beyond survival. The louse and the tape worm make a fairly successful adaptation to environment, and Steinbeck's *paisanos* of Monterey are almost as parasitic. It is a merry prank to knock out a slat of the fence between Danny's yard and that of the widow who lives next door, so that her chickens may stray through the gap, get lost in the weeds, be captured, and find their destiny on Danny's table. We understand that in this circle property is in disrepute, but in the interim before the advent of total communism, proprietorship in chickens must be respected. Adjustment to environment by thieving is temporary and inadequate. The philosophy of the Monterey *paisanos* lacks range.

Danny and his community have their own code, conventions, taboos, scruples, a film of religion, courtesies, and refinements. They practice the art of relaxation with paradoxical zeal. The best of their ethics is impulsive kindness—as evidenced by their hospitality to the Pirate and their kindness to Teresina and her innumerable brood of children of doubtful paternity. The kindness involved burglary on a considerable scale, to be sure; but the humane motive may be entered on the credit side of the ledger. It is not too strained an interpretation to read this book as a jolly satire of respectable society. Treat the average community as follows: Eliminate the institution of property; reduce marital fidelity to a minimum—or less; raise the per capita consumption of alcohol many degrees; instead of doing your exploitation legally and on a grand scale, do it by petty larceny and burglary; let your charities be matters of sporadic impulse; and spread over the whole a veneer of religion. You then have a parallel between the reputable world and the community of paisanos. The proportion of good and evil favors the average community—and that is important; but the ingredients are the same. There—in Tortilla Flat—but for the grace of God, goes Main Street. And did not Kipling tell us that the Colonel's lady and Judy O'Grady are sisters under the skin?

III

I wish to cancel the violent prejudice against Steinbeck in the minds of good people. But this is too defensive and apologetic a process. It would be a gross injustice to ignore the affirmative phase of Steinbeck's work.

The obligation of the novelist to morality is precisely that of the scientist to truth: objectivity and impartiality. Since the writer of fiction has to do with human values, he must needs possess sympathies and antipathies, so that the achievement of objectivity and impartiality is far more difficult for him than for the chemist or the physicist. Appreciation of human nature in all its variety has never been achieved—not even by Chaucer or Browning, not even by Shakespeare. If we applaud the scientist for restricting his field, we should permit the novelist to select his province and have his favorite types. We should insist only that he tell us the whole truth within the limits he chooses.

Steinbeck's selection includes mainly the rebels, the outcasts, the underdogs of our society—ranch-hands, Okies, fruit-pickers, cotton-pickers, small farmers in California. He represents these as victims of injustice, the special forms of injustice being chiefly results of the mechanization of agriculture. In California the conditions of land tenure and the character of the product cause and magnify all the evils that industrialism had brought earlier to factory towns: poverty and extreme wealth, over-production, bad housing and sanitation, strikes, armed conflict, perversion of justice in the interest of owners, destruction of property and life, danger of violent revolution.

This is Steinbeck's theme in In Dubious Battle. Mainly, he treats it with impartiality, despite the strength of his sympathy with the laborers and the small farmers. To be sure, the owners and their minions—police, checkers, vigilantes, even judges and clergymen—get short shrift in his pages; but why should they not? The technique of the art of fiction precludes anything else. The story is told from the angle of the leaders of the strike—Mac, Jim Nolan, and the others. From their point of view their opponents showed nothing but cruelty, chicanery, cant, and tyrannical power, whatever private virtues they may have had. The mind of a novelist—or reader—is not a camera of universal focus. Only a small part of the picture appears in exact detail.

Steinbeck's treatment of the strikers is not flattering. Most of them are coarse; a few are cowards and turncoats; some are shortsighted and self-indulgent. In the mass they are subject to inconstant gusts of emotion—now ferociously valiant, now whimpering with discomfort and fear. They remind one of Tennyson's etching of the populace:

> The people here, a beast of burden slow,
>   Toiled onward, pricked with goads and stings;
> Here played, a tiger, rolling to and fro
>   The heads and crowns of kings;
>
> Here rose an athlete, strong to break or bind
>   All force in bonds that might endure,
> And here once more like some sick man declined,
>   And trusted any cure.[4]

The leaders are steadfast almost to the point of fanaticism, but they are no heroes of romance, complete with every imaginable strength and grace. They lie; they foment strife for the sake of their cause; they take advantage of every atrocity committed by their opponents, in order to inflame the hearts of their followers. They fight the devil with fire. The charge that the novelist has loaded the dice will not hold. Indeed, the realism of his treatment puts weapons into the hands of the oppressors and gives persons who ought most to ponder his disclosures a pretext for disregarding them.

Steinbeck's treatment of mass emotion in *In Dubious Battle* is masterly. In comparison with it the mob scenes of Dickens,[5] Mark Twain,[6] and Galsworthy[7] seem melodramatic. In this connection one should read "The Vigilante." As a story this piece has little merit; its value is its insight into the mind of a mob. It is concerned with the mental state of a mediocre person who has just taken part in a lynching. The aftermath, not the event, is the theme; and the aftermath is like that of a sexual debauch—satiation, fatigue, disgust. The picture is not pretty, but it has useful information concerning one of the major scandals of American civilization.

Concerning Steinbeck as a moralist one has some misgivings. Revulsion from hypocrisy and prudery carries him to a violent extreme. For example, he treats prostitution as a merry jest—as in the story of the two *paisano* sisters in *The Pastures of Heaven*. One of the men in *Of Mice and Men* expresses preference for a "clean cat-house" over marriage as a means of satisfying and regulating the appetite of sex; and in the same story the social graces of a "madam" are celebrated with no little enthusiasm. Of course these sentiments need not be attributed to Steinbeck himself, although in the preface of *Tortilla Flat* he attempts to place the "hure lady" and her patrons on the plane of respectability. Adulteries and casual sex adventures are condoned—sometimes with an indulgent smile, as negligible peccadillos; sometimes with approval, as revolts against too rigorous domestic discipline; sometimes with applause, as means of obtaining money or food from fatuous female sympathizers with the radical cause. One story, "The Murder"[8] (if it may be taken seriously), is a total anachronism. An injured husband vindicates his honor by neatly puncturing the skull of his wife's lover with a rifle bullet and beating his wife within an inch of her life with a bull whip. The sheriff puts the murderer under arrest, as a matter of form, but assures him that no conviction ever results in such cases. And the couple live happily ever after. This tale contains every element of an antiquated morality, including the double standard of sex, for the husband was not himself a model of marital fidelity. Long ago Maeterlinck made an eloquent protest against the pseudo-duty of a husband's vindicating his honor and gave us a vivid dramatic version of the protest in the last act of *Monna Vanna*. Steinbeck's story is a reversion to barbarism. The massive impression of his fiction is that sex (as among animals) is an innocent necessary appetite, in little need of control or regulation.

And this is the clue to the defects of Steinbeck's ethics. Man has been defined as "the animal that laughs, and that loves all the year round." The second clause of the differentia suggests that, unlike that of other animals, man's reproductive instinct is not regulated by nature and restricted to its natural purpose—the production of children. Moreover, the prolongation of infancy in the human species makes necessary the institution of the family—a permanent relation between parents. Animal promiscuity does not comport with this institution.

Steinbeck's sex morality is not even primitivism or animalism. It is human license, and would, if allowed to prevail, destroy humanity. It is supported, in Steinbeck's writings, by a fantastic nature mysticism or by an almost equally fantastic humanism. The humanism involves the conception of "group-man"—the soul of aggregate humanity, which has interests and passions of which individual men and women—cells in the body of group-man—can discern only the vaguest hints. For example, individuals, as pioneers on their journey to California, desire new acres for settlement; group-man desires only "westering," for what end one may only guess. Adequate discussion of these religious ideas must be postponed; but they should receive passing attention, if only to indicate that Steinbeck's immoralities are not mere incidents in his thinking, or the mere violent swing of the pendulum away from social conventions. They are grounded in a comprehensive immature philosophy—or perhaps in two such philosophies.

IV

It is unfortunate that these phases of Steinbeck obscure the timely value of his work. His human sympathies and his artist's perceptions are far better than his lax morality of sex or his confused philosophizing. His indignation against "the oppressor's wrong, the proud man's contumely, the insolence of office, and the spurns that patient merit of the unworthy takes" is all to the good. His moral value is an achievement, not a theory—the achievement of dramatizing the plight of migrant laborers, which is only one example (perhaps the worst) of the injustices of our civilization. Shakespeare made a vast contribution to the humanization of mankind, with only the faintest traces of metaphysics or even of a social and political philosophy. He was—if you choose—a noncritical humanist. Sympathy and imagination did the trick. And it would probably be well for all artists to emulate Shakespeare in this respect, at least until their more analytical philosophies have had time to mature. Meanwhile, we may be grateful to Steinbeck, that he has applied his sympathies and imagination to neglected areas of American life.

We Americans worship with elaborate rites at the shrine of efficiency. It is profitable to compare the icons of that religion that most of us carry in our minds with those of Steinbeck. What picture forms in our minds when we pronounce the dear polysyllable efficiency? Is it not that of a corporation executive or a super-banker, seated behind an imposing desk in a luxurious office, with a battery of telephones in front of him and a row of push buttons under his hand? He is supported by a corps of secretaries, one of whose principal duties is to protect the great man from irrelevant intrusions and enable him to think the vast thoughts appropriate to his station. This is not Steinbeck's picture of efficiency. He thinks of a small thrifty hard-working farmer or ranch-owner, of his employee, the ranch-hand, expert in horses, of the old "top-faller"—a lumberman who had spent a long life of labor, danger, and skill and whose main grievance was that now in his old age he must surrender his pride of occupation and descend to the ignoble work of picking apples in the orchard of a corporation. Steinbeck might take Slim, the crack mule skinner, as the type of efficiency, or even young Anderson, the proprietor of a lunch wagon, who could serve a tasty stew, with pie, for a quarter, and knew how to toast a hamburg sandwich to an appetizing turn. Steinbeck might think of Tom Joad, who was a driver and motor-mechanic expert enough to drive a ramshackle jalopy from Oklahoma to California without breakdown or mishap. Steinbeck delights to recognize the efficiency of such obscure persons. By this recognition he does democracy a service. On the whole they do their jobs far better than the corporation magnate does his, and in the aggregate their labors are quite as important to the national well-being. Walt Whitman catalogues these inarticulate Americans, with notes of admiration; but he seldom shows them in action. Steinbeck's portrayals are motion pictures; he shows the men at the job. Perhaps he can teach us that, pre-eminently in a democracy, they deserve both praise and pudding.

These sympathies have taken the novelist into the class conflict. In Dubious Battle is the story of a strike of fruit growers on a California ranch. This strike is a peculiarly instructive event. On the side of capital the whole county—courts, police, government, Associated Farmers, banks, the more powerful makers of sentiment, vigilantes, even the clergy—was organized in favor of the large ranch owners. On the side of the strikers were the smaller fruit-growers and many sympathizers in the towns, who, however, dared not express their sympathy openly. There was no union; indeed, the laborers strongly distrusted the radicals who incited and attempted to organize the strike. A strike is war on a small scale, with all the advantage of money, munitions, and the favor of government on one side. Only one condition favored the strikers— the perishability of fruit. Fruit must be harvested within a few days, and a force of scab labor must be brought from a distance. The time factor gave the strikers a slight advantage. Fruit-growers cannot close the plant, store the product, and await a favorable turn of events, like factory-owners. The laissez-faire doctrine, based on the assumption of equality of bargaining power between employer and laborer, unrealistic as it is, has a slight show of validity in the employers' need of many workers at the time of harvest. If the strikers can beg enough food from sympathizers to keep themselves alive for a few days and can prevent scabs from entering the orchards, the employers must come to terms. But their small advantage availed them nothing. Government, money, the courts, and the weight of public sentiment were too strong for them. If government had faithfully discharged the function assigned to it by the classical theory—that of safeguarding impartially the legal rights of both parties—the outcome might have been different. But government was no impartial umpire, enforcing the rules of the game; it became a tool of the more powerful interests. The failure of the strike demonstrates the hopeless situation of unorganized labor. Political democracy fails in an emergency, because nothing remotely like economic equality is to be seen.

V

On the score of morality it is all to the good that the novelist penetrate to the heart of his characters, especially if his characters are beyond the respectable pale. Good people express loathing for the persons in *Of Mice and Men* and *The Grapes of Wrath*. Why should one associate with such people in books, since one avoids them in life? To waive the question whether it is right utterly to shun the company of immoral persons, one may reply that fiction is useful largely as a means of extending one's knowledge of men beyond the possible or expedient range of experience. It is unwise for most people to be among tigers in the jungle; caged in a zoo the animals may be admired and studied in safety. The art of fiction is an animal cage—and something more, to be sure; it permits an intimate study of evil beasts.

But the novelist does more than this for defective and degraded characters. He throws a light into their souls. The dream of Lennie and George, of a few acres and a little house, where they might live in comfort and independence—that is the gleam of positive light from within. It is not an extravagant aspiration, and not a lofty one; but it is deeply human. If it could have been realized, it might have developed into something nobler. People of no opportunities move toward the future in short stages; too often the next meal is the limit of their flights. But a human being is progressive: if his necessities are supplied, he begins to think of ideals. The pair of friends could never become great men, since one was a half-wit and the other a rude unlearned man; but they might have become good neighbors and useful citizens.

The novelist of insight confers more benefit on humanity by the interpretation of characters than by the advocacy of reforms. Since he must have imagination and heart, he is drawn almost inevitably into current conflicts. These are the temporary shapes which the age-long interests of humanity assume. New obstacles are set up in the path of men and women, but these new obstacles are mainly a new outer form of the old. The special issues change and disappear, like fashions of dress; but the substance of human nature changes slightly and slowly and the direction of its aspirations is constant. The permanent value of drama and fiction is the revelation of the permanent essence. To be sure, this essence must be clothed in the garb of the times. Novelists must sense the conflicts of their own age and sometimes take sides in them. But Tolstoi's greatest work was done as an artist, not a reformer, and the same is probably true of Galsworthy. Probably it is true even of Dickens and certainly of Howells. On the other hand, there is something deficient in a novelist who shows no interest in the struggles of his own age; he is too detached and cold. Even Henry James, the expatriate and denizen of the ivory tower, manifests a moralist's interest in the uprooted Americans he met in Europe.

Steinbeck has associated his name with the migrant laborers and other underprivileged groups. He espouses their cause. In his writings so heavy an emphasis falls on their hard lot that other aspects of his work are ignored. But the problem of the migrants is more than a current problem. It is the occasion that brings heroism to light. The Okies and the striking fruit-pickers do and dare as well as suffer. Tom Joad and Jim Nolan would be heroes in whatever period and social class their lot might be cast. Ma Joad would be womanly and maternal in any station. If she had been a duchess, she would have labored with heroism for the integrity of the family and would have had a comprehensive vision of the serious social obligations of her class. The scene of her farewell to Tom, in the latter part of *Grapes of Wrath*, is of the pure essence of motherhood. The pathos is profound and free from a taint of sentimentality. The courage and devotion of the woman are sublime. With a more fortunate rearing and a better education Mac and Jim would have been leaders in some cause of social betterment. Less conspicuous characters are equally human—the ranch-hand in "The Red Pony," the boy hero, his parents, and his grandfather. The boy is a more complete embodiment of the essence of boy than even Mark Twain's Tom Sawyer.

"A field full of folk" is the subject matter of literature. One returns to the dictum of Howells, the humanitarian—a dictum inspired by the reading of Tolstói: "Men are more like than unlike one another. Let us make them know one another better, that they may be all humbled and strengthened with a sense of their fraternity."[9] For thousands of readers Steinbeck has accomplished this. Thanks to him we sense the wrongs, the virtues, the potential strength of thousands of our fellow citizens whom we had not known. His writings make for democracy.

1. "The Snake" and "Johnny Bear," in *The Long Valley*.
2. "St. Katy the Virgin," in *The Long Valley*.
3. *Twelfth Night*, II, iii, 124-7.
4. *The Palace of Art*.
5. *Barnaby Rudge*, chap. liv and later chapters.
6. *Huckleberry Finn*, chap. xxii.
7. *The Mob*, Act IV.
8. In *The Long Valley*.
9. *Criticism and Fiction* (1891), p. 188.

Edwin Berry Burgum

THE SENSIBILITY
OF JOHN STEINBECK

THE NOVELS of our most distinguished novelist of the thirties, John Steinbeck, with one exception treat of farmers, impoverished workers or vagabonds, present life supposedly through their eyes and create a sympathy for them. They are the most conspicuous examples of a shift of attitude, general to the thirties, from the traditional absorption of American fiction with the problems and personages of the middle classes to an intense curiosity about the poor.

This magnetic attraction which the lower classes began to exercise upon the American writer induced a variety of responses. Only in a few instances did he see them as they saw themselves. Commonly the aura of his sympathy was discolored by envy or pity or any number of distortions set up by the outside view. The novelist seemed to bring the hesitancies and confusions of the petty bourgeoisie into the new attachment. The poor appeared at some times possessed of a mysterious strength which should be admired and imitated, at others victimized by circumstances and therefore to be wept for; but most popularly they seemed caught in a common maelstrom of disaster, against which the best protection was the resignation of mutual pretense that it did not exist. The novelist who presented the widest range of these fluctuations was Steinbeck. Although always remaining of a benevolent intention, he swung in his various novels from the extreme of a deep and legitimate admiration for working people to that in which all values are paralyzed in the apathy of the sentimental.

When Steinbeck's novels are taken in the order of publication, these oscillations of attitude form an interesting pattern. His earliest novel, *To a God Unknown*, published in 1933, exhibited as much fascination

EDWIN BERRY BURGUM was for some years professor of literature at New York University. "The Sensibility of John Steinbeck" first appeared in the Spring, 1946 issue of Science and Society, *with which periodical Mr. Burgum has had a long association as writer and editor. The author later incorporated the essay in his book* The Novel and the World's Dilemma, *which was published by Oxford University Press in 1947. Mr. Burgum has given his permission for the reprint of the essay here.*

with the erotic compulsions of farms workers as the writings of D. H. Lawrence or the poetry of his fellow Californian, Robinson Jeffers. The violence of these turbulent passions faded into the mild casual vagabondage of *Tortilla Flat*. But immediately afterwards, with *In Dubious Battle* the stridency returned, only directed outward from the sexual to the social, in the violence of labor conflict. *Of Mice and Men* represented a compromise between the two. Though the sociological interest had faded into the background, it had determined that the characters be no longer vagabonds nor their heightened emotions of erotic significance. When the national consciousness of the economic depression had reached its height and the country was supporting the New Deal as its remedy, Steinbeck combined elements of both *Of Mice and Men* and of *In Dubious Battle* into a social novel of larger canvas and happier ending. Later, when the war against fascism demanded a still more comprehensive social awareness, he broke under the strain in *The Moon is Down*, and lapsed into the amiable superficiality of *Tortilla Flat* with *Cannery Row*. These oscillations, furthermore, have been on two different planes. Besides the familiar one between violent and mild emotions in the personal lives of his characters, there has been an oscillation between the decadence represented by an amused tolerance for ignorance, poverty and depravity and a recovery from decadence in the social novels.

Steinbeck's career, therefore, has been a most unusual one. It has been an exception both to the usual development of the significant novelist and to the mechanical stereotype of the professional craftsmen of popular fiction. Our better writers express what they seem forced to say in the process of their personal maturation; whereas the popular writers repeat the formula the public seems to want. Doubtless in an ideal situation the two approaches would merge. But in a society constituted like our own, the profound approach to fiction has been personal, and those who have sought to meet the needs of the larger public have been aware only of shallow and conventional ones. Steinbeck, belonging in neither group, exhibits the qualities of both, and thus advertizes the instability of our society more graphically than any other novelist.

On the whole one feels that he has been more absorbed in the expert presentation of his theme than in laboring to fathom its hidden potentialities. In a more stable society he might well have been content to write without exception well-made novels like *Cannery Row*. As it is, his efficiency in combining words into stories is of no mean importance. It testifies that we have achieved as high a level of general culture as France, where a sophisticated use of words as tools to secure an emotional effect has long existed, in felicitous contrast to the lugubrious crudity of the amateur spirit in the popular Anglo-Saxon prose tradition. This gift of Steinbeck's is proof of how much more the French tradition has contributed to our cultural development than the English. But Steinbeck's sensitiveness has not been limited to a ready perception of what the public wants and so facile a satisfaction of it. He has shown a capacity to be moved by the deeper urges in the body public when those urges have come to the surface in a time of national crisis and have been moulded for the time being into a pattern of national unity. Cannery Row should not obscure the achievement of The Grapes of Wrath in reflecting such a temporary unity in the acceptance of the New Deal; so successful an achievement, indeed, that it became the only novel of the thirties which was both a best seller and a darling of the critics.

The parallel between Tortilla Flat, at the beginning of his career, and his latest novel, Cannery Row, is Steinbeck's evidence of our psychological reconversion after the strain of war. The same types of people do the same sort of thing they did ten years before, and the author smiles upon them with the same sort of indulgence. A pedant might define the mood as the American picaresque, if the emphasis were not less on the sharpness of wit in these vagabonds than on a sentimental admiration for their carefree way of life. Rather, one should say, it is the gentlest reductio ad absurdum of the Lawrence ideal. For here are people who have found the correct receipt for living as Lawrence preached. To live for the belly urge alone is most comfortable when the belly is not too urgent; just as living from the belly urge alone by a relentless logic suggests living off somebody else. And so Steinbeck's Mexicans have no inner conflicts. They know that they have turned the laugh on Lawrence by their common sense. They recognize that happiness is more consistent, spreads over a broader area of time, when one does not overstimulate by conscious attention those deep urges from within, but takes them, after Lawrence's bidding, as they come. Indeed they are aware that in this case there is room also for many other minor urges, for food or sleep or walking slowly or merely sitting in the shade or the sunshine as the day may proffer.

They are quite free from contamination by the evils of modern life since they are immune to that last contamination in Lawrence, the very urgency of his demand. They have the wisdom of an ignorance paradoxically beyond the grasp of Lawrence's genius, like the illiterate Negroes of the Louisiana bayous whom Anderson came at length to celebrate. In Anderson some echo of appreciation for their folk songs, for the poetry of the imaginative life, remains. But these Mexicans, like

Saroyan's Greeks, are also beyond the discipline set up automatically by the orderliness of song. They enjoy in all simplicity, without any lurking melancholy misgivings, the chaotic comfort of their prosaic souls. Content ordinarily to wait, like certain lower organisms, for pleasure to come their way in the form of food or chance acquaintance, they break this passivity and avoid monotony by taking the initiative when it is easy, by raiding a nearby chicken coop or dropping in upon some friend who has a job, a larder and a weak will. Experience has taught them that the world as it is is quite good enough for their purposes, and they do not dilute the purity of their pleasure either, like Saroyan, by an undercurrent of melancholy or, like Lawrence, by the sententiousness of reflection. They have long since learned to avoid situations beyond their control, and to intuit the kindred spirit in those they choose as friends beneath the conventionalism, which, by obligating a job, makes friendship profitable. They seek out those who work from habit rather than conviction; or, shall I say from a cowardice or a compliance which, in the area of friendship, leaves them the victims of any moderate good-natured pressure.

Within such a compliant milieu the modesty of their demands and the contagion of their irresponsibility provide them the final luxury of freedom. They achieve a more complete experience of our national ideal than any other citizens; for they are as free from spiritual compulsions as those of ambition or prestige. And they are excellent propagandists for this ideal since, by taking it for granted in their lives, they insidiously reduce those they associate with to their own level. A few moments after these rogues have invaded your premises, you forget their tenacious fawning, the insistence of their inertia, the hypocrisy of their friendship, the underhandedness of their methods. The selfishness of their aims is swallowed up by the insignificance of them. And you end by feeling at home in their droll indifference for the conventions.

Decadence could hardly go farther. But its presence is concealed from the reader for other reasons than the charm with which Steinbeck invests his vagabonds. We do not recognize the decadence because our Puritan tradition has accustomed us to find it only in the flaunting of sexual abnormality. And I think we also neglect to feel its presence because we secretly envy them. They are not merely like our middle-class selves in our Milquetoast fawning upon our betters, our similar patience in waiting for somewhat larger crumbs to fall our way, the indirection of our boldness behind the boss's back. Our very consciousness of superiority permits us, under the cover of what we take for a literary interest, secretly to envy them. For in them we see these aspects of ourselves, freed from the fetters of duty, and thus capable of being used actively to serve themselves. They use the manners of a servant not to serve but to receive. Their cunning may be as low as their literacy, but it gains their ends; and it capitvates us when we are sick of the toiling and the thinking that remain always insufficient for our more comprehensive goals. Peering through the haze of the picturesque, we do not notice that these rogues lack bath tubs and breakfast cereals; we see only that they are living the life of Reilly while we drag behind us the chain of hectic obligations and dull conformities.

This siren call to drifting was succeeded shortly by the shock of its opposite. If the atmosphere of *Tortilla Flat* was that of a lumpenproletarian Watteau, offering the idyllic domesticity of shacks on vacant lots or unusually commodious abandoned sewer pipes, the light of *In Dubious Battle* is a battery of Kliegs from Hollywood, that cruel photographic clarity of the California sunshine. But this sharp light is appropriate to the new action. It throws into bold outline the conflict between employer and employed when that conflict has reached its most strident crisis, in a strike of unionized workers of the most unskilled category. But the light does not shine with corrosive impartiality upon the just and the unjust alike. Though it emphasizes the sharpness of will on both sides, it etches (like the famous snap-shot of the Republic Steel "massacre") the brutality of the motorized state police as they charge the migrant workers of the California orchards. At the same time it becomes a challenge to the manhood of the strikers, symbolizing the cruel indifference of nature. It forces them to realize they must depend upon their own energies and join together to utilize them to the uttermost. It strips life of the subterfuges of *Tortilla Flat*; by setting the tone of the book, it forces us to face reality without blinking, or not at all. It acclimatizes us to live on a higher level than our usual complacency; so that we do not pity the strikers for their suffering or their defeat, and their courage in defeat leaves us strong with its unspent residue.

In the dreary lot of so-called proletarian novels of the thirties, one would go far to find another more lifelike and satisfying than *In Dubious Battle*. The usual charge against such novels is that they oversimplify their characters, especially the union organizer who plays the role of hero. But any forthright physical activity demands a simplification of the personality. It must be freed, if it is to function efficiently, from the scrupulosities and indecisions, the peripheral and personal interests, which form the attraction of the introspective novel. To complain of the imperfection of characterization in the novel of action, therefore, is usually testimony that the action is badly handled; that it has not taken over from the characterization those hesitancies and impetuosities and contradictions which are the necessary preludes to a decision. In the novel of action it is not the characterization but the action which is too simple. Not only has Steinbeck properly developed his plot; when he puts it in the black and white outlines of the California sun, he beguiles the esoteric reader by affording him a completely coherent esthetic experience to compensate for the loss of his customary thrill from introspection. No documentary film, in which the sophisticated observer swallows the document because the photography is so good, could be more successful to win support for the striking foreign-born workers in the great fruit-growing factories of the California plains.

After this novel Steinbeck did not revert to the carefree decadence of *Tortilla Flat*. *Of Mice and Men*, combining elements from all his previous novels, is his most characteristic work. George and Lenny, his new heroes, are ignorant workers of native stock. But their disorders of personality arouse Steinbeck's pity rather than amusement, and they do not form his sole interest in them. These men have modest aspirations for their welfare for which he also has respect and attention. Awareness of social issues, though it no longer forms the backbone of the novel as in *In Dubious Battle*, remains to condition both the motivation and the progress of the story. The psychological and the sociological combine (as they do normally in life) to afford a well-rounded characterization. But characterization does not become an end in itself. Achieved through the incisiveness of conversation, it becomes an integral part of the action. Though George and Lenny have their ambitions, they are scarcely in a position to attain them. They are caught between the dual pressures of their own limitations and those imposed by their station in society. The tone of the novel, therefore, is neither the extreme of tension between groups that characterized *In Dubious Battle* nor the opposite extreme of relaxing of tension found in *Tortilla Flat*. The sharpness of tension is dispersed by the fact that in this novel every relationship involves it in its own way. The tone of the novel is that precarious equilibrium where various minor tensions for the time being check one another off, where men are uneasy within themselves and in uneasy association with one another, but manage to maintain some sort of control until the storm breaks in the final crisis.

On the sociological side, *Of Mice and Men* assumes that these tensions are set up by the nature of capitalism. The cockiness of Curley, the son of the ranch owner, his willingness to fight at the drop of the hat, is not merely a trait of his individual personality. It is a trait that his position in society encourages; in fact, there is his real strength, it turns out, in his power to fire a worker, for as an individual he is a coward, beneath his braggadoccio. In a similar way the one skilled worker on the ranch, the mechanic Carlson, because he is difficult to replace, can assume an arrogance forbidden the others. He is the one employee who might dare to avail himself of the advances of Curley's wife, and the one who, free also to lord it over his less expendable fellow workers, orders Slim's dog to be put to death. The other workers are compliant either because they are old or afraid of losing their jobs. Only Lenny, whose intelligence is too limited to enable him to recognize these realities, among the common ranch hands, stands up against the boss's son, and, when challenged, crushes his hand in his iron grip.

Lenny has the strength to resist. But it is George who has the brains and the ambition. He is the most complex of the characters because he has not accepted his position, but carries around with him the longing to save money, buy a small form, work as his own boss in an air of freedom. His ideal has infected his friend Lenny, and, breaking through the barrier of race prejudice because of the need for allies, it is taken over by the old Negro, who has lived alone in ostracism from the ranch hands. But three such as these form an alliance that is pathetically inadequate, and we forsee, implicit in the constellation, its eventual doom.

But the pathos of ineffectual struggle towards an ideal is overshadowed by the reader's interest in the difficult relationship between George and Lenny. Their friendship is an obligation imposed upon George by Lenny's aunt, and it frequently irritates George since Lenny has always got them both into trouble in the past. George has no obscure desire to be ruined. The psychology of the friendship is presented with deft sufficient outline by Steinbeck. George's generosity of spirit responds to Lenny's need for him, and his self-esteem is increased by the knowledge that Lenny will obey him without question, provided he is around to give the command. What leaves George under constant tension is the knowledge that he cannot always be around, and Lenny is always destroying what he loves, hysterically overexerting his great strength to ward off what he fears, or what George has taught him to fear. The mouse he pets in his pocket (as though the world, even George, would not sanction so much affection if they knew about it), he stifles to death. Under George's injunction to behave himself and not ruin their chances to save money for the farm where he can have unlimited small animals to play with, Lenny's fear of his own clumsiness mounts to a new pitch. And it is not lessened when he senses that all the ranch hands resent the advances the new wife of Curley appears to be making them. When, with that zest for the sexually abnormal which is an irresistible undercurrent of Steinbeck's personality, Curley's wife is especially attracted to Lenny because he seems so grossly masculine, Lenny loses control of himself. He has not been affected by her sexual attraction, merely by the fact that George has told him he must keep from involvement with her. When she asks him to stroke her hair, he finds it as soft as the mouse's head. She draws back in fear at so unusual an interest, and he strangles her out of a strange melange of urges in which desire to possess utterly so soft an object is intensified by his sense of guilt at doing what he has been told not to do. After such an accident, all plans for a farm become impossible. Knowing that the law of the frontier must overtake Lenny and will destroy him, seeing the lynch mob of his own fellow workers gather under the boss' direction, George's last act of friendship is to kill Lenny to save him from the more cruel death at the hands of the mob and to pretend to the mob that he has been one of them in his action. Thus abjectly the forces of destiny in the novel reduce the struggling manhood of George to impotence. The generosity of his action must parade as a prevarication, and he must appear reduced to the level of brutality from which he had sought escape into the freedom of economic independence.

Thus much of awareness of the uselessness of ambition among men as underprivileged as George, thus much cynical justification for the drifting and vagabondage of the men of *Tortilla Flat*, distills from the course of the narrative. But it is only the appropriate setting for the story of two men. Steinbeck has not yet reached the social consciousness of his next novel and is in a state of reaction from the strenuousness of *In Dubious Battle*. It would therefore be impossible to take the action of these mice and men as symbolic of the working class. Indeed, to find in Lenny a symbol of the power of the proletariat would be to reduce any confidence in the working class to an absurdity. Nor could any one but the most cynical opponent of the labor movement find in George the directive intelligence of the organizer, manipulating, however vainly, the brute force of the well-intentioned but uncontrollable laborer.

On the contrary, our acceptance of the story will depend upon our attitude towards the two heroes as personalities, and in particular upon our reaction to Lenny. To some readers his strangeness is fascinating. Steinbeck leaves his motivation obscure; he does not make it explicit like that of George. He apparently desires to hold us by the very mysteriousness of Lenny's motives, to arouse a kind of awe for him as we witness this uncanny union of brute strength and childlike affection. But other readers may feel that in Lenny, Steinbeck's tendency towards the sentimental reaches its artistic culmination. And though they rec-

ognize the deftness with which he achieves his end, the precision that
can create clarity or ambiguity of effect at will, they will nevertheless
dislike the end. But at least it must be admitted that no character in
Steinbeck is more characteristic of his peculiar talent. And the novel
becomes a testimonial to the transformation of the picaresque tradition
when it comes into contact with the American sensitiveness to the
plight of the underprivileged. In more religious countries such a character would take on mystic proportions, such as Silone gives to his
imbecile in *The Blood beneath the Snow*. It is precisely here, in his
capacity to arouse awe without mysticism, that Steinbeck proves how
essentially American is his talent. He leaves Lenny somehow entirely
natural and human, and yet essentially a mystery, the mystery of the
unfit in a practical world. The hopelessness of the petty bourgeoisie and
its confusion before the problems of the depression era are truly symbolized in Steinbeck's attitude of sympathy for Lenny. And we are all
to a certain extent Georges in the spontaneity of our protective reaction, unless, that is to say, we have a clearer conception of democracy
and are ready for *The Grapes of Wrath*. But we can scarcely feel much
sympathy for Lenny and admire Tom Joad.

What, one suspects, led Steinbeck to acquire this political information when he came to write *The Grapes of Wrath*, was not the inclina-
tion of his own temperament, but the tremendous pull of the social
situation upon him. He seems, like one of his own characters, to have
been pulled together by sharing the wholesome reaction of the country
under the leadership of President Roosevelt. The novel came at the
time when, in reaction to the shock of the depression, the country
united, as never before in our history, in a common recognition of the
desperateness of our internal affairs and the need for radical measures
to restore order and security to our society. Under these pressures
Steinbeck kept his sentimentality in check until the final scene of his
novel. Then a meretricious desire to italicize the action got the better
of him, and he introduced the only bit of symbolism in the book (save
for the dubious turtle on the road at the beginning). The scene of the
proffer of the mother's milk to the starving old man, on the practical
level, is a useless gesture of aid, and to be acceptable must be taken
as pure symbolism. But since there has been no preparation for symbolism in the antecedent action, the reader follows the attitudes the
book has set up in him, and rejects the conclusion as an unpleasant bit
of realism instead.

Otherwise the novel is a fascinating exhibition of Steinbeck's technical versatility. Just as its composition was stimulated by the temporary
comradeship between the poor who had nothing and those who saw

themselves losing what they had; so too, by the use of diverse literary styles, its appeal was directed to virtually every level of taste in the book-reading public. The reader habituated to the rigid consistency of style characteristic of our best writing (such as is found in Hemingway) may dislike the lush loose style of many passages, the shift into the slick superficial narration of our magazines of national circulation. But it is precisely the presence of the second-rate, the way in which popular techniques are interwoven into the story, which gives this novel, from another point of view, its significance. For the time being we had laid aside our differences of opinion, and our practice of acting through the competition of groups. But even though we had thus achieved in a general way an emotional unity, it was impossible to lay aside our ingrained preferences for different kinds of writing. The sophisticated still liked the clipped and sinewy style, the man in the street still preferred the loose sentimentality of old habit. At best the cooperation tended slightly to bring the two closer: to make the sophisticated more tolerant of the unsophisticated, and to drive the man in the street into a willingness to pull himself together, put his mind to work, bring (for once) to his reading of fiction the act of attention it deserves, change him into a more sophisticated reader. The effect upon the one group was to make it more tolerant of a less esthetic, a broader social conception of the novel; upon the other it was to improve its esthetic insight in the process of satisfying its practical demands. The result was that the novel was more than a best seller. It raised the standard of taste by being the best written of best sellers.

Students of style, therefore, may take pleasure in going through *The Grapes of Wrath* and discovering that hardly any style practised today is missing from it. The introductory panels, through which Dos Passos sought to present the background against which the story is written, are there. Passages are there in the introspective technique of Joyce; others reminding of the curt understatement of Hemingway; others which echo the diapason rhetoric of Thomas Wolfe. But at the same time there are stretches of narrative which might have come out of *Gone with the Wind* or a serial in the *Saturday Evening Post*. Approaching the book in the warm atmosphere of national unity, the sophisticated reader, delighted by such recognitions, was pulled out of his fanatical devotion to a particular style into a more catholic appreciation. Once the unity of the period was lost, doubtless, the old limitations reasserted themselves, and a rereading of the novel today will afford fewer readers so tolerant a reaction. But however one reacts to its style, it will be difficult at any time not to be impressed by the structure of the book. Here again Steinbeck met the social crisis more successfully than any other author, met it within the artistic sphere as successfully as Roosevelt in the political, and thus once more illustrated the dependence of good form upon a valid understanding of objective events. One would be hard put to find in our recent fiction another novel, which, judged by purely esthetic standards, had a better achieved plot. Always sensitive to the problems of expression, Steinbeck proves equal to the challenge of his material. And his plot is as dialectic as the events of those disturbing days. It is divided into two contrasting yet interacting lines of development, both vertically and horizontally.

The first half of the book is a contrast between the attitudes of the Joad family and that of Tom under the guidance of his preacher friend, Casy. Tom has just been released from the Oklahoma State Prison. He had killed a man in self-defense, and Steinbeck sympathizes with Tom's own conviction that he has been unjustly treated. Young Joad leaves prison in a mood of undirected rebelliousness which may become delinquency (as his mother fears), or may be channeled into a more constructive activity. His good fortune is to meet the preacher Casy who (in that subtle defiance of popular prejudices so characteristic of Steinbeck) has given up being an evangelist because he found his orgies of pious words always ending with the seduction of some woman in his audience. Enough of the impulse which led him to preach has survived to demand that he solve his dilemma in some socially desirable way. By sharing a common problem of social adjustment with Tom, he becomes a force to prevent a possible false solution on Tom's part through delinquency. In both men, therefore, experience promotes a healthy scepticism; error stimulates an educative process. So Tom returns home to a family which has neither erred nor learned anything, and finds that they are being driven by drought and depression from their small holding. But accepting the traditional belief in the promise of American life, they have concluded that their ruin is a blessing in disguise. They plan to follow the rainbow they have looked at for years to the pot of gold at its end in sunny California. There is always prosperity for the man who will bestir himself to work for it, and nowhere more abundantly than in the golden valleys of the Pacific. Tom, however, with Casy at his elbow, is not so sure, and thus the opposition of forces in the first half of the novel becomes clear. As the family in its jalopy draws nearer to California, the more fantastic becomes its delusion of prosperity. But Tom has been using his eyes and ears, and his cynicism has increased in like proportion. Death has taken one member of the family; desertion another. The climactic event is meeting a man who has returned and who is able to tell them that the circular they have seen offering jobs is a falsehood. None of them will believe the evidence except Tom. And so, after they have crossed the desert and ascended the hill for their first view of the promised land, they seem to have the testimony of their own eyes, and it is everything they have wished for. The fields stretch for miles in serried rows, succulent with milk and honey; and they descend in a mood for hosannas.

But their optimism proves a delusion parallel to the erotic one Casy had earlier found in our evangelical tradition. The second half of the story forms the vertical division of the novel, the dialectic complement of the first, now that facts intrude to shatter their dream. The land is already owned and occupied, and there are no jobs on it. They are now forced to accept reality, as Tom has had a growing suspicion they would find it. And the horizontal division also reverses its dialectic contrast. But when Tom takes the ascendency over his family, his growth into a rational optimism has already replaced their fallacious hopes, and comes to dominate the abyss of despair and confusion into which they have suddenly fallen. This new optimism has two justifications. The national government has established a model camp for unemployed transient workers, where they are encouraged to govern themselves, and thus can recover their self-respect while they hunt for jobs. But since their stay at the camp must be limited to make way for others, it affords only a taste of what a democratic society might be.

The enduring factor in the new optimism is that, under Tom's guidance, they begin to trust themselves. Tom has come across Casy again, and learns from him a second and more important lesson. For Casy has at last found himself. He has become a union organizer of the field workers, and in a strike similar to the one of *In Dubious Battle* he is being pursued by the state police. Once more the initial action is repeated, but on a more meaningful level. Under a bridge, Tom sees Casy killed by the police in the moonlight, and in spontaneous retaliation kills one of the attacking band. Returning to the transient camp that night, Tom realizes that the critical step in his education has been passed. He has learned that one who would co-operate with the proper intention of government as represented in the existence of the camp must still fight for his rights against uncooperative forces in the community. Specifically for him this means his succeeding Casy as a union organizer. When he discovers that the police have identified the license of the family car, he knows that he must act elsewhere with a change of identity. But before he leaves, in a midnight conversation with his mother, he is able to make her feel and understand the authenticity of his newly born conviction. Capable at last of learning from events, she can resume her old direction of the family in a new spirit, since she has always with her this awareness of her son's resolute functioning somewhere for their ultimate salvation.

The action of the second half of the book rises into this dialectic contradiction of the first. Immediate events become more desperate. They have outstayed their time at the camp; yet the search for work continues futile, and they drift from place to place. But only the obtuse reader will be deceived by the overt nature of the action. As their material circumstances deteriorate, in their inner selves they are no longer despondent. Tom's shadow hovers over them, from somewhere in the outside world, where his mother is certain he is fighting for the welfare of poor people like themselves. And it would be a strange sort of American who could find this new conviction as spurious as the old fallacy; grounded, as it is, in the belief that a democratic government must respond to the pressure of the people and cooperate to secure their needs.

Indeed, the novel is more than a reflection of the democratic spirit in America. It reflects that spirit as the principles of the Atlantic Charter have made it the ideal of a world community, at a time when throughout the world the most backward of peoples are passing through a process of suffering and enlightenment similar to that of the Joads. The novel mirrors more than the psychology of the common people of the United States. It sets the pattern of enlightenment which has instigated the movements for independence in Africa, in Java, in China, in Burma, indeed in all places where people of good intent are oppressed by poverty. And one may expect that in due time it will be widely translated.

One cannot be quite so certain that its spirit will be found again in later works by Steinbeck. When the second World War arose, its gigantic issues proved too heavy a strain upon his talent. *The Moon is Down* is an instance of a new literary phenomenon brought about by the absorption in social issues which the state of the world imposes upon the public mind. A certain order of writers, with the most laudable intention, will themselves into a response in fiction, which either runs counter to those deeper and already fixed attitudes from which they write, or, in spite of their plan, reveals the reality of the objective situation. For example, the American public says and appears to believe that it has been fighting a war against fascism. The writer attempts to compose an anti-fascist novel, but certain emotional qualities seep through and corrupt the plot and characterization as planned; and the total effect of the novel is in the end not anti-fascist. In such a case either the novelist or the public is trying or pretending to be anti-fascist against the grain of more deep-seated motivations. When the discrepancy is in the public, and not merely a limitation of the author, the novel is bound to be a valuable sociological document. But in either case, it is a poor novel since it will lack artistic unity. *The Moon is Down* is an outstanding example of this tendency. A first-rate novel will remove the contradiction by making us clearly aware of it. The author will present it quite consciously as existing in the objective situation or he will fail to share it because his own orientation of personality is so fortunate as to dictate from a level below the consciousness the proper discriminations.

Otherwise sentimentality is bound to enter when the social viewpoint becomes obscure, and the author will achieve an effect the opposite to what he planned. *The Moon is Down* ends with the triumphant assertion of the native underground, and it is certainly intended to make us hate the Nazi system. Its plan is to contrast Nazism and democracy as two opposed social systems so that we hate the one and love the other. Instead it advocates by inference a third system which is neither Nazism nor democracy but a vague kind of aristocratic government. For it must be remembered that fiction argues not through logic but the sympathies which are stimulated. We accept the philosophical or political systems implicit in the actions and personalities of the men and women we are drawn to like. And in this novel we sympathize with the Junker general who controls the occupied town, more fully and with fewer reservations than with any other character. He is a kindly cultivated man, well-balanced and efficient, without a trace of the arrogance and brutality we rightly associate with the Prussian Junker officer class. He is Prussian only in the sense that he feels an obligation to do his duty even when it is distasteful to his temperament and contrary to his better judgment. He knows the Nazi way is no way to control a foreign population, but he has no objections to their economic exploitation as a political system. Nor is it part of the Nazi plan to use more force than needed; they prefer the willing obsequious assent; only when this is wanting do they become ruthless. When the Junker turns cruel it is true that our liking for him disappears. But since we find no one else to like better, he remains in our memory as the ideal governor: given the political system appropriate to his personality, given his own emancipation from the serfdom of Nazism and the restoration of the aristocratic formulas traditional to his training, and he would provide us with a happy, orderly world. The only other person we have to choose from is the native mayor of the village, and by contrast his principles are doubtful and his personality contemptible. His principles deny all leadership to the elected official; they transform him into a mechanism for carrying out the "will of the people" as though the perspective of his office had nothing to contribute to good government.

But he requires to be prodded by his people to act, since his functioning ideal is that of the compromiser; and he goes to his martyrdom in the best Social Democratic tradition of the leaders of the Weimar Republic.

The treatment of minor characters in the novel increases this discrepancy between the ideas the novel purports to serve and the veritable predilections its narration sets up. Several of the German soldiers are also kindly individuals, wishing only to stop fighting and go home, longing for love and pained to find that the system which holds them in its grip makes them objects of hatred. One such, indeed, seeks this love from a native girl who seems to reciprocate, and leads him on only to murder him. We recoil with distaste from such duplicity, which can hardly be excused by her secret hatred for the Nazis who have killed her husband. It is instead a perversion of the personality in the literary tradition of the Salomes and the Cencis and those others whose case for revenge is obscured by pathological stimuli craving the cruel sensation. And this single episode on the side of the resistance seems indeed to lend to the final conflagration of the village something more than the healthful retaliation of the scorched earth. Nazi and underground alike share the same pathology, though to highly varying degrees; just as high principle, whether in German or native ranks, is stained with the same tincture of impotent compliance.

Indeed throughout Steinbeck's work blood lust of the perverse runs like a thread that now dominates the pattern and again fades into the tranquility of exhaustion and acceptance. In most of the novels both extremes dissolve in the soft snare of sentimentality. Only in The Grapes of Wrath do they merge in such a way as to remove the taint of degeneration and become an altogether praiseworthy demand for a self-fulfillment in which action ceases to be associated with brutality and the ideal with helplessness. It is to be hoped that the course of American life will develop the potentialities that made possible The Grapes of Wrath. For Steinbeck, like his own characters, will pursue the weak side of his talent unless the forces that play upon him are imperative to rally the strong.

John S. Kennedy

JOHN STEINBECK:
LIFE AFFIRMED AND DISSOLVED

JOHN STEINBECK is generally regarded as the most versatile of contemporary American fiction artists. This distinction is not undeserved, for he has tried his hand at a number of forms. During the first decade (1929-1939) of his fame, he had ten books published, and it was only in the last of these that he returned to a mood and manner previously used. There have been other repetitions since. But his first nine works were markedly different one from another in matter and tone and style. He shifted sharply and with a show of ease from costume drama to fantasy at once earthy and lyric to knockabout farce to abrasive naturalism to argument none too successfully disguised as narrative, proving that he could do more or less creditably in a number of fictional forms, even if in none did he demonstrate the mastery and finesse of indisputable greatness.

But though his books might show contrast in form, pace and diction, they inevitably had certain things in common. For example, binding together the now rather extensive body of novels, short stories, sketches, plays, is the California setting, and specifically the Salinas Valley setting, of most of his productions.

Steinbeck was born in Salinas, the white town in "the huge green Salinas Valley," on February 27, 1902. He was of German-Irish-Yankee stock, his father being treasurer of Monterey County and his mother a school teacher. After graduating from the Salinas high school, he went intermittently to Stanford University, but his education for his career as a novelist was chiefly gathered in a series of jobs as agricultural worker, laboratory assistant, and manual laborer. He broke into print as a contributor to the Salinas high school paper, and, after leaving Stanford, came East and worked as a newspaper reporter in New York and at various odd jobs. It was only after his return to California, while

JOHN STEINBECK: LIFE AFFIRMED AND DISSOLVED first appeared as a chapter of Fifty Years of the American Novel, edited by Harold C. Gardiner, S. J., and published by Charles Scribner's Sons in 1951. The essay is reprinted here by permission of Charles Scribner's Sons, holder of the copyright, and by that of the author.

still in his middle 'twenties, that he wrote his first published book, *Cup of Gold* (1929), an historical romance about Sir Henry Morgan, the English pirate. His second book, *The Pastures of Heaven* (1932), had a California setting, as have most of those which followed. Just now Steinbeck is reported to be finishing a long novel, which he is said to consider his *chef d'oeuvre*, and, appropriately enough, its tentative title is *Salinas Valley*. Willa Cather would generally be considered a less versatile writer, yet she has dealt tellingly with a wider range of places: Nebraska, Virginia, the Southwest, New York, Quebec.

Far more important than the common scene in Steinbeck is the common theme. Something of the sort is discernible, of course, in the output of any writer, however many-sided. In Steinbeck's case the common theme may be called "reverence for life." Albert Schweitzer, the Protestant missionary who gained international renown by burying himself in the African jungle, says that the core of his creed is "reverence for life." If Steinbeck were in the habit of giving interviews to explain his purpose in writing (the very reverse is the case), he might well say that he aims at expressing and inculcating "reverence for life." At least, the student of his work as a whole easily discovers this concern running through it. To judge the worth of the idea, one must know what Steinbeck means by life, and it will be the chief object of these paragraphs to try to find out. But first, it may be observed that Steinbeck's preoccupation with life and living is perhaps the main reason for his popularity and influence.

Dozens of his contemporaries write consistently better than he, with greater subtlety and polish, greater depth and force. He can produce pages of beauty and impact, preceded and followed by pages of sheer trash, the emptiness of which is only accentuated by the pseudo-grandeur or pseudo-primitivism of the diction. He can be acutely sensitive and true for a chapter, then embarrassingly sentimental and cheaply trite. He can write dialog with authenticity and bite, and go on to more dialog which is reverberant rhetorical noise. He can juxtapose a penetrating analysis of human feeling, especially of sense impression, and painfully artificial fabrication. In short, he has at least as many faults as he has felicities in his talent; his books are by no means rigorously weeded.

Still, he has won both critical and popular acclaim, largely, it would appear, because he is, within limits, an affirmative writer. So many novelists in the 'thirties and 'forties have followed Hemingway's example of necrophilia. Their violent narratives have culminated by forcing the protagonist into a cul-de-sac, death, quick, arbitrary, grim and final extinction, and thus have been a reflection and a propagator of bleak despair with meaningless overtones of defiance. Other artists in fiction have been wryly fastidious chroniclers of picayune but lethal futilities, arguing that life amounts to no more than a steady series of defeats which may be individually no more than pinpricks but which add up to slow, unavoidable bleeding to death.

Steinbeck is different. He does not fit into any of the categories of negativism prevalent in this age's fiction. He is no Pollyanna—far from it. He depicts human existence as conflict, unremitting and often savage battle. But he suggests that life is worth living, flagellant and baffling though it may be. When, as rarely happens, he produces a memorable character like Ma Joad, that character has an irrepressible will to live, even under heart-breakingly adverse conditions, is resourceful and indomitable before the hostility of a world apparently bent on his or her extermination. In a time when the prevalent note in creative literature is that of despondency and abandonment to malign fate, whether armed with sledgehammer or scalpel, Steinbeck's assertion of the resiliency and tough durability of life has set him off from the generality.

Moreover, his prepossession with life, rather than ideologies, has made it impossible to pigeonhole him politically, which is not true of many another novelist.

He did run afoul of the critical habit, prevalent in the 'thirties and early 'forties, that rated fiction principally, if not exclusively, according to the political bias a man's work showed or might be tortured into showing, or the political capital which partisans might, honestly or dishonestly, make of it. Thus *The Grapes of Wrath* (1939) was attacked by the politically conservative as out-and-out Communist propaganda. It was nothing of the sort, even if Communists, despite their distrust of Steinbeck, did use its stark picture of the plight of the dispossessed as graphic evidence of the crimes and the certain collapse of capitalism.

Steinbeck had written of Communists not unsympathetically and had hit at reactionary Red-baiters in earlier books, but had clearly demonstrated his critical awareness of the bad features of the Communist mentality and methods in the novel, *In Dubious Battle* (1936), dealing with an abortive strike by migrant fruit pickers of whom monolithically organized owners would take pitiless advantage. Mac, the veteran Communist who foments and manipulates the strike, voices the familiar propaganda about the Communists' love for all workers and their disinterested toil to assure to every last mortal a life worthy of a man. And the appeal which communism makes to the unorientated and destitute by manifestly doing something while no help for the suffering comes from any other quarter, is forcefully depicted. But Doc, the character who, it is manifest, speaks for Steinbeck, debunks the legend of the Communists' altruistic humanitarianism; and the Party's cold-blooded exploitation of misery, as well as its callous use of the most despicable means to its power-seeking ends, is graphically shown. Steinbeck evidently rejected communism because communism throttled life.

Hence the accusation that Steinbeck was pro-Communist had to be doubted on the basis of what he had written, even before one read *The Grapes of Wrath*. And a careful dispassionate reading of the latter novel showed there was no justification for the charge that it contained solid chunks of undisguised Communist doctrine. The book said, at unconscionable length and with some resort to sensationalism and melodrama, something incontrovertibly true: namely, that thousands upon thousands of Americans were being cruelly victimized and heinously degraded by a system, crazily inept at least in part, which destroyed masses of ordinary people for the inordinate and socially unjust and detrimental enrichment of remote, impersonal corporations. Steinbeck, aroused over the trampling of human life, put this strongly in accents of burning anger and disgust. He did not have to be a Communist to do so, and indeed it was an appalling commentary on the inhumanity or stupidity of the comfortably circumstanced that his indictment of a reeking evil should be answered only by wholly irrelevant name-calling.

But it was not very long until Steinbeck was under fire for precisely the opposite reason and being styled a sort of crypto-Nazi. This happened when *The Moon Is Down* was published as a novel and produced as a play in 1942. The United States was then at war, the Axis tide was still running strong, and many influential American publicists had agreed to make a mockery of exact truth for the duration. Steinbeck was writing of occupied Norway (he had visited the country, as he had Russia, a few years before), and his Nazi characters emerged as something like human beings, by no means admirable, but by no means demoniac either. For not making them intrinsically and uniformly monstrous, at a time when some of our most celebrated writers were trying to whip Americans up to a frenzy of indiscriminate hatred, Steinbeck was pilloried.

The allegations first of Communist, then of Nazi, sympathies would appear to cancel each other out. But then again, they could lead one to believe that there might be a certain paradoxical justification for such seemingly contradictory charges. Communism and nazism have in common a commitment to collectivism, differing though they do as to the auspices under which it should be conducted. Was Steinbeck in favor of some sort of collectivism? It is plain from his books that he does not favor the familiar forms of economic or political collectivism, be they controlled by foreign dictators or native capitalists. For example, he writes scathingly of the monopolist who thwarts the poor Mexican in *The Pearl* (1947). He hits hard, for another example, at that centralization which would make of American agriculture no more than a mass-production scheme for the aggrandizement of urban shareholders, and this precisely because life is demeaned and quenched in the process.

In *The Grapes of Wrath* he has a tenant farmer say something in which it not preposterous to find a faint echo of Leo XIII's teaching on property in his encyclical letter *On the Condition of the Working Classes*:

> If a man owns a little property, that property is him, it's part of him, and it's like him. If he owns property only so he can walk on it and handle it and be sad when it isn't doing well, and feel fine when the rain falls on it, that property is him, and some ways he's bigger because he owns it . . . But let a man get property he doesn't see, or can't take time to get his fingers in, or can't be there to walk on it—why, then property is the man . . . , stronger than he is. And he is small, not big. Only his possessions are big.

Is it fantastic to see some similarity between this and the words of Pope Leo:

> When man spends the industry of his mind and the strength of his body in procuring the fruits of nature, by that act he makes his own that portion of nature's field which he cultivates—that portion on which he leaves, as it were, the impress of his own personality; and it cannot but be just that he should possess that portion as his own, and should have a right to keep it without molestation?

Steinbeck emphasizes the natural bond between life and productive property, the need that man has of a bit of earth to give him sustenance and dignity. He had touched on this earlier, as in *Of Mice and Men* (1937), in which Candy says:

> Everybody wants a little bit of land, not much. Jus' som'thin' that was his. Som'thin' he could live on and there couldn't nobody throw him off of it. I never had none. I planted crops for damn near ever'body in this state, but they wasn't my crops, and when I harvested 'em, it wasn't none of my harvest.

This is a legitimate complaint against a derangement which has contributed greatly to the dehumanization of man.

But later in *The Grapes of Wrath* Steinbeck seems to approve and recommend collectivism of a different sort, a collectivism which, according to him, would foster, rather than crush, life. The Okies have had their ramshackle but cherished homes and their small patches of earth snatched away from them by the insatiable behemoth of big-scale agriculture. What is wrong with this, it is suggested, is not the pooling of hundreds of family-size farms, but the fact of the alien ownership of the amalgam. Steinbeck does not oppose mechanized collective farming in itself. "Is a tractor bad?" he asks. "Is the power that turns the long furrows wrong? If this tractor were ours it would be good—not mine but ours. If our tractor turned the long furrows of our land, it would be good. Not my land, but ours." And there is much more in the same vein, urging a sort of popularly chosen and controlled socialism, which Steinbeck heatedly advocates without ever bothering to consider its pitfalls or its possible deleterious consequences.

This idea is not to be dismissed out of hand as absurd or pernicious. The social character of property, the legitimacy and desirability of social ownership of what is indispensable to the common good, the incomparable value and profoundly Christian character of voluntary cooperation and joint endeavor—these are not being called into question. But Steinbeck means something more, something different. Just here we are coming to grips with the central point in Steinbeck's concept of life: namely, that its fullness is found only in the group and never in the individual. While he regards with disfavor a superimposed collectivism, he believes ardently in the primacy of the collectivity. Permeating his works is this idea, which is the very heart of his philosophy of life: that the concrete person is in himself virtually nothing, whereas the abstraction "humanity" is all.

Consider some examples from books published over a span of years, and you will observe the persistency and growth of this attitude. In *To a God Unknown* (1933), Rama says:

> I tell you this man is not a man, unless he is all men. The strength, the resistance, the long and stumbling thinking of all men, and all the joys and suffering too, cancelling each other out and yet remaining in the contents. He is all these, a repository for a little piece of each man's soul, and more than that, a symbol of the earth's soul.

In *In Dubious Battle*, Doc tells Mac, "You might be an expression of group-man, a cell endowed with a special function, like an eye-cell,

drawing your force from group-man . . . Yes, it might be worthwhile to know more about group-man, to know his nature, his ends,
his desires." Later, he asks another character, "Can't a group of men
be God?" In *The Red Pony* (1937), the westward migration of the pioneers is described as "a whole bunch of people made into one big
crawling beast." In *The Grapes of Wrath* Tom Joad, quoting the ex-
preacher Casy, declares:

> Says one time he went out into the wilderness to find his own soul,
> and he foun' he didn' have no soul that was his'n. Says he foun' he jus'
> got a little piece of a great big soul. Says a wilderness ain't no good,
> 'cause his little piece of soul wasn't no good 'less it was with the rest,
> an' was whole.

It might be said that Steinbeck is doing no more than asserting, in
a rather vaporous way, the solidarity of the human race, the continuity
and interdependence of the species, the indubitable fact that all men
are brothers and members one of another, or referring to the workings
of mob psychology. But it is none of these things that he is getting at.
Rather, he is ever more strongly affirming that, in the last analysis, man
has no individual identity, that the human person as such, separately
created and distinct from all others, does not in fact exist. Commitment to this idea may well be reaction against the unbridled, atomistic
individualism which has wreaked havoc in society as a whole and in
innumerable lives, and which, as his books indicate, Steinbeck recognizes as disastrous for mankind. But he has swung to and remains at
the opposite extreme, that amalgamism which deprives the individual
of initiative, responsibility, value, and even metaphysical being, and
makes him no more than a cell in a supposititious monstrosity called
"group-man" or an inextricable aspect of a pseudo-mystical entity called
the "great big soul." It is the "great big soul" which, for Steinbeck,
is life.

Indeed, he goes further than blotting out the boundaries of personality which mark off one man from another. He declares that, for man
to be whole, he must be indistinguishably at one with all that exists.
Casy, in *The Grapes of Wrath*, says: "There was the hills, an' there was
me, an' we wasn't separate no more. We was one thing. An' that one
thing was holy." Here again, one might dismiss objections, on the
ground that all that exists, whether organic or inorganic, is interrelated
and should be in harmony. There is an intimate interrelationship of all
the levels of a universe made through, and bearing the mark of, the one
Eternal Word. But Steinbeck is nowhere clear as to the essential, quali-
tative difference between man and the rest of created beings.

This can be plainly seen in what Edmund Wilson has called Steinbeck's "animalizing tendency." Wilson says that "constant in Mr. Steinbeck is his preoccupation with biology" and points out "his tendency in his stories to present life in animal terms." The tendency is one which Wilson applauds in Steinbeck as in Erskine Caldwell. Discussing the latter's *Tragic Ground* in the *New Yorker* in 1944, Wilson observed that its evaluation of man was "one symptom of a change in attitude which Western man is in our time undergoing in regard to his role on the earth." He went on:

> Even thirty-five years ago such books would hardly have been written. Today we read them for their humor and charm (e.g., a twelve-year-old girl working in a brothel), accepting incest and murder as quite innocent, and undisturbed by such casual cruelty as that of the hero of the present novel when he decides to go home by himself and leave his ailing wife alone, because it is made to seem as unconscious and natural as the self-preserving egoism of animals. The point is that we can read about all this today without anything more than a smile or a qualm because we are prepared, as our grandfathers were not, to study human behavior on the animal level.

Another critic, Alfred Kazin, says that Steinbeck approaches "the modern social struggle as a tragicomedy of animal instincts." And the same view was voiced by still a third critic, John Chamberlain. Reviewing *Cannery Row* (1945) for *Harper's Magazine*, he wrote:

> Cannery Row is an amoral place, and Steinbeck is amoral in his approach to it. Between the boys of the Palace Flophouse and the tomcats they catch for Doc there is little discernible difference, and the girls of Dora's Bear Flag bordello might be out of the Elsie Dinsmore books for all that Steinbeck cares. In Steinbeck's world whores are interchangeable with angels, and pimps with saints. From his marine biological expeditions Steinbeck has caught a naturalist's view of life as consisting of struggle, color, intensity, violence, feeding, and orgasm. Moral and ethical choices are merely man's way of making things difficult for himself; the animals know better. . . . The Steinbeck attitude results in books that are devoid of human meaning. Cannery Row is exciting and pleasurable because it has salt, color and movement. But you can say as much for a circus or a zoo.

I quote these three critics at such length because none of them is likely to be taxed with religious fanaticism or moralistic narrow-mindedness, as is the case when someone like myself says that he finds in certain books a reduction of man to the merely animal level. A trio of leading non-religious commentators on letters agrees as to Steinbeck's concept of man's stature and status, and two of them rather like the novelist's appraisal of our species.

The reader of Steinbeck's works is always coming on plainly stated parallels between men and animals. In its most blatant and hideous form, this can be seen in that story of nightmarish horror, *The Snake*. In *The Pearl*, just after describing how the greedy bourgeoisie gang up on their peasant victim, Steinbeck writes:

> Out in the estuary a tight woven school of small fish glittered and broke water to escape a school of great fishes that drove in to eat them. And in the houses the people could hear the swish of the small ones and the bouncing splash of the great ones as the slaughter went on. . . . And the night mice crept about on the ground and the little night hawks hunted them silently.

In *The Red Pony*, dogs hunting mice are compared with troops hunting Indians. In *Of Mice and Men*, the shooting of a decrepit old dog and the shooting of a decrepit old man are linked. In *In Dubious Battle*, the killing of a dog and the killing of a Negro are similarly linked, as are dogs fighting and men fighting, the slaughtering of men and the slaughtering of sheep. In *The Grapes of Wrath*, there is the same pairing of behavior and treatment between dogs and men, horses and men, and other forms of animal life and men. Examples could be cited from book after book, but the foregoing are enough to give substance to the statement that habitually and characteristically Steinbeck sets human conduct and animal conduct side by side, on the same plane, not simply as commentaries one on the other but as indications of the same nature in the two apparently disparate sorts of creature.

Man is, of course, an animal. But he is an animal with a difference. He is a rational animal, a moral animal. Steinbeck seems to agree to man's rationality when he says, in *The Grapes of Wrath*, "Fear the time when Manself will not suffer and die for a concept; for this one quality is the foundation of Manself." And yet he incessantly presents man as a creature, indeed a captive, of instincts and appetites only, blindly desiring and striving, not reasoning, judging, choosing but automatically responding to impulses and attractions.

As for man's being moral, Doc (who, to repeat, is Steinbeck's spokesman in *In Dubious Battle*) says: "My senses aren't above reproach, but they're all I have . . . I don't want to put on the blinders of 'good' and 'bad,' and limit my vision." In *The Grapes of Wrath*, Casy says of sexual promiscuity: "Maybe it ain't a sin. Maybe it's just the way folks is . . . There ain't no sin and there ain't no virtue. There's just stuff people do. It's all part of the same thing." Pa Joad echoes this with, "A fella got to do what he got to do." And Ma Joad says, "What people does is right to do." As John Chamberlain suggests, this idea represents a conclusion Steinbeck has drawn from his observation of marine life. Reporting on one of his expeditions, he states in *Sea of Cortez* (1941):

> The true biologist deals with life, with teeming boisterous life, and learns something from it, learns that the first rule of life is living . . . He knows that morals are too often diagnostic of prostatitis and stomach ulcers. Sometimes he may proliferate a little too much in all directions, but he is as easy to kill as any other organism, and meanwhile he is very good company, and at least he does not confuse a low hormone productivity with moral ethics.

And so in man, according to Steinbeck, what counts, what alone matters, is life, its preservation, its transmission. In his latest work, *Burning Bright*, which appeared both as a novel and as a play in 1950, Joe Saul suspects he is impotent and desponds. He is over the threshold of middle age, and he has not done the one capital thing—passing on physical life. His second wife, much younger than he, seeks to allay his self-contempt by getting a lusty youth named Victor to father a child which she will tell Joe Saul is his own. This she does on the advice of Friend Ed (plainly another Steinbeck mouthpiece), who is a model of wisdom and natural goodness. Thinking his manhood is vindicated, Joe Saul exults. But then Victor threatens to tell him the truth and is promptly murdered by Friend Ed. Joe Saul gets from a doctor conclusive proof that he is impotent, and upbraids his wife for deceit and infidelity. But Friend Ed persuades him that what his wife did was fine and beautiful and, when the child is born, Joe Saul greets it as his own, declaiming that every man is the father of every child and every child the offspring of every man. Life is vindicated, life goes on, and whatever violence is done the moral code is of no moment alongside that fact.

The thoughtful reader is appalled by the complete severance of man from morality which the book's argument represents. He reflects that fundamentally what is amiss with these characters is failure or refusal to recognize and accept God's will and word: as regards physical defects, the exclusiveness of marriage, the disposition of life. And this leads one to inquire about the novelist's attitude to religion.

We have already noted the idea, mentioned in *In Dubious Battle*, that the human collectivity, men *en masse*, may be all that is meant by the term "God." Several times in Steinbeck's works one finds the idea that a character has outgrown prayer because, with enlightenment, he no longer knows what or whom to pray to. This is the case, for example, with the scientist in *The Snake* and the ex-preacher in *The Grapes of Wrath*. "No, I can't pray to anything," says the first, and the second says, "I don't know . . . who to pray to." On the other hand, the ignorant, superstitious people of whom Steinbeck is writing in *The Pearl* and *The Long Valley* (1938) pray because it is part of an immemorial behavior-pattern which, quite as uninformed as their forebears, they unquestioningly accept.

These benighted men and women, incidentally, are Catholic, and it is interesting to see how Steinbeck treats Catholicism. It is not understandingly or sympathetically. In *The Pearl*, the Church is a symbol for obscurantism and the unscrupulous milking of the poor. Kino, an indigent fisherman, finds an enormous pearl, perhaps the greatest the world has ever known. Immediately everyone is scheming to get it away from him. Among the lusters after it is the priest. Up to now, Kino and his wife have not been able to be married in Church because they never had enough money to pay the fee; likewise, their baby has not been baptized because they could never meet the "cost" of the ceremony. Kino is bitter about this, as he is about the priest's preaching which, in effect, is no more than a browbeating attempt to keep the people shackled in their poverty, since its drift is that God's clear and immutable will for them is the squalor and hunger of the sub-human existence in which the upper classes have them imprisoned. But now that Kino has the pearl, the priest comes, smiling and reptilianly wily, to the fisherman's wretched shack—for the first time.

From a different racial background and a somewhat different social stratum is Jim Nolan, the tormented young man in *In Dubious Battle*, who, in revolt against the system which, he says, has ruined his whole family, joins the Communist Party and goes to his death in the fruit pickers' strike. His father abominated religion and would not hear of his worn-out wife's going to the Catholic church. He prevented her from attending Sunday Mass, but sometimes during the week, while he was at work, she would slip into the church for a few minutes' prayer. In the end, however, she turned away from the Church, refusing the priest on her death bed. The only religion that Jim knows is the Catholic, and this he knows very imperfectly. But he detests it. It might be parenthetically remarked that Steinbeck and his Jim Nolan are both unaware of Pius XI's strictures on a system which so cripples human nature as to deter it, if not alienate it, from the practice of religion.

When, alight with enthusiasm over the strike, Jim talks to Doc, the latter says to him, "You've got something in your eyes, Jim, something religious." Jim furiously replies, "Well, it isn't religious. I've got no use for religion," and later, "I don't believe in religion."

It may be remembered that, a few years ago, Steinbeck published in Collier's magazine an article retelling the story of the apparitions of Our Lady of Guadalupe. This he related with every evidence of reverence, and he lavished upon it all the resources of his best poetic style. A reader unfamiliar with the rest of his writings might possibly have considered the piece the work of a Catholic. But, taken in the Steinbeck context, it was merely his presentation not of an historical fact, but of a lovely myth to which simple people in whom Steinbeck is interested and whom he has again and again used as subjects for his fiction, give credence. This, he is saying, is what such folk believe. Thus, the bus driver in The Wayward Bus (1946) always has a likeness of Our Lady of Guadalupe in the vehicle as a kind of amulet or fetish; his life show that he does not conform to the code which the image symbolizes.

Nowhere does Steinbeck give evidence of adequate knowledge of the Catholicism on which he touches with evident disfavor in his various productions. He seems much more familiar with the cruder sort of evangelical Protestantism, and this is acidly treated in his books.

For example, there is an indictment of it in To a God Unknown. Again, there is Casy in The Grapes of Wrath, once an evangelist holding rambunctious revival meetings, half glory-shouting and half sexual orgies, throughout the hinterland. When, at the beginning of the book, Tom Joad is returning home after a stay in prison, he meets Casy by the wayside and is surprised to hear that the preacher has given up that work. "I was a preacher," Casy tells him. "Reverend Jim Casy— was a Burning Busher. Used to howl out the name of Jesus to glory. And used to get an irrigation ditch so squirmin' full of repented sinners half of 'em like to drownded. But no more . . . Just Jim Casy now. Ain't got the call no more. Got a lot of sinful idears—but they seem kinda sensible."

He further explains his abandonment of the ministry:

> I love people so much I'm fit to bust, sometimes. And I says, "Don't you love Jesus?" Well, I thought an' thought, an' finally I says, "No, I don't know nobody name' Jesus. I know a bunch of stories, but I only love people" . . . I figgered about the Holy Sperit and the Jesus road. I figgered, "Why we got to hang it on God or Jesus? Maybe," I figgered, "maybe it's all men an' all women we love; maybe that's the Holy Sperit —the human sperit—the whole shebang."

Casy gave up baptizing because nobody seemed to feel any different as a result of it. He had once baptized Tom and now asks him, "Well—did you take any good outa that baptizin'? . . . Did you take any bad from it?" And Tom answers, "No-o-o, can't say as I felt anything." Casy has also come to discredit the notion of sin. "Maybe we been whippin' the hell out of ourselves for nothin'." His apologia for withdrawing from religious endeavor goes on for paragraphs and pages, but perhaps the point is just as strikingly made by the single gesture of Pat Humbert in *The Pastures of Heaven* (1932), when, seeking to disengage himself from the dead hand of the past which has always kept him from enjoying life, he picks up the old family Bible and hurls it out into the yard to rot in the rain.

Steinbeck may justly be said to belong to that populous group of contemporary novelists who, rejecting as proscrustean and unlivable a peculiar, diluted blend of Calvinism and Lutheranism, think that, in exposing such freakishness, they are refuting authentic Christianity. They look upon what is a caricature of authentic Christianity, find it wanting, repudiate it, and suppose that they have thereby pulled the props out from under the real article, whereas in fact they have left this untouched. Casy's ramblings are a case in point. They reveal that what he thought to be essential Christianity was, in fact, no more than an inorganic agglomeration of bits and tatters torn away from the original, and inoperative and incapable of standing searching scrutiny. The privativism which Casy, Pat Humbert, and other Steinbeck characters find and disavow in what they take to be integral Christianity is actually a disease at the heart of a faint and fragmentary copy of genuine Christianity. Thus, the notion of grace which Casy scorns, is a travesty on the Christian doctrine of grace. The former holds grace to be entirely subjective, no more than an emotional impulse, a nervous compulsion, muscular response to stimuli, while the latter holds it to be objective, a distinctively spiritual power and presence. If you ridicule the first because, in practice, it leads to grotesque and sometimes disastrous doings, you still have not rebutted, indeed you have not even considered, the second.

Steinbeck, therefore, nowhere comes to grips with the basic, pristine Christian religion. Hence he never takes into account what it has to say about human nature, human life, human destiny. He is not conversant with its moral code as a whole. He is not familiar with its bearing upon the human predicament, the light it casts upon it and the resources it brings to mortals for managing and solving it.

His last book, *Burning Bright*, harshly highlights all that is weakest in Steinbeck as a philosopher and a writer of fiction. Even if one could do the impossible and agree that adultery is no more than an outdated word so long as life is propagated, there is the question of Victor's fate. Friend Ed, goodness and wisdom personified, recommends that Victor be used and then coolly kills the young man when convenience calls for that. There is no slightest hint that the murder is a wicked injustice. The brutality, the icy amorality of this is one of the most shocking things in all Steinbeck's output, the more shocking because it comes from a supposedly mature man and is surrounded with resounding generalities about the sacredness of life. Yet it is scarcely surprising in view of the sophistry in which, in his succession of works, Steinbeck has become ever more tightly entangled. And, by the way, one might here stress the fact that it is the sophistry, rather than the foul speech, which is most regrettable in Steinbeck's fiction. *Burning Bright* is almost entirely free of the vulgar, obscene, or blasphemous dialog which characterizes so many of Steinbeck's books. It is only the coarse Victor who recalls, and that but faintly and briefly, the profane and filthy language of the figures which dominate, and are constantly articulate in the idiom of lewdness, in several of the other novels. The rest of the principals use no offensive words, indeed their talk has an exalted ring to it, and yet the ideas they express are far worse than mere lurid utterance. To reproduce verbatim the gutter language of people who are virtually mute unless they resort to lascivious lingo is hardly to be compared with the communication of a philosophy of life which is totally fallacious. The reporting of the sordid does not begin to do the harm stemming from a false interpretation of man. Two such dissimilar writers as T. S. Eliot and Somerset Maugham have both emphasized that the novelist and playwright are primarily commenting on life in terms of a certain set of postulates and principles. Too often the reader does not advert to this fact, does not sift out and assess the author's concept of life, but is content to praise or blame on the basis of, say, what he considers the decency or indecency of speech used.

In *Burning Bright*, too, may be seen at its worst Steinbeck's failure with characters. He has written about fifteen volumes of fiction by now, yet given us almost no memorable characters. Ma Joad is a possible exception, but it is hard to name even half-a-dozen more. For the most part the men and women in Steinbeck's narratives are hazy, faceless, pithless. They are not sharply drawn, clearly projected, unmistakably themselves, or recognizable from one's experience however catholic. They have no forms, in the philosophical sense, which is but another way of saying that they have no souls. There are about them certain superficial peculiarities which make for a measure of material individuation, but almost nothing making for personality. They are heavily documented types, not living people. Nor is this merely a deficiency in imagination or technique. It springs from Steinbeck's conviction that a man or woman is just "a little piece of a great big soul." It has been said of Steinbeck that he is not a creative artist; if this is true, it is to be attributed to his missing the point of God's several creation of humans, each a separate entity, each a microcosm and a mystery which cannot be wholly fused or confused with any other. There is not anything abstract about God's attitude toward men, but there is about Steinbeck's.

Also in *Burning Bright* there is on display Steinbeck's tendency to cause his characters to speak in bombast. This novel abounds in the most stilted, overblown, porous talk that a reader is likely to encounter anywhere. It is hardly more than an accumulation of big, empty words through which an aimless wind blows, making unintelligible noises. Here Steinbeck is manifesting his penchant for the amorphous notion orotundly uttered. Imprecision in thinking is matched by imprecision in expression. The gutless abstraction emerges as a vapor of speech.

This is the irony of John Steinbeck's work: that, in his concern for Manself and Life, he has dissolved both for want of exact and plenary knowledge of what they are. He who would affirm the dignity of man, deals that dignity a shattering blow by denying man the dimensions and the personality which alone confer a dignity that is intrinsic and not an accident of circumstance, the attributes of sovereign intellect and unforced free will which alone make man more than the beasts that perish. He who would extol Life and win its reverence, strips it of whatever differentiates it from mere biological existence. And yet, over and over again in Steinbeck's writing, there are crude intimations of something beyond what, when he is being definitive, he sets as the terms of man's being. One could wish that the novelist would rigorously examine these, for it is only from apprehension and appreciation of them that there can come the clarity and strength which his work lacks.

Earlier in this paper there was reference to the resemblance which might be found between Leo XIII's doctrine of property and the ideas which Steinbeck expresses on the subject. It would be excellent for Steinbeck, both as a thinker and as an artist, if his concept of man were not so wholly at odds with that set forth by the Holy Father in his discussion of property. "Beyond the appeal of their instincts," says Pope Leo,

> the brute creation cannot go, for they are moved to action by sensibility alone, and by the things which sense perceives. But vastly dif-

ferent is the nature of man. He possesses, on the one hand, the full perfection of animal nature, and therefore enjoys, at least as much as the rest of the animal race, the fruition of the things of the body. But animality, however perfect, is far from being the whole of humanity. . . . It is the mind, or the reason, which is the chief thing in us who are human beings. It is this which makes a human being human, and distinguishes him essentially and completely from the brute.

The judgment one must pass on Steinbeck is this: that he is a sentimentalist. This may seem the wildest sort of misstatement, but it is literally true. Clifton Fadiman once said that the classification of Steinbeck as a hard-boiled writer is incorrect; if there must be a comparison with eggs, Steinbeck is soft-boiled. Fadiman was referring to the maudlin note sounded habitually in Steinbeck's work, as, for example, in the mawkish pages of *Of Mice and Men* or in the sickly conclusion of *The Grapes of Wrath*. But Steinbeck's sentimentality is something that goes beyond the facile tear-jerking which Fadiman decries. It is a way of regarding humanity, the way of feeling rather than of reason. "Steinbeck the realist" is a misnomer, for the flight from reason which, in common with so many of his contemporaries, he has indulged in, has prevented him from seeing reality as it is, in its entire fullness and proportioning and significance.

Freeman Champney

JOHN STEINBECK, CALIFORNIAN

JOHN STEINBECK is one of the few American writers who can be discussed in both past and present. He has done important work for fifteen years or so and he is still developing and experimenting. So much criticism and analysis of his work have been published that writing any more seems a little silly—we have several times as many passable literary critics now as we have halfway good creators. But most of the critics are Easterners and have discussed Steinbeck's books with little or no knowledge of the country in which he grew up and which he writes about. Even a casual direct contact with this country and its people suggests that this background is the most important thing to know about Steinbeck and that it explains much of his writing better than any amount of remote analysis. It also explains things about the East by comparison and contrast.

The Salinas Valley roughly parallels the coast, thirty miles or so inland, for most of its length of about a hundred and twenty miles. It is one of the smaller of California's central valleys, which run up and down the state between mountain ranges. The enclosing hills have the steep slopes and the barren, rounded crests which have evoked so many anatomical comparisons. During much of the year they are brown and dry, turning green during the rainy winter. The river, the highway, and the Southern Pacific Railroad chase each other down the valley floor. The river itself, like most California rivers, is normally sandy, brush-choked, and nearly dry but carries a great volume of floodwater when the big rains come. At the lower end of the valley the flat bottomland is cut into great fields of lettuce, broccoli, alfalfa, sugar beets, and other truck crops. Cattle are raised on the slopes of the hills. Salinas (where

FREEMAN CHAMPNEY has been manager of the Antioch Press for almost twenty years. He is also business manager of The Antioch Review and is one of three members of the editorial board of that magazine who have been with it since its inception in 1941. In the late 1930's he edited The Writers' Forum. Mr. Champney lived for several months in Steinbeck's California country, out of which experience he wrote "John Steinbeck, Californian," which is reprinted here by his permission and that of The Antioch Review, where it appeared first in the Fall, 1947 issue.

Steinbeck was born and raised) is about ten miles inland from the river's mouth in Monterey Bay. It is the county seat and the trading and shipping center for the lower part of the valley. It looks a little more metropolitan than the raw valley towns but not much more.

Cattle-raising has been a valley occupation since the days of the missions but the intensive cultivation of vegetables—especially lettuce, which takes up more than 50,000 acres—has outranked it in importance for some time. But the nostalgic glamor of the cowhand days is clung to. You see fifty lean men in sombreros, tight jeans, and riding boots for every visible horse. Once a year Salinas stages "California's Biggest Rodeo" and cashes in handsomely on its nostalgia.

Lettuce, however, is the big industry of the valley, and its growing, packing, and shipping follow the highly capitalized pattern of California agriculture that Carey McWilliams has accurately called "Factories in the Field." In 1936 a strike by lettuce packing shed workers was crushed at a cost of around a quarter of a million dollars. Civil liberties, local government, and normal judicial processes were all suspended during the strike and Salinas was governed by a general staff directed by the Associated Farmers and the big lettuce growers and shippers. The local police were bossed by a reserve army officer imported for the job and at the height of the strike all male residents of Salinas between 18 and 45 were mobilized under penalty of arrest, were deputized and armed. Beatings, tear gas attacks, wholesale arrests, threats to lynch San Francisco newspapermen if they didn't leave town, and machine guns and barbed wire all figured in the month-long struggle which finally broke the strike and destroyed the union.

So much for John Steinbeck's birthplace, where he lived his first nineteen years. From Salinas it is about fifteen miles through a pass in the Santa Lucia Range to the Monterey Peninsula. This fantastic area contains some of the most picturesque country in the world and an assortment of humanity almost as bizarre and much less permanent. Monterey itself is tough and raucous. Its harbor shelters the purse-seiners of the sardine fleet; farther west the shore is solid with the processing plants (Cannery Row) that receive the catch. The fishermen and cannery workers are Italian, Portuguese, Japanese, a few Chinese, and the paisanos of *Tortilla Flat*. Nearby is the army post of Fort Ord and the main business section along Alvarado Street is thick with ratty-looking bars. Sardine fishing and the canneries are highly speculative, feast-or-famine affairs. Beyond this variable economic base, Monterey has its honkeytonks for the military and a considerable volume of tourist business (they come to see the fishing boats and the historic adobes and absorb the legends of the rancho and mission days).

Just west of Cannery Row is the city of Pacific Grove. Its recent history stems from the days when it was a Methodist camp-meeting ground, complete with a fence, and duly locked against the sinful world at curfew. Today it has become rather nondescript middle-class—a haven for retired Middlewesterners of the staider sorts and a respectable residential town. Its moralistic past lingers on in covenants in real estate deeds forever prohibiting the sale of liquor, and in books in the public library from which the profanity has been scratched with a righteous nail file (apparently; maybe it was a hat pin or a corset stay). Public night life in Pacific Grove is limited to a few dreary milkshake dens and occasional prowling teenagers trying to make noises like juvenile delinquents.

Across the wooded ridge of the Peninsula is Carmel-by-the-Sea. Originally an artists-and-writers colony, Carmel has become a fashionable center for all sorts of people with cultural pretensions and a surplus of money. It is quaint and arty and individualistic and grimly "unspoiled." Down the coast from Carmel is the craggy and desolate Big Sur country (once Robinson Jeffers' special literary domain). Most of the shore line between Pacific Grove and Carmel, and most of the wooded hills behind it, are part of the Del Monte Properties—an exclusive real estate development purveying summer homes and de luxe lodge accommodations to the financial aristocracy of California.

The Monterey Peninsula has a lively bohemian-artist-writer class. The ones with money live in Carmel. The others in the hills above Monterey, in the Big Sur country, or anywhere else where rents are low and the folkways relaxed. The mild climate makes a minimum of clothes and housing quite tolerable. The shifting population, the resort atmosphere, and the lack of strenuous industry all give a certain glamor and acceptability to the bohemian life. It even has a certain economic importance as part of the tourist bait.

One other environmental feature should be mentioned: the Bay swarms with marine life. Even a casual observer of the tide pools gets some of the feeling for biological diversity, fecundity, and struggle which has played so important a part in Steinbeck's thinking.

II

John Steinbeck grew up in Salinas and after four years at Stanford University he lived at various times in Carmel and Pacific Grove and kept a fishing boat in Monterey Harbor. More perhaps than any important contemporary American writer, except William Faulkner, his writing has grown out of a special region. It is a region, however, that contains such polar extremes as the hard materialism of Salinas and the bohemianism of the Peninsula. Both have obviously been important in Steinbeck's writing but Salinas came first and is most apparent.

The cultural climate of the Salinas Valley is typical of California agriculture. A tradition of personal individualism goes along with a strongly collectivized economy. As Carey McWilliams has pointed out, the great California valleys show few resemblances to traditional American rural life. The "school-house on the hilltop, the comfortable homes, the compact and easy indolence of the countryside" are noticeably absent. Instead there are the vast orchards, vineyards, and ranches, meticulously tended, irrigated, and smudged but showing little close functional connection with human life. They are (most of them) really farm factories, and their financing and cultivation, and the marketing of their output, have become highly collectivized activities, managed by and for the great owners and packers, the banks, and the utilities. As in most big business, ownership and management are usually sharply separated. The exploitation of labor has exceeded anything known in Western civilization since the early mill towns of England. The operators of this paradise have usually been able to use or usurp the sovereign powers of local or state government whenever necessary to wipe out a threat to their absolutism.

Economically, socially, and culturally it has been an ugly state of affairs. In its extremes of wealth and destitution, in the absence or impotence of any middle group representing the public interest, and in the domination of the organs of civil life by irresponsible private greed, it has been one of the few areas of American life that has closely approximated the Marxian predictions about capitalist society. The proletariat was kept homeless, voteless, and close to or below the starvation point, with the gulf between it and the dominant group widened by racial differences. Civil liberties were nonexistent whenever they remotely threatened the *status quo*. The whole system was impersonal and relentless and individual men of good will on either side were helpless to do much about it. There was no liberal, middle-of-the-road answer that had much reality to it. It is not surprising that Steinbeck's reaction to this aspect of his environment was to explore communist answers in *In Dubious Battle*.

The book is the story of two communists and the strike they organized and directed in the apple country. It is a very "dubious battle" indeed. They don't expect to win the strike—in fact they prefer it that way. Their job is to give the strikers an experience of working together and a feeling of their united strength, and to convince them of the implacable nature of their enemy by a bath of blood that will turn as many of them as possible into all-out revolutionaries. All available tricks and deceits are thrown into the game and friends and sympathizers are sacrificed ruthlessly. (The forces of "law and order," to be sure, play their hand as dirtily as they can and leave little to be done in the way of creating grievances and incidents.) One of the communists is killed as the strike begins to disintegrate and the book ends with his faceless corpse propped up on the platform to help his comrade stir up the men to a final burst of violence. It is a study of tactics that make sense only for the long-term end of bloody revolution.

Characteristically, however, Steinbeck's interest in the communists has always been more a matter of what makes them tick as people than of abstract ideology. Why should they go out to face certain beating and possible death from the enemy and betrayal and hatred from the people they are trying to organize? It is this question of motivation that runs through *In Dubious Battle*, is singled out in the story, "The Raid" in *The Long Valley*, and echoes in Casy in *The Grapes of Wrath*. As near as Steinbeck comes to an answer is Casy's quoting of the "fella in the jail house":

> You didn't do it for fun no way. Doin' it 'cause you have to. 'Cause it's you. . . . Anyways you do what you can . . . the on'y thing you got to look at is that ever' time they's a little step fo'ward, she may slip back a little, but she never slips clear back. You can prove that, an' that makes the whole thing right. An' that means they wasn't no waste even if it seemed like they was.

But there is also the note of doubt, of conflict between faith and skepticism. The doctor of *In Dubious Battle*, who will give everything he's got to help the strikers but who has no real faith in the cause, is one side of the conflict in Steinbeck himself. Interestingly enough, Steinbeck never seems to question the adequacy of the Marxian analysis—he accepts class war and inevitable revolution as the way things are and will be. His doubts go deeper, really; they are doubts as to the nature of mankind itself. The first party for "Doc" in *Cannery Row* is a symbolic dramatization of a feeling that runs all through Steinbeck's writing. Mack and the boys give a surprise party for Doc to show him how much they like him. But Doc doesn't get home when they think he will and the party "she got out of hand." Doc finally gets back to his devastated laboratory and Mack tells him:

> It don't do no good to say I'm sorry. I been sorry all my life. This ain't no new thing. It's always like this. . . . I had a wife. Same thing. Ever'thing I done turned sour. . . . If I done a good thing it got poi-

soned up some way. If I give her a present they was something wrong with it. She only got hurt from me.

There are many variations of this "every man kills the thing he loves" theme in Steinbeck. *Of Mice and Men* is little else. The doctor of *In Dubious Battle* says:

> There aren't any beginnings. Nor any ends. It seems to me that man has engaged in a blind and fearful struggle out of a past he can't remember, into a future he can't foresee nor understand. And man has met and defeated every obstacle, every enemy except one. He cannot win over himself. How mankind hates itself. . . . We fight ourselves and we can only win by killing every man.

I would suggest that both Steinbeck's acceptance of Marxian dogma as accurate prophecy and his distrust of humanity are outcomes of his California background, and that a broader perspective on American life offers evidence of another sort.

The historical analysis of Marxism calls for a steady intensification of class warfare, in which the lines are drawn more and more sharply, compromise and gradualism become less and less possible, until the stand-up-and-slug-it-out day of revolution comes. After which all things will be different. A lot of our most able writers have accepted this prognosis for America at one time or another. Often, perhaps, they have done so because its drive-to-a-showdown jibes so neatly with their own personality unbalance. The mixture of social revolt, idealism, spiritual homelessness, and unresolved tension that has been so characteristic of serious American writing since the first World War demands an explosive crisis to bring itself to a tolerable, if only temporary, equilibrium. But it has been an outstanding quality of American evolution since the Civil War that the march of events has by-passed every crisis and that the great showdown never comes. Time and again things have built up to the boiling point, only to subside as new developments broke up rigidities and diverted energies. The revolutionary effects of mass production and technology, and the tremendous reshuffling caused by two world wars seem to have been the factors most responsible.

This by-passing of crises has not been so characteristic of California history as of the country as a whole but I think it can be shown that it has happened there as well—and in one of the worst crisis-spots. When *The Grapes of Wrath* and *Factories in the Field* appeared it looked as if nothing could avert an all-out battle between revolution and fascism in California's great valleys. Conditions were intolerable, tensions were incandescent, and both sides seemed ready and eager to fight it out. But the war raised food prices, created a labor shortage, and brought badly-needed industrial ballast to the California economy. The situation may, of course, come to a new boiling point in the future. But the larger picture has changed and goes on changing and there is no showdown.

This blind dynamic of American growth—this refusal to harden into a static shape—is one of the great and hopeful things about this country. It doesn't make things easier for the writers, however, and may be one reason for the short creative life-expectancy of the best of them.

III

American civilization, with its extraordinary melting pot and its many regional variations, is a risky thing to generalize about. But there is certainly a central core of character, custom, and belief that has been the dominant national strain. Americans, by and large, tend to be optimistic, pragmatic, outgoing, gregarious, energetic, and moral. We believe in the home, in education and self-betterment, in religion and moral responsibility; we take eagerly to the new in technics and distrust the new in social and political institutions; we rate character above intelligence and horse sense above theory. Wherever we have lived for several generations without too much upheaval, these characteristics have become part of a way of life, or a social tradition, or whatever you care to call it, which has a life and strength of its own and shapes the individuals who grow up in it. In spite of variations and breakdowns, this condition of settled society has, for better or worse, made us what we are. It is what we have to start with and to go on from.

American society, in this sense, is probably strongest in the Middle West. It is noticeably weaker in the Far West and especially weak in Steinbeck's country. There are obvious reasons for this: it is only a hundred years since California was largely unmapped, undeveloped, and very thinly inhabited. It is still subject to upheaval by a great wave of immigrants every twenty years or so and a steady inflow between waves. In the years when it was absorbing the first great comings of Americans, the rigors of the journey, the isolation of the section from the country back East, and the strangeness of the life and the countryside all tended to dilute and efface the habits and culture that the immigrants brought with them. For the most part, the existence of a settled and mature society is exceptional and the typical state of affairs is a condition of formless flux or of unbalanced extremes.

Furthermore, this condition isn't merely a matter of a time lag. The settled American society that we talk about is itself in process of change —so abrupt a series of changes that we can almost say that it is breaking up around our ears. It has lost much of its relevance to the conditions of modern life and it is by no means certain that it will be adaptable enough to make a transition of any smoothness to meet new needs. Since the Far West experienced this pattern of social integration only partially when it was in its prime in the East, now that it is falling apart we can hardly expect to see much more growth of it. Most of the country's intellectuals—which includes the writers—have been cheering on this social breakup for the last twenty-five years. They have carried on a running battle against the restrictions and compulsions of settled society, usually in the name of individual freedom. One of the major differences between the East and the West is that in the East this anti-society drive has about run its course, while in the West it seems to be just getting under way.

The intellectuals of the East have learned that freedom is more complicated than getting away from family and neighbors, or from "the system." The "freedom from" battle has become a rout and such questions as "freedom for what?" and "How do we escape this freedom that we cannot handle?" are the order of the day. It is being discovered—the hard way—that a settled society offers securities and supports without which few individuals can remain integrated.

The Far West, however, is kicking up its heels in an individualistic binge very much like the bohemianism of Greenwich Village of the '20's. The little magazines are feeling their cultural oats in what would look like a real renaissance if we hadn't seen the same thing and its aftermath in the East. In Steinbeck's home country, there are more than a few devotees of what a recent *Harper's* article calls "The New Cult of Sex and Anarchism."

Steinbeck has always had a keen awareness of the importance of the social cement of common purpose as far as small groups are concerned. That he has never extended it to society as a whole is probably because there has been little visible reason in California life for considering such a projection anything but fanciful. And the Marxist slant on things, of course, has its poetic summation in Dos Passos' "All right we are two nations." As Mac puts it in *In Dubious Battle:*

> Men always like to work together. There's a hunger in men to work together. Do you know that ten men can lift nearly twelve times as big a load as one can? It only takes a little spark to get them going. Most of the time they're suspicious, because every time someone gets 'em working in a group the profit of their work is taken away from them; but wait till they get working for themselves.

Lord knows we have come close enough to being two nations often enough (or three, or four, or no nation at all). But always the change

and the reshuffling have gone on and when the chips were down we
have been one nation. On the other hand, most parts of California have
never been places to get any such feeling and if we don't find it in
Steinbeck there's no reason we should expect to. Steinbeck's California
contains little fragments of the American character, detached from the
whole and dragged over the mountains and the desert with the other
immigrant baggage and overdeveloped by the golden sun and the ache
of homesickness. The big shots and vigilantes of Salinas show one sort
of overdeveloped fragmentation; the fierce Christers of Pacific Grove
another. Most of the distribution curves between the mountains and
the sea are violently skewed.

Which brings us to another one of Steinbeck's favorite black and
white oversimplifications; as he puts it in *Sea of Cortez:*

> the so-called and considered good qualities are invariably concomitants
> of failure, while the bad ones are the cornerstones of success.

The same idea is somewhat better expressed by Doc in *Cannery Row:*

> The things we admire in men, kindness and generosity, openness,
> honesty, understanding and feeling are the concomitants of failure in
> our system. And those traits we detest, sharpness, greed, acquisitiveness,
> meanness, egotism and self-interest are the traits of success.

The duplication shows how fond Steinbeck is of this idea. It may be a
reasonable reaction to the Salinas growers and their flunkies, but as an
unqualified statement about American life it is absurd. It probably had
considerable truth in it in the "Robber Baron" period after the Civil
War, when the relatively simple and self-sufficient village economies of
agriculture, handcraft and trade were disappearing before the thrust of
big business combinations. There were huge rewards then in financial
piracy and mercantile buccaneering. But the very process that has
changed the typical American career from individual enterprise to
wage- or salary-earning for one bureaucracy or another has brought
about a lessening of acquisitive pressures. It is still true enough that a
man who puts money-getting at the top of his agenda will usually
accumulate more of it than a man who doesn't. But unless it is "failure"
not to be a millionaire, there are plenty of fields of activity in which the
generous virtues are no handicap. In fact, one of the most characteristic
"types" in modern life is the go-getter who never quite makes the grade,
is always busily outfoxing himself, and affords endless amusement to
his more relaxed colleagues.

This key idea of Steinbeck's is, I submit, a California aberration.

That it is a key idea is pretty obvious. It crops out in the way he hates his middle-class characters. (There are no capitalist giants in Steinbeck's writing—except for occasional beautifully scatological references to Hearst.) His middle-class men are mean, pudgy creatures, blinking pinkly through spectacles, the slaves of their small anxieties and their neurotic and sexually frigid wives. The lunch-wagon woman in *The Grapes of Wrath* dismisses them collectively as "shitheels." (It should be remembered too that California is perpetually full of tourists, and that to the gawked-at native the American Tourist is not a sympathetic type.)

This hatred of the genteel, the solvent, and the fancypants is, of course, the other side of the sentimentalizing of the paisanos of *Tortilla Flat* and the bums of *Cannery Row*. Which is one of the things Steinbeck is famous for. It doesn't require too complicated an explanation. Everything Steinbeck has written shows the urgency of his need to "bite deeply into living." His environment, however, showed him only a mean, life-denying greed and respectability firmly in the saddle. He tried for a while to find answers and a spiritual home for himself in the dream of social revolution. But the Revolution has its own austerities and narrow righteousness and there was always his deep distrust of humanity's capacity for surpassing itself. But when he had rejected Man as Success and Man as Citizen, and couldn't quite accept Man as Reformer or Revolutionary, what was left? Well, there was Man as Animal, and to be satisfactory he had to be without any other pretensions. Hence Danny and Pilon and Mack and the boys. It is noticeable, however, that even Steinbeck cannot sustain the celebration of Man as Animal for long without slipping into a semi-lyrical sort of fantasy-prose in which the complexities and consequences of real life are lost in the happy fog of a literary mood. It is undeniable that an important section of the traditional American character got itself badly warped by trying to ignore Man as Animal. Writers of our generation have supplied a corrective reaction which was certainly needed but has just as certainly been a little more than adequate.

There is one of Steinbeck's books, however, in which his tensions and conflicts seem to have reached an affirmative equilibrium. The people in *The Grapes of Wrath* are whole (Man as Man, for a change); they live with the natural balance of biological, social, and spiritual needs and assertions that makes the human being. There is no anxiety over leftist means and ends, no agonizing about the self-hate in man. For all its sprawling asides and extravagances, *The Grapes of Wrath* is a big book, a great book, and one of maybe two or three American novels in a class with *Huckleberry Finn*.

I think it is significant that *The Grapes of Wrath* is about folks who have the cement of settled society in them. For all their exile and destitution, they are a *people*, and they act as a people to an extent that is unique in Steinbeck's writing and in the California life which he knows best. I suggest that it is this social integration—which Steinbeck has felt and reproduced amazingly well—which is the greatness of this book. Further, this social integration provides the answers to the dichotomies and oversimplifications which torture so much of Steinbeck's other writing. Against it as a frame of reference, being a responsible citizen and a jobholder becomes merely playing an honest and dignified part in the common life—rather than the mean abdication of freedom and vitality that is implied by the glorification of Mack and the boys. The tortured obsession about men killing the thing they love shows up as the self-pitying indulgence of a romantic individualism gone sour. The answer to it is in Ma Joad's advice to Uncle John about his sins:

> Tell 'em to God. Don' go burdenin' other people with your sins. That ain't decent. . . . Go down the river an' stick your head under an' whisper 'em in the stream.

The pattern of life that Steinbeck found in the Joads—their strength as a people—has been undergoing the attrition of the city and the machine for several generations. Much of it is gone for good and much that remains is moribund. No amount of nostalgic yearning is going to regenerate it. But the lesson we are painfully learning today is that some sort of settled society—with habits, folkways, common aspirations, sanctions and taboos—is an essential part of human life. The rampant individualism of the frontier days is not only too irresponsibly anarchic for modern economic society but it fails to provide the social fabric that supports individual sanity. A kind of dynamic balance between society and the individual is what we need and the danger of too much individualism is that it can create a reaction to the other extreme. It should go without saying that the social integration we need will have to be relevant to today's conditions of living. But that is a long way from saying (as so much of our literature has said for the last twenty-five years) that all society, or all "capitalist" society, is rotten to the core and must be swept into the ashcan of history before things can be better.

IV

There is a coldness about *The Wayward Bus* that reviewers have variously found unpleasant and a welcome change from previous emotional lushness. The book has few "sympathetic" characters and these are chiefly distinguished by a sort of hard, despairing honesty. One of the best reviews that have appeared[1] points out that the key to Steinbeck's approach in this book is explicitly stated in *Sea of Cortez*.

In a rough way, *Sea of Cortez* occupies about the same place in Steinbeck's work that *Death in the Afternoon* does in Hemingway's. Both are relaxed musings about life and art, written as breathers between novels. There is also something of a parallel in Hemingway tying *Death in the Afternoon* to the lore of the bull ring while Steinbeck uses a cruise to the Gulf of California—to collect tide-pool invertebrates—as his framework. The ritual violence of bull-fighting was Hemingway's peacetime laboratory for the study of death and pure emotion. Marine biology has had a similar fascination for Steinbeck.

The part of *Sea of Cortez* that concerns us here is Steinbeck's speculation about what he calls "nonteleological thinking." This seems to be a mixture of philosophical relativism, the rigorous refusal of the scientist to be dogmatic about hypotheses, and a sort of moral fatalism. To quote:

> What we personally conceive by the term "teleological thinking" . . . is most frequently associated with the evaluation of causes and effects, the purposiveness of events. This kind of thinking considers changes and cures—what "should be" in the terms of an end pattern (which is often a subjective or an anthropomorphic projection); it presumes the bettering of conditions, often, unfortunately, without achieving more than a most superficial understanding of those conditions. In their sometimes intolerant refusal to face facts as they are, teleological notions may substitute a fierce but ineffectual attempt to change conditions which are assumed to be undesirable, in place of the understanding-acceptance which would pave the way for a more sensible attempt at any change which may still be indicated.
>
> Nonteleological ideas derive through "is" thinking, associated with natural selection as Darwin seems to have understood it. They imply depth, fundamentalism, and clarity—seeing beyond traditional or personal projection. They consider events as outgrowths and expressions rather than as results; conscious acceptance as a desideratum, and certainly as an all-important prerequisite. Nonteleological thinking concerns itself primarily not with what should be, or could be, or might be, but rather with what actually "is"—attempting at most to answer the already sufficiently difficult questions *what* or *how*, instead of *why*.

This is fairly heavy going but it is clear enough that Steinbeck is objecting to wishfulness obscuring facts, and understanding being limited by preconceived notions of what should be the case. No one can quarrel with this. There is a strong implication, however, that to think in terms of "why" and "what might be" is not only risky but downright sinful. This implication is even stronger in the following:

> It is amazing how the strictures of the old teleologies infect our observation, causal thinking warped by hope. It was said earlier that hope is a diagnostic human trait, and this simple cortex symptom seems to be a prime factor in our inspection of our universe. For hope implies a change from a present bad condition to a future better one. The slave hopes for freedom, the weary man for rest, the hungry for food. And the feeders of hope, economic and religious, have from these simple strivings of dissatisfaction managed to create a world picture which is very hard to escape. Man grows toward perfection; animals grow toward man; bad grows toward good; and down toward up, until our little mechanism, hope, achieved in ourselves probably to cushion the shock of thought, manages to warp our whole world. . . . To most men the most hateful statement possible is, "A *thing is because it is.*" Even those who have managed to drop the leading-strings of a Sunday-school deity are still led by the unconscious teleology of their developed trick.

It should be apparent from these quotations why I said that Steinbeck's "is-thinking" has a large content of moral fatalism. If the height of wisdom is "things are because they are" and thinking in terms of cause and effect and of changes for the better are Sunday-school fatuities, we come to an attitude towards life remarkably oriental and passive. It is not the attitude with which we normally contemplate our house catching fire—nor our world catching fire. For that matter, it is not an attitude which would lead anyone to build a house in the first place—or to do any other creative job based on "what might be." Nor will observation which shuns the "why" of things see very much in the long run. Its only logical end is pure mysticism—a search for objectivity winding up in the absolute subjective.

This line of thought is not new in Steinbeck's writing. The doctor of *In Dubious Battle* is something of a nonteleological thinker. But previously it had been a sort of intriguing sideline. In *Sea of Cortez* it becomes the main channel and in both *Cannery Row* and *The Wayward Bus* Steinbeck is obviously trying to see what he can with nonteleological literature. I can only speculate as to why his slant on things took this particular turn at this particular time. But the *Sea of Cortez* cruise took place in the spring and early summer of 1940, when the Nazis were overrunning France and the Low Countries. Steinbeck's attitude to the war then was that it was:

> a war . . . which no one wants to fight, in which no one can see a

gain—a zombie war of sleep-walkers which nevertheless goes on out of all control of intelligence.

So he collected his invertebrates and watched the teeming tide-pool struggle of eat-and-be-eaten and wondered whether a school of fish mightn't properly be considered an organism in its own right (like "group-man"), and he thought further about war and men:

> When it seems that men may be kinder to men, that wars may not come again, we completely ignore the nature of our species. If we used the same smug observation on ourselves that we do on hermit crabs we would be forced to say, with the information at hand, "It is one diagnostic trait of Homo Sapiens that groups of individuals are periodically infected with a feverish nervousness which causes the individual to turn on and destroy, not only his own kind, but the works of his own kind. It is not known whether this be caused by a virus, some airborne spore, or whether it be a species reaction to some meteorological stimulus as yet undetermined." Hope, which is another species diagnostic trait—the hope that this may not always be—does not in the least change the observable past and present. When two crayfish meet, they usually fight. One would say that perhaps they might not at a future time, but without some mutation it is not likely that they will lose this trait. And perhaps our species is not likely to forgo war without some psychic mutation which at present, at least, does not seem imminent. And if one places the blame for killing and destroying on economic insecurity, on inequality, on injustice, he is simply stating the proposition in another way. We have what we are. . . . So far the murder trait of our species is as regular and observable as our various sexual habits.

It seems likely that the war was, for Steinbeck, overwhelming evidence of the irrational, self-destructive drive of the human race; that it killed—or at least submerged—the faith and buoyancy that filled The Grapes of Wrath; and that it drove him back on the toughminded nihilism of "is-thinking." As noted above, the "golden mean" and the "middle way" are no part of Steinbeck's temperament. When he abandons Man as Man for Man as Biological Freak he goes all the way. He jettisons not only hope and progress but cause and effect as well. Which leaves the vertebrates of The Wayward Bus, animated by the simpler forms of protoplasmic irritability, and deprived of even a biological dignity by their silly pretensions that they are up to something noble.

Steinbeck's current "is-thinking" has a lot in common with the search for verbal simplicity and for the hard, clean reality of the physically tangible that characterized Hemingway's writing after the previous war. Both are spiritually weary, sick of abstractions and ideologies, and both find comfort in the evocation of what can be seen, felt, heard, smelled, and tasted. In Steinbeck, this retreat to physical reality takes the form of descriptions of the countryside and its wild life and a meticulous reporting of physical action—especially skilled action. In *The Wayward Bus* some of his reporting is a repetition of what he has done better elsewhere. The repairs to the bus that open the book are of a piece with the burnt-out connecting rod bearing in *The Grapes of Wrath* (including the same superstition about skinned knuckles). The Chicoy lunchroom also has a prototype in the previous book and Mrs. Pritchard had a preview in the story called "The White Quail." But much of the book is fresh and new and if Steinbeck's faith in mankind is at a low ebb, his skill as a writer is becoming keener. There is more precision and control in the prose and the structure than in his other books and it ends with little of the melodrama that has wound up most of his previous novels.

The Wayward Bus is, if less *intensely* regional than some of his other books, the most broadly descriptive of California's countryside and the queer assortments of people encountered there. The accidental grouping of a collection of "characters" in a situation which "brings them out" is more than a novelist's trick. It is itself fairly typical of California life. It symbolizes the endless coming and going, the fragmentary social integration, and the human diversity of the region. In fact, it would be quite plausible to say that Steinbeck's "is-thinking" can be explained without reference to any background of disillusionment in revolution and mankind—that it is simply the way life looks to a thoughtful Californian who has outgrown his youth.

V

In many ways the American West might be a good place in which to see our future cultural pattern shape up. The lack of settled society which we dwelt on above may facilitate new cultural fusions and social forms. Just as America itself diverged widely from its European sources because it encountered the first impact of the industrial revolution with less of a cushioning of habit and institutional inertia than the old country, so the West may adapt to the continuing thrust of change more directly and flexibly than the more static East. There are many rigid extremes in the West, of course, and California in particular has many people who come out only to die, or to postpone dying. But the general configuration is one of flux and change and it is a region to which many come in the hope of some sort of vaguely splendid fulfillment. There is still something of the selective process which colonized and settled

America at work and California is a setting in which an inchoate mass of aspiration and restless hope will have to either find new patterns of living or drown itself in the Pacific.

One important area where the West seems to show a hopeful flexibility is in the relation between the intellectual and the common man. In most of the country the cleavages between these two classes is one of the sharpest and most disastrous gulfs in American life. The intellectual is a specialist in abstract thought. He typically works from the general to the particular (and sometimes never arrives at the particular at all) and is articulate to a point where he is often unable to perceive any reality for which he lacks a word. The nonintellectual, on the other hand, deals with particulars almost exclusively. He ordinarily uses abstractions and generalizations only in an uncritical, proverbial way that he has picked up from someone else. For the most part, he is incapable of abstract thinking—being unable to use words precisely or to perceive the niceties of logic. But the intellectual so overvalues words and logic, and generalizes from such a narrow base of experience that his conclusions are often irrelevant and sometimes absurd. More serious, he is usually cut off by his overspecialized work and personality from any broad, functional give-and-take with society as a whole. Consequently, his shortcomings of understanding tend to be self-reinforcing and he becomes more and more isolated culturally from everyone but other intellectuals. Society, meanwhile, is deprived of effective intellectual leadership from its most talented (in this direction) members and becomes ripe for totalitarian manipulation.

This vicious circle is of special importance to writers because they are, in the nature of things, intellectuals, and their job is to give meaning and relationship to the raw stuff of life. And since most readers, critics, and publishers of serious literature are also intellectuals, and since a successful writer usually moves completely out of his social and cultural origins into the rarefied air of the literary world, the unhappy social and individual effects of intellectual isolationism are all too characteristic of contemporary literature.

All of this has to do with Steinbeck because—almost alone among important contemporaries—he seems to have no hankering for the literary life or the isolationism of a typical intellectual. The people he writes about are primarily nonintellectuals and his acquaintance with such people and his intuitive feeling for what makes them tick are probably his greatest strength as a writer. He presumably classifies the typical professional intellectual along with the other middle-class "shit-heels" as inferior and inadequate human beings. His best field is the subrational and the inarticulate and many of the reviews of *The Way-*

ward Bus show that this anti-intellectualism produces confusion among the critics who are called upon to classify and evaluate his writing.

The brilliant Mr. Barzun, for instance, discussed the book in a recent issue of *Harper's* with a mixture of disdain and incomprehension. The characters of *The Wayward Bus* meet no vital counterparts in Mr. Barzun's frame of reference—exceptionally qualified though he is in the worlds of learning and abstractions—and he could only blather about Steinbeck's using the naturalist tradition without bothering to understand it. On the other hand, there have been some reviews of the book which overpraised it with the maudlin hysteria of someone's maiden aunt trying to live dangerously.

It is typical of Steinbeck—and it is typical of California—that he can study biology and speculate about teleology without losing his interest in, or fellowship with, Mack and the boys. His biggest contribution as a writer may turn out to have been the exploration and colonization of the no-man's-land between intellectual and nonintellectual, rational and subrational. Similarly, the ferment of California may come to play a similar part in the future of America.

As we have suggested above, Steinbeck's *Sea of Cortez* musings suggest that he has grown weary of trying to make responsible sense of life and is experimenting with "nonteleological" reporting. But even the most arid stretches of *The Wayward Bus* pretty well demonstrate the impossibility of writing in a state of abstract omniscience from which cause and effect and good and bad have been filtered. Even among the dip-net heterogeneity of this novel's catch, he obviously likes some and dislikes others, and he finds it necessary to explain how they got the way they are. Both Steinbeck and California are relatively young. I suggest that both may have their most creative days ahead of them. And that it would be intelligent to study them in relation to each other.

1. By Toni Jackson Ricketts in *What's Doing On The Monterey Peninsula*, a small California magazine which began as tourist bait and has matured in a little over a year into a first-rate regional publication. She knows Steinbeck well and her statements about his intent can be accepted as sound. [See p. 275, below.]

152

Stanley Edgar Hyman

SOME NOTES
ON JOHN STEINBECK

THE HEATED CONTROVERSY over John Steinbeck's *The Moon Is Down*, which has been raging in the press since the book's publication in March, has been concerned almost wholly with misleading or extraneous issues. Reviewers and letter writers have centered their discussion around two general questions: Is the book true to Nazi conquest? and, Does it aid in the anti-Nazi struggle? Obviously, no book is "true" to anything as large and many-faceted as Nazi conquest; the only question that can be asked is what truth or part of truth does Steinbeck present, and why. As critics of the book admitted, men like Lanser and Tonder, the doubting Nazi and the neurotic Nazi respectively, undoubtedly exist in the German Army (Ambassador Dodd describes several Lansers in his book, someone pointed out) but what percentage of the army can they be said to represent? Tonder, for example, although described by Steinbeck as "trained in the politics of the day, believing the great new system invented by a genius so great that he never bothered to verify its results," is so far unaffected by the Aryan ideal as to (1) love dark women, (2) quote Heine, and (3) be completely unimpressed by Goebbels' releases.

Steinbeck's "truth" about the Nazis would seem to be a "truth" about a small group of German army officers (privates are hardly mentioned in the book, and the action revolves wholly around a group of five officers), and of that group only the tiny percentage of unconvinced, hysterical, passive, or desperate officers. These people are probably all "true"; that is, their parallels exist. But why is Steinbeck interested in them? The other question, whether the book aids in the fight against the Axis, is so complicated, depends so much on the

STANLEY EDGAR HYMAN teaches literature at Bennington College, has been on the editorial staff of The New Republic, and is a staff writer for The New Yorker. In The Armed Vision, a book on the methods of modern literary criticism, he published the criticism of critics Steinbeck once expressed a hope for. "Some Notes on John Steinbeck," reprinted here by permission of Mr. Hyman and The Antioch Review, appeared in June, 1942, in that quarterly.

answer to the first question, on a knowledge of just what literature helps the war and how, and on the answer to a really tough question, whether Steinbeck is concerned with aiding in the fight against the Axis, that it is not a thing to be answered off the top of any letter-writer's head.

If those are the wrong questions, what are the right questions? First, of course, the two old standbys: What does the book actually deal with? and, Why was it written? The answers to them are in the body of Steinbeck's other work, in the nature of his preoccupations and interests, and are most readily available in his recent *Sea of Cortez*, which was a direct and invaluable nonfiction statement of his beliefs and ideas, at least at that time. One thing *The Moon Is Down* is not about, it may be said definitely, is the German conquest of Norway. The conquerors do seem to be German, although the words "German," "Nazi," and "Hitler" are never used.[1] That is, they wear gray helmets, they are at war with England, and they fought in Belgium and France twenty-odd years before.

Steinbeck, however, has taken great pains (which seem to have been wasted) to make the invaded country not Norway: it is distinctly stated as having been invaded during the conflict between Germany and the Soviet Union, that is, after June, 1941, and in the autumn (Norway was invaded in the spring, April of 1940, more than a year before the attack on Russia). What we know about the country is that it is a cold northern land, it is fairly close to England (men escape and row to England in boats), it is possibly Scandinavian (its citizens have such names as Orden, Morden, Winter, Corell) and that it is invaded in the autumn of 1941 or any autumn after that. Since no country even remotely answering to that description has been invaded since the attack on Russia, the book is obviously describing a hypothetical attack in the future, on Sweden or on some nonexistent northern country. The mythical nature of this country is made more manifest, as Isidor Schneider pointed out in another connection, by the fact that this strange seaport town in this strange country seems to have no political parties, no trade unions, and no organizations of any kind, either democratic, fifth-column, or neutral.

A major clue to the meaning of *The Moon Is Down* is its form. From internal evidence it seems to have been written first as a play, and then rewritten as a novel, with each of the eight scenes made into a chapter. The directions are obviously directions for stage business, the setting is stage setting, and the dialogue is clearly written as stage dialogue. The easiest way to demonstrate this is to take any chapter ending, where the dramatic structure becomes particularly obvious in terms of Curtain, and change all past tenses to the theatrical present. Here, for example, is the ending of Chapter Two, with nothing altered but tense, punctuation, and the omission of the word "says":

> Lanser (standing up slowly and speaking as though to himself): So it starts again. . . .
> Prackle: What do you say, sir?
> Lanser: Nothing. . . . (He turns to Loft) Please give my compliments to Mayor Orden. . . .
> (Major Hunter looks up, dries his inking-pen carefully, and puts it away in a velvet-lined box.)

It needs nothing but the notation "Slow Curtain" after it.

It is worth noting that *Of Mice and Men* was also a short playlike novel with what the publisher's blurb calls "the disciplines of time and place" (all its action takes place from dusk Thursday to dusk Sunday) although, unlike *The Moon Is Down* it appears to have been first written in novel form and then dramatized. The fact that at two definite places in Steinbeck's work his material seems to have worked itself naturally into a dramatic form is important, and in this connection it is interesting to observe Thomas Mann's explanation for his use of the play form in "Royal Highness." He says in his preface to *Stories of Three Decades*:

> I was driven to the dialogue form, I suppose, on account of the dialectical matter of this study of the Renaissance; the historical setting only serves as pretext for an exposition of opposed elements in my own nature.

It is not hard to demonstrate that Steinbeck was "driven" to the dialogue form by a necessity similar to Mann's, the conflict between two points of view in himself and his work having grown so sharp as to require direct pro and con talking, and that his two plays are consequently pivotal points in his work, expressing that conflict most sharply, and, incidentally, each signalizing a marked break or change of direction.

Another pertinent problem about *The Moon Is Down* is its rather strange title. Stylistically, it is right in the tradition of Steinbeck titles (two strongly accented words), but in terms of meaning, it seems less significant than either some flat and transparent naming, like *The Grapes of Wrath*, or a place name like *Sea of Cortez*. Reviewers have been quick to point out that the moon hardly enters the book (actually it is mentioned twice, both times, amusingly enough, as throwing little light, and neither time very significantly). James Thurber, in his sharp and discerning review in *The New Republic*, claimed that the title is too ethereal, that a war story should have a title like *Guts in the Mud*, and that Steinbeck may have started from this dreamy title and so found himself writing what Thurber refers to as "Robert Nathan's best book."[2]

Actually the title is a quotation from Shakespeare, as the dramatic critics discovered after a decent interval. It is in the second line in Act II, Scene 1, of *Macbeth*, and is spoken by Fleance to Banquo, in reply to his question: "How goes the night, boy?" The whole line is "The moon is down; I have not heard the clock." It would thus mean that the night is dark, and, considering Macbeth's subsequent murder of Duncan, ominous. The only significant line in the passage is Fleance's next speech, which tells Banquo, with unconscious meaningfulness, that it is later than he thinks. All of which is only mildly impressive, since the relationship between Macbeth's murder of his king and the Nazi occupation of a small seacoast town is cloudier than seems necessary, and it would seem to be worth while to look for other meaning for the title in the rest of Steinbeck's work.[3]

Actually, the symbol of the moon means a great deal to John Steinbeck, and it runs through his work like a recurrent theme. In *Cup of Gold*, Steinbeck's first novel, he equates it with unattainable ambition of a sexual nature. Merlin, the old wise man of Wales, gives his wisdom to Henry Morgan:

> "I think I understand," he said softly. "You are a little boy. You want the moon to drink from as a golden cup; and so, it is very likely that you will become a great man—if only you remain a little child. All the world's great have been little boys who wanted the moon; running and climbing, they sometimes caught a firefly. But if one grows to a man's mind, that mind must see that it cannot have the moon and would not want it if it could—and so, it catches no fireflies."

Later, "the golden cup" that the moon is to Morgan becomes the town he sacks, Panama (which the Spaniards call the Cup of Gold), and specifically a very desirable woman in it. Thus the moon and the golden cup (the symbol of his taking Panama is the capture of a literal golden chalice) both represent the Grail, a rather traditional female sex symbol. Later in the book, the moon is used as a setting for an attempted seduction of Morgan, and another character in the book tells him of a very interesting conjecture about how the inhabitants of the moon might have very unusual *necks* (this neck-moon business turns up later).

In *To a God Unknown*, Steinbeck's early mystic novel, the moon is frankly described as a female sex symbol (a golden moon is pierced, apparently by a sharp pine tree, which is withdrawn as the moon arises) and is then equated with fertility when it is used as a sign for rain in a time of drought, and when a pregnant woman rides out to a mystic grotto of fertility on a horse named Moonlight. It is sterility as well as fertility, however, and one of the characters, who has been obsessed with nightmares of "a bright place that is dry and dead" where people come out of holes and pull off his arms and legs, commits suicide (hanging himself by the neck) when he gets his first look through a telescope and finds that the moon is the dry place of his dreams. Incidentally, To a God Unknown is the only one of Steinbeck's books where I was able to find the specific sentence, "The moon is down." It occurs, very significantly, when a magic spring, the only water remaining in a land of drought, is finally running dry, and one character gives the protagonist Joseph bulletins about the moon to match his bulletins about the state of the spring ("The moon is going down," "The moon is down," and so on).

In Tortilla Flat, the moon dripping blood is one of the legendary signs celebrating the death of Danny, the superhuman and lecherous hero. In In Dubious Battle, the Doctor says: "You say I don't believe in the cause [Communism]. That's like not believing in the moon." In the short story "The Murder" in The Long Valley, the moon is identified with a wife's adultery, and finally lights her in bed with her lover before her husband's eyes. In The Grapes of Wrath, the moon is identified with sexual passion when it drives a pair of lovers to embrace, and it later shines on Tom Joad when he goes out to meet Casy, witness and avenge Casy's death, and assume Casy's personality and mission. In Sea of Cortez, Steinbeck states explicitly his theory that the moon, next to the sea, is the strongest "racial" or mystic memory in us, with the lunar rhythm deeply rooted in our unconscious, and that "all physiological processes might be shown to be influenced by the tides" (or moon), as is menstruation and, in some animals, the phenomenon of sexual heat.

It should be apparent from this evidence that the moon has a very special significance for Steinbeck, that it associates for him a whole context of factors: women, the unattainable, the Grail, fertility and sterility at once (in To a God Unknown they are both aspects of the same thing, the mystic female Earth symbol which is central to the book), mystic factors of racial unconsciousness, the relationship between Tom and Casy, and a Cause. Thus, when Steinbeck calls his book The Moon Is Down he means less that Duncan is about to be murdered, that it is dark and later than you think, than that his personal moon is down, the moon of Henry Morgan's romantic individualism, of the mystic and unattainable Woman-Grail, of a Cause or Mission, and of a whole past nexus of preoccupations.[4]

The basic problem in Steinbeck's work is the familiar one of the individual (that is, John Steinbeck as artist) in relation to society. In that sense, all his books are social. Around this problem, the books move in two marked trends, from extreme unsociality or individualism to a height of sociality, and then back again to individualism with a new name, this time scientific isolation. The first pivotal point is the play-novel *Of Mice and Men* and the second pivotal point is the play-novel *The Moon Is Down*.

In Steinbeck's first general "period," up to *Of Mice and Men*, the growing sociality is expressed by a constant search for "solutions," each one of which is tried, rejected, and symbolically killed off. *Cup of Gold*, a characteristic first novel about a bold bad pirate, experiments with the completely individualistic strivings of Henry Morgan. They fail, and Morgan dies in ironic bourgeois domesticity. *Pastures of Heaven*, the next book, tries the viewpoint that nature and the "natural" life are worth while, and only man is vile. This also fails, and of its two principal exponents, one, the amiable idiot Tularecito is committed to an asylum for the criminal insane, and the other, Junius Maltby, is convinced by well-meaning neighbors that raising his boy in natural freedom is harmful to the child, and is driven back to the city. In *To a God Unknown*, Steinbeck toys with formal religion, pagan rites, and every other supernatural device he can get his hands on, with no greater success. In *Tortilla Flat*, Steinbeck carries his natural man of *The Pastures of Heaven* to an extreme, the completely amoral California *paisanos*, whose activities consist almost entirely of sleeping, drinking, and copulation (one of them states the totality of their desires as "wine, food, love and firewood"). In *In Dubious Battle*, Steinbeck picks up and rejects the solution offered by his concept of the Communist Party.

The general characteristics of this "period" are a growing preoccupation with the common or working people, the milieu moving from the pirates and slave-owners of *Cup of Gold*, through the middle-class landowners of *Pastures of Heaven* and *To a God Unknown*, to the migratory workers of *In Dubious Battle*. Along with this, the individual "hero" declines, from Henry Morgan, who is a proper Nazi führer (several years before the Nazis came to power), through Joseph in *To a God Unknown*, a mystic individualist, to Danny, in *Tortilla Flat*, who leads the *paisanos* in terms of friendship, and Mac and Jim of *In Dubious Battle*, who lead the workers by working alongside them. The strong emphasis on the rejection of solutions in this period comes through most clearly in *To a God Unknown*, where Steinbeck gives each of them a chance to bring rain in a drought: the folk try weather signs, the priest prays, the bartender offers to put out a free barrel of whiskey, and Joseph manipulates his mystic pagan symbols. All fail, and finally only Joseph's sacrificial suicide brings the rain.

Steinbeck's social attitude toward the end of this period, as it jells, seems to be best expressed by the Doctor in *In Dubious Battle*.[5] This doctor is a mystery to the Communists in the book. He works constantly with the Party, he never receives compensation, and he seems to have no faith in their doctrines but to be always ready to help them. Finally he tells Mac and Jim his beliefs. "I want to see the whole picture," he says.

> I want to see. When you cut your finger, and streptococci get in the wound, there's a swelling and a soreness. That swelling is the fight your body puts up, the pain is the battle. You can't tell which one is going to win, but the wound is the first battleground. If the cells lose the first fight the streptococci invade, and the fight goes on up the arm. Mac, these little strikes are like the infection. Something has got into the men; a little fever has started and the lymphatic glands are shooting in reinforcements. I want to see, so I go to the seat of the wound. . . . Group men are always getting some kind of infection. This seems to be a bad one.
>
> I want to see, Mac. I want to watch these group-men, for they seem to me to be a new individual, not at all like single men. A man in a group isn't himself at all; he's a cell in an organism that isn't like him any more than the cells in your body are like you. I want to watch the group and see what it's like. People have said, "Mobs are crazy, you can't tell what they'll do." Why don't people look at mobs not as men, but as mobs? A mob nearly always seems to act reasonably, for a mob.

Later he explains why he helps, in addition to "observing," social "wounds":

> Maybe if I went into a kennel and the dogs were hungry and sick and dirty, and maybe if I could help those dogs, I would. Wouldn't be their fault they were that way. You couldn't say "Those dogs are that way because they haven't any ambition. They don't save their bones. Dogs always are that way." No, you'd try to clean them up and feed them. I guess that's the way it is with me. . . .

His own part, though, is never revolutionary, always stated in terms of "helping." In regard to social change, he has Huxley's dogmatic faith in the identity of means and ends:

> But in my little experience the end is never very different in its nature

from the means. Damn it, Jim, you can only build a violent thing with violence.

At the end of the first "period" is *Of Mice and Men*, the turning point away from sociality and the beginning of the second trend. Thus *Of Mice and Mean*, despite the superficial radicalism of *In Dubious Battle* and *The Grapes of Wrath*, is actually the most social of Steinbeck's books.[6] What has proved misleading about it is that the book functions on two marked levels, the symbolic and the real, and that despite their vastly different directions and meanings, it has proved hard for most readers to keep them separate. On the symbolic level, *Of Mice and Men* is backward-looking, to Steinbeck's rejection of social formulas. Symbolically, it deals with the attempt of George, who seems to be Steinbeck's type for the radical (he is physically much like Mac in *In Dubious Battle*, he constantly emphasizes the sacrificial nature of his leadership, he does the "talking") to lead Lennie, a symbol of the masses, to a utopia. George has the same faith in his ability to lead Lennie that Steinbeck attributes to his radicals leading the masses. ("Jus' tell Lennie what to do and he'll do it if it don't take no figuring. He can't think of nothing to do himself, but he sure can take orders.") But Lennie fails him, he is too strong and untrustworthy, too subject to temptation, and the utopia fails with him.[7]

However, on the real level, the book is forward-looking, into the next period of declining sociality and decreasing faith in the efficacy of change. Realistically, what fails is simply the attempt of a worker, George, to get out of his class into the small owning class. This obvious, foolhardy ambition collapses, the vessel of George's discontent (Lennie), is killed off, and at the end Steinbeck hints at the formation of a new alliance between George and the adjusted worker functioning successfully within his class, Slim. Thus the two meanings of the book look in opposite directions, one disposing of Steinbeck's old preoccupations and the other anticipating the new. This same conflict, like Mann's, is expressed literally in the dialogue-dialectic of the play itself, with one character always saying "You can't get your little farm" and another always answering "I can too." The play structure of the book also facilitates such symbolic effects as George's constant game of *solitaire*, his regular repetition of how without Lennie he could "get along so easy" (he could have a girl, or go to a whorehouse, or get drunk, or eat good food), and the structure whereby all the other characters, each representing a point of view, point out how pleasant it is to "talk" to Lennie because instead of listening he thinks only of his own desires.

Steinbeck's second "period," from *Of Mice and Men* through *Sea of*

Cortez, is a period of declining and, finally, vanishing sociality. The emphasis shifts from social change by active agitation, to change by science and education, to, finally, a scientific isolation. At the same time, the concept of "hero" or leader, that had almost vanished in the earlier period, returns and augments. The difference between the labor leaders of *In Dubious Battle*, suggesters from the ranks, and Casy and Tom Joad in *The Grapes of Wrath*, men who "come" to the workers with a "gospel," makes this evident. The first book prefigures the second in many ways (it has a young worker, Joey, trying to solve his social problem by studying to be a postman, like Connie's utopian correspondence school course; it has a morally good, social murder, Sam's, that anticipates Tom Joad's) so that the differences are particularly significant. The aim of *In Dubious Battle* is expressed in its epigraph from Milton, Satan's lines:

> What though the field be lost?
> All is not lost—the unconquerable will,
> The study of revenge, immortal hate,
> And courage never to submit or yield:
> And what is else not to be overcome?

It relies on a future militancy, an eventual triumph in the future on the basis of the failure of the present—a revolutionary aim. The ideal of *The Grapes* is the utopian New Dealism of the government camp, which may be a different society symbolically, but which is nevertheless achieved realistically by benevolent and paternal government action.

The first book in this new "period" is a collection of short stories, *The Long Valley*, first published in a limited edition called *The Red Pony* (Steinbeck's first, and, fortunately, last attempt at that Edna Millay trick). These stories appear to have been written over a period of years, rather than at the same time (as were the stories that constitute his second book, *The Pastures of Heaven*), and are only bound together loosely by their common setting in the Salinas Valley. One of them, "St. Katy the Virgin," seems to have been published separately in book form as early as 1936. Many of them show evidence of having been written after *Of Mice and Men*, but some, like "The Vigilante" and "The Raid," appear to have been written earlier, about the time of *In Dubious Battle*, and share with it a preoccupation with respectively, the nature of the mob and the nature of radical martyrdom. Their general theme seems to be, as Edmund Wilson has pointed out, an identification of people with animals, and their various "solutions" range over the whole width of Steinbeck's work, from the study of an individual rebellion like Morgan's in *Cup of Gold* ("Flight") to an essay in the scientific isolation Steinbeck reaches in *Sea of Cortez* ("The Snake").

The Grapes of Wrath, Steinbeck's major work of this period, has been so generally misunderstood that critics are still able to howl as every new work fails to repeat what they thought of as its magnificent social vision. Actually, as a careful reading makes clear, the central message of *The Grapes* is an appeal to the owning class to behave, to become enlightened, rather than to the working class to change its own condition. "Hungry men will take your land if you allow them to stay hungry," he says repeatedly; "Marx and Lenin are results, not causes." He summarizes:

> And the great owners, who must lose their land in an upheaval, the great owners with access to history, with eyes to read history and to know the great fact: when property accumulates in too few hands it is taken away. And that companion fact: when a majority of the people are hungry and cold they will take by force what they need. And the little screaming fact that sounds all through history: repression serves only to strengthen and knit the repressed.

He reminds them (as Dollfuss' supporters learned to their sorrow when Hitler moved in, after Dollfuss had broken up the Austrian workers' organizations and killed their leaders) that the workers are their strength, their defense:

> We could have saved you, but you cut us down, and soon you will be cut down and there'll be none of us to save you.

It has been remarked of the book that Ma is the most developed character and Casy probably the most significant, but that Tom automatically becomes the focus of the book, and that it disintegrates at the end when he leaves. The rather simple explanation for this is that Tom expresses Steinbeck himself.[8] With this in mind, it is interesting to note that Tom as a person has two distinct personalities, a public and a private one, the public one a cruel toughness that he displays to strangers (like the truckdriver who gives him his first ride, and the one-eyed junkyard attendant he insults) and the private one a surprising tenderness he displays to his family.[9] (This disposes of the contradiction that bothered some readers of *The Grapes* when it first appeared, the fact that Tom first appears in the book as anything but sympathetic.) It is worth noting that at the end, Tom's much vaunted "conversion" to labor agitation actually amounts to no more than a mystic identification with humanity, a watering-down of Debs's famous declaration of identification with the oppressed, that he will "be" wherever there is starvation, militancy, or any emotion, and that when society is finally altered into a state where "our folks eat the stuff they raise and live in the houses they build," he will be there, too. Just how this new state will be achieved is never mentioned, although Steinbeck's own belief (at the time) seems to be in slow social evolution, expressed by Casy's statement that "ever' time they's a little step fo'ward, she may slip back a little, but she nevers slips clear back."[10]

In "The Forgotten Village," the self-made movie that is Steinbeck's next work after The Grapes of Wrath, even these thin wisps of a "social" solution disappear. "The Village" emphasizes the ignorance of biology and preventive medicine that characterizes a Mexican village, shows how that ignorance may be remedied, implies that the young boy who has gone away to study will come back and remedy it, and quits for the day. It gives no hint of any necessity for social or economic change, no sense of any correlation between educational progress and social progress.

Sea of Cortez (the "leisurely journal of travel and research" written in collaboration with Edward F. Ricketts of the Pacific Biological Laboratories) at the end of this line, is markedly the least social of Steinbeck's books. (It is also, though perhaps for other reasons, his least commercially successful book since he became known.) For Steinbeck, the book is a literal rebirth in which he kills off all his remaining social compulsion and emerges into a perfect scientific vacuum. He himself makes the rebirth nature of the book quite clear, emphasizing constantly that the trip was a dreaming, a sleep, a death. ("We felt [on leaving] a little as though we were dying"; "the . . . water runs out of time very quickly, and a kind of dream sets in"; "answers which if faced realistically, would give rise to . . . a possible rebirth"; "the trip had been like a dreaming sleep.") On the trip, he looks back scornfully at the social ideas he once held, decides that the effect of any collective state would be to eliminate "the swift, the clever, and the intelligent," and substitute stepped-up reproduction ("replacement parts in a shoddy and mediocre machine") for any other achievement; recalls that "once we thought that the bridge between cultures might be through education, public health, good housing, and through political vehicles—democracy, Nazism, communism—but now it seems much simpler than that. . . ." He writes a final elegy to concepts of social progress:

> Perhaps the pattern of struggle is so deeply imprinted in the genes of all life conceived in this benevolently hostile planet that the removal of obstacles automatically atrophies a survival drive. With warm water and abundant food, the animals may retire into a sterile sluggish happiness. This has certainly seemed true in man. . . . If these things are true in a biologic sense, what is to become of the warm fed protected citizenry of the ideal future state?

Once, in *In Dubious Battle*, Steinbeck felt that the man of science (the Doctor) had a responsibility at least to "help," and one of his pet resentments was against the doctor (who appears in *In Dubious Battle* and is mentioned again in the short story "The Raid") who refused to treat men because they were radicals. Once, in *The Grapes of Wrath*, he felt that the scientist had some sort of responsibility to the land, these men who were able to produce fertility and then saw it destroyed, burned, plowed under or thrown into the river, because of the economic system. Now he feels that the scientist's only responsibility (and it cannot be emphasized too strongly that "scientist" in *Sea of Cortez* means Steinbeck) is to the rigors of non-teleological thought and the comforting cynicism of ecological balance, and his only danger is that bogy of bogies, "the emotional content, the belief."

All through the book Steinbeck rationalizes the purpose of the trip ("the impulse which drives a man to poetry will send another man into the tide pools"; "it will enlarge the world picture"; "we search for . . . truth . . . understanding"). Finally he admits that the trip was simply pleasant, that it brought a freedom from the world, from "the fear and fierceness and contagion of war and economic uncertainty." "Here was no service to science, no naming of unknown animals," he admits at the end, "but rather—we simply liked it."[11]

Steinbeck admits that the trip (during the crucial spring of 1940, when Denmark, Norway, Holland, Belgium, and France fell to the Nazis) was a refuge from the war, from everything "modern" (that is, contemporary). He says:

> The world and the war had become remote to us; all the immediacies of our usual lives had slowed up. Far from welcoming a return, we rather resented going back to newspapers and telegrams and business. We had been drifting in some kind of dual world—a parallel realistic world; and the preoccupations of the world we came from, which are considered realistic, were to us filled with mental mirage. Modern economies; war drives; party affiliations and lines; hatreds, political and social and racial, cannot survive in dignity the perspective of distance.

In *Sea of Cortez* Steinbeck admits no slightest stake in the war, no trace of anti-Nazism. The war is simply "a zombie war of sleep-walkers"; war production is "men preparing thoughtlessly, like dead men, to destroy things." He gives his perspective: "Six thousand miles away the great bombs are falling on London and the stars are not moved thereby." He regards war as inevitable to mankind and as natural as eating or reproducing; "a murder trait . . . as regular and observable as our various sexual habits." He tries a mock-serious scientific statement:

It is one diagnostic trait of *homo sapiens* that groups of individuals are periodically infected with a feverish nervousness which causes the individual to turn on and destroy, not only his own kind, but the works of his own kind. It is not known whether this be caused by a virus, some air-borne spore, or whether it be a species reaction to some meteorological stimulus as yet undetermined.

Not only are Steinbeck's views on war in *Sea of Cortez* those of the completely objective observer, with no stake in either side or any issues, but his scientific view of human behavior is not too far from justification of Nazism.[12] Typically he writes:

There is a strange duality in the human which makes for an ethical paradox. We have definitions of good qualities and of bad; not changing things, but generally considered good and bad throughout the ages and throughout the species. Of the good, we think always of wisdom, tolerance, kindliness, generosity, humility; and the qualities of cruelty, greed, self-interest, graspingness, and rapacity are universally considered undesirable. And yet in our structure of society, the so-called and considered good qualities are invariable concomitants of failure, while the bad ones are cornerstones of success. . . . In any animal other than man we would replace the term "good" with "weak survival quotient" and the term "bad" with "strong survival quotient." Thus, man in his thinking or reverie status admires the progression toward extinction, but in the unthinking stimulus which really activates him he tends toward survival.

If *Sea of Cortez* contradicts much of Steinbeck's earlier work, it is in almost shocking contrast to the next book, *The Moon Is Down*. *Sea of Cortez* was published in December of 1941. A few days after publication we went to war. Three months later, *The Moon Is Down* appeared, having all the appearance of what the trade calls a "quickie." *The Moon Is Down* marks a sudden and abrupt return to sociality, to a faith in the mass of people, but this time transcended to a higher level; out of the state of California, out of America (for the first time since the early scenes of his first novel, which are in Wales), out of the class struggle into the international struggle. This, then, is the reason for the play form. Like *Of Mice and Men*, *The Moon Is Down* is a pivotal work looking backward to the old beliefs (the scientist's isolation, lost to Steinbeck by our entry into the war) and forward to the new sociality (whatever it may turn out to be); containing within it the shell of the old as well as the seeds of the new. And just as the conquered people are the spokesmen for the new sociality, the Nazis are the spokesmen for Steinbeck's scientists! That, very simply, is why they make such half-hearted villains. They are not really Nazis at all, just Steinbeck's scientists disguised as Nazis, with the same disinterest in (not contempt for!) the people, the same "job to do" that fails to take human factors into account, the same ecological good sense ("four or five farms ought to be joined together"), the same biologist's approach to ethics and behavior in general.

That is why the book is so unconvincing; that is why the tone of reassurance that "free men can never be conquered" (they may lose battles, they may be slow, they may be unprepared and disarmed, but they will somehow win), is so hysterical; and that is why the book literally forced itself into dramatic form, facilitating the direct clash in dialogue of those two elements in Steinbeck's mind. The only problem here is that writing a book, even a short book that makes half a million dollars, requires some measure of conviction, and there is no evidence that Steinbeck has changed his mind about any of the things he believed in Sea of Cortez. In purely ecological terms (and Steinbeck has come forward flatly as a convinced and vocal ecologist), the Nazis ought to win, since their "survival quotient" is higher, and that would constitute an automatic ecological "justification" for their winning. And yet, despite ecology, the Nazis in The Moon Is Down are somehow defeated, are somehow to be unnerved, by a pure act of faith on Steinbeck's part (which, if it were not for his expressed contempt for all teleologies, might possibly be called teleological). It seems almost a shame that when fifteen years of effort, concentrated in ten books, have finally managed to cleanse Steinbeck of all taint of sociality, and he emerges in Sea of Cortez as the naked scientific mind, such an unexpected bionomic factor as the attack on Pearl Harbor should force him into a brand-new transition.

Whether in actual value the book will do more to inspire or to disarm the struggle against the Axis is still debatable. Unfortunately, the deeper compulsions that inspired it, the crucial dilemma in Steinbeck that came so near to resolution in Sea of Cortez and has now been forcibly reopened, have forced the book into a form where its effect will probably be somewhere along the line from the useless to the downright dangerous. No book that bases its hopes for the conquered peoples on such physical weapons as dynamite and chocolate, such mental weapons as sabotage so intelligent and inventive that it need never be organized, and such spiritual weapons as a God that is always on the side of the freer battalions, is likely to help in the war effort. Steinbeck may have finally managed, at the cost of great labor, to get his personal moon "down," and he may even (though the noticeable commercialism of the new book makes it highly unlikely) emerge from this book to greater and more directed writing than he has ever achieved, but in regard to this book, at least, the moon is so high up in the clouds as to be invisible.

1. Steinbeck's naming and absence of naming is very interesting. His book about the Communist Party, *In Dubious Battle*, never uses the word Communist. None of the principal characters in *The Moon Is Down* has first names, except the Mordens (who require it, since there are two of them) and the local Quisling. None of the principal characters in *Tortilla Flat* had last names (except Jesus Maria, who would seem to need one). Curley's wife in *Of Mice and Men* never had any other name but that.

2. One group to whom the title has been a godsend are the popular song-writers, who immediately dashed off a popular song along the lines of "The White Cliffs of Dover," or "My Sister and I."

3. For the suggestion of this line of inquiry, as well as for many other ideas in this article, I am indebted to Professor Leonard Brown of Syracuse University, who was kind enough to place his stimulating and intensive study of Steinbeck at my disposal.

4. It is obvious that almost any problem raised by *The Moon Is Down* can be solved in this manner, since Steinbeck has published a rich enough body of work to constitute almost his autobiography.

5. Before the publication of *Sea of Cortez*, Edmund Wilson hazarded a guess that this Doctor spoke for Steinbeck. Now, in *Sea of Cortez*, this is confirmed, and the views Steinbeck states as his own turn out to be almost word for word those he gave the Doctor five years before.

6. It was also his first extensive commercial success.

7. The utopian dream is not dead, it still functions as belief (Candy tries to carry it on, and it is still deep in Crooks' mind) but for all practical purposes it has failed.

8. There is a curious piece of evidence that Steinbeck identifies himself with Tom. One of the short stories in *The Long Valley*, a little sketch called "Breakfast" (dealing with a hospitable family, glowing with pride in having work, food, and a new baby, who offer breakfast to a stranger), is used again in *The Grapes*. As a story, it is in the first person, and the person commenting on it as a beautiful experience he once had is a person of some literacy, presumably Steinbeck. In *The Grapes*, it becomes an experience of Tom's, word for word, with only the philosophic comments omitted. Obviously, if Steinbeck feels enough similarity between his and Tom's attitudes to transfer an experience that seems to be his own to Tom, it is not unlikely that Tom can speak for him.

9. In this connection, it would be useful to know who the people of the *The Grapes of Wrath* dedication are, the Carol who *willed* it, and the Tom who *lived* it.

10. The suggestion that the workers use armed violence, or the threat of armed violence, made in *The Grapes* (in the story of the Akron rubber worker's "turkey shoot") is particularly curious, since even in Steinbeck's most "revolutionary" book, *In Dubious Battle*, the workers never consider armed resistance, and when they do capture guns they markedly fail to use them.

11. Like the old man in *To a God Unknown*, who tries rationalizing his sacrificing of animals to the sun, and finally admits that he does it simply because it makes him feel "glad," that he likes to do it.

12. Some of the ideas and concepts expressed in *Sea of Cortez* are so sharply at variance with ideas and concepts in the earlier Steinbeck works as to raise the inevitable question whether they might not be Ricketts' ideas, only attributed to Steinbeck because of the editorial "we" in which the book is written. Obviously they might, but this does not explain why Steinbeck chooses to take responsibility for them with the covering "we," unless they coincide with his own beliefs.

Woodburn O. Ross

JOHN STEINBECK:
EARTH AND STARS

JOHN STEINBECK, having achieved significant literary stature,[1] has been the subject of several critical studies which are of more scholarly interest than book reviews and popular essays. Harry T. Moore has published a small volume about Steinbeck,[2] valuable particularly for the factual information which it offers. Frederic I. Carpenter has studied Steinbeck's relation to American thought in two articles, "The Philosophical Joads,"[3] and "John Steinbeck, American Dreamer,"[4] the latter perhaps somewhat extreme in its interpretation. Maxwell Geismar has brilliantly traced the development of Steinbeck's social attitudes,[5] and Joseph Warren Beach has illuminated his techniques.[6]

No one, however, has yet attempted to isolate the essential ideas and attitudes of Steinbeck which have determined the directions which his fiction takes and the terms in which he discusses characters and events. This study is meant to present these attitudes and to add something to Mr. Carpenter's description of Steinbeck's ideological background. I shall consider as basic attitudes of Steinbeck those which appear frequently in his work and which are fundamental in the sense that most of what he has to say is directly related to them. First allowing Steinbeck to speak in his own person from *Sea of Cortez*,[7] the only extensive expository work which he has published, concerning each of the attitudes thus selected, I shall discuss most of the novels in the light of these attitudes[8] and touch upon some similarities and differences between Steinbeck and Auguste Comte.

I

Steinbeck objects to causal, or, as he calls it, teleological thinking. For one thing, it frequently involves the *post hoc, ergo propter hoc*

WOODBURN O. ROSS *has been a member of the English Department of Wayne University since 1936. "John Steinbeck: Earth and Stars" appeared originally in Studies in Honor of A. H. R. Fairchild, published in 1946 as a volume of the University of Missouri Studies. It is reprinted here by permission of Fred C. Robbins, Secretary of the University of Missouri Studies, and of the author.*

fallacy. (*Sea of Cortez,* p. 140.) For another, causes are actually so complex as to make any attempted statement of them virtually meaningless, with the result that teleological thinking is frequently associated with superficial understanding of what actually exists. (pp. 134-6.) But lastly —and it is here that Steinbeck becomes most eloquent and, so far as I know, makes his only contribution to the subject—he finds that

> non-teleological methods more than any other seem capable of great tenderness, of an all-embracingness which is rare otherwise. Consider, for instance, the fact that, once a given situation is deeply understood, no apologies are required. There are ample difficulties even to understanding conditions 'as is.' Once that has been accomplished, the 'why' of it (known now to be simply a relation, though probably a near and important one) seems no longer to be preponderantly important. It needn't be condoned or extenuated, it just 'is.' It is seen merely as part of a more or less dim whole picture . . . With the non-teleological treatment there is only the love and understanding of instant acceptance; after that fundamental has been achieved, the next step, if any should be necessary, can be considered more sensibly. (pp. 146-7.)

We do not have to pause here to consider the absurdity of arguing teleologically the undesirability of teleological thinking. But there are two aspects of the doctrine which Steinbeck is here advancing which are pertinent to our present purposes: he is accepting the scientific method of thinking, which seeks to limit itself to what is actually observed and to avoid as far as possible all metaphysical considerations (See *Sea of Cortez,* p. 136.); and he is revealing an unusual, an intense, affection for the objective world, which, as we shall see, colors all his thinking and, carried to an extreme, seriously compromises his rational, scientific position.

At first this position certainly appears secure. Mr. Edmund Wilson has already called attention to Steinbeck's apparent scientific interests.[9] The reasons given in *Sea of Cortez* for the authors' setting out upon the expedition of which it is a chronicle express genuine scientific curiosity:

> One of the reasons we gave ourselves . . . was to observe the distribution of invertebrates, to see and to record their kinds and numbers, how they lived together, what they ate, and how they reproduced. . . . Our curiosity was not limited, but was as wide and horizonless as that of Darwin or Agassiz or Linnaeus or Pliny. We wanted to see everything our eyes would accommodate, to think what we could, and, out of our seeing and thinking, to build some kind of structure in modeled imitation of the observed reality. (*Sea of Cortez,* p. 2.)

The fact that the book itself contains a three hundred page annotated phyletic catalogue and bibliography is further evidence, though, of course, it must not be forgotten that Mr. E. F. Ricketts, a biologist, is co-author.

But despite his scientific predilections and his expressed objections to other than purely descriptive thinking, Steinbeck soon assumes an attitude toward the objective world which is almost mystical. We have seen evidence of his loving acceptance of whatever is. Actually, though Steinbeck himself never seems quite aware of the fact, he does not love everything, but only what he considers "natural." Thus, in *Sea of Cortez* he defends the thieving of little boys, the impolite giggling of little girls who are sincerely amused, drinking, lust, laziness. He distrusts the complexities and heaped-up artificialities of modern life. "It is a rule of paleontology," he writes, for instance,

> that ornamentation and complication precede extinction. And our mutation, of which the assembly line, the collective farm, the mechanized army, the mass production of food are evidences or even symptoms, might well correspond to the thickening armor of the great reptiles—a tendency that can end only in extinction. (p. 88.)

But if Steinbeck experiences a spontaneous and sympathetic outpouring of himself toward whatever he considers natural, some natural objects provoke in him a response yet more striking. I must quote at length something that he says about boats near the beginning of *Sea of Cortez*:

> Apparently the builder of a boat acts under a compulsion greater than himself. Ribs are strong by definition and feeling. Keels are sound, planking truly chosen and set. A man builds the best of himself into a boat—builds many of the unconscious memories of his ancestors. Once, passing the boat department of Macy's in New York, where there are duck-skiffs and little cruisers, one of the authors discovered that as he passed each hull he knocked on it sharply with his knuckles. He wondered why he did it, and as he wondered, he heard a knocking behind him, and another man was rapping the hulls with *his* knuckles, the same tempo—three sharp knocks on each hull. Can this have been an unconscious testing of the hulls? Many who passed could not have been in a boat, perhaps some of the little boys had never seen a boat, and yet everyone tested the hulls, knocked to see if they were sound, and did not even know he was doing it. (p. 15.)

The sound of doves, too, moves Steinbeck deeply:

> The quality of longing in this sound, the memory response it sets up,

is curious and strong. And it has also the quality of a dying day. One wishes to walk toward the sound—to walk on and on toward it, forgetting everything else. (p. 185.)

And at least twice in Sea of Cortez he speaks of the peculiar effects which particular spots of land produce. His feeling for the land, in fact, will prove to be one of the dominant motifs of his novels.[10]

The explanation which he gives for such curious reactions is usually the one implied in the long quotation just above—they are the result of unconscious memories. Perhaps this explanation is correct; but an important fact is that even at the moment of giving it Steinbeck himself admits the possibility that it is not rationally justifiable:

> It appears that the physical evidence for this theory . . . is more or less hypothetical . . . and that critical reasoning could conceivably throw out the whole process and with it the biologic connotations, because of unknown links and factors. (p. 33.)

Now this represents a notable falling off from the purely descriptive thinking which Steinbeck recommends above. Strictly speaking, he should not be thinking teleologically at all, much less doing so without proper evidence. The truth seems to be that because of his training in rational thought he feels himself obliged to account rationally for an irrational emotion inspired in him by certain objects. They have a significance which he cannot properly explain. The word "fetishism" is shocking when applied in a non-Freudian sense to the thinking or feeling of a modern author. But Steinbeck's reactions to some places and things demand the use of the term. He treats them as fetishes, objects possessing unusual—in some instances, even magical—powers. The reader who is not convinced by the quotations offered above may consult the description of Steinbeck's application of these ideas given below in the discussion of To a God Unknown.

His fetishism is, as is natural, accompanied by some doubts as to the ultimate importance of reason. He calls it a "poor blunt weapon." "Conscious thought," he says, "seems to have little effect on the action or direction of our species." And in another place he adds, "Ideas are not dangerous unless they find seeding place in some earth more profound than mind."

We appear almost to have finished a kind of circle. We began by finding Steinbeck laying down rigid rules of empirical thought, then found him thinking as his affections dictated anyway, and now hear him declaring the very limited effectiveness of reason. Actually his difficulty is this, and it is the basic problem of his novels: How is man, with his powerful affections and intuitions, to adjust himself properly to a universe which he can understand only rationally? Reason and affection or intuition make powerful claims and they are sometimes contradictory. How is one to decide between them? Steinbeck has been attempting to give primacy to reason and actually giving it to intuitions based upon his affections.

But we have not yet seen the most striking example of his willingness to transcend reason. He is much concerned with groups as entities. He writes, for instance:

> There are colonies of pelagic tunicates which have taken a shape like the finger of a glove. Each member of the colony is an individual animal, but the colony is another individual animal, not at all like the sum of its individuals. Some of the colonists, girdling the open end, have developed the ability, one against the other, of making a pulsing movement very like muscular action. Others of the colonists collect the food and distribute it, and the outside of the glove is hardened and protected against contact. (p. 165.)

Here is another description of fish:

> The schools swam, marshaled and patrolled. They turned as a unit and dived as a unit. In their millions they followed a pattern minute as to direction and depth and speed. . . . We cannot conceive of this intricacy until we are able to think of the school as an animal itself, reacting with all its cells to stimuli which perhaps might not influence one fish at all. And this larger animal, the school, seems to have a nature and drive and ends of its own. It is more than and different from the sum of its units. . . . In the little Bay of San Carlos, where there were many schools of a number of species, there was even a feeling (and 'feeling' is used advisedly) of a larger unit which was the interrelation of species with their interdependence for food, even though that food be each other. A smoothly working larger animal surviving within itself —larval shrimp to little fish to larger fish to giant fish—one operating mechanism. And perhaps *this* unit of survival may key into the larger animal which is the life of all the sea, and this into the larger of the world. (p. 240.)

Passages in which Steinbeck interprets groups as being themselves separate animals—perhaps until they merge with larger groups—occur several times in Sea of Cortez, and the most extreme interpretation of them is warranted. He definitely feels some groups of individuals to be other and separate individuals. But this conclusion is intuitive and not rational, for the science of biology offers it no support. He is dabbling

. in mystical ideas of unity. This is another aspect of his feeling for the objective world. He is meeting it not merely with a sense of affection for it and a sense of its mysterious significance, but with a conviction of its ultimate unity and, of course, of his unity with it.

Let us now consider the effect of these ways of thinking upon Steinbeck's fiction.

II

After the immature and unimportant *Cup of Gold*, Steinbeck's next novels were *To a God Unknown*, 1933, and *Tortilla Flat*, 1935. These are variant treatments of the same theme, the relation of man to nature.

The earlier is by far the more extreme in its statement. We have seen above that Steinbeck is moved by a profound feeling of relation to certain objects, which results in their becoming virtually fetishes to him. *To a God Unknown*, as its title implies, is the description and illustration of a mysterious religious attitude which is presented as inexplicable, "a naked thing" which would be distorted by the clothes of rational thought. But the religion is identifiable as fetishism; it is only the explanation of its value which is inexpressible. Joseph Wayne leaves the Vermont farm on which he was born to take up new land in a valley in California. He feels an amazing passion for this land:

> He stamped his feet into the soft earth. Then the exultance grew to be a sharp pain of desire that ran through his body in a hot river. He flung himself face downward on the grass and pressed his cheek against the wet stems. His fingers gripped the wet grass and tore it out, and gripped again. His thighs beat heavily on the earth. (*To A God Unknown*, p. 14.)

He builds his house beneath a giant oak, and to this tree, too, he has a sense of mystical relatedness. In some fashion the soul of his father, whom he left behind in Vermont and who has since died, has become a part of the tree:

> . . . The great stree stirred to life under the wind. Joseph raised his head and looked at its old, wrinkled limbs. His eyes lighted with recognition and welcome, for his father's strong and simple being, which had dwelt in his youth like a cloud of peace, had entered the tree.
> Joseph raised his hand in greeting. He said very softly, 'I'm glad you've come, sir. I didn't know until now how lonely I've been for you.' The tree stirred slightly. (p. 31.)

There is a glade on Joseph's land, in which are a huge moss-covered stone and a little spring; and Joseph feels that this glade too has inexplicable religious significance:

> 'Be still a moment, Tom,' he said languidly. 'There's something here. You are afraid of it, but I know it. Somewhere, perhaps in an old dream,[11] I have seen this place, or perhaps felt the feeling of this place.' He dropped his hands to his sides and whispered, trying the words, 'This is holy—and this is old. This is ancient—and holy.' (pp. 55-6.)

The book also is based partially upon Steinbeck's theory of groups, particularly upon the final reaches of that theory, the notion that ultimately everything is to be seen as a single organism. As *To a God Unknown* ends, Joseph, lying upon his holy rock, kills himself by opening the arteries of his wrists—kills himself in order to end the drouth which has come upon the land by sacrificing his own life. The method probably is not one which most readers would view as promising; but it works:

> The pain was sharp at first, but in a moment its sharpness dulled. He watched the bright blood cascading over the moss, and he heard the shouting of the wind around the grove. The sky was growing grey. And time passed and Joseph grew grey too. He lay on his side with his wrist outstretched and looked down the long black mountain range of his body. Then his body grew huge and light. It arose into the sky, and out of it came the streaking rain. 'I should have known,' he whispered. 'I am the rain.' And yet he looked dully down the mountains of his body where the hills fell to an abyss. He felt the driving rain, and heard it whipping down, pattering on the ground. He saw his hills grow dark with moisture. Then a lancing pain shot through the heart of the world. 'I am the land,' he said, 'and I am the rain. The grass will grow out of me in a little while.' (pp. 321-2.)

Naturally in a book such as this, filled with fetishistic and mystic ideas, rational thought gets rather brusque treatment. Characters know significant things intuitively, without knowing how they know them. Joseph feels that his father is dead and is correct; he knows intuitively when his tree has been girdled; Thomas, his brother, knows "instinctively where a straying beef would stray." The novel thus is avowedly dedicated to mystery; it make no attempt to interpret life rationally. But it is a perfectly sincere work and represents essentially an attitude which, as we have seen, Steinbeck still holds, though possibly in a somewhat less extreme fashion, today.

Tortilla Flat is rooted in Steinbeck's love for whatever seems to him natural, as opposed to the artificial, and is therefore primitivistic. But

Steinbeck's primitivism is different from that of the eighteenth century. The natural life does not lead to virtue; it defines it. What the natural, the uncomplicated, the economically disinterested man does is, in the context of *Tortilla Flat*, right. Necessarily the usual moral values are here inverted. The paisanos of Monterey, who are the characters of the book, may lie, steal, and fornicate at random to the applause of the author—almost. An important reservation is established by the very tone of the book. Steinbeck enters a kind of disclaimer by writing in a mock-heroic vein. He thus implies that he doesn't quite mean what he says; it is all in fun; he isn't dealing with the real world anyway. To put it another way, he is not willing here to face intellectually the implications of his intuitively established attitude. The second paragraph of the book sets the tone:

> In Monterey, that old city on the coast of California, these things are well known, and they are repeated and sometimes elaborated. It is well that this cycle be put down on paper so that in a future time scholars, hearing the legends, may not say as they say of Arthur and of Roland and of Robin Hood—'There was no Danny nor any group of Danny's friends, nor any house. Danny is a nature god and his friends primitive symbols of the wind, the sky, the sun.' This history is designed now and ever to keep the sneers from the lips of sour scholars. (*Tortilla Flat*, p. 10.)

Both *To a God Unknown* and *Tortilla Flat* thus avoid the world of actual experience which furnishes the data with which the mind ordinarily deals—the first by its constant emphasis upon intuitional knowledge, the other by its tone.

But it was inevitable that a novelist with the interest in carefully conducted observation which we have seen that Steinbeck entertains should write novels in which the rationally perceived world, the world of ordinary experience, is dominant. Such a book is *In Dubious Battle*, 1936, Steinbeck's next work. It appears to be simply a realistic story of a strike of fruit-pickers in California, a strike inspired and engineered by so-called radicals but made possible only by the exploitation of the workers. The motives of Mac, the organizer, and Jim Nolan, his assistant, are clearly presented, and the changing states of mind of the strikers are carefully analyzed. All this seems to be a faithful recording of significant aspects of observable life. But beneath the surface there is something different. Much of the action, it turns out, develops around one of Steinbeck's familiar themes—that of the group as an entity. The concept is repeatedly dealt with in the novel. (pp. 73, 261,

274-5, 323, besides the passage cited below.) The doctor who has come
to oversee the health of the strikers' camp says to Mac, for instance:

> 'Group-men are always getting some kind of infection. This seems to
> be a bad one. I want to see, Mac. I want to watch these group-men, for
> they seem to me to be a new individual, not at all like single men. A
> man in a group isn't himself at all, he's a cell in an organism that isn't
> like him any more than the cells in your body are like you. I want to
> watch the group, and see what it's like. People have said, "mobs are
> crazy, you can't tell what they'll do." Why don't people look at mobs •
> not as men, but as mobs? A mob nearly always seems to act reasonably,
> for a mob. . . . You might be an effect as well as a cause, Mac. You
> might be an expression of group-man, a cell endowed with a special
> function, like an eye cell, drawing your force from group-man, and at
> the same time directing him, like an eye . . .' (pp. 150-51.)

Here is the doctrine of the group as an individual expressed as definitely
as in *Sea of Cortez*. And, as there, the concept is a mystical one. There
may not appear to be much difference between saying that men in
groups behave differently from men acting alone, and saying that
groups are themselves separate animals. But the one idea represents an
observable fact and the other is an intuitive conclusion. Steinbeck's
position is the latter; and his assuming it here introduces an element of
unreality into the very core of what is otherwise a hard, factual
narrative.

His next novel, *Of Mice and Men*, 1937, is the story of two friends,
Lennie, extremely powerful in body but with no mind at all, and
George, small but intelligent. The speech and, in the main, the actions
of the characters form realistic patterns. Land hunger dominates the
friends—this time a rational desire for a home, but certainly related to
Steinbeck's sometimes fetishistic attitude toward the land. And there
appears again his irrational intuition that whatever is "natural" is good.
Lennie literally has no mind; consequently, being incapable of artificiality of conduct, he is completely "natural." Steinbeck is attracted to this
kind of man,[12] and represents George as being closely attached to
Lennie. But George's feeling is not convincing because it is not that of
most men in real life. Again Steinbeck's affections dictate his attitude
toward his material and prevent his adopting a completely realistic attitude; the world as he would have it is not the world in which most
people live.

In *The Grapes of Wrath*, 1939, Steinbeck's longest work, beneath
his eloquent pleading of the cause of the dispossessed and beneath his
realistic portrayal of the plight of the Joads are to be found all the atti-

•tudes which we have associated with him. Land hunger is a constant theme, and occasionally the love of an individual for his land is represented as being so strong as to amount to an identification of himself with it. "Grampa an' the old place," says Casy the preacher, for instance, "they was jus' the same thing . . . He died the minute you took 'im off the place . . . He was that place, an' he knowed it. . . ." (*The Grapes of Wrath*, p. 199.) The conduct of the Joads is reasonably uninhibited—that is, natural—and their social position, somewhat similar to that of the Monterey paisanos, keeps them from being a part of the social artificialities which Steinbeck distrusts.

The theme of group-man again becomes a theory of the Whole, which is given important status in the book through the utterances of Casy and Tom Joad. Steinbeck's position here is practically pantheistic; he speaks definitely of a spiritual rather than a physical Whole. Thus, near the end of the book Tom says to Ma:

> 'Guess who I been thinkin' about? Casy! He talked a lot. Used ta bother me. But now I been thinkin' what he said, an' I can remember—all of it. Says one time he went out in the wilderness to find his own soul, an' he foun' he didn' have no soul that was his'n. Says he foun' he jus' got a little piece of a great big soul. Says a wilderness ain't no good, 'cause his little piece of soul wasn't no good 'less it was with the rest, an' was whole. . . . I'll be all aroun' in the dark. I'll be ever'where—wherever you look. Wherever they's a fight so hungry people can eat, I'll be there. Wherever they's a cop beatin' up a guy, I'll be there. If Casy knowed, why, I'll be in the way guys yell when they're mad an'—I'll be in the way kids laugh when they're hungry an' they know supper's ready. An' when our folks eat the stuff they raise an' live in the houses they build—why, I'll be there. See? God, I'm talkin' like Casy.' (pp. 570 and 572.)

Casy himself declares that the unity of man and nature and of man with man is holy and that what destroys this unity is evil:

> '. . . There was the hills, an' there was me, an' we wasn't separate no more. We was one thing. An' that one thing was holy. . . . I got thinkin' how we was holy when we was one thing, an' mankin' was holy when it was one thing. An' it on'y got unholy when one mis'able little fella got the bit in his teeth an' run off his own way, kickin' an' draggin' an' fightin'. Fella like that bust the holiness.' (p. 110.)

Why did Steinbeck's imagination lead him to make the need of the poor for unity an important—probably the most important—theme in *The Grapes of Wrath* (See specifically p. 206.) and to ground his development of this theme in notions of mysterious spiritual unities? It seems manifest that his thoughts took this direction because he had long entertained feelings about curious physical unities and found it easy to apply them to the world of spirit.[13]

A similar explanation shows Steinbeck's next novel, *The Moon Is Down*, 1942, in a new light. The book is an unusual description of the strength of a democratic group under the occupation of foreign troops. Orden, the mayor of the occupied community, is to an almost incredible extent the mirror of public opinion and the executor of the popular will. It is not that he chooses deliberately to act in these capacities; it is rather as if he literally cannot usurp authority which is not his or fail to meet the responsibilities of his office. And the people are peculiarly one-minded. At first they are puzzled; how ought they to respond to the invader? And then gradually bewilderment turns to anger and anger inspires the complete ostracism of the enemy by day and the methodical sabotage of his installations by night. With but few exceptions the populace sees as one man.

Now to many it must have seemed that the union of the mayor and the people is too close to be true and that the people are far too completely in agreement. But as soon as one asks oneself why Steinbeck was moved to cast his defence of democracy in these terms the difficulties disappear. We have here, of course, group-man in action again. The invaded community is like the schools of fish which "turned as a unit and dived as a unit." The mayor is a cell of this single animal which has a highly specialized function, as did Mac of *In Dubious Battle*.

Steinbeck's two remaining novels require little discussion. *Cannery Row*, 1945, is merely a repetition of *Tortilla Flat* in everything except tone. But whereas in the earlier book Steinbeck jestingly avoided making a serious defence of the paisanos, in *Cannery Row* a similar group living by similar values is unhesitatingly accepted. "It's a puzzler why Steinbeck should have wanted to write or publish such a book at this point in his career," writes Mr. F. O. Matthiessen.[14] May not this change in tone suggest the answer? May it not be that Steinbeck, having hesitated in 1935 to accept the inversion of commonly held values to which his love of the natural impelled him, now wished to do the whole thing over again without his tongue in his cheek? Five years of war may have left him with no hesitations at all concerning the values of civilized artificiality.

His latest work, *Pearl of the World*, published in *The Woman's Home Companion* for December, 1945, is not important, but reflects once more his love of the primitive life. In *Sea of Cortez* he repeats in a single page the story of a native of Lower California who found an unbelievably large pearl and was pursued by greedy men until he threw it back into the ocean. (pp. 102-3.) Such a tale is manifestly Steinbeckian raw material, and *Pearl of the World* is the finished product.

One of the best remarks uttered concerning the work of Steinbeck is, I think, that of Mr. James T. Farrell, who says that *Of Mice and Men* has "all the mannerism and none of the substance of genuine realistic writing."[15] This judgment is applicable to all of Steinbeck's work since 1932 except *To a God Unknown* and *Tortilla Flat*, which make almost no attempt at realism. But the contempt for Steinbeck as a half-abandoned writer of slick entertainment which Mr. Farrell goes on to express is completely unwarranted. Steinbeck's difficulty is that, as I have explained, he is a man of two worlds. As a believer in the inductive, scientific method he must record what he sees, he must write realistically. But as a man of powerful affections and intuitions he must reflect irrational attitudes which are justifiable only in terms of the desires of the human spirit. He is therefore at the same time brutal and tender, rational and irrational, concrete and abstract. His imagination provides for humanity a home in the universe which his senses do not perceive.

III

Steinbeck's fundamental attitudes represent in part, of course, his assimilation and modification of the attitudes of thinkers who have preceded him. The task of describing an author's intellectual heritage at all completely is an enormous one, and I have no intention of attempting such a description here. But I do wish to take a tentative step in that direction. In discussing Steinbeck's background I am continuing work initiated in an article referred to above, "The Philosophical Joads," by Mr. Frederic I. Carpenter, though Mr. Carpenter restricted himself to dealing with American ideas reflected in *The Grapes of Wrath*.

Clearly Steinbeck has been affected in some manner by the ideas of several thinkers—Hume, Rousseau, and Emerson, for example. But there is at least one man to whom he bears a striking resemblance, as I hope to show—Auguste Comte, the father of sociology and of positivism. I make no claim that Steinbeck has ever read Comte. Both men developed their attitudes during socially troubled times, and it is possible that they spontaneously arrived at certain similar positions. Or it may be that Comte has influenced Steinbeck indirectly, through other men. But in any event the two may be described as being in many respects in the same stream of thought. Let us compare them.

Steinbeck objects to casual, or teleological, thinking. But the objection to thinking in terms of causes rather than descriptive laws is basic to Comte's positive system, and Comte was of course extremely influential in promoting this point of view. Thus he writes in the *Cours de philosophie positive:*

> We see, through what precedes, that the fundamental character of the positive philosophy is to regard all phenomena as subject to invariable natural laws, the precise ascertainment of which, and the reduction of which to the smallest number possible are the end of all our efforts. At the same time the search for what are called causes—first causes or final—must be considered fruitless. In our positive explanations, even the most perfect, we make no pretense whatever to discover the generating causes of phenomena, since we would then only push back the difficulty one stage; we intend only to analyze with exactitude the circumstances of their production and attach one to the other in their normal relations of succession and similarity.[16]

Steinbeck, further, regards the rational mind as exercising relatively little influence over human conduct. In this, too, he follows Comte, who writes in the *Système de politique positive:*

> The mind is not supposed to control, but to serve; when it thinks to dominate, it serves, in reality, the personality . . . without being able to avoid supporting some passion or other. In fact, reality demands above all force, and reason offers nothing but light; force must come from elsewhere.[17]

Certain differences between the two men concerning the relations of the intellect and the affections will be mentioned below.

Steinbeck loves the dispossessed and emphasizes their social virtues. Comte writes in the *Système de politique positive:*

> The habitual mode of life of the proletarian is much more appropriate to the spontaneous development of our better instincts. . . . When the final systematization of opinion and custom shall have determined the character proper to that immense base of modern society, one will find that the various domestic feelings must naturally have developed there rather than among the middle classes, which are too preoccupied with personal schemes to appreciate such worthy ties. But the principal moral efficacy of the proletarian life concerns the social sentiments proper, all of which are exercised there daily, even from the early childhood of the individual. It is there that one finds ordinarily the best models of true friendship—even among those whom a constant poverty, too often depreciated by our aristocratic customs, seems to condemn to the least moral elevation.[18]

Ma Joad, struggling incessantly to preserve her family, and Rosasharn, feeding a dying man at her own breast, are certainly drawn to just such a theory as this.

We have seen that Steinbeck's feeling for certain natural objects causes him to turn them practically into fetishes. Curiously enough, Comte regards genuine, primitive fetishism as representing the attitude of the mind, next to positivism, most suitable for man. By treating each object separately instead of establishing classes, fetishism encourages accurate observation and permits man to reach conclusions about nature more accurate than those of the priest or the metaphysician. (Have we here some kind of explanation of Steinbeck's ability to move quickly back and forth between the positivistic and fetishistic attitudes?)

And, lastly, we have seen Steinbeck's fascination with the idea that groups should be regarded as separate entities. In his *Système de politique positive* Comte seeks to establish the worship of the Great Being,
•Humanity. The individual fades into relative unimportance; indeed, he is actually an abstraction of the mind, and only a group composed of all men has real existence:

> The new Great Being does not depend at all . . . upon a purely subjective abstraction. The notion of it results, on the contrary, from an exact objective understanding; for the individual, properly speaking, exists only in the too abstract intellect of the metaphysician. After all, nothing is real but humanity. . . .[19]

The individual—and we have seen Steinbeck sometimes depicting him thus—is merely an organ of the whole which is the sum of the individuals.

Steinbeck and Comte, then, are similar in that both insist upon the necessity of thought based solely upon observation, both deny the power of reason to control man, both believe that the proletariat as a class is the principal repository of the social virtues, both are in some fashion inclined toward fetishism, and both believe in the real existence of entities which transcend and include the individual. Steinbeck is at least to some extent in the positivistic tradition.

But differences between the two men underscore certain of Steinbeck's qualities and suggest some differences between nineteenth and twentieth century thought. In the first place, Steinbeck relegates reason far more completely to the background than does Comte. Comte clearly makes reason the servant of the affections, but only in this sense: the affections select the field within which reason is to function, the problems which it is to solve. The only faculty, however, which can utter judgments remains the reason. Indeed, no further subordination of the reason than this is possible to Comte, for his whole system is a celebration of the triumphs of the scientific method, which is going to save Humanity.

In Steinbeck confidence in what can be accomplished by reason dwindles. He questions the ultimate value of science, even while insisting upon the value of its methods. He writes in *Sea of Cortez:*

> . . . The Indian might say, 'What good is this knowledge? Since you make a duty of it, what is its purpose?' We could have told our people the usual thing about the advancement of science, and again we would not have been questioned further. But the Indian might ask, 'Is it advancing, and toward what? Or is it merely becoming complicated? You save the lives of children for a world that does not love them. . . . We would not want a child to escape pneumonia, only to be hurt all its life.' The lies we tell about our duty and our purposes, the meaningless words of science and philosophy, are walls that topple before a bewildered little 'why.' (p. 209.)

And Steinbeck appears to allow the affections to dictate judgments. Else how, because he loves the natural, can he permit the overturning of conventional moral values, and how, because he loves trees, can he soberly deposit the soul of a man in a tree? In short, by enhancing Comte's emphasis upon the deficiencies of reason Steinbeck becomes basically an irrationalist, belonging in this respect to a group of writers whose most successful spokesmen have been D. H. Lawrence and Aldous Huxley.

The other difference between Comte and Steinbeck which I wish to mention concerns an aspect of their attitudes toward society. In the *Système de politique positive* Comte writes concerning his proposed social reforms:

> This decisive regeneration consists above all in the substitution of duties for rights, in order better to subordinate the individual to society. The word *right* ought to be as completely removed from the proper language of politics as the word *cause* from the language of philosophy. Of these two theologico-metaphysical notions, the one is henceforth immoral and anarchic, just as the other is irrational and sophistic.[20]

But Steinbeck's orientation is in precisely the opposite direction. He has almost nothing to say about the duties of citizens, much about their rights. "We have a right to protect our property, and we'll do it," cries the leader of the orchard owners of *In Dubious Battle*. "There aren't any rules a hungry man has to follow," reply the strikers. The Joads in *The Grapes of Wrath* are pursuing their right to work and to own land, and "the boys" in *Cannery Row* are asserting their right to live the life of their choice. In this respect, too, Steinbeck, differing from the nineteenth century Comte, is, I think, in harmony with much twentieth century thought.

1. Mr. Elmer Davis calls Steinbeck "still the best prospect in American letters," *Saturday Review of Literature*, XVIII (Sept. 24, 1938), 11. According to the *Publishers' Weekly*, CXXXVII (April 13, 1940), 1494, *The Grapes of Wrath* has been translated into Danish, Dutch, French, Norwegian, Portuguese, Spanish, German, Polish, and Russian. Steinbeck has been attracting attention in Latin America. See Lidia Besouchet, "Amando Fontes y Steinbeck," *Nosotros* (Sept., 1942, no. 78), pp. 323-5; Maria Rosa Oliver, "La Novella Norte Americana," *Sur* (Aug., 1939, no. 59), pp. 33-47; Victoria Ocampo, "Ratones y Hombres de Steinbeck," *Sur* (April, 1940, no. 67), pp. 85-9.

2. *The Novels of John Steinbeck: A First Critical Study* (Normandie House, Chicago, 1939).

3. *College English*, II (Jan., 1941), 315 ff. [See p. 241, below.]

4. *Southwest Review*, XXVI (1941), 454 ff. [See p. 68, above.]

5. *Writers in Crisis: The American Novel between Two Wars* (New York, 1942), pp. 239 ff.

6. *American Fiction, 1920-1940* (New York, 1942), pp. 309 ff. [See p. 80, above, and p. 250, below.]

7. John Steinbeck and Edward F. Ricketts, *Sea of Cortez, a Leisurely Journal of Travel and Research* (Viking Press, New York, 1941).

8. I shall not deal with *Cup of Gold*, Steinbeck's first novel, because it is an immature work in which his philosophy has hardly begun to shape itself; and I shall also omit the two volumes of short stories, *Pastures of Heaven* and *The Long Valley*, because it would be impossible to deal with a large number of short stories in a paper the length of this one. But the reader may easily apply the theories here advanced to the latter works.

9. "The Californians: Storm and Steinbeck," *New Republic*, CIII (Dec. 9, 1940), 785.

10. In this connection see H. T. Moore, *op. cit.*, p. 15.

11. Cf. Steinbeck's notion about racial memory, mentioned above.

12. Every reader of Steinbeck will recall the frequency with which idiots appear on his pages. See, as examples, the story of Tularecito in *Pastures of Heaven* and "Johnny Bear" in *The Long Valley*.

13. It is difficult to say just when this development in Steinbeck's thinking or feeling took place. Since the unity about which he talks is always mysterious, it is nearly impossible to be certain of his meaning. It seems to me, however, that he usually is thinking of a physical unity—a group of individuals forms a single animal, each individual being a specialized part. But the conclusion of *To a God Unknown*, quoted above, is extremely difficult to interpret. And what is one to make of the soul of a man which becomes a part of a tree?

14. *New York Times Book Review* (Dec. 31, 1944), p. 1.

15. "The End of a Literary Decade," *American Mercury*, XLVIII (Dec., 1939), 414.

16. *Cours de philosophie positive* (6 vols., Paris, 1877), I, 16-17. [In the original appearance of this article the quotations were given in French. The author, Woodburn O. Ross, has translated all the quotations from Comte into English for this book.]

17. *Système de politique positive, ou traité de sociologie instituant la religion de l'humanité* (4 vols., Paris, 1851-4), I, 16. See also pp. 14, 91.

18. *Ibid.*, I, 132.

19. *Ibid.*, I, 334.

20. *Ibid.*, I, 361.

Frederick Bracher

STEINBECK AND
THE BIOLOGICAL VIEW OF MAN

JOHN STEINBECK'S interest in biology, and particularly in marine zoology, is of long standing. Presumably his studies at Stanford University awakened an interest which was intensified by his long friendship and association with Edward F. Ricketts, formerly a professional collector of biological specimens at Monterey. Steinbeck worked with Ricketts at odd intervals for nearly twenty years, and in 1940 the two organized a collecting expedition to the Gulf of California. *Sea of Cortez,*[1] "a leisurely journal of travel and research," was one of the fruits of this trip. It is a very fruitful book for the student of Steinbeck, for it contains the substance of many conversations with Ricketts—conversations which, over a period of years, did much to shape Steinbeck's thought and determine his values. Moreover, the book emphasizes the biological cast of Steinbeck's thinking and, by elaborating a number of biological ideas, underlines their frequent brief appearances in the novels.

Sea of Cortez consists of two parts: a running narrative of the voyage interspersed with conversations and speculations, and an illustrated scientific description of the marine organisms found. The narrative and speculative part, which is of greatest interest here, was written up from two journals, one by Steinbeck and the other by Ricketts, and it is a genuine work of collaboration. Its form preserves the rhythm of the voyage—feverish collection and preservation of specimens, followed by periods of leisurely talk as the boat goes to a new station. The book is full of speculations on the nature of life—not the formal hypotheses of the responsible scientist speaking ex cathedra, but the casual insights and guesses and hints suggested to an alert mind by the facts of marine biology, and preserving the flavor of good conversation.

What appears in Steinbeck's novels is not primarily these specula-

FREDERICK BRACHER *is professor of English at Pomona College, Claremont, California. He has made some revisions in his essay "Steinbeck and the Biological View of Man" for its appearance in this volume. It is reprinted by permission of Mr. Bracher and of* The Pacific Spectator, *in the Winter, 1948 issue of which it first appeared.*

tions (though many of them do appear), but rather a point of view, in
the literal sense of that phrase—a way of looking at things characteristic
of a biologist. It comprises Steinbeck's typical attitude toward the characters in his novels and also the attitudes of some of the characters
themselves. In particular, it appears as the typical values and virtues of
Steinbeck's "heroes"—not necessarily the protagonists of the novels,
but the characters with whom the reader is obviously intended to sympathize. The manifestations in the novels of this point of view throw
light on the development of Steinbeck's thinking, yet, in a welter of
comment on Steinbeck's economic, social, moral, and political views,
there has been very little mention of this basic attitude toward man.
Edmund Wilson[2] with characteristic acuteness has discussed Steinbeck's pre-occupation with biological processes, and Alfred Kazin[3]
suggests that Steinbeck's interest in the animal nature of man leads to
oversimplification and a failure to create fully human characters.

More recently, Toni Ricketts[4] has pointed out that *Sea of Cortez*
contains an explicit statement of the philosophical position underlying *Of Mice and Men*. This book, according to friends with whom
Steinbeck discussed its plan and intention, was originally entitled
"Something That Happened" and was intended to exemplify the "non-
teleological" attitude toward human behavior which is elaborated in
Sea of Cortez. The article goes on to show how this attitude helps to
clarify the author's intentions in *The Wayward Bus*. But there is more
to Steinbeck's basic point of view than an avoidance of "cause" thinking; and a study of Steinbeck's biological interests throws light on more
of his work than *The Wayward Bus*.

The central metaphor is the tide pool. As an amateur collector,
Steinbeck has for years been looking into tide pools and studying the
ecology of the marine organisms inhabiting them. He has looked with
curiosity and interest, growing into enthusiastic affection. Here is life
in a lusty, primitive form, yet clearly related to the life of that larger
organism, man, who, no longer limited to tide pool or mud flat and
incomparably more complex and potential, is nevertheless formed of
the same kinds of living cells, subject to the same primitive drives, and
a part of an ecological pattern as determinate as that of the tide pool,
though infinitely more complicated.

Why should not man be examined with the affectionate detachment
of the biologist? "We have looked into the tide pools and seen the
little animals feeding and reproducing and killing for food . . . . but
we do not objectively observe our own species as a species, though we
know the individuals fairly well." Most novelists are humanists, in
some sense of the term; when they go beyond studies of individual

human beings, it is to human society and its values. Steinbeck looks at man, both individually and in groups, as only one more manifestation of the life which teems throughout earth and sea. Other naturalistic writers, to be sure, have tried to regard man with the coldly objective eye of the scientist and to show his kinship with the so-called lower forms of life. What distinguishes Steinbeck is the specifically biological flavor of his naturalism. It shows itself in incidental coloring (biological allusions, metaphors, and analogies—as when the Joad family group themselves like the parts of a living cell around the truck, the ● nucleus), but mainly in the warmth of Steinbeck's enthusiasm for life in all its forms. Doc, in *Cannery Row*, tips his hat to the dogs he passes on the street, and the gesture is hardly an exaggeration of Steinbeck's respectful tenderness toward living things. As Preacher Casy puts it, "All that lives is holy."

Moreover, the strong vein of mysticism which runs through the novels from *To a God Unknown* to *The Wayward Bus* sets them off from the conventional naturalistic novel. That Steinbeck is fascinated by biological mysteries—the "pulse" of plankton concentrations, the absence of marine life in certain "burned" areas, the existence of localities hostile to man—is made clear in almost every chapter of *Sea of Cortez*. Facts, unquestionable but inexplicable in terms of accepted scientific concepts, excite him to semimystical speculations on the nature of life itself. Nor need the facts be unimpeachably established. Even though it may be a fact, it is probably impossible to prove the existence of supersensory emanations (like those supposedly given off by dying organisms) which other animals can recognize. Fact or not, Steinbeck is so fascinated by the idea that he elaborates it in *Sea of Cortez* and uses it in various forms in the novels. The aura emitted by Camille Oaks in *The Wayward Bus* is an extreme example. What Steinbeck seems to be saying is that life is more mysteriously wonderful than even the biologists have realized; and his insistence on the unity ● of all life leads invariably to a religious attitude.

> And it is a strange thing that most of the feeling we call religious, most of the mystical outcrying which is one of the most prized and used and desired reactions of our species, is really the understanding and the attempt to say that man is related to the whole thing, related inextricably to all reality, known and unknowable . . . . that all things are one thing and that one thing is all things—plankton, a shimmering phosphorescence on the sea and the spinning planets and an expanding universe, all bound together by the elastic string of time. It is advisable to look from the tide pool to the stars and then back to the tide pool again.

It is probably worth noting that the characters in *The Wayward Bus*, however much their behavior may suggest the tide pool, are struggling, in spite of difficulties and betrayals, toward St. John of the Cross (San Juan de la Cruz). In *Cannery Row* Steinbeck prays to "Our Father who art in nature," and the heroes of the novels are admirable in Steinbeck's eyes because they live according to the principles revealed to the scientist by this Immanent Deity.

In spirit, if not always by profession, the typical Steinbeck hero is a biologist. The most obvious example is Doc, in *Cannery Row*, who, despite the disingenuous disclaimer that "the people in this book are, of course, fictions and fabrications," is a replica of Edward Ricketts. Ricketts' home and place of business, the Pacific Biological Laboratory, appears in *Cannery Row* as the "Western Biological Laboratory." It is diagonally across the street from Wing Chong's general store, thinly disguised in the book as "Lee Chong's." The actual locale is described literally and minutely—canneries, old pipes and boilers, tumbledown shacks. Even today, walking along the northern end of Cannery Row is like stepping into the pages of the book. There is only one major departure from actuality: the curious tourist will be misled as to the location of the "honest, old-fashioned sporting house" of Dora Flood.

Steinbeck is reported[5] to have said that all characters in his work represent people he has known, and Ricketts is the source of several characters and a kind of archetype of the later Steinbeck hero. He appears in easily recognizable form in "The Snake," one of the short stories in *The Long Valley*, in which his scientific attitude and values are contrasted with those of the neurotic woman who buys a rattlesnake. He is pretty clearly the pattern for the doctor in *The Moon Is Down*, and perhaps also for the young doctor of *In Dubious Battle*.

In *The Grapes of Wrath*, the manager of the federal camp for migrant workers displays one of the characteristic attitudes of the biologist-hero: he cares for his charges with affectionate comprehension of their failings and their virtues, and, as one of the migrants remarks, "He don't believe in sin. . . . . Says the sin is bein' hungry. Says the sin is bein' cold." For that matter, Preacher Casy follows the general pattern: he is an outsider, a disinterested though friendly observer, and the insights he grows into sound remarkably like the nonteleological attitude of *Sea of Cortez*.

> "I says, 'Maybe it ain't a sin. Maybe it's just the way folks is. Maybe
> we been whippin' the hell out of ourselves for nothin'!' . . . . Before I
> knowed it, I was sayin' out loud, 'The hell with it! There ain't no sin
> and there ain't no virtue. There's just stuff people do. It's all part of the

same thing. And some of the things folks do is nice, and some ain't nice, but that's as far as any man got a right to say.' "

This is a colloquial version of "is" thinking—the attempt to concern oneself "not with what should be, or could be, or might be, but rather with what actually is—attempting at most to answer the already sufficiently difficult questions *what* or *how*, instead of *why*." "Cause-thinking," say Steinbeck-Ricketts, is almost always co-existent with "blame-feeling," and while to the average man nonteleological methods may seem detached, hardhearted, or even cruel, actually they are "capable of great tenderness, of an all-embracingness which is rare otherwise." Casy, though certainly neither a biologist nor a scientist, arrives at the attitude which, for Steinbeck, is essential to the good scientist: "the love and understanding of instant acceptance."

Juan Chicoy in *The Wayward Bus* lives a philosophy, instead of thinking or talking one; but the attitude of warmly interested yet objective examination appears explicitly in the contrast between Chicoy and his wife:

> All relations and all situations to Alice were person-to-person things. . . . . There was no shading. . . . . But Juan, now, he could shut everything out and look at each thing in relation to the other. Things of various sizes and importance. He could see and judge and consider and enjoy. Juan could enjoy people. Alice could only love, like, dislike, and hate. She saw and felt no shading whatever . . . . Juan's eyes were distant and amused. This was a matter of horror to Alice. She knew he was seeing her, not as an angry woman who darkened the world, but as one of thousands of angry women to be studied, inspected, and, yes, even enjoyed.

What all of these characters have in common is the ability to practice the nonteleological methods described in chapter 14 of *Sea of Cortez*. This chapter, which Steinbeck has inserted, as an Easter Sunday sermon, into the log of the voyage, is based on a previously written but unpublished essay by Ricketts, and according to the author it has been widely misunderstood. An obvious corollary of the avoidance of cause-thinking and blame-feeling would be an inability to take sides—not necessarily the agonized indecision of a Hamlet, but a quietistic acceptance of a larger pattern, of which the two opposed sides are necessary parts. Mr. Ricketts insists that this corollary is not justified and that nonteleological thinking is, in fact, the only solid basis for positive action. In the novels, Steinbeck never resolves some of the paradoxes involved in a nonteleological approach. If, as Casy says, "There ain't

no sin and there ain't no virtue; there's just stuff people do," it is difficult to see why "some of the things folks do is nice and some ain't
nice," or how one is justified in an attempt to change society. Despite
Steinbeck's fervent desire to correct social injustices, the admirable
characters in his novels are distinguished by their all-encompassing love
and comprehension, and their inability to be devoted partisans.

The young doctor of In Dubious Battle is contrasted sharply with
the dedicated Communist organizers, who are the main characters in
the book. Dr. Burton is not a Party man; Mac comes finally to the
puzzled conclusion that Burton is too far left to be a Communist. But
he works with the party and serves the strikers tirelessly and at considerable personal risk. He "believes" in the cause in the same way that he
believes in the moon—it is. But he has no illusions as to its ultimate
rightness, or success.

> "Listen to me, Mac. My senses aren't above reproach, but they're all
> I have. I want to see the whole picture—as nearly as I can. I don't want
> to put on the blinders of 'good' or 'bad' and limit my vision I
> want to be able to look at the whole thing."

Dr. Burton compares social injustice to the physiological injustice of
syphilis or amoebic dysentery, and he insists that to cure either, one
must first study and see. Nor is it enough to study the pathogenic
organisms in the test tube; one must observe them in interaction with
a body and grasp the whole pattern. Hence he goes to the seat of the
wound, the strike, and he studies the vigilantes as enthusiastically as he
does the strikers.

In explaining to Mac why he works for the strikers without really
believing in their cause, Dr. Burton touches on one of the speculations
elaborated in Sea of Cortez. This is the idea of group-man, and it is
an idea which has deeply stirred Steinbeck's imagination. Apparently
it developed out of conversations with Ricketts, and some of the
biological data out of which the concept grew are recorded in Between
Pacific Tides, "an account of the habits and habitats of some five
hundred of the common, conspicuous seashore invertebrates of the
Pacific Coast."[6] In a discussion of the aggregating, or intertwining,
habits of brittle stars (Amphiodia occidentalis) Ricketts refers to
studies made by Dr. W. C. Allee[7] which "lead us to the border line of
the metaphysical." Groups of brittle stars bring about "a degree of resistance to untoward conditions that is not attainable by isolated individuals," by giving off a protective material which passes through
ordinary filter paper and persists after the filtrate is boiled. It is appar-

ently similar to antibodies, and it is capable of conferring protection from poisons to isolated animals which, by themselves, cannot produce the protective substance. Rickets uses this discovery to explain his own observation that, while individual anemones can be readily anesthetized, a group shows great resistance and even ultimately renders the pans in which they are kept unfit for use in anesthetizing. To summarize, there is evidence that a group of animals performs biological functions of which the individual animals are incapable.

The idea is elaborated in several sections of *Sea of Cortez*, perhaps best in connection with certain colonies of pelagic tunicates (*Pyrosoma giganteum*) which have assumed a shape like the finger of a glove.

> Each member of the colony is an individual animal, but the colony is another individual animal, not at all like the sum of its individuals. Some of the colonists, girdling the open end, have developed the ability, one against the other, of making a pulsing movement very like muscular action. Others of the colonists collect the food and distribute it, and the outside of the glove is hardened and protected against contact. Here are two animals, and yet the same thing—something the early Church would have been forced to call a mystery.

But this oneness in variety is a mystery only by the standard of human reason, with its rigid dependence on the law of contradiction. Whether or not we grasp the relationship (and there are many analogies to assist us, from the individual cells of the human body to the mass behavior of a school of fish), the fact remains that in some instances a collection of individuals has a group-life of its own.

Dr. Burton in *In Dubious Battle*, applies this idea to man.

> "I want to watch these group-men [the strikers], for they seem to me to be a new individual, not at all like single men. A man in a group isn't himself at all, he's a cell in an organism that isn't like him any more than the cells in your body are like you. . . . . It might be like this, Mac: When group-man wants to move, he makes a standard. 'God wills that we re-capture the Holy Land'; or he says, 'We fight to make the world safe for democracy'; or he says, 'We will wipe out social injustice with communism.' But the group doesn't care about the Holy Land, or Democracy, or Communism. Maybe the group simply wants to move, to fight, and uses these words simply to reassure the brains of individual men. I say it *might* be like that, Mac."

The nature, ends, and desires of group-man are not the same as those of the individual. "The pleasure we get in scratching an itch causes death to a great number of cells. Maybe group-man gets pleasure when individuals are wiped out in a war." Though the strikers constitute a group-animal, they may also be only one part of a still larger group-animal—the total society of which they are one force. Similarly, the school of fish, "an animal itself, reacting with all its cells to stimuli which perhaps might not influence one fish at all," may be a part of a larger unit which is, as explained in *Sea of Cortez*,

> the interrelation of species with their interdependence for food, even though that food be each other. A smoothly working larger animal surviving within itself—larval shrimp to little fish to larger fish to giant fish —one operating mechanism. And perhaps *this* unit of survival may key into the larger animal which is the life of all the sea, and this into the larger of the world.

To study group-man, a scientist must try his best to keep from being a mere cell in that organism. The tragedy is that an individual is not able to isolate himself completely from the larger organism, nor yet control it; and he is affected, often mortally in Steinbeck's novels, by what group-man does. So, in *Of Mice and Men*, George does, knowingly, what group-man makes it necessary for him to do, even though it is bad in itself. So, in *The Grapes of Wrath*, men do evil things driven by the demands of an organism which they compose, but which is larger than themselves.

> "The bank is something else than men. It happens that every man in a bank hates what the bank does, and yet the bank does it. The bank is something more than men, I tell you. It's the monster. Men made it, but they can't control it."

The grandfather who was "The Leader of the People" (*The Long Valley*) is left an empty shell when the westering group-animal of which he was a part has spent its force. And the Nazis in *The Moon Is Down* are not so much evil in themselves (to the great annoyance of many reviewers) as cells in a group-animal bent on evil of an immensity impossible to any single human being.

Though Steinbeck clearly hates capitalist exploitation and attacks bourgeois virtues, he is far from being an orthodox leftist. The inconclusive struggle between strikers and the town is truly a dubious battle; and while the reader's sympathy is directed unmistakably toward the strikers, Dr. Burton is there to remind us to be shocked at the mechanized inhumanity of the Communist organizers. The exploitation of the apple pickers is undoubtedly bad, but so are cancer and tetanus. The cruelty of the vigilantes is bad, but Steinbeck makes it clear that they are only tools of the owners; they are parts of an organism larger than themselves, and they follow the drives and direction of the larger organism. So with the owners and vigilantes of *The Grapes of Wrath*. Steinbeck hates the system of which they are natural manifestations, but his severest charge against them personally is that they have become de-humanized, have lost the vitality and initiative and adaptability of good biological specimens of the human species. This, it appears from the novels generally, is the true sin against the Holy Ghost—to become so sunk in the social organism as to lose one's biological individuality.

In contrast, Steinbeck's heroes, from Tom Joad to Juan Chicoy, are first and foremost themselves, strongly aware of their identities and armed with the biological virtues necessary to protect their individualities. They are humorous, strong, lecherous, and versatile. Particularly lecherous. "If the reader of this book is 'genteel'," says Steinbeck in *Sea of Cortez*, "then this is a very vulgar book, because the animals in a tide pool have two major preoccupations: first, survival, and second, reproduction. They reproduce all over the place." Steinbeck's heroes, it is hardly necessary to point out, also reproduce all over the place, but there is almost no picture of romantic love in the later novels. Steinbeck persistently writes of sex relations in physical terms only, and the sex act is presented as a pure good in itself, whether it takes place in the muddy streets of Tortilla Flat, on a truck traversing U.S. Highway 66, in the stern and stately whore-house of Dora Flood, or in a barn on the detour to San Juan de la Cruz. From this point of view, sex is bad only when the normal biological drives are subverted in the interest of gentility or some man-made convention. If the sex life of Mr. and Mrs. Pritchard in *The Wayward Bus* is unwholesome, that is because Mrs. Pritchard is herself a defective organism, and Mr. Pritchard has been mechanized and dehumanized into a kind of automaton.

The antithesis of Mr. Pritchard is the man who has learned to live in accordance with the precepts of Our Father who art in nature; and Steinbeck pays tribute to his hero in *Sea of Cortez*:

> What good men most biologists are, the tenors of the scientific world —temperamental, moody, lecherous, loud-laughing, and healthy. . . . . The true biologist deals with life, with teeming, boisterous life, and learns something from it, learns that the first rule of life is living. . . . . He must, so know the starfish and the student biologist who sits at the feet of living things, proliferate in all directions. Having certain tendencies, he must move along their lines to the limit of their potentialities.

Steinbeck's heroes do proliferate in all directions, on the biological level at least. They eat enormously, when they can get the food, and

Grandpa Joad, a natural man if ever there was one, dreams of squash-ing a whole bunch of grapes on his face and letting them run off his chin. All of them drink with enthusiasm, and their love-making is already sufficiently notorious. Those who have the capacity for it, like Tom Joad, throw themselves with sensuous delight into work. All of Steinbeck's "good" people have the capacity for gorgeous loafing, and the spontaneous enthusiasm of their play, as at a dance, is the one bright spot in the somber chronicle of the Dust Bowl migrants. Their common lack of spiritual complexity and subtlety is compensated, from the biological point of view, by their vitality, viability, and adaptability.

This last quality is important in Steinbeck's thinking. The ability to adapt to new conditions is one of man's most valuable biological attributes, and the loss of it might well lead to man's extinction. Steinbeck's bourgeois characters are in a dangerous rut. Mr. Pritchard, in *The Wayward Bus*, is dependent on his level of society, not merely for the means of existence, but for self-assurance and self-respect. Alone, in the Chicoys' lunchroom, facing strangers not of his own class, he is uncertain how to act, and he covers his confusion by the automatic act of cleaning his fingernails. He is further embarrassed by the ques-tions of Ernest Horton:

> "You know, we're supposed to be a mechanical people. Everybody drives a car and has an icebox and a radio. . . . . But let a little dirt get in the carburetor and—well, a car has to stand there until a mechanic comes and takes out the screen. . . . . Can you set the timer on your car? . . . . Suppose you had to stay out here two weeks. Could you keep from starving to death? . . . . Could you kill a cow?" Ernest in-sisted. "Could you cut it up and cook it?"

Like the other adolescents on the way to Hollywood, Mr. Pritchard takes refuge in a comforting, and neatly censored, fantasy.

Steinbeck's explanation of Mr. Pritchard's biological inadequacy is given in *Sea of Cortez*:

> Perhaps the pattern of struggle is so deeply imprinted in the genes of all life conceived in this benevolently hostile planet that the removal of obstacles automatically atrophies a survival drive. With warm water and abundant food, the animals may retire into a sterile, sluggish happiness. This has certainly seemed true of man.

And again:

> In a thoroughly collectivized state, mediocre efficiency might be very

great, but only through the complete elimination of the swift, the clever, and the intelligent, as well as the incompetent. Truly collective man might in fact abandon his versatility.

The middle class, Steinbeck seems to be repeating in his novels, has abandoned its versatility, and its values are atrophied into a sluggish desire for comfort and security.

In sharp contrast to Mr. Pritchard, Steinbeck's heroes have retained the ability to take care of themselves, and the self-assurance that goes with it. Slim, the jerk-line skinner in *Of Mice and Men*, knows he is good, and he accepts the deferential respect of the ranch hands with aristocratic graciousness. Equipped with a revolver, a roll of bandage, a bottle of iodine, a vial of lavender smelling salts, and a pint of whisky, Juan Chicoy feels fairly confident of handling most situations. He knows how to do what needs to be done, whether it be changing a ring gear in the differential, straightening out the kitchen of his lunchroom, pulling his bus out of the mud, or helping a strongly-sexed young woman to find satisfaction. He proliferates in all directions, and his strength and assurance are contagious, helping to make a man out of his pimply assistant. Other men are kept alert, strong, and self-reliant by a benevolently hostile environment. Steinbeck implies that there are many heroes among the underprivileged, and they are not necessarily masculine. Ma Joad is an heroic figure because she is so good a biological specimen. Her will to survive is strong, not merely for herself but for the family as a unit. Like her companions, she has humor, generosity, and tolerance. As a whole, the Dust Bowl migrants have been made tough and resourceful by adversity, and like Steinbeck's symbolic turtle, they struggle ahead despite temporary setbacks carrying the seeds of all that is good in man, as the turtle unwittingly bears the barley seeds on his shell.

Mack, in *Cannery Row*, emphasizes somewhat different virtues. Like the other Steinbeck heroes, he is a natural leader, competent and versatile. When he travels, Mack always carries salt and coffee, but he would not think of taking food into the country, knowing that the country is where food comes from. Still, his real strength, like Thoreau's, comes from renunciation. Mack's economy is as simple as that at Walden Pond; he knows what he wants, but he always considers whether or not its cost is excessive. He has no puritanical objection to high living (and the genteel might find his thinking plain indeed); but most of the things valued by the middle class—mechanical gadgets, security, cleanliness, prestige, comfort—Mack finds too expensive.

What can it profit a man to gain the whole world and to come to his property with a gastric ulcer, a blown prostate, and bifocals? Mack and the boys avoid the trap, walk round the poison, step over the noose, while a generation of trapped, poisoned, trussed-up men scream at them and call them no-goods, come-to-bad-ends, blots-on-the-town, thieves, rascals, bums.

Mack and the boys, in short, are strong enough to be able to relax, to take their pleasures simply and easily, without feeling the necessity for calling them something else. Like the *paisanos* of Tortilla Flat, they are artists in living, though they work with a limited palette, industrial society being what it is and the price of essentials like leisure, simplicity, and honor being so high. They have the repose of healthy animals, or of primitive men. Not that Steinbeck has any illusions about the noble savage. His picture of the fishing Indians of the Gulf of California stresses their superstitions and suffering.

> It is not implied that this fishing Indian lives a perfect or even a very good life. A toothache may be to him a terrible thing, and a stomach-ache may kill him. Often he is hungry, but he does not kill himself over things which do not closely concern him.

The inhabitants of Tortilla Flat and Cannery Row have this in common with the fishing Indian of the Gulf: they have no wish to become involved in the contradictions of a civilization which drives itself to the verge of nervous breakdown finding new ways to cure the sick and kill the healthy, to pamper the body and stultify the spirit.

Mack and the boys and the fishing Indian know that laziness is as natural to man as busy-ness, that a living organism needs repose as well as stimulation, and that leisure and an easy mind are essential to the life of the spirit.

> "Only in laziness," say Steinbeck-Ricketts, "can one achieve a state of contemplation which is a balancing of values, a weighing of oneself against the world and the world against itself. A busy man cannot find time for such balancing. We do not think a lazy man can commit murders, nor great thefts, nor lead a mob. He would be more likely to think about it and laugh."

Furthermore, laziness and the contemplation which it permits do not merely keep men out of mischief; they are productive of the best kind of activity. "One could argue, particularly if one had a gift for laziness, that it is a relaxation pregnant of activity, a sense of rest from which directed effort may arise, whereas most busy-ness is merely a kind of nervous tic." Two acquaintances of Steinbeck provide illustrations: a woman who frantically empties ashtrays and a man with a compulsion to straighten rugs and pictures and to arrange books and magazines in neat piles. Suppose the latter should relax, "with his feet up on a chair and a glass of cool beer beside him." He might well be led to speculate on the relativity of straightness and the folly of imposing his narrow sense of rightness on a rug. His relaxation might even become pregnant of the kind of activity so prevalent in the tide pools.

"Suppose I should try to straighten people," and here he sips deeply. "Helen C., for instance, is not neat, and Helen C."—here he goes into a reverie—"how beautiful she is with her hair messy, how lovely when she is excited and breathing through her mouth." Again he raises his glass, and in a few minutes he picks up the telephone. He is happy; Helen C. may be happy; and the rug is not disturbed at all.

If Steinbeck's attitude here is only half-serious, it is nevertheless part serious; and the bitterness of his Foreword to the Modern Library edition of *Tortilla Flat* shows that the account of Danny and his friends was not intended to be merely amusing. The *paisanos* of Tortilla Flat are suitable material for myth on the Arthurian pattern because their virtues are so simple and their vices almost nonexistent from a biologist's point of view. Danny and his friends are the direct antithesis of the middle class: they do what they want to do, and they cheerfully pay the price for leisure and independence. Steinbeck likes them, as he likes all viable biological specimens. He refuses to criticize them by the standards of modern, industrialized man, and he is bitterly resentful of the patronizing attitude of middle-class tourists who find them "quaint" and picturesque.

Steinbeck is said to have agreed with Malcolm Cowley that, if *Cannery Row* is a kind of literary cream puff, it is a remarkably poisoned cream puff. The poison would seem to be the implicit attack on middle-class values which may be found in all the novels. The outright criticisms of our economic system to be found in *The Grapes of Wrath* and *In Dubious Battle* may sting certain Chambers of Commerce into outraged apologetics, but the real poison in the novels is concealed beneath the readability which has made them best sellers. Though many readers may gulp the cream puff without indigestion, the virus remains latent there—a glorification of the biological virtues and an implicit attack on most of the things dear to the hearts of the respectable.

When Steinbeck goes beyond the simple biological virtues, it is to a set of values equally nonhumanistic: the mystical. Steinbeck oscillates between two poles: the tide pool and the stars; and of the area between the animal and the saint, which most novelists have taken for their province, he has relatively little to say. The starfish plays his part in the scheme of things well enough, and for any man who is as good an animal as the starfish, Steinbeck has an honest respect. But man is differentiated from the starfish by his ability to see his part, as well as play it. Only men (though not all men) are able to achieve the understanding that "man is related to the whole thing." The concluding summary of the trip to the Gulf is a tribute to this conscious identification of the self with all reality:

> The shape of the trip was an integrated nucleus from which weak strings of thought stretched into every reachable reality, and a reality which reached into us through our perceptive nerve trunks. The laws of thought seemed really one with the laws of things. . . . The real picture of how it had been there and how we had been there was in our minds, bright with sun and wet with sea water and blue or burned, and the whole crusted over with exploring thought. . . . . The brown Indians and the gardens of the sea, and the beer and the work, they were all one thing and we were that one thing too.

To be aware of the whole thing and to accept one's part in it is, for Steinbeck, the saving grace which may lift man out of the tide pool. His heroes—George, saving Lennie from the mob; Doc, committing the idiot boy who loves him; Juan Chicoy, turning back to pull the bus out of the mud; even Camille Oaks, wearily enduring her attractiveness—all share the main "non-teleological" virtue: the ability to see what "is" (which includes what needs to be done) with "the love and understanding of instant acceptance."

1. Quotations in this article from the writings of John Steinbeck and from *Sea of Cortez*, by John Steinbeck and Edward F. Ricketts, are used by permission of the Viking Press.

2. *The Boys in the Back Room*, San Francisco: The Colt Press, 1941.

3. *On Native Ground*, New York: Reynal and Hitchcock, 1942.

4. Antonia Seixas, "The Non-teleological Bus," *What's Doing* (Monterey Peninsula—San Francisco), March, 1947. [See p. 275, below.]

5. Fred B. Millett, *Contemporary American Authors*, New York: Harcourt, Brace and Co., 1944.

6. Edward F. Ricketts and Jack Calvin, *Between Pacific Tides*, Stanford University Press.

7. W. C. Allee, *Animal Aggregations*, University of Chicago Press.

Blake Nevius

STEINBECK: ONE ASPECT

IN *SEA OF CORTEZ* Steinbeck records the disappointment of the people of Monterey when a local scientist identified the decomposed body of a "sea serpent," washed up on the beach at Moss Landing, as that of a shark:

> They so wanted it to be a sea-serpent. Even we hoped it would be. When sometime a true sea-serpent, complete and undecayed, is found or caught, a shout of triumph will go through the world. "There, you see," men will say, "I knew they were there all the time."

The fact remains, they are not there. We know it, and Steinbeck knows it, but he is driven to the sentimental conclusion that "men really need sea monsters in their personal oceans." The Old Man of the Sea is one of them:

> In Monterey you can find many people who have seen him. . . . . So far, he has never been photographed. When he is, probably Dr. Bolin will identify him, and another beautiful story will be shattered. For this reason we rather hope he is never photographed, for if the Old Man of the Sea should turn out to be some great malformed sea lion, a lot of people would feel a sharp personal loss—a Santa Claus loss.

Although Steinbeck proceeds to invest his metaphor with more complicated meanings, I believe most readers will accept it as it stands as a fair description of his attitude toward illusion. He both cherishes and rejects it. From the boy Henry Morgan, dreaming in his Welsh valley, filled with "a desire for the thing he could not name"—for the Indies of his imagination—to Juan Chicoy, yearning toward the Mexico of his boyhood, Steinbeck's characters with few exceptions stand, in their personal visions of the world, in much the same realtionship to reality. Although they are victimized by their illusions, which are ultimately

BLAKE NEVIUS is a member of the English Department of the University of California at Los Angeles. His essay on Steinbeck first appeared in the Summer, 1949 issue of The Pacific Spectator. It is reprinted here by permission of Mr. Nevius and of the Managing Editor of The Pacific Spectator.

powerless in the face of reality, it is clear that through them they have realized whatever beauty, grace, and meaning life holds for them.

For this reason none of them experiences the usual sense of freedom when he is released from the grip of illusion and enters the world of reality. Their loss is indeed "a Santa Claus loss." Henry Morgan, robbed of his final dream in Panama, becomes an unattractive mediocrity. Exiled to Jamaica, he spends his declining years being bullied at home by his wife and, by way of compensation, dispensing questionable justice in court to his former comrades-in-arms. The stories comprising *The Pastures of Heaven* treat disillusionment in the same wistfully ironic tone. One by one, through the operation of the Battle farm curse, the valley inhabitants are made aware of a reality which is inimical to their peace of mind, a reality which, by impressing upon such happily amoral characters as the Lopez sisters, Raymond Banks, and Junius Maltby the conventional moral truth of their motives and situations, succeeds in driving them from the valley.

It is only when its hard facts and uncongenial duties are forgotten that life begins to blossom outward. As soon as Pat Humbert's dour and demanding parents are buried, the roses come suddenly alive again and cover his house. Peter Randall, the Salinas County farmer of the short story "The Harness," is enslaved to an ideal of duty and respectability wrought by his wife. When she dies, he improvidently sows his acres with sweet peas, then settles back on his front porch to enjoy them. The best things in life come to those who throw off the harness—so much is apparent. But the harness always goes back on. The dream ends and reality takes over, and Peter Randall finds himself involuntarily carrying out his dead wife's wishes. So it is always in Steinbeck's world. Juan Chicoy, in *The Wayward Bus*, relinquishes his dream of Mexico and returns to his jealous dipsomaniac wife and the drab routine of his business.

If American novelists are preoccupied with themes of disillusionment, it is not merely because the novel in general is concerned with the progress from illusion to reality, but because they view their fellow Americans essentially as dreamers who are easily subject to disenchantment, as idealists whose ideals are seldom realizable, as sentimentalists whose happiness is threatened by their refusal to approach life rationally. For those novelists in the New England tradition who were writing before World War I—Hawthorne, Howells, James—disillusionment was likely to be merely the prelude to regeneration; for their successors—Hemingway, Fitzgerald, and Dos Passos—it was the single, inescapable fact of existence, and consequently they dispensed with salvation. But in both cases illusion was regarded as an obstacle to the liberation of the individual mind and personality.

Steinbeck, however, like the later Willa Cather, argues that there is a saving grace in illusion because without it life may be insupportable. Such is the value of the Hawkins sisters to the community described in "Johnny Bear." "It wouldn't be good for any of us if the Hawkins sisters weren't the Hawkins sisters," Alex Hartnell tells the narrator. The Hawkins mansion, the Hawkins respectability, and the Hawkins philanthropies provide the one bulwark between the community and a total invasion of the grim reality which its foggy, swamp-bound atmosphere menacingly implies. They are, in Hartnell's words, "the safe thing."

> The place where a kid can get gingerbread. The place where a girl can get reassurance. They're proud, but they believe in things we hope are true. And they live as though—well, as though honesty really is the best policy and charity really is its own reward. We need them.

When the myth of the sisters' respectability is exploded, the community is suddenly and justifiably frightened.

Aware of its saving value, many of the characters of Steinbeck's later stories try determinedly to protect the illusion from the encroachment of reality. Colonel Lanser of *The Moon Is Down* is, as I hope to indicate, the supreme example, but they range in importance down to Henri, the would-be painter of Cannery Row, who has been building a boat for seven years but refuses to finish it because he hates water.

Traditionally, illusion in the novel has been conceived of in terms of an aberration of the individual will, brought about either by a failure of values in the religious or moral realm or by a failure of insight in a given social situation. In the broadest sense, we may say that in the first case the illusion stems from an imperfect relationship between man and God, and in the second, from an imperfect relationship between man and man. In this country, so long as the novel remained under the domination of New England, illusion was represented as primarily inherent in the worship of false gods—property, social position, power, success—in the failure of the individual to align his will with the discernible will of the God of Nature or the God in Nature. As a result of the unbroken influence of Puritan thought, the corruption and eventual rehabilitation of the will furnished a seemingly inexhaustible theme, and this was true because it was not treated primarily in theological terms but instead lent itself to infinite adaptation. On the other hand, the novel of manners, which has developed more successfully abroad, is concerned, as Lionel Trilling recently has suggested, with the problem of illusion and reality as it is revealed by "the shifting and conflict of social classes," a field of investigation that has never really interested American novelists. In either case, a corrective view is generally implied, because there is some recognition of the fundamental nature of the illusion.

With Steinbeck no such emphatic recognition is possible. It is very nearly obtained in the finest of his novels, *In Dubious Battle*, through the skeptical mediation of Doc Burton, who realizes that illusion is generated on both sides by the conflict of interests between owners and strikers, and who, unlike most of Steinbeck's characters, is willing to probe for the source of the infection. But the relatively searching and dispassionate kind of analysis which Steinbeck applied to the situation in this novel has not been repeated in his later work.

Steinbeck's failure is further defined by the fact that evil, which is generally thought of as the product of illusion, is granted no basis for existence in his world. It has no source in the illusion, but arises spontaneously and unpredictably, like a cloud, enveloping and infecting everything in its wake for a while, then disappearing as unaccountably as it came. Of Estera de la Luna, one of the *Western Flyer's* points of call in the Sea of Cortez, he writes:

> We felt that this had not been a good nor a friendly place. Some quality of evil hung over it and infected us. . . . . It had been a bad place —bad feelings, bad dreams, and little accidents. The look and feel of it were bad.

Steinbeck's philosophical justification of this passage may be found in the same book, for *Sea of Cortez* is in large part an attempt to rationalize a view of life which derives essentially from the author's particular nervous response to people and environment. Briefly, its philosophical passages constitute an attack on teleological reasoning, which seeks to discover causes and concerns itself with the purposiveness of events. The burden of Steinbeck's counterstatement is that "the truest reason for anything's being so is that it *is*." Nonteleological, or "is" thinking, as Steinbeck calls it, is of use to him primarily as an antidote to optimists, moralists, and reformers, who attempt to ameliorate conditions before they have achieved even the most superficial understanding of them, and as a means of clearing the air for a detached but sympathetic approach to human nature.

At the same time, applied to the problem of evil, it becomes a convenient pretext for begging the question. Thus, in *The Pastures of*

Heaven evil assumes the guise of the Battle farm curse which, through the agency of Bert Munroe, spreads through the whole community, poisoning the lives of its inhabitants and driving them from their false Eden. It has no source in human nature. It simply exists. It "is." And in this early collection of stories Steinbeck, at a loss to account for its origin in terms of the usual myths, treats it with the incipient irony that marks his first two books. The whirlwind of dust which Richard Whiteside accepts as a favorable omen from God is the granddaddy of the whirlwind which, two generations later, catches up the vagrant sparks from a bonfire and destroys the house he has built for the dynasty to succeed him. And of course the irony of the concluding framework episode, in which the tourists look down on the valley and picture it individually to themselves as a happy refuge from the world, is if anything overstressed.

In "Johnny Bear," the disaster which is to overtake the community when its saving illusion is destroyed is announced by a series of unaccountable accidents at the construction camp: the digger sinks into the swamp, a crew member loses both legs, a leverman develops blood poisoning. In *Cannery Row*, following the abortive party at which Mack and the boys wreck Doc's laboratory, the community is similarly plagued by accidents: "It was a bad time. Evil stalked darkly in the vacant lot. There is no explaining a series of misfortunes like that." Then with as little preparation the pall is lifted, and Steinbeck commemorates the change in some of his most embarrassing prose:

> Now a kind of gladness began to penetrate into the Row and to spread out from there. Doc was almost supernaturally successful with a series of lady visitors. . . . . The puppy at the Palace was growing like a beanpole. . . . . The benignant influence crept like gas through the Row. . . . . The sea lions felt it and their barking took on a tone and cadence that would have gladdened the heart of St. Francis. Little girls studying their catechism suddenly looked up and giggled for no reason at all. . . . .

Although Steinbeck has moved from irony to sentimentality, his vision of evil—if it may be called that—is essentially unaltered.

Instances could be multiplied, but *The Grapes of Wrath* offers a crucial one. Here, when we ask what Steinbeck is attacking, we are again confronted with a blank wall. Society as it is constituted in this country? Hardly. There is little criticism of specific evils except that of absentee ownership. Human nature? Steinbeck, following the logic of "is" thinking, is inclined to be lenient: men act brutally toward less fortunate men out of fear for their possessions. No ultimate assignment of responsibility for the Okies' plight is possible. Of the owners who drove them from their land, some, says Steinbeck, were kind, some angry, some cold, some afraid, some "hated the mathematics that drove them," and all of them "were caught in something larger than themselves." The tractor driver who plowed up the land got his orders from the agent; the agent, from the Bank; the Bank, from the East. "But where does it stop?" cries the tenant. "Who can we shoot?" And the driver replies: "I don't know. Maybe there's nobody to shoot. Maybe the thing isn't men at all."

That there is an antagonism at the heart of the world is apparent, but that is all that can be affirmed. Steinbeck is admittedly opposed to the investigation of first causes: "The whole picture is portrayed by *is*, the deepest word of ultimate reality, not shallow or partial as reasons are, but deeper and participating, possibly encompassing the Oriental concept of *being*." Like the Hindus he acknowledges the possibility of differentiating between good and evil, since evil implies the absence of good, but insists that they be regarded as aspects of the same whole. The preacher Casy, in *The Grapes of Wrath*, is the prophet of Steinbeck's middle period:

> "There ain't no sin and there ain't no virtue. There's just stuff people do. It's all part of the same thing. And some of the things folks do are nice, and some ain't nice, but that's as far as any man got a right to say."

Western philosophy, in so far as it remains untouched by the implications of modern science, conceives of good and evil as separate, warring forces and therefore is ultimately trapped, in dealing with the problem of evil, by the question "why," which demands an assignment of responsibility. From first to last Steinbeck refuses to be trapped. "I want to see the whole picture—as nearly as I can," Doc (Steinbeck) Burton tells Mac, in *In Dubious Battle*. "I don't want to put on the blinders of 'good' and 'bad' and limit my vision."

Steinbeck illustrates vividly the kind of moral impasse to which the idea of relativity applied to the field of cultural investigation has brought us while at the same time widening the grounds of tolerance in a way we can only approve. Since what is good in terms of our culture may be a positive bad in another, we can safely apply the term "good" only to those motives which appear in common at the most primitive level. This is precisely what Steinbeck does. His *paisanos* in *Tortilla Flat*, Mack and the boys in *Cannery Row*, and most of the characters in *The Wayward Bus* gain a certain vitality (which his less earthy characters do not have) as a result of their uninhibited response to organic drives; but this involves their almost complete emancipation from social responsibility and a disregard of everything which culture has added to human life. The novels of Steinbeck's middle period, *In Dubious Battle*, *Of Mice and Men*, and *The Grapes of Wrath*, in a large measure avoided this simplification; but when the impulse generated by social change, which so vitalized his work in the late 'thirties, passed, he returned in *Sea of Cortez* and in the stories which followed it to an earlier and apparently more characteristic point of view.

The danger which this kind of thinking entails for the artist should be clear from the failure of *The Moon Is Down*. Now that the controversy over the question of Steinbeck's possible disservice to the Allied cause at a critical moment is buried, the question of his artistic failure can be discussed more calmly. Although for the first time since *Cup of Gold* Steinbeck broke away from the California valley and the isolated rural community of his earlier, successful stories, the unfamiliar setting of this new novel posed less of a problem than did the necessity of dealing with characters in whom the qualities of intelligence and the operation of cultural values were manifested to a high degree.

"Honor and peace to Pilon," Steinbeck had written in *Tortilla Flat*, "for he had discovered how to uncover and to disclose the good that lay in every evil thing." In *The Moon Is Down* Pilon's creator seems to have approached his task in much the same spirit. As I have noted, the nonteleological approach is valuable to Steinbeck in so far as it tends to eliminate moral judgments and to substitute what he calls the ideal of "understanding-acceptance." Applied to the situation described in *The Moon Is Down*, it produced a supposedly representative group of Nazis (we may call them that for the sake of convenience) who at their worst appear to us as misguided idealists and rather unpleasant barracks-mates. Omitting Colonel Lanser, they are: Major Hunter, the engineer, a happy, humorless automaton; Captain Bentick, "a family man, a lover of dogs and pink children and Christmas," an Anglophile, unsuccessful in his profession; Captain Loft, an unimaginative disciplinarian who "had no unmilitary moments"; and Lieutenants Prackle and Tonder, "sentimental young men," the former a foe of degenerate art who can scowl like the Leader, the latter "a bitter poet who dreamed of a perfect, ideal love of elevated young men for poor girls" and longed to die romantically on the field of battle. "These," Steinbeck concludes, "were the men of the staff, each one playing war as children play 'Run, Sheep, Run' . . . ." Here, in other words, is The Enemy —innocuous, a bit ludicrous, playing a game. "Of them all, only Colonel Lanser knew what war really is in the long run."

It is in the characterization of Lanser that Steinbeck's determined fair-mindedness operates most disastrously. I am willing to grant that his failure may be one of emphasis rather than intention, but his refusal to ground his action clearly on the moral dilemma faced by this polite, cultured, world-weary, supposedly humane individual, who is responsible as a soldier but irresponsible as a human being, is fatal to that intention if it existed. As a matter of fact, one is hardly justified in speaking of Lanser's "dilemma," for he has rationalized himself clear of the threat of alternatives. Although he presents himself to Mayor Orden as a man untroubled by memories, he carries with him the bitterest recollection of the first World War and of his part in it.

> Lanser had been in Belgium and France twenty years before and he tried not to think what he knew—that war is treachery and hatred, the muddling of incompetent generals, the torture and killing and sickness and tiredness. . . . . Lanser told himself that he was a soldier, given orders to carry out. He was not expected to question or think, but only to carry out orders. . . . .

Because of his evasions, his refusal to accept responsibility as an individual for what he does, preferring to take refuge in the fact that he is acting under orders, he is—given his other qualities of intelligence and sensitivity—a potentially tragic or ironic figure. He is driven to the most ignoble kind of expedient: forced to condemn to death a man whom he admires, he looks for consolation to the iron pattern of the military which he feels is imposed on his actions as an individual. He is no more responsible for Orden's death, Steinbeck would evidently have us believe, than the agent of the Bank is for the dispossession of the tenant farmers of The Grapes of Wrath. Nor does the responsibility rest ultimately with the German High Command any more than it does with the Bank.

That Steinbeck is unable to conceive of Lanser's predicament in either tragic or ironic terms or to make it the center of interest in his plot is perhaps an index of his own predicament, which is dangerously like that of Lanser. He is not only required to make the same evasions, but seems to be equally unaware of their significance. In his latest characters evasion has become a settled habit of mind. Juan Chicoy, longing to desert his wife and return to Mexico, shuffles off the decision onto the Virgin of Guadalupe.

> You know that I have not been happy and also that out of a sense of duty that is not natural to me I have stayed in the traps that have been set for me. And now I am about to put a decision into your hands. I cannot take the responsibility for running away from my wife and my

little business. . . . . I am on this road not of my own volition. I have
been forced here by the wills of these people who do not care anything
for me or for my safety and happiness. . . . .

And yet this is Steinbeck's "man of complete manness," the one character in the allegory who commands his admiration, the successor to
Mac in In Dubious Battle, Slim in Of Mice and Men, and Doc in
Cannery Row, imperturbable men who can do things with their hands
and are equal to every situation.

In a qualified sense Steinbeck's attitude is merely symptomatic; it
helps illustrate to what degree the novelists of the 'twenties and 'thirties
succeeded in extricating themselves from the New England tradition.
With the last vestiges of puritanism discredited, they were no longer
compelled to face the problem of evil squarely or to recognize the ideal
of individual responsibility as the basis of conduct. If among them only
Faulkner has tried to any extent to reshape the puritan myth into a
myth peculiarly his own in terms of which he can order and dramatize
the experience he presents in his novels, at least no other writer of
comparable reputation has resorted to the sentimental evasion of
Steinbeck.

Woodburn O. Ross

JOHN STEINBECK:
NATURALISM'S PRIEST

IN A PREVIOUS ARTICLE on the work of Mr. John Steinbeck I tried to describe his basic ideas and mental processes and to interpret the "meaning" of his fiction, in a general way, in their light.[1] I wish now to approach his work from another point of view, trying to interpret not so much in terms of meanings as in those of values.

I

The triumph of naturalism as a popular philosophy has been so complete that many of us have perhaps forgotten the horror with which western Europe began to realize the implications of the new biology in the later nineteenth century. The very foundations of spiritual values seemed about to be swept away. A somewhat eminent Victorian, A. J. Balfour, writing in The Foundations of Belief (1894), puts the matter this way: According to the naturalistic philosophy

> . . . not only does there seem to be no ground, from the point of view of biology, for drawing a distinction in favour of any of the processes, physiological or psychological, by which the individual or the race is benefited; not only are we bound to consider the coarsest appetites, the most calculating selfishness, and the most devoted heroism, as all sprung from analogous causes and all evolved for similar objects, but we can hardly doubt that the august sentiments which cling to the ideas of duty and sacrifice are nothing better than a device of Nature to trick us into the performance of altruistic actions.

But if, on the one hand, naturalism leveled values, on the other, by pointing to nature rather than to God as the source of value, it really deprived mankind of any suitable foundation for a moral code. Balfour says:

WOODBURN O. ROSS wrote "John Steinbeck: Naturalism's Priest" for College English, where it appeared in May, 1949. It is reprinted here by permission of Frederick L. Gwynn, editor of College English, and by permission of Mr. Ross. Another essay by Ross, "John Steinbeck: Earth and Stars," appears in the present volume.

I lay down two propositions . . . : (1) That, practically, human beings being what they are, no moral code can be effective which does not inspire, in those who are asked to obey it, emotions of reverence; and (2) that, practically, the capacity of any code to excite this or any other elevated emotion cannot be wholly independent of the origin from which those who accept that code suppose it to emanate.

Needless to say an impersonal nature inspires in him and, he thinks, in the rest of humanity none of these necessary emotions of reverence.

The development of the naturalistic point of view in the twentieth century has been accompanied by many of the results which Balfour feared. Western society now does experience difficulty in distinguishing between "the most calculating selfishness" and "the most devoted heroism," not simply because it is deceived by hypocrites, but because all ethics have tended to become purely relative and because permanent objective criteria by which acts can be measured are lacking. Theodore Dreiser states the case of the naturalist well in *The Titan*. Ethical principles, he explains, represent only a balance among the tensions to which the natural man is subject, and they certainly possess no transcendent validity. And in *Death in the Afternoon*, Ernest Hemingway, baffled by the difficulty of finding any adequate basis for morals, falls back upon the ultimate simplicity of "I know only that what is moral is what you feel good after."

On the other hand, persistent attempts have been made by some to resuscitate the sense of reverence, of a need for worship, and to use it, at least to some extent, to support principles of conduct. In literature such attitudes have been represented, for example, by the work of D. H. Lawrence, who completely rejected the rational sources of twentieth-century materialism and placed his trust in dark, subjective gods; and by that of Aldous Huxley, who has turned his face toward the East and has found in the ancient religions of India and China confirmation of the validity of the intuitive, mystical faith in which a small minority of his own people have always been willing to trust.

I suggest that much of the significance of the work of John Steinbeck lies in his partial affiliation with this movement. It is true, apparently, that to most readers he is a novelist interested in social reform. This interpretation of his work rests primarily upon certain obvious portions of *The Grapes of Wrath*, *Of Mice and Men*, *In Dubious Battle*, and, perhaps, upon the pamphlet *Their Blood Is Strong*. But these works were products of the great depression, and he has written nothing like them since. Indeed, Steinbeck shows a distinct tendency to shift his apparent interests with the times. But beneath his frequent changes of subject, at which reviewers marvel, he has maintained relatively un-changed certain fundamental attitudes, which have controlled his treat-ment of his subjects. It is these attitudes which we shall now consider, and we shall find that they lead us far from any discussion of social reform.

II

Unlike D. H. Lawrence and the current Aldous Huxley, Steinbeck is, up to a certain point, the complete naturalist; he accepts the scien-tists' representation of life. Sea of Cortez, in fact, suggests that his inter-est in biology verges on the professional. He emphasizes in his stories and novels the value of human acts and attitudes which he considers in harmony with natural law. Junius Maltby in The Pastures of Heaven pays for his love of the natural life with the lives of his wife and two children and, to the scandal of the neighbors, raises a third child with-out regard to artificial, civilized values; and Steinbeck apparently sym-pathizes with Maltby throughout. He leads the reader to dislike the stiff, unnatural garden of Mary Teller in The Long Valley. His friendly description of "natural" conduct in Tortilla Flat and Cannery Row is, of course, familiar. To a great extent, though not completely, Steinbeck accepts the ethical implications which many have seen in natural sci-ence. One need only mention, for instance, the Lopez sisters in The Pastures of Heaven and refer again to "the boys" of Cannery Row and to the Joads to make this fact clear. His position, in so far as he is a naturalist, appears to be the commonplace one that, since humanity is a product of natural forces and since the profoundest biological urge is the urge for life, for survival and reproduction, then virtue consists in whatever furthers these ends. "There would seem," he writes in Sea of Cortez, "to be only one commandment for living things: Survive!"

Steinbeck's naturalistic ideas have clearly done much to determine the character of the fiction which he writes. Yet to describe him as a naturalist is in one sense false. The description is incomplete; for, while never repudiating the points of view which I have just described, he amalgamates them with others which many would consider contradic-tory; and the resulting body of thought is, I think, significant.

In trying to describe this other side of his work, I shall begin with a quality which is the result of an emotional bias rather than an intellec-tual conviction. Steinbeck's writing is outside the strict scientific, natu-ralistic tradition, in that it is not objective. Steinbeck loves whatever he considers "natural" and is keenly sensitive to its emotional values. In Sea of Cortez one of the reasons which he advances against teleo-logical thinking is that thinking in terms of ends obscures spontaneous affection for whatever is, an affection which is the most important reaction that man should have to the world about him. He clearly loves human beings whom he considers to be living natural lives—the Joads, the paisanos, "the boys," and the characters of deficient mentality who appear often in his pages. A sensitiveness to the atmosphere of a piece of land, a recognition of a mysterious spirit of place, is a striking quality of his work. His love of the natural extends to naturalistic ethics; he loves natural behavior. He writes in *Sea of Cortez*:

> We sat on a crate of oranges and thought what good men most biologists are, the tenors of the scientific world—temperamental, moody, lecherous, loud-laughing, and healthy. . . . He must, so know the starfish and the student biologist who sits at the feet of living things, proliferate in all directions. . . . Your true biologist will sing you a song as loud and off-key as will a blacksmith, for he knows that morals are too often diagnostic of prostatitis and stomach ulcers.

The sympathetically drawn Grampa, in *The Grapes of Wrath*, is almost as virtuous as a biologist:

> He fought and argued, told dirty stories. He was as lecherous as always. Vicious and cruel and impatient, like a frantic child, and the whole structure overlaid with amusement. He drank too much when he could get it, ate too much when it was there, talked too much all the time.

Second, Steinbeck's ethical system, which, as we have thus far seen it, finds ultimate virtue only in obedience to the natural law which demands reproduction and survival, is in reality complicated by the introduction of a second major virtue, whose demands must be expected at times to be contrary to those of the former. It is altruism. Altruism is one basis of the satisfaction which the beaten-up radicals feel in "The Raid," a story in *The Long Valley*. It is certainly entangled among the inspiring emotions experienced by the narrator in "Breakfast." It is one of the forces motivating Mac and Jim Nolan, the strike organizers in *In Dubious Battle*. It frequently controls the actions of the poor in *The Grapes of Wrath*—perhaps, indeed, too frequently for the novel to be wholly convincing. It is dramatically expressed by the final act of Rose of Sharon, as she feeds a starving man at her own breast. Indeed, I believe that throughout the entire body of Steinbeck's work he excites admiration for characters who in some fashion love their brothers as constantly as he does for those who prove that they can be natural. But he does not support his emphasis upon altruism by any scientific reasoning. The cause of his acceptance of this virtue seems to lie in his own affections, in his love of all nature, human included.

In the third place, Steinbeck has developed ideas about the unity of the cosmos which may fairly be called "mystical," ideas which, of course, ultimately go considerably beyond what his scientific naturalism would support but which are, I think, connected with his love of the natural. His notion of the unity of things is complicated, but in its simplest aspects, as might be expected, it is presented as a conclusion which goes but little beyond what is warranted by scientific observation. In reporting in Sea of Cortez, for example, the semiscientific expedition which he made to the Gulf of Lower California with Mr. E. F. Ricketts, he writes:

> There are colonies of pelagic tunicates which have taken a shape like the finger of a glove. Each member of the colony is an individual animal, but the colony is another individual animal, not at all like the sum of its individuals. Some of the colonists, girdling the open end, have developed the ability, one against the other, of making a pulsing movement very like muscular action. Others of the colonists collect the food and distribute it, and the outside of the glove is hardened and protected against contact. Here are two animals, and yet the same thing—something the early Church would have been forced to call a mystery.

Most of this passage could have been written by any conventional scientist, intent upon reporting his unusual observation of this circumstance in nature; but at the end there is a hint of Steinbeck's seeing hidden meanings, not quite understood.

Another passage, however, still from Sea of Cortez, will make more clear what he is thinking:

> . . . It seems apparent that species are only commas in a sentence, that each species is at once the point and the base of a pyramid, that all life is relational to the point where an Einsteinian relativity seems to emerge. And then not only the meaning but the feeling about species grows misty. One merges into another, groups melt into ecological groups until the time when what we know as life meets and enters what we think of as non-life: barnacle and rock, rock and earth, earth and tree, tree and rain and air. And the units nestle into the whole and are inseparable from it. Then one can come back to the microscope and the tide pool and the aquarium. But the little animals are found to be changed, no longer set apart and alone. And it is a strange thing that most of the feeling we call religious, most of the mystical outcrying which is one of the most prized and used and desired reactions of our species, is really the understanding and the attempt to say that man is

related to the whole thing, related inextricably to all reality, known and unknowable. This is a simple thing to say, but the profound feeling of it made a Jesus, a St. Augustine, a St. Francis, a Roger Bacon, a Charles Darwin, and an Einstein. Each of them in his own tempo and with his own voice discovered and reaffirmed with astonishment the knowledge that all things are one thing and that one thing is all things. . . .

Scientific interests lie behind all these passages; Steinbeck is concerned with the organization and the interpretation of the observations which he and his colleague made. But he cannot rest content with the naturalist's world of sense experience. His grasping at mystical insight grows more evident as one reads. The very list of names which he gives above is suggestive of the ideological blend which he is trying to make: "Jesus . . . St. Francis . . . Charles Darwin."

Finally, let me quote one more passage from *Sea of Cortez*, one which goes still further in implying on the part of Steinbeck a mystical belief in the oneness of creation:

> Sometimes we asked of the Indians the local names of animals we had taken, and then they consulted together. They seemed to live on remembered things, to be so related to the seashore and the rocky hills and the loneliness that they are these things. To ask about the country is like asking about themselves. "How many toes have you?" "What, toes? Let's see—of course, ten. I have known them all my life, I never thought to count them. Of course it will rain tonight. Of course, I am the whole thing, now that I think about it. I ought to know when I will rain."

I have selected material demonstrating Steinbeck's mystical ideas of the unity of things entirely from *Sea of Cortez*, because this work is expository and the ideas are consequently presented here more directly than elsewhere in his work. But to forestall a possible objection to the effect that this attitude of his may have been transitory, let me point out that the conclusion of *To a God Unknown*, one of his earliest novels, asserts the unity of the hero with the universe—as a matter of fact, he is said to be the rain—and that *The Moon Is Down*, one of the latest of his novels, sees an invaded community as a group strikingly like his schools of fish which "turn as a unit and dive as a unit."

Steinbeck never explains the nature of the unity of the cosmos which he perceives. How can his colonies of fish form a single creature? What is the nature of the consciousness of this larger being? In just what sense is a man the rain? Manifestly, he lacks data with which to answer; indeed, he is never able rationally to prove that the unity about which he speaks exists at all. But the fact that his notions about the unity of things are very incomplete and rest upon feeling, insight, intuition, rather than upon reason is neither here nor there. The fact is that as an artist he believes in these things. They represent a part of Steinbeck which is not controlled by scientific rationalism.

The fourth and last aspect of Steinbeck's thought which cannot be called naturalistic is yet harder to describe. We have already seen him referring to part of the organization of nature as "something the early Church would have been forced to call a mystery." A sense of mystery, of significance which is not quite open to rational understanding, appears at least occasionally in Steinbeck. It is more than a perception of a strange unity in the universe, though, as what we have just seen would indicate, the exact nature of the unity is indeed a part of the mystery. It is a feeling that there is a meaning in things which forever eludes explanation in terms of knowledge which is simply organized sense experience. Some words of Elizabeth, the wife of Joseph Wayne, in *To a God Unknown*, help to show what Steinbeck feels. She says at the close of a festival described in the book:

> It was such an odd day. There was the outwardness, the people coming and the mass and the feasting and then the dance, and last of all the storm. Am I being silly, Joseph, or was there a meaning, right under the surface? It seemed like those pictures of simple landscapes they sell in the cities. When you look closely, you see all kinds of figures hidden in the lines. Do you know the kind of pictures I mean? A rock becomes a sleeping wolf, a little cloud is a skull, and the line of trees marching soldiers when you look closely. Did the day seem like that to you Joseph, full of hidden meaning, not quite understandable?

Steinbeck's perception of a mysterious significance in things is responsible for another episode in the book. Near the end of the story Joseph comes upon a strange man who lives at the end of a little peninsula jutting out into the Pacific Ocean. He lives there in order to be the last man on the continent to see the sun go down; and each evening as it sinks he kills some animal as a sacrifice. "You really want to know why I watch the sun—why I kill some little creature as it disappears?" he says. ". . . I don't know. . . . I have made up reasons, but they aren't true. I have said to myself, 'The sun is life. I give life to life. I make a symbol of the sun's death.' When I made up these reasons I knew they weren't true." Joseph broke in, "These were words to clothe a naked thing, and the thing is ridiculous in clothes."

III

Now much of Steinbeck's basic position is essentially religious, though not in any orthodox sense of the word. In his very love of nature he assumes an attitude characteristic of mystics. He is religious in that he contemplates man's relation to the cosmos and attempts, although perhaps fumblingly, to understand it. He is religious in that he seeks to transcend scientific explanations based upon sense experience. He is religious in that from time to time he explicitly attests the holiness of nature. Sometimes it is a mysterious plot of land which inspires him. In *To a God Unknown* Joseph Wayne, coming upon a curiously secretive glade, says to his brother: "Be still a moment, Tom. . . . There's something here. You are afraid of it, but I know it. Somewhere, perhaps in an old dream, I have seen this place, or perhaps felt the feeling of this place. . . . This is holy—and this is old. This is ancient—and holy." In *The Grapes of Wrath* Casy finds holiness in the unity of nature: ". . . There was the hills, an' there was me, an' we wasn't separate no more. We was one thing. An' that one thing was holy. . . ." And later he sees holiness in life itself: "All that lives," he says, "is holy." Steinbeck even finds holiness in "natural" conduct which, measured by conventional standards, would be found immoral. "Gonna lay in the grass, open an' honest with anybody that'll have me," says Casy. "Gonna cuss an' swear an' hear the poetry of folks talkin'. All that's holy, an' that's what I didn' understan'. All them things is good things."

Overtones of a religious character are to be heard in Steinbeck's latest book, *The Wayward Bus*. It is, I think, significant that the phrase "El Gran Poder de Jesus" has been painted over on the bumper of the bus and the word "Sweetheart" put in its place. The bumper-palimpsest is, I take it, a symbol of the substitution by a wicked generation of a superficial interest in sex for a profound sense of the nature and reality of things. It is likewise worth noticing that Juan Chicoy, the hero, communes with an image of the Virgin as he drives. This is not to imply that Steinbeck represents him as an orthodox Christian. But to Juan the image is a kind of talisman, something in which he does not believe rationally but to which the depths of his mind do respond. A primitive part of his nature, uncomplicated by reason, finds in this image itself, in an animistic fashion, power, wisdom, and sympathy. Steinbeck seems to approve of these "natural," half-religious, half-superstitious gropings of Juan. They are of a piece with the rest of the unintellectual, instinctive conduct which makes him the hero of the book. Again, the command "Repent" printed on the cliff above the stalled bus can hardly be without symbolic significance. Steinbeck never says what is to be repented of. But, if one reads the book in the context of Steinbeck's previous work, one may be sure that the warning is directed not against any conventional sins but against failure to accept life and nature as they are and against failure to love life and man, to feel the mystery and unity of creation.

IV

Nineteenth-century fears that the development of naturalism meant the end of reverence, of worship, and of "august sentiments" are not warranted in the case of Steinbeck. He has succeeded in taking the materials which undermined the religious faith of the nineteenth century and fusing them with a religious attitude in the twentieth, though a religious attitude very different from what the orthodox in the nineteenth century would have thought possible. Nature as described by the scientist becomes not merely the foundation of a revolutionary ethic; it also supplies, as many in the nineteenth century thought it could not, the basis of a sense of reverence which affectively supports the new ethic, now surprisingly turned altruistic. Steinbeck is, I think, the first significant novelist to begin to build a mystical religion upon a naturalistic base. The important question, as yet, of course, unanswerable, is to what extent he, or the mystical movement with which he has affiliations, will prove influential in this century. Certainly, the Western world is gasping in the religious vacuum into which it has been plunged. It seeks an affective relationship with the universe. Steinbeck's answer is arresting for the reason that it does not require the West to forget or deny what it has learned about nature in the last hundred years, as, for instance, D. H. Lawrence's solution did. Steinbeck is in the current of positive scientific thought; in that respect he does not swim upstream. Yet he is both rational and irrational: he accepts all that reason can tell him and permits his intuition and affections to add what they will to the world created by reason and to determine his position toward the universe as it then appears.

This new religious attitude which Steinbeck, at least in some vague way, has been able to construct for himself out of unpromising materials bears on it the marks of its perilous birth. It is extremely primitive. It rejects more than two thousand years of theological thought. It abandons all attempts to discern final purposes in life. It virtually reduces man again to animism; for, unlike Wordsworth, Steinbeck does not see through nature to a God beyond; he hears no intimations of immortality; for him there is no spirit which rolls through all things. There is only nature, ultimately mysterious, to which all things belong, bound together in a unity concerning whose stupendous grandeur he can barely hint. But such a nature Steinbeck loves, and before it, like primitive man, he is reverent.

In brief, the significance of Steinbeck's work may prove to lie in the curious compromise which it effects. It accepts the intuitive, nonrational method of dealing with man's relation to the universe—the method of the contemporary mystics. But, unlike them, it accepts as the universe to which man must relate himself the modern, scientifically described cosmos.

1. [See p. 167, above.]

Claude-Edmonde Magny

STEINBECK, OR THE LIMITS
OF THE IMPERSONAL NOVEL

*S*TEINBECK has already begun to appear much less important in American literature than he might have a few years ago and *The Wayward Bus*, his latest novel, is not such as to restore his prestige. However, its very defects (using the word in its most etymological sense) have a typical significance; it seems to represent the best, as well as the most limited, of what the American novel offers us.

The first attraction we find in Steinbeck stems from the extreme simplicity of his art as revealed by the very choice of his novelistic means: the social milieu in which he chooses his characters, their intellectual level, the very limited vocabulary which they use in their speech, and the not much larger one which is used by the author in developing his plot.

The collection of short stories called *The Long Valley* presents a fairly complete epitome of the works of Steinbeck. The stories which make up the book are definitely linked together; their relationship is proved by the single title which covers them all without belonging to

CLAUDE-EDMONDE MAGNY, *graduate in philosophy of l'École Normale Supérieure, taught French literature for four years at Cambridge University before becoming Professor of Philosophy in a lycée in Paris. She has published* Histoire du Roman Français depuis 1918 (1950) *and has written an Introduction for an anthology of the writings of Arthur Rimbaud. One of the most important reviews of Steinbeck's East of Eden was the one she wrote for Perspectives U. S. A., No. 5.*

L'Age du Roman Américain, from which the essay on Steinbeck reprinted here is taken, was awarded the Sainte-Beuve Prize for a work in criticism in 1948. "The Limits of the Impersonal Novel" was translated into English by Françoise Gourier of the Department of Modern and Classical Languages at the University of New Mexico.

any one in particular. Linked as they are by a common color and atmosphere, they are also tied by at least one of the three unities necessary to classical tragedy, that of place. Although they differ considerably in length, subject, and the very technique of narration, the thirteen stories all take place in the same region, the one dearest to Steinbeck's heart, the valley of Salinas, in California, where he was born. And the secret relationship created by this common background is far deeper than a simple topographic location. It seems that the author was particularly inspired by that valley, *his* valley, and that speaking of his native country made him give his very best, his most representative at any rate, and his most essential, forcing him to use to their utmost the gifts which make him unique among American novelists.

Historically speaking, Steinbeck is a realistic novelist of the depression era. But he did not feel and live the economic depression (which, for example, changed Hemingway's inspiration so deeply) in the implacable mineral universe of big cities, but in the tender landscapes of the "long valley," under the mild Californian climate, among its peaceful orchards. Whence this note of serenity, which is never absent from his stories, however darkly objective the events he relates may be. It is impossible for him to reach as sordid a realism, as absolute a despair as that we find, for instance, in the novels which James T. Farrell has dedicated to the corrupt city childhood of his Young Lonigan.

Simplicity, ease, tenderness, such are the words which spring to our lips to characterize his art. We like his work for its spontaneous harmony with the deeper rhythms of natural life (without showing the constantly tense and slightly emphatic pantheism of a Giono, that Italian writer eternally frustrated by d'Annunzian laurels), but still capable of raising its normally moderate voice to the epic protest (probably slightly over-simplified) which *The Grapes of Wrath* raises against the capitalistic society. In Steinbeck, evil is always devoid of ambiguity: man is good by nature, and it seems at times that the sight of Californian orchards endowed him with the same noble optimism which Rousseau found in the Clarens vineyards. In the very development of his style we feel the peaceful confidence of a man treading the countryside, *his* countryside, with a steady, kindly stride, assured that he will arrive at a halting place in the evening, wherever it may be. And that confidence is what enables him to lean without fear over the abyss of existence: thanks to it, he can voice in *In Dubious Battle* his indictment of the scandals of American society without attaining the weariness of a Dos Passos, or, as the short stories of *The Long Valley* unfold, without trembling he can contemplate the depths of the human soul, relate in "The Murder," a tragedy of love, show us a man returning from a lynching in "The Vigilante," or paint in "The Snake" the sadistic instincts of a woman who has live rats fed to a snake, and he does these things without troubling us deeply or forcing us to despair of Man. Steinbeck has a kind of heavenly saintliness, a pre-Edenic innocence which stems from the fact that he moves with most ease in sub-human relationships. Contact with his books (I do not say imitation of them) is bound to be rewarding, almost refreshing, to a literature like ours, so exclusively devoted to the individual and his psychological complexities. Steinbeck, creator of the unforgettable Lennie, the retarded giant who, in *Of Mice and Men*, strangles mice and men when he means to caress them, seems incapable of painting human beings in their individualities as men; he sees them only in their animality, or as members of a mass where they are dissolved and no longer themselves. The moments of extreme emotion in *The Great Valley*, for instance, are those when a group of famished men eat bacon and drink coffee in "Breakfast," or when in "The Chrysanthemums" Eliza explains to the itinerant peddler her feelings while pruning her flowers as she squeezes under her finger the condemned buds and describes the kind of symbiosis which occurs between man and plant. The heroine of "The White Quail" identifies herself with the bird she sees in her garden and thus finds her inner self in the loss of her individuality; one could write, as an epitaph to the whole works of Steinbeck, what the old pioneer of "The Leader of the People" tells to his grandson Jody as a conclusion to his stories about Indians:

"I tell those old stories, but they're not what I want to tell. I only know how I want people to feel when I tell them. It wasn't Indians that were important, nor adventures, nor even getting out here. It was a whole bunch of people made into one big crawling beast." Steinbeck enables the reader to feel wonderfully that "transformation into a crawling beast," in a way that French Unanimism, from Charles Vildrac to Jules Romains, rarely reached. This is the real value of *In Dubious Battle* or *The Grapes of Wrath*. With this latter book, Steinbeck has successfully brought to life—as did Dos Passos in *U. S. A.*, but by totally different means—the impersonal novel. It might be possible to explain by sociological means (rather than biographical) this cleavage between generations, this change of atmosphere, so noticeable when one goes from the tense style of Faulkner to the ample period of Steinbeck's sentence. Faulkner and Dos Passos resist the surrounding world; they bear witness against it as much as they can. They seem to be painting, in spite of themselves, a reality which they dislike. That reality, that world-as-it-is, has been assumed by Steinbeck from the very beginning, in its horror as well as in its grandeur. His personality is "consonant," as the graphologists call it (or, if you prefer, "syntonic" although the syntony is rather primitive compared to "our schizoid civilization"). He is completely reconciled to the impersonality of what he wants to paint; he does not attempt to express anything else, while one always seems to hear, through the prose of Dos Passos, the stifled muttering of the unrepentant individualist, of that old Adam who cannot resign to death.

In Dos Passos it is not only the attention, or even the affection, of the reader that we see diverted from the collective reality toward an individual character, but that of the author as well. For Dos Passos, extreme collectivism of man remains a malediction. Steinbeck will immediately find its grandeur.

It took him some ten years, however, before he became fully conscious of this deep will, which had probably been his from the very beginning, of de-personalizing the novel; it is possible to detect it in an implicit state in his early works which rather than being centered upon individual human beings, are constructed around a group: racing circles in *Cup of Gold*, poor people in *Tortilla Flat*, which is the name of a populous district in Monterey. *Of Mice and Men* takes us one step further toward the negation of human individuality, presenting us, so to speak, a hero in two persons, formed by the indissoluble couple of George and Lennie, the man and the monster, conscience and bestiality. In the same manner, *In Dubious Battle*[1] will be constructed around another pair, Mac and Jim, two men linked not so much by a personal friendship as by their common participation in the same task: the organization of the Lumpenproletariat of the United States, those amorphous masses of agricultural or unemployed workers, of tramps-of-all-trades, a floating population which no professional organization protects. And the true subject, the true "hero" of the book, is no longer the individual fate of Mac or Jim, but the story of their common task; the novel is the *Iliad* of that strike of fruit-pickers beyond which we can foresee an even vaster, more impersonal adventure of which this is but an episode. Unlike Dos Passos' Glen Spotswood, whose unrepentant individualism too often holds our attention at the expense of the proletarian adventure as a whole, Mac and Jim are only the leaders, as well as the privileged observers, the half-agent, half-patient consciences, the participants with whom both writer and reader will identify themselves while observing the adventure. The novelist must have a particular conscience to use as a camera, and it would be too strongly against our customs (and those of the writer), it would upset our vision too much, if he suddenly abandoned the central hero, the traditional "likeable character" whose point-of-view will be adopted by the reader.

Moreover, Mac and Jim find their true definition, their very essence, in the fact that they have been freed from themselves; not bcause they have been dispossessed in the purely passive or negative manner of Dos Passos' characters, but because they have voluntarily given up their individualities. Such is the meaning of the funeral oration given by Mac over Jim's body, in a last effort to make his friend useful to the Cause—words which end the book and could be its moral: "Comrades! He didn't want nothing for himself—"

In *The Grapes of Wrath*, the evolution toward impersonality goes even further: the book hardly contains any "likeable character" (or at least one eminently so, in the scholastic sense of the word), any hero, not even a leader (as were Mac and Jim). The only characters given a little more individuality and particularization than the others are obscure people, arbitrarily chosen by the novelist, and these could be, without much damage to the book as a whole, replaced by others of a very different sort; they are simple pieces on a chess-board, engaged in a tragedy which is far beyond their comprehension, which they have not created and can never dominate. The deep subject of the book is the odyssey (corresponding to the *Iliad* of *In Dubious Battle*) of the emigrants from Oklahoma, small farmers dispossessed by the banks because, in order to yield income in a capitalistic system, the raising of cotton must be highly industrialized; dispossessed of their ancestral land, attracted by the fallacious promises of big Californian land-owners, they migrate west to hire out as agricultural workers. Steinbeck's artistic effort consists of setting before our eyes the drama of this completely impersonal being which constitutes their social group, this "being-on-the-march," if there ever was one, in the strictest sense of the word. As it is necessary to compromise with novelistic traditions, he will show us its tragedy mostly through the story of one of the units of the collectivity, this kind of "novelistic atom" (already trans-individual) made up of the Joad family. But sometimes it seems to be nothing but a concession to our habits as readers: whole chapters, and not the least successful, deal, not with the Joads, but with anonymous individuals, who happen to be completely (or nearly so) similar to them; if by chance, one of them were not called by his Christian name, or associated with some specific episode in his life, we might not realize that we are no longer dealing with one of the usual protagonists of the drama,[2] but that is unimportant.

Thus, one of the most harmonious chapters, esthetically speaking, of the novel, offers only a very tenuous connection (not to say an imperceptible one) with the plot proper: it retells for a few hours the life of one of the cafe-gas stations scattered along the interminable, perfectly straight highways. There come the truckers, for a drink and a chat, or the wealthy couple with expensive cars, for much disdained refreshments (out of boredom more than actual need). There also we occasionally see one of the emigrants, unable to reach the nearest town for lack of money or gas, shyly asking that a loaf of bread be sold to him. (We are free to believe, if we wish, that it is Tom Joad. The story is even interrupted by almost didactic chapters, in which the collective being is presented directly, where the collectivity of expropriated farmers is the express subject of the book.) Nothing "happens," if you wish, in these pages; on the whole, there is a rather small number of "events" in the book, considering its length. The episode is nevertheless necessary to the complete book, but for poetic reasons rather than novelistic ones.

It is for the same reason, because the epic interest has taken over the novelistic one that the book, so to speak, does not "end," or rather ends without our being told what happens to the main characters, nor even what will be the fate of the mass of the emigrants.

The last lines of *In Dubious Battle* had already left us in doubt as to the fate of Mac after Jim's death, as well as to the final issue of the strike which made the very subject of the book. Individuals go by; the group (or the cause) remains. The strike itself (as Mac repeated a dozen times in the course of the book) is only one episode in the organization of the proletariat, one panel of an immense fresco of which Steinbeck, limited by the servitude of his art, can show us only a fragment; whether the strike is won or lost is only an almost anecdotal detail. As for Mac's fate, it is even less important; whether he dies or goes on further to organize the mass of unskilled workers will have little effect on the final goal.

In the same manner *The Grapes of Wrath* ends on a purely poetic image which in no way brings the plot to a conclusion: Steinbeck shows us "Rose of Sharon" (the young woman, with a fresh biblical name, is the Joad's youngest daughter), who has just given birth to a still-born infant, breast-feeding a half-starving man who has been sheltered by her mother during a flood, and whose tense stomach can only digest milk, which no one has any money to buy him. (Steinbeck's angelic simplicity, which I mentioned before, will be even better appreciated if we compare the archaic ingenuity of his treatment of a situation that could easily become scabrous with the slightly off-color treatment which our Maupassant conceals under feigned objectivity in a very similar episode.) We are told neither what happened to Tom, the eldest son and the protagonist, wanted by the police, nor what the Joad family will do, nor even what the fate of the mass of expelled farmers will be. This may be because a collectivity has no real story, no personal fate in the sense that an individual does; if this story is to be presented in a literary work, it is impossible not to decide purely arbitrarily on the place where the tale of the changes of this "advancing being" will stop. It is also probably because the novel, when it stops to deal with individuals, is no longer a narrative but a descriptive art, just as the great Russian pictures, for the same reasons, tend more and more to become documentaries, satisfied with showing statically the impersonal reality they treat without relating it.

Thus we perceive, in its very beginnings, the tendency which seems more and more to lead the great American writers away from fiction toward a kind of reporting mixed with abstract considerations: this is what Dos Passos did in 42nd Parallel and The Big Money or Erskine Caldwell in Some American People and in You Have Seen Their Faces (with the help of Margaret Bourke White's photographs); but we see at the same time the danger of that type of work, lack of novelistic interest for the reader for the very reason that the books are not tied to a plot. The temptation of the arabesque, of the lovingly refined detail, threatens Steinbeck as the danger of a "beautiful photograph" threatens the skillful producer, too much in love with his profession. In this regard, it is interesting to compare the story entitled "Breakfast" (in The Long Valley) with the version of the same episode incorporated in The Grapes of Wrath. The scene is extremely simple: the narrator discovers at sunrise a camp where two men are preparing breakfast, while a young woman feeds her baby; they invite him to share their meal, but, beyond the intense and simple pleasure of nourishment, beyond the sudden communion between them all, the narrator seems to feel in that scene a deep poetry which he cannot quite bring to light and communicate to the reader; the story ends awkwardly and shamefacedly with the writer's admission of consciousness that he has failed in his mission, which is precisely to express the unexpressible, to bring to light and communicate the uncommunicable: "That's all. I know, of course, some of the reasons why it was pleasant. But there was some element of great beauty there that makes the rush of warmth when I think of it." On the contrary, when the identical scene takes place in The Grapes of Wrath, attached to the main character of Tom and incorporated into his life as one of its events (and no longer presented as a self-sufficient image of beauty), Steinbeck no longer needs to stress in intellectual terms its poetical significance: the whole episode acquires meaning from within, but thanks to its context and its imminent beauty it reveals itself on its own.

The reason is that a scene, or a story, is not moving in itself; it becomes so because of its relationship to our eyes and to our human conscience by which it is finally perceived. (The individualistic and "petit-bourgeois" art had at least the merit of remaining human—sometimes too human, unfortunately!) Steinbeck can speak of animals and plants, or orchards and mice better than he does of men. Whence the constant threat to his art, the most serious of all dangers to the impersonal novel, lack of humanity.

On the other hand from this very impersonality stem his essential qualities: grandeur and serenity. Since individual existences do not count, then the endings of *In Dubious Battle* or of *Of Mice and Men*, however bloody they may be, cannot be sad: they are in the order of things. It does not matter that Jim is killed or that the strike fails (Mac knew from the very beginning, anyway, that it was doomed to failure): things go on as usual, slightly ameliorated by Jim's sacrifice, which is hardly a sacrifice since it is not a true loss. Jim does not value his own life; it only acquired real meaning after his joining the party; only then did he begin to *exist*. The personal existence of Malraux's characters, on the contrary—it is undoubtedly to Malraux that Steinbeck can be best compared—is almost too strong; they know that their life is unique, that it represents man's only possession; when they sacrifice it, it is a truly heart-rending tragedy, even if it remains silent. They are still *engagés* in humanity; it is their personal story which makes the plot of the work. If they do achieve this separation from their personality, as does Katov at the end of *La Condition Humaine*, the reader observes this development under his very eyes; we are not spared a single one of the stations of their Cross. In Steinbeck, on the other hand, the depersonalization of the heroes has already taken place when the story begins, either because their interior evolution is ended, as is the case of Mac and Jim, or because, like the Joads, they have never reached full consciousness of their separate individualities but have remained, so to speak, infra-individuals.

Malraux's grandeur is thus diametrically opposed to that of Steinbeck, and that difference can be found in the very rhythm of their styles, very integrated in Steinbeck, blunt and full of despair in Malraux. The bewildering greatness of the end of *La Condition Humaine*, or of Hernandez' death in *L'Espoir* is due to the fact that physical sufferings and death are real, irreparable things for the author. Faced with human sufferings, Steinbeck shows the profound indifference of nature. Thus he is enabled to write scenes which would be practically intolerable in any other writer, as for example in *In Dubious Battle*, when Mac systematically disfigures, with his fists, without anger, simply because it must be done, an adolescent boy, nearly a child, while remaining likeable to the reader. The simple theme of *Of Mice and Men* is atrocious if abstractly expressed; but the tragedy fades even from the final scene; there remains only a kind of abstract pity for the human condition, such as we sometimes feel in Shakespeare. In Malraux or Dos Passos, on the contrary, the sufferings of the heroes never cease to appear as metaphysically *unatonable*. In his Letter To Reynolds, Keats mentions this "blind purgatory" made of helpless pity for universal sorrow, which any artist must experience. It seems that Steinbeck and his heroes have found their way out of their purgatory, while Malraux and Dos Passos are still there. Whence the very different accent given to the social preoccupations of the former, since any metaphysical revolt is totally inexistent in them; we are not tempted to pity Mac or Jim when they are from the start so far above anything that might happen to them. We find in them a kind of serene majesty, the equivalent of which can only be found in a few of Shakespeare's characters, such as the Mark Anthony of *Anthony and Cleopatra*. Steinbeck has achieved a complete transfiguration of all the horrible, ugly, or vulgar elements of reality, with such success that they no longer appear ugly and horrid except to the abstract intellect which would arbitrarily isolate them from their literary expression.

This explains also his wonderful use of slang and clichés, of the most deformed and debased language, which enables him to express, better than would any austere intellectual vocabulary, such great single realities as manly fraternity, death, communism, heroism, or charity. With Steinbeck, we are never embarrassed by any detail of daily existence, for we feel beyond them from the start. Like Keats, Steinbeck, while refusing escapism, has found the best protection in absolute immanence. It would be interesting to analyze the literary processes through which that transfiguration takes place: the interior rhythm of the work, the fugue technique in *Of Mice and Men*, with its regular reappearances of subject and counter-subject. Balzac was proud of having composed his novels like Rossini: one might say that *Of Mice and Men* is composed like Bach and that Steinbeck has found the same serene gravity.

But that is true only of his great successes, of the privileged moments of his works. Every author shows a central point, a sort of great divide from which flow both defects and qualities. This center of gravity is, for Steinbeck, sub-human impersonality. There is a fundamental ambiguity in his works which prevents us from knowing for certain whether his heroes are beyond, or simply on this side of clear consciousness and distinct individuality. It is too obvious that if this ambiguity is real in Mac and Jim, it could not possibly be so in the cases of Lennie (*Of Mice and Men*), of the moron in the short story entitled "Johnny Bear," of Pilon and Danny (*Tortilla Flat*) or of all the bad boys (ne'er-do-wells) of *Cannery Row*; they are simply and unequivocally slightly above average mankind, and they do not transcend it in any way.

There is to be found the essential limitations of Steinbeck's art. He has an extraordinary power to catch and paint man in his most elementary terms, terms that also seem bound to be the most essential, those that bring him closer to other men, or even to other beings; but in the end, this power turns against him. His range of expression is strangely limited by the collapse of his syntax, which is incapable of expressing logical connections if ever so slightly abstract and by the inadequacy of his vocabulary (not from choice, as with Racine, but out of necessity; and it matters little, in the end, whether this necessity stems from the nature of the subject chosen, or from the artist's means). Reading the strangely rudimentary language used by his main characters, I am reminded of a remark made by an American writer:

"Some one who was studying the American language once made an exhaustive study of the vocabularies of women who wrote constantly for movie magazines. Each of them, she discovered, had at her disposal to express the whole emotional gamut from ravishment to disgust exactly a hundred and fifty words." (*America at the Movies* by Margaret Farrand-Thorpe.) Or one thinks of the monkeys studied by Köhler (who had only, at best, around fifteen onomatopes to express their emotions) or Etiemble's recent remarks: "With eight hundred and fifty English words and a few grammatical rules, they have constructed a language through the very poverty of which the Anglo-Saxons are hoping to conquer the globe. It is called Basic-English."

Shakespeare and the Bible have been rewritten, using only the eight hundred and fifty words selected after a fashion. As the *New York Times* (or is it the *London Times?*) said: "From now on, Shakespeare would become 'grand reading for everybody.'" Whoever tries to rewrite Steinbeck's books in Basic English will certainly have fewer problems than the "translator" of the Bible or of *Madame Bovary*.

If Steinbeck's characters seldom achieve true novelistic reality, it is precisely because they are so little individualized, so little individuals, and finally so little human. Their emotions always remain obscure and somewhat opaque, situated it seems, under the diaphragm or around the solar plexus; it is hard to picture them, even in a distant time, reading a clear consciousness of themselves. As a result, their creator fails whenever he tries to paint more complex individualities, such as, after all, we have to meet in modern civilization. That is probably why *The Moon Is Down* is such an abstract, unintentionally semi-caricatural book, too over-simplified to be convincing; in the end, practically everything in the book acquires a false ring, particularly to European ears.

There is something else which Steinbeck's universe sadly lacks, what Denis de Rougemont so accurately called the "Devil's share"—or, if you prefer a less theological language, the sense of evil. After considering Steinbeck's work, we find an increased strength in the terrible and prophetic statement of Walter Rathenau: "America has no soul and will not deserve one until it consents to plunge into the abyss of human suffering and sin." (Quoted by Gide in his Diary).

(It would be interesting at this point to elucidate a mystery, probably historical in its essence, which goes beyond literature and probably reaches the very core of contemporary American civilization: the mysterious disappearance in the modern American conscience of that "sense of evil," so deep and acute in Hawthorne or Melville, but seemingly so vehemently repressed from the collective soul after the middle of the 19th century. This repression probably explains, to a large extent, the complete failure for the contemporary reader of that part of Melville's work, from *Moby Dick* to *Billy Budd*, which appears most valid to us, or the fact that the U. S. was found unlivable by Henry James or T. S. Eliot, both of whom were unable to find there the spiritual climate they needed.)

Without undertaking here the psychoanalysis of the American soul which would undoubtedly be required to attempt even a simple description of that mystery, but returning to our level of literary criticism and to Steinbeck, we may say that there is something false and suspicious, at any rate monstrous, in the very innocence of Steinbeck's heroes: Lennie's sadism, or his *Schadenfreude* (whatever name one wishes to use) might be made literarily acceptable by its unconsciousness; it is nevertheless just as atrocious as is Lennie's death. And the falsely picaresque aspect of the adventures told in *Tortilla Flat* does not remain entertaining for long. The 20th-century man cannot reduce himself to a purely vital existence without punishment or without a fundamental mutilation of his whole being.

Because of this very amputation, Steinbeck's universe and the artistic domain in which he can succeed will be perforce very limited. His familiar means of expression will fail him as soon as he wishes to bring to life other groups besides the agricultural workers of California, the 18th century pioneers of the West, or paisanos of Monterey: a universe mostly made up of sadists, tramps or congenital morons. We are almost glad when he honestly returns to the simple painting of pure animality: it is not by chance that the best stories of *The Long Valley* have animals rather than men as true "heroes," as centers of attention and sympathy, and that they are entitled *The White Quail, The Snake,* or *The Red Pony.* But one cannot help wondering whether there are very great possibilities open to a "novelist of animality," however perfect his art may be and however deep the bond of sympathy between his subject and himself.

1. A beginning of that duplication of the hero can be found already in *Tortilla Flat,* where we are dealing with two central characters, Pilon and Danny, a pair no less indissoluble than Lennie and George, if for very different reasons; so much so that the book ends with their separation through Danny's death and deification, when he becomes a kind of mythical hero of *Tortilla Flat.*

2. In its results, the method is quite similar to the use made by Dos Passos of the 'Camera Eye': the center of interest moves from one of the central characters to an anonymous person (without our having been warned, exactly in the Orson Welles manner, when the spectator's attention finds itself centered on the middle or background). We are suddenly brought within the conscience of "Mr. X"—the "one" of Heidegger, if you wish—we are presented with his life, his interior monologue.

IV. THE GRAPES OF WRATH

Martin Staples Shockley

THE RECEPTION OF
THE GRAPES OF WRATH
IN OKLAHOMA

MOST OF US remember the sensational reception of *The Grapes of Wrath* (1939), Mr. Westbrook Pegler's column about the vile language of the book, Raymond Clapper's column recommending the book to economic royalists, Mr. Frank J. Taylor's article in the *Forum* attacking factual inaccuracies, and the editorial in *Collier's* charging communistic propaganda. Many of us also remember that the Associated Farmers of Kern County California, denounced the book as "obscene sensationalism" and "propaganda in its vilest form," that the Kansas City Board of Education banned the book from Kansas City libraries, and that the Library Board of East St. Louis banned it and ordered the librarian to burn the three copies which the library owned. These items were carried in the Oklahoma press. The *Forum's* article was even reprinted in the Sunday section of the Oklahoma City *Daily Oklahoman* on October 29, 1939, with the editor's headnote of approval.

With such publicity, *The Grapes of Wrath* sold sensationally in Oklahoma bookstores. Most stores consider it their best seller, excepting only *Gone With the Wind*. One bookstore in Tulsa reported about one thousand sales. Mr. Hollis Russell of Stevenson's Bookstore in Oklahoma City told me, "People who looked as though they had never read a book in their lives came in to buy it."

Of thirty libraries answering my letter of inquiry, only four, including one state college library, do not own at least one copy of the book, and the Tulsa Public Library owns twenty-eight copies. Most libraries

MARTIN STAPLES SHOCKLEY *is a member of the Department of English of North Texas State College at Denton. "The Reception of The Grapes of Wrath in Oklahoma" first appeared in January, 1944, in American Literature. It is reprinted here by permission of the managing editor of that periodical, Arlin Turner, as well as by permission of Mr. Shockley. Elsewhere in the present volume will be found Mr. Shockley's "Christian Symbolism in The Grapes of Wrath."*

received the book soon after publication in the spring of 1939. Librarians generally agreed that the circulation of The Grapes of Wrath was second only to that of Gone With the Wind, although three librarians reported equal circulation for the two books, and one (Oklahoma Agricultural and Mechanical College) reported The Grapes of Wrath their most widely circulated volume. The librarians often added that many private copies circulated widely in their communities, and some called attention to the extraordinary demand for rental copies. A few libraries restricted circulation to "adults only." About half the libraries mentioned long waiting lists, Miss Sue Salmon of the Duncan Public Library reporting that "Even as late as the spring of 1940 we counted 75 people waiting." Mrs. Virginia Harrison of A. and M. College stated that the four copies there "were on waiting list practically the entire time up to March 19, 1941." After over two hundred students had signed the waiting list for the two copies in the University of Oklahoma library, faculty members donated several additional copies to the library.

The Grapes of Wrath was reviewed throughout Oklahoma to large and curious audiences. A high-school English teacher wrote that he had reviewed the book three times, at a ladies' culture club, at a faculty tea, and at a meeting of the Junior Chamber of Commerce, receiving comments ranging from one lady's opinion that Ma Joad was a "magnificent character," to a lawyer's remark that "Such people should be kept in their place." When Professor J. P. Blickensderfer reviewed the book in the library at the University of Oklahoma, so many people were turned away for lack of standing room that he repeated the review two weeks later, again to a packed audience.

Much of what has passed in Oklahoma for criticism of The Grapes of Wrath has been little or nothing more than efforts to prove or to disprove the factual accuracy of Steinbeck's fiction. One of the minority supporters of the truth of Steinbeck's picture of the Okies has been Professor O. B. Duncan, Head of the Department of Sociology at A. and M. College. In an interview widely printed in Oklahoma newspapers, Professor Duncan discussed the economic and social problems which are involved.

> The farm migrant as described in Steinbeck's Grapes of Wrath, Duncan said, was the logical consequence of privation, insecurity, low income, inadequate standards of living, impoverishment in matters of education and cultural opportunities and a lack of spiritual satisfaction.
> "I have been asked quite often if I could not dig up some statistics capable of refuting the story of the Grapes of Wrath," Duncan related.

"It cannot be done, for all the available data prove beyond doubt that the general impression given by Steinbeck's book is substantially reliable."[1]

Billed as "The one man, who above all others, should know best the farm conditions around Sallisaw," Mr. Houston Ward, county agent for Sequoyah County, of which Sallisaw is the county seat, spoke over radio station WKY in Oklahoma City on March 16, 1940, under the sponsorship of the State Agriculture Department. Under the headline "Houston B. Ward 'Tells All' About *The Grapes of Wrath*," the press quoted Mr. Ward on these inaccuracies:

> Locating Sallisaw in the dust bowl region; having Grandpaw Joad yearning for enough California grapes to squish all over his face when in reality Sallisaw is in one of the greatest grape growing regions in the nation; making the tractor as the cause of the farmer's dispossession when in reality there are only 40 tractors in all Sequoyah county. . . . "People in Sequoyah county are so upset by these obvious errors in the book and picture, they are inclined to overlook the moral lesson the book teaches," Ward said.[2]

Numerous editorials in Oklahoma newspapers have refuted or debunked Steinbeck by proving that not all Oklahomans are Joads, and that not all Oklahoma is dust bowl. The following editorial, headed "GRAPES OF WRATH? OBSCENITY AND INACCURACY," is quoted from the Oklahoma City *Times*, May 4, 1939:

> How book reviewers love to have their preconceived notions about any given region corroborated by a morbid, filthily-worded novel! It is said that *Grapes of Wrath*, by John Steinbeck, shows symptoms of becoming a best seller, by kindness of naive, ga-ga reviewers. It pictures Oklahoma with complete and absurd untruthfulness, hence has what it takes. That American literary tradition is still in its nonage . . . is amply proved by the fact that goldfish-swallowing critics who know nothing about the region or people pictured in a novel accept at face value even the most inaccurate depiction, by way of alleged regional fiction. No, the writer of these lines has not read the book. This editorial is based upon hearsay, and that makes it even, for that is how Steinbeck knows Oklahoma.

Mr. W. M. Harrison, editor of the Oklahoma City *Times*, devoted his column, "The Tiny Times," to a review of the book on May 8, 1939. He wrote:

> Any reader who has his roots planted in the red soil will boil with indignation over the bedraggled, bestial characters that will give the

ignorant east convincing confirmation of their ideas of the people of the southwest. . . . If you have children, I'd advise against leaving the book around home. It has *Tobacco Road* looking as pure as Charlotte Brontë, when it comes to obscene, vulgar, lewd, stable language.

Usually the editors consider the book a disgrace to the state, and when they do not deny its truth they seek compensation. One editor wrote:

> Oklahoma may come in for some ridicule in other states because of such movie mistakes as *Oklahoma Kid* and such literature as the current *Grapes of Wrath*. Nationally we may rank near the bottom in the number of good books purchased, and in the amount we pay our teachers. But when the biggest livestock and Four H club show comes along each year the nation finds out that somebody amounts to something in Oklahoma.[3]

On September 25, 1941, during the Oklahoma State Fair, the *Daily Oklahoman*, of Oklahoma City, carried a large cartoon showing the Oklahoma farmer proudly and scornfully reclining atop a heap of corn, wheat, and pumpkins, jeering at a small and anguished Steinbeck holding a copy of *The Grapes of Wrath*. The caption: "Now eat every gol-durn word of it."

Considerable resentment toward the state of California was felt in Oklahoma because California had stigmatized Oklahoma by calling all dust bowl migrants—even those from Arkansas and Texas—"Okies." One lengthy newspaper editorial was headed "So California Wants Nothing But Cream"[4] and another "It's Enough to Justify a Civil War."[5] On June 13, 1939, the *Daily Oklahoman* carried under a streamer headline a long article on the number of Californians on Oklahoma's relief rolls. In Tulsa, employees of the Mid Continent Petroleum Company organized the Oklahoma's California Hecklers Club, the stated purpose being to "make California take back what she's been dishing out." The club's motto was "A heckle a day will keep a Californian at bay." A seven-point program was adopted, beginning, "Turn the other cheek, but have a raspberry in it," and ending, "Provide Chamber of Commerce publicity to all Californians who can read."[6] The Stillwater *Gazette* in editorial approval wrote of the club: "*The Grapes of Wrath* have soured and this time it's the Californians who'll get indigestion."[7]

Numerous letters from subscribers have appeared in newspapers throughout Oklahoma. Some are apologetic, some bitter, some violent. A few have defended Steinbeck, sympathized with the Joads, and praised *The Grapes of Wrath*. Some take the book as text for economic, social, or political preachments. Miss Mary E. Lemon, of Kingfisher, wrote:

> To many of us John Steinbeck's novel, *The Grapes of Wrath*, has sounded the keynote of our domestic depression, and put the situation before us in an appealing way. When the small farmers and home owners—the great masses upon which our national stability depends— were being deprived of their homes and sent roaming about the country, knocking from pillar to post; when banks were bursting with idle money, and insurance companies were taking on more holdings and money than they knew what do with, Steinbeck attempted a sympathetic exposition of this status.[8]

Mr. P. A. Oliver, of Sallisaw, wrote no less emphatically:

> *The Grapes of Wrath* was written to arouse sympathy for the millions of poor farmers and tenants who have been brought to miserable ruin because of the development of machinery. . . . The people are caught in the inexorable contradiction of capitalism. As machinery is more and more highly developed, more and more workers are deprived of wages, of buying power. As buying power is destroyed, markets are destroyed. As the millions of workers are replaced by machinery in the industrial centers, the markets over the world collapse. The collapse of world markets destroyed the market for the cotton and vegetables produced by the poor farmers and tenants of Sequoyah county. Sequoyah county is a part of the world and hence suffered along with the rest of the capitalistic world in the collapse of capitalistic business. The day of free enterprise is done. The day of the little farmer is done. Had it not been for government spending, every farmer in the United States, every banker, every lawyer, every doctor, and all other professional workers and wage earners would long since have joined the Joads on the trail of tears. Better do some serious thinking before you ridicule the Joads.[9]

From September 22 to 25, 1940, a Congressional committee headed by Representative Tolan of California held hearings in Oklahoma's capitol investigating the problem of migratory workers. Apparently Oklahoma viewed with suspicion this intrusion, for as early as August 16, a newspaper editorial stated that

> Anticipating an attempt to "smear" Oklahoma, Governor Phillips is marshalling witnesses and statistics to give the state's version of the migration. He has called on Dr. Henry G. Bennett and faculty members of the Oklahoma A. and M. college to assist in the presentation.

Oklahoma has a right to resent any undue reflections on the state. If the hearing develops into a mud-slinging contest, Oklahoma citizens have a few choice puddles from which to gather ammunition for an attack on the ham-and-egg crackpot ideas hatched on the western coast.[10]

On September 9 the *Daily Oklahoman* of Oklahoma City carried a story giving the names of the members of the committee which the governor had appointed to prepare his report. The paper stated that "Governor Phillips announced his intention to refute the 'Okies' story when the committee of congressmen come here to study conditions causing the migration." During the hearings, front-page stories kept Oklahomans alert to Steinbeck's guilt. On September 20, the *Daily Oklahoman* reported with apparent relief that "The fictional Joad family of *The Grapes of Wrath* could be matched by any state in the union, according to testimony." Next morning the same paper's leading editorial on "Mechanized Farms and 'Okies'" stated that mechanized farming was not responsible for conditions represented in *The Grapes of Wrath*. The editorial concluded, "It is a disagreeable fact, but one that cannot be ignored by men earnestly seeking the truth wherever found, that two of the chief factors that produce 'Okies' are AAA and WPA."

Under the heading "'Grapes' Story Arouses Wrath of Governor," the Oklahoma City *Times* on October 2, 1939, printed the story of a correspondence between His Excellency Leon C. Phillips, Governor of Oklahoma, and an unnamed physician of Detroit, Michigan. The unnamed physician wrote, as quoted in the paper:

"Is it at all conceivable that the state of Oklahoma, through its corporations and banks, is dispossessing farmers and sharecroppers . . . ? I am wondering whether you, my dear governor, have read the book in question." To which the governor warmly replied: "I have not read the thing. I do not permit myself to get excited about the works of any fiction writer. In Oklahoma we have as fine citizens as even your state could boast. . . . I would suggest you go back to reading detective magazines. . . ."

The following news item is quoted from the Stillwater *Gazette* of March 23, 1940:

Thirty-six unemployed men and women picketed Oklahoma's state capitol for two hours Saturday calling on Governor Phillips to do something about conditions portrayed in John Steinbeck's novel, *The Grapes of Wrath*. One of their signs stated "Steinbeck told the truth." Eli

Jaffee, president of the Oklahoma City Workers' alliance, said that "we are the Okies who didn't go to California, and we want jobs." Phillips refused to talk with the group. He said that he considered that the novel and the movie version of the book presented an exaggerated and untrue picture of Oklahoma's tenant farmer problem as well as an untruthful version of how migrants are received in California.

If His Excellency the Governor had been reticent as a critic of literature, the Honorable Lyle Boren, Congressman from Oklahoma, was no way abashed. The following speech, reprinted from the *Congressional Record*, was published in the *Daily Oklahoman*, January 24, 1940:

Mr. Speaker, my colleagues, considerable has been said in the cloak-rooms, in the press and in various reviews about a book entitled *The Grapes of Wrath*. I cannot find it possible to let this dirty, lying, filthy manuscript go heralded before the public without a word of challenge or protest.

I would have my colleagues in congress, who are concerning themselves with the fundamental economic problems of America know that Oklahoma, like other states in the union, has its economic problems, but that no Oklahoma economic problem has been portrayed in the low and vulgar lines of this publication. As a citizen of Oklahoma, I would have it known that I resent, for the great state of Oklahoma, the implications in that book. . . .

I stand before you today as an example in my judgment, of the average son of the tenant farmer of America. If I have in any way done more in the sense of personal accomplishment than the average son of the tenant farmer of Oklahoma, it has been a matter of circumstance, and I know of a surety that the heart and brain and character of the average tenant farmer of Oklahoma cannot be surpassed and probably not equalled by any other group.

Today, I stand before this body as a son of a tenant farmer, labeled by John Steinbeck as an "Okie." For myself, for my dad and my mother, whose hair is silvery in the service of building the state of Oklahoma, I say to you, and to every honest, square-minded reader in America, that the painting Steinbeck made in his book is a lie, a black, infernal creation of a twisted, distorted mind.

Some have blasphemed the name of Charles Dickens by making comparisons between his writing and this. I have no doubt but that Charles Dickens accurately portrayed certain economic conditions in his country and in his time, but this book portrays only John Steinbeck's unfamiliarity with facts and his complete ignorance of his subject. . . .

Take the vulgarity out of this book and it would be blank from cover to cover. It is painful to me to further charge that if you take the obscene language out, its author could not sell a copy. . . .

I would have you know that there is not a tenant farmer in Oklahoma that Oklahoma needs to apologize for. I want to declare to my nation and to the world that I am proud of my tenant-farmer heritage, and I would to Almighty God that all citizens of America could be as clean and noble and fine as the Oklahomans that Steinbeck labeled "Okies." The only apology that needs to be made is by the state of California for being the parent of such offspring as this author. . . .

Just nine days after Congressman Boren's speech had appeared in print, a long reply by Miss Katharine Maloney, of Coalgate, appeared on the Forum page of the Oklahoma City Times. I quote a few brief excerpts from Miss Maloney's letter:

If Boren read The Grapes of Wrath which I have cause to believe he did not, he would not label John Steinbeck a "damnable liar." John Steinbeck portrayed the characters in his book just as they actually are. . . . Why, if Boren wants to bring something up in congress, doesn't he do something to bring better living conditions to the tenant farmer? . . . This would make a better platform for a politician than the book.

Not only politics, but the pulpit as well were moved by the book. One minister in Wewoka was quoted as praising it as a "truthful book of literary as well as social value, resembling in power and beauty of style the King James version of the Bible."[11] His was decidedly a minority opinion. The other extreme may be represented by the Reverend W. Lee Rector, of Ardmore, who considered The Grapes of Wrath a "heaven-shaming and Christ-insulting book." As reported in the press, the Reverend Mr. Rector stated:

"The projection of the preacher of the book into a role of hypocrisy and sexuality discounts the holy calling of God-called preachers. . . . The sexual roles that the author makes the preacher and young women play is so vile and misrepresentative of them as a whole that all readers should revolt at the debasement the author makes of them." The pastor complained that the book's masterly handling of profanity tends to "popularize iniquity" and that the book is "100 percent false to Christianity. We protest with all our heart against the Communistic base of the story. . . . As does Communism, it shrewdly inveighs against the rich, the preacher, and Christianity. Should any of us Ardmore preachers attend the show which advertises this infamous book, his flock should put him on the spot, give him his walking papers, and ask God to forgive his poor soul."[12]

Other Oklahomans resented the filming of the story. Mr. Reo

M'Vickn wrote the following letter, which was published in the Oklahoma City *Times* on January 26, 1940:

> After reading the preview of *Grapes of Wrath* (Look, January 16) I think the state of Oklahoma as a whole should take definite steps to prevent the use of the name of our state in such a production. They are trying to disgrace Oklahoma and I for one am in favor of stopping them before they get started.

Oklahoma Chambers of Commerce had already tried to stop the filming of the picture. The following story is taken from the Oklahoma City *Times*, August 7, 1939:

> Neither Stanley Draper, secretary-manager of the Oklahoma City Chamber of Commerce, nor Dr. J. M. Ashton, research director of the State Chamber of Commerce, wants Twentieth Century Fox Corporation to make *Grapes of Wrath* in the "dust bowl." . . . Enough fault was found with the facts in Joseph [sic] Steinbeck's book on the "okies." . . . So the two Chamber of Commerce men think someone should protest the inaccurate and unfair treatment the state seems to be about to receive in the filming of the picture. Draper is going to suggest the mayor of Oklahoma City protest, and Ashton will ask the governor to do likewise. . . .

On September 1, 1941, the *Daily Oklahoman* carried a four-column headline, "Lions to Attack 'Okie' Literature." The news story described the nature of the attack:

> Those who write smart and not so complimentary things about Oklahoma and Okies had better watch out, because the 3-A district governor of Oklahoma Lions clubs and his cabinet, at their first session here Sunday, discussed an all-out counter-offensive. . . . The district governor and a dozen members of his cabinet agreed in their meeting at the Skirvin hotel that something should be done to offset *Grapes of Wrath* publicity. . . .[13]

The opinions and incidents which I have presented are representative, by no means inclusive. There are, I should say, two main bodies of opinion, one that this is an honest, sympathetic, and artistically powerful presentation of economic, social, and human problems; the other, the great majority, that this is a vile, filthy book, an outsider's malicious attempt to smear the state of Oklahoma with outrageous lies. The latter opinion, I may add, is frequently accompanied by the remark: "I haven't read a word of it, but I know it's all a dirty lie."

The reception of *The Grapes of Wrath* in Oklahoma suggests many interesting problems, particularly pertinent to contemporary regional literature in America. Any honest literary interpretation of a region seems to offend the people of that region. Ellen Glasgow, though herself a Virginian, has been received in her native state with a coolness equal to the warmth with which Virginians have welcomed Thomas Nelson Page. Romanticizers of the Old South are local literary lions, while authors who treat contemporary problems are renegades who would ridicule their own people for the sake of literary notoriety.

A tremendous provincial self-consciousness expresses itself in fierce resentment of "outsiders who meddle in our affairs." One consistent theme in the writings of Oklahomans who attacked *The Grapes of Wrath* was that this book represents us unfairly; it will give us a lot of unfavorable publicity, and confirm the low opinion of us that seems to prevail outside the state. Rarely did someone say, "We should do something about those conditions; we should do something to help those people." Generally they said, "We should deny it vigorously; all Oklahomans are not Okies."

Properly speaking, *The Grapes of Wrath* is not a regional novel; but it has regional significance; it raises regional problems. Economic collapse, farm tenantry, migratory labor are not regional problems; they are national or international in scope, and can never be solved through state or regional action. But the Joads represent a regional culture which, as Steinbeck shows us, is now rapidly disintegrating as the result of extra-regional forces. It may well be that powerful extra-regional forces operating in the world today foreshadow the end of cultural regionalism as we have known it in America.

1. Oklahoma City *Times*, Feb. 5, 1940.   2. *Ibid.*, March 16, 1940.   3. *Ibid.*, Dec. 5, 1939.   4. *Ibid.*, Nov. 28, 1938.   5. *Ibid.*, Aug. 6, 1938.   6. Stillwater Gazette, April 26, 1940.   7. *Ibid.*   8. Oklahoma City *Times*, Dec. 22, 1939.   9. Sallisaw *Democrat-American*, March 28, 1940.   10. *Payne County News* (Stillwater), Aug. 16, 1940.   11. Letter in my possession.   12. Oklahoma City *Times*, March 30, 1940.   13. The governor of district 3-A of the Lions clubs of Oklahoma is Dr. Joseph H. Marshburn, Professor of English in the University of Oklahoma.

Frederic I. Carpenter

THE PHILOSOPHICAL JOADS

A POPULAR HERESY has it that a novelist should not discuss ideas—especially not abstract ideas. Even the best contemporary reviewers concern themselves with the entertainment value of a book (will it please their readers?), and with the impression of immediate reality which it creates. *The Grapes of Wrath*, for instance, was praised for its swift action and for the moving sincerity of its characters. But its mystical ideas and the moralizing interpretations intruded by the author between the narrative chapters were condemned. Presumably the book became a best seller in spite of these; its art was great enough to overcome its philosophy.

But in the course of time a book is also judged by other standards. Aristotle once argued that poetry should be more "philosophical" than history; and all books are eventually weighed for their content of wisdom. Novels that have become classics do more than tell a story and describe characters; they offer insight into men's motives and point to the springs of action. Together with the moving picture, they offer the criticism of life.

Although this theory of art may seem classical, all important modern novels—especially American novels—have clearly suggested an abstract idea of life. *The Scarlet Letter* symbolized "sin," *Moby Dick* offered an allegory of evil. *Huck Finn* described the revolt of the "natural individual" against "civilization," and *Babbitt* (like Emerson's "Self-Reliance") denounced the narrow conventions of "society." Now *The Grapes of Wrath* goes beyond these to preach a positive philosophy of life and to damn that blind conservatism which fears ideas.

I shall take for granted the narrative power of the book and the vivid reality of its characters: modern critics, both professional and popular, have borne witness to these. The novel is a best seller. But it also has ideas. These appear abstractly and obviously in the interpretative interchapters. But more important is Steinbeck's creation of Jim Casy, "the

THE PHILOSOPHICAL JOADS *is reprinted here by permission of Frederic I. Carpenter and by that of W. Wilbur Hatfield, former editor of College English, where the essay first appeared in January, 1941. Another essay by Mr. Carpenter, "John Steinbeck: American Dreamer," appears earlier in the present collection.*

preacher," to interpret and to embody the philosophy of the novel. And consummate is the skill with which Jim Casy's philosophy has been integrated with the action of the story, until it motivates and gives significance to the lives of Tom Joad, and Ma, and Rose of Sharon. It is not too much to say that Jim Casy's ideas determine and direct the Joads's actions.

Beside and beyond their function in the story, the ideas of John Steinbeck and Jim Casy possess a significance of their own. They continue, develop, integrate, and realize the thought of the great writers of American history. Here the mystical transcendentalism of Emerson reappears, and the earthy democracy of Whitman, and the pragmatic instrumentalism of William James and John Dewey. And these old philosophies grow and change in the book until they become new. They coalesce into an organic whole. And, finally, they find embodiment in character and action, so that they seem no longer ideas, but facts. The enduring greatness of *The Grapes of Wrath* consists in its imaginative realization of these old ideas in new and concrete forms. Jim Casy translates American philosophy into words of one syllable, and the Joads translate it into action.

I

"Ever know a guy that said big words like that?" asks the truck driver in the first narrative chapter of *The Grapes of Wrath.* "Preacher," replies Tom Joad. "Well, it makes you mad to hear a guy use big words. Course with a preacher it's all right because nobody would fool around with a preacher anyway." But soon afterward Tom meets Jim Casy and finds him changed. "I was a preacher," said the man seriously, "but not no more." Because Casy has ceased to be an orthodox minister and no longer uses big words, Tom Joad plays around with him. And the story results.

But although he is no longer a minister, Jim Casy continues to preach. His words have become simple and his ideas unorthodox. "Just Jim Casy now. Ain't got the call no more. Got a lot of sinful idears—but they seem kinda sensible." A century before, this same experience and essentially these same ideas had occurred to another preacher: Ralph Waldo Emerson had given up the ministry because of his unorthodoxy. But Emerson had kept on using big words. Now Casy translates them: "Why do we got to hang it on God or Jesus? Maybe it's all men an' all women we love; maybe that's the Holy Sperit—the human sperit—the whole shebang. Maybe all men got one big soul ever'body's a part of." And so the Emersonian oversoul comes to earth in Oklahoma.

Unorthodox Jim Casy went into the Oklahoma wilderness to save his soul. And in the wilderness he experienced the religious feeling of identity with nature which has always been the heart of transcendental mysticism: "There was the hills, an' there was me, an' we wasn't separate no more. We was one thing. An' that one thing was holy." Like Emerson, Casy came to the conviction that holiness, or goodness, results from this feeling of unity: "I got to thinkin' how we was holy when we was one thing, an' mankin' was holy when it was one thing."•

Thus far Jim Casy's transcendentalism has remained vague and apparently insignificant. But the corollary of this mystical philosophy is that any man's self-seeking destroys the unity or "holiness" of nature: "An' it [this one thing] on'y got unholy when one mis'able little fella got the bit in his teeth, an' run off his own way. . . . Fella like that bust the holiness." Or, as Emerson phrased it, while discussing Nature: "The world lacks unity because man is disunited with himself. . . . Love is its demand." So Jim Casy preaches the religion of love.

He finds that this transcendental religion alters the old standards: "Here's me that used to give all my fight against the devil 'cause I figured the devil was the enemy. But they's somepin worse'n the devil got hold a the country." Now, like Emerson, he almost welcomes "the dear old devil." Now he fears not the lusts of the flesh but rather the lusts of the spirit. For the abstract lust of possession isolates a man from his fellows and destroys the unity of nature and the love of man. As Steinbeck writes: "The quality of owning freezes you forever into• 'I,' and cuts you off forever from the 'we.' " Or, as the Concord farmers in Emerson's poem "Hamatreya" had exclaimed: " 'Tis mine, my children's and my name's," only to have "their avarice cooled like lust in the chill of the grave." To a preacher of the oversoul, possessive egotism may become the unpardonable sin.

If a society has adopted "the quality of owning" (as typified by absentee ownership) as its social norm, then Protestant nonconformity may become the highest virtue, and even resistance to authority may become justified. At the beginning of his novel Steinbeck had suggested this, describing how "the faces of the watching men lost their bemused perplexity and became hard and angry and resistant. Then the women knew that they were safe . . . . their men were whole." For this is the paradox of Protestantism: when men resist unjust and selfish authority, they themselves become "whole" in spirit.

But this American ideal of nonconformity seems negative: how can men be sure that their Protestant rebellion does not come from the devil? To this there has always been but one answer—faith: faith in the instincts of the common man, faith in ultimate social progress, and faith in the direction in which democracy is moving. So Ma Joad counsels the discouraged Tom: "Why, Tom, we're the people that live. They ain't gonna wipe us out. Why, we're the people—we go on." And so Steinbeck himself affirms a final faith in progress: "When theories change and crash, when schools, philosophies . . . . grow and disintegrate, man reaches, stumbles forward. . . . Having stepped forward, he may slip back, but only half a step, never the full step back." Whether this be democratic faith, or mere transcendental optimism, it has always been the motive force of our American life and finds reaffirmation in this novel.

II

Upon the foundation of this old American idealism Steinbeck has built. But the Emersonian oversoul had seemed very vague and very ineffective—only the individual had been real, and he had been concerned more with his private soul than with other people. *The Grapes of Wrath* develops the old idea in new ways. It traces the transformation of the Protestant individual into the member of a social group— the old "I" becomes "we." And it traces the transformation of the passive individual into the active participant—the idealist becomes pragmatist. The first development continues the poetic thought of Walt Whitman; the second continues the philosophy of William James and John Dewey.

"One's-self I sing, a simple separate person," Whitman had proclaimed. "Yet utter the word Democratic, the word En-Masse." Other American writers had emphasized the individual above the group. Even Whitman celebrated his "comrades and lovers" in an essentially personal relationship. But Steinbeck now emphasizes the group above the individual and from an impersonal point of view. Where formerly American and Protestant thought has been separatist, Steinbeck now faces the problem of social integration. In his novel the "mutually repellent particles" of individualism begin to cohere.

"This is the beginning," he writes, "from 'I' to 'we.' " This is the beginning, that is, of reconstruction. When the old society has been split and the Protestant individuals wander aimlessly about, some new nucleus must be found, or chaos and nihilism will follow. "In the night one family camps in a ditch and another family pulls in and the tents come out. The two men squat on their hams and the women and children listen. Here is the node." Here is the new nucleus. "And from this first 'we,' there grows a still more dangerous thing: 'I have a little food' plus 'I have none.' If from this problem the sum is 'We have a little food,' the thing is on its way, the movement has direction." A new social group is forming, based on the word "en masse." But here is no socialism imposed from above; here is a natural grouping of simple separate persons.

By virtue of his wholehearted participation in this new group the individual may become greater than himself. Some men, of course, will remain mere individuals, but in every group there must be leaders, or "representative men." A poet gives expression to the group idea, or a preacher organizes it. After Jim Casy's death, Tom is chosen to lead. Ma explains: "They's some folks that's just theirself, an' nothin' more. There's Al [for instance] he's jus' a young fella after a girl. You wasn't never like that, Tom." Because he has been an individualist, but through the influence of Casy and of his group idea has become more than himself, Tom becomes "a leader of the people." But his strength derives from his increased sense of participation in the group.

From Jim Casy, and eventually from the thought of Americans like Whitman, Tom Joad has inherited this idea. At the end of the book he sums it up, recalling how Casy "went out in the wilderness to find his own soul, and he found he didn't have no soul that was his'n. Says he foun' he jus' got a little piece of a great big soul. Says a wilderness ain't no good 'cause his little piece of a soul wasn't no good 'less it was with the rest, an' was whole." Unlike Emerson, who had said goodbye to the proud world, these latter-day Americans must live in the midst of it. "I know now," concludes Tom, "a fella ain't no good alone."

To repeat: this group idea is American, not Russian; and stems from Walt Whitman, not Karl Marx. But it does include some elements that have usually seemed sinful to orthodox Anglo-Saxons. "Of physiology from top to toe I sing," Whitman had declared, and added a good many details that his friend Emerson thought unnecessary. Now the Joads frankly discuss anatomical details and joke about them. Like most common people, they do not abscond or conceal. Sometimes they seem to go beyond the bounds of literary decency: the unbuttoned antics of Grandpa Joad touch a new low in folk-comedy. The movies (which reproduced most of the realism of the book) could not quite stomach this. But for the most part they preserved the spirit of the book, because it was whole and healthy.

In Whitman's time almost everyone deprecated this physiological realism, and in our own many readers and critics still deprecate it. Nevertheless, it is absolutely necessary—both artistically and logically. In the first place, characters like the Joads do act and talk that way—to describe them as genteel would be to distort the picture. And, in the second place, Whitman himself had suggested the necessity of it: just as the literature of democracy must describe all sorts of people, "en masse," so it must describe all of the life of the people. To exclude the common or "low" elements of individual life would be as false as to exclude the common or low elements of society. Either would destroy the wholeness of life and nature. Therefore, along with the dust-driven Joads, we must have Grandpa's dirty drawers.

But beyond this physiological realism lies the problem of sex. And this problem is not one of realism at all. Throughout this turbulent novel an almost traditional reticence concerning the details of sex is observed. The problem here is rather one of fundamental morality, for sex had always been a symbol of sin. *The Scarlet Letter* reasserted the authority of an orthodox morality. Now Jim Casy questions that orthodoxy. On this first meeting with Tom he describes how, after sessions of preaching, he had often lain with a girl and then felt sinful afterward. This time the movies repeated his confession, because it is central to the motivation of the story. Disbelief in the sinfulness of sex converts Jim Casy from a preacher of the old morality to a practitioner of the new.

But in questioning the old morality Jim Casy does not deny morality. He doubts the strict justice of Hawthorne's code: "Maybe it ain't a sin. Maybe it's just the way folks is. Maybe we been whippin' the hell out of ourselves for nothin'." But he recognizes that love must always remain responsible and purposeful. Al Joad remains just "a boy after a girl." In place of the old, Casy preaches the new morality of Whitman, which uses sex to symbolize the love of man for his fellows. Jim Casy and Tom Joad have become more responsible and more purposeful than Pa Joad and Uncle John ever were: they love people so much that they are ready to die for them. Formerly the only unit of human love was the family, and the family remains the fundamental unit. The tragedy of *The Grapes of Wrath* consists in the breakup of the family. But the new moral of this novel is that the love of all people—if it be unselfish—may even supersede the love of family. So Casy dies for his people, and Tom is ready to, and Rose of Sharon symbolically transmutes her maternal love to a love of all people. Here is a new realization of "the word democratic, the word en-masse."

III

"An' I got to thinkin', Ma—most of the preachin' is about the poor we shall have always with us, an' if you got nothin', why, jus' fol' your hands an' to hell with it, you gonna git ice cream on gol' plates when you're dead. An' then this here Preacher says two get a better reward for their work."

Catholic Christianity had always preached humility and passive obedience. Protestantism preached spiritual nonconformity, but kept its disobedience passive. Transcendentalism sought to save the individual but not the group. ("Are they my poor?" asked Emerson.) Whitman sympathized more deeply with the common people and loved them abstractly, but trusted that God and democracy would save them. The pragmatic philosophers first sought to implement American idealism by making thought itself instrumental. And now Steinbeck quotes scripture to urge popular action for the realization of the old ideals.

In the course of the book Steinbeck develops and translates the thought of the earlier pragmatists. "Thinking," wrote John Dewey, "is a kind of activity which we perform at specific need." And Steinbeck repeats: "Need is the stimulus to concept, concept to action." The cause of the Okie's migration is their need, and their migration itself becomes a kind of thinking—an unconscious groping for the solution to a half-formulated problem. Their need becomes the stimulus to concept.

In this novel a kind of pragmatic thinking takes place before our eyes: the idea develops from the predicament of the characters, and the resulting action become integral with the thought. The evils of absentee ownership produce the mass migration, and the mass migration results in the idea of group action: "A half-million people moving over the country. . . . And tractors turning the multiple furrows in the vacant land."

But what good is generalized thought? And how is future action to be planned? Americans in general, and pragmatists in particular, have always disagreed in answering these questions. William James argued that thought was good only in so far as it satisfied a particular need and that plans, like actions, were "plural"—and should be conceived and executed individually. But Charles Sanders Peirce, and the transcendentalists before him, had argued that the most generalized thought was best, provided it eventually resulted in effective action. The problems of mankind should be considered as a unified whole, monistically.

Now Tom Joad is a pluralist—a pragmatist after William James. Tom said, "I'm still layin' my dogs down one at a time." Casy replied: "Yeah, but when a fence comes up at ya, ya gonna climb that fence." "I climb fences when I got fences to climb," said Tom. But Jim Casy believes in looking far ahead and seeing the thing as a whole: "But they's different kinda fences. They's folks like me that climbs fences that ain't even strang up yet." Which is to say that Casy is a kind of transcendental pragmatist. His thought seeks to generalize the prob-

lems of the Okies and to integrate them with the larger problem of
industrial America. His solution is the principle of group action guided
by conceptual thought and functioning within the framework of democratic society and law.

And at the end of the story Tom Joad becomes converted to Jim
Casy's pragmatism. It is not important that the particular strike should
be won, or that the particular need should be satisfied; but it is important that men should think in terms of action, and that they should
think and act in terms of the whole rather than the particular individual. "For every little beaten strike is proof that the step is being
taken." The value of an idea lies not in its immediate but in its eventual
success. That idea is good which works—in the long run.

But the point of the whole novel is that action is an absolute essential
of human life. If need and failure produce only fear, disintegration follows. But if they produce anger, then reconstruction may follow. The
grapes of wrath must be trampled to make manifest the glory of the
Lord. At the beginning of the story Steinbeck described the incipient
wrath of the defeated farmers. At the end he repeats the scene. "And
where a number of men gathered together, the fear went from their
faces, and anger took its place.And the women sighed with relief . . .
the break would never come as long as fear could turn to wrath." Then
wrath could turn to action.

IV

To sum up: the fundamental idea of The Grapes of Wrath is that
of American transcendentalism: "Maybe all men got one big soul
ever'body's a part of." From this idea it follows that every individual
will trust those instincts which he shares with all men, even when these
conflict with the teachings of orthodox religion and of existing society.
But his self-reliance will not merely seek individual freedom, as did
Emerson. It will rather seek social freedom or mass democracy, as did
Whitman. If this mass democracy leads to the abandonment of genteel
taboos and to the modification of some traditional ideas of morality,
that is inevitable. But whatever happens, the American will act to
realize his ideals. He will seek to make himself whole—i.e., to join
himself to other men by means of purposeful actions for some goal
beyond himself.

But at this point the crucial question arises—and it is "crucial" in
every sense of the word. What if this self-reliance lead to death? What
if the individual is killed before the social group is saved? Does the
failure of the individual action invalidate the whole idea? "How'm I

gonna know about you?" Ma asks. "They might kill ya an' I wouldn't know."

The answer has already been suggested by the terms in which the story has been told. If the individual has identified himself with the oversoul, so that his life has become one with the life of all men, his individual death and failure will not matter. From the old transcendental philosophy of identity to Tom Joad and the moving pictures may seem a long way, but even the movies faithfully reproduced Tom's final declaration of transcendental faith: "They might kill ya," Ma had objected.

"Tom laughed uneasily, 'Well, maybe like Casy says, a fella ain't got a soul of his own, but on'y a piece of a big one—an' then—'

" 'Then what, Tom?'

" 'Then it don' matter. Then I'll be aroun' in the dark. I'll be ever'where—wherever you look. Wherever they's a fight so hungry people can eat, I'll be there. Wherever they's a cop beating up a guy, I'll be there. If Casy knowed, why, I'll be in the way guys yell when they're mad, an'—I'll be in the way kids laugh when they're hungry an' they know supper's ready. An' when our folks eat the stuff they raise an' live in the houses they build—why, I'll be there. See?' "

For the first time in history, The Grapes of Wrath brings together and makes real three great skeins of American thought. It begins with the transcendental oversoul, Emerson's faith in the common man, and his Protestant self-reliance. To this it joins Whitman's religion of the love of all men and his mass democracy. And it combines these mystical and poetic ideas with the realistic philosophy of pragmatism and its emphasis on effective action. From this it develops a new kind of Christianity—not otherworldly and passive, but earthly and active. And Oklahoma Jim Casy and the Joads think and do all these philosophical things.

Joseph Warren Beach

JOHN STEINBECK:
ART AND PROPAGANDA

THE GRAPES OF WRATH is probably the finest example produced in the United States of what in the thirties was called the proletarian novel. This is a somewhat loose term to designate the type of novel that deals primarily with the life of the working classes or with any social or industrial problem from the point of view of labor. There is likely to be a considerable element of propaganda in any novel with such a theme and such a point of view. And it often happens that the spirit of propaganda does not carry with it the philosophical breadth, the imaginative power, or the mere skill in narrative which are so important for the production of a work of art. Upton Sinclair is an example of a man of earnest feeling and admirable gifts for propaganda who has not the mental reach of a great artist nor the artist's power of telling a plausible story and creating a world of vivid and convincing people. One sometimes has the feeling with Sinclair that he starts with a theory and then labors to create characters who will prove it; that his interest in the people is secondary. And that is a bad start with a writer of fiction.

With Steinbeck, it is the other way round. He has been interested in people from the beginning, from long before he had any theory to account for their ways. What is more, he is positively fond of people. More especially he has shown himself fond of men who work for bread in the open air, on a background of fields and mountains. They have always appealed to him as individuals, and for something in them that speaks to his esthetic sense. He sees them large and simple, with a luster round them like the figures in Rockwell Kent's engravings. He likes them strong and lusty, ready to fight and ready to make love. He likes to see the women nursing their babies. He likes to see people enjoying

JOSEPH WARREN BEACH prepared "John Steinbeck: Art and Propaganda" as well as his essay "John Steinbeck: Journeyman Artist," which appears elsewhere in the present volume, as a chapter of his American Fiction: 1920-1940, *published in 1941 by the Macmillan Company. Mr. Beach has given his permission for the appearance here of this essay and has made a few revisions in the text.*

their food, however coarse, and sharing it with others, what there is of it. And when they are in distress. . . .

When people are in distress, you want to help them. If the distress is so widespread that anyone's help is a mere drop in the bucket, you begin to reflect on the causes. You develop theories. The people in distress themselves begin to ponder causes, the rights and wrongs of the case, and they develop theories. Their theories may not be scientific, but they have the merit of growing out of a real experience. The best of social philosophies, so far as fiction is concerned, is that which comes spontaneously to the lips of people trying to figure out a way through life's labyrinth. The best sort of story from the point of view of sociology is one that by the very nature of its incidents sets you pondering the most fundamental human problems.

Steinbeck has always had a liking for brave men, men who could fight when occasion served, who could take their punishment, and who would risk their lives without repining in the cause of justice and human solidarity. He likes men who have the courage, the cunning and the singleness of mind that make them leaders. That is what attracts him to labor organizers. Already in 1936 he published *In Dubious Battle*, which is one of the best of novels dealing with industrial disputes. It is the story of a strike in the apple orchards of California— of communist organizers who move in on a district where the wage has been cut below a living standard and lead the men in a desperate fight for higher pay.

It is not a communist tract; it was not favorably received by the party, I believe, in spite of the highly sympathetic way in which he treats the party leaders. The ideology is somehow wrong. Too much space is given to the doctor who comes to see to the sanitary arrangements of the labor camp. This doctor is too much of a philosopher, and too much of a sociologist—regarding himself and his communist friends too coolly as products of forces which have been at work through all history, creatures of mob sentiment, and seeing this particular fight as but an incident in a never-ending struggle and perpetual balance of powers. The communist organizers are a little too frank in acknowledging that their object is not so much to win this fight as to develop class consciousness in the workers and make recruits for the revolution. They are men of normal feeling, and they grieve over those who are killed or mutilated. But they eagerly seize on blood and death and use them to fan the fires of wrath and violence. Such is the technique of the class struggle; and while the author does not pass judgment on it, he shows it up perhaps too clearly for the purpose of propaganda.

It is not a good communist tract, but as between labor and commercial profit the author's sympathies are on the side of labor. The law, the guns, and the dirty tricks are all with the big producers. You are made to feel the absolute necessity as well as the rightness of organization among the workers. The alternative is starvation for themselves and their children. As for the organizers, what is never in doubt in this book is their good faith, their courage, and their self-devotion. All these are brought to their peak in Jim, the new recruit, who in the course of these few days of the strike develops fine qualities of leadership, and whose death at the end gives him the status of a martyr. His comrade does not fail to exploit his death in the speech he makes over his dead body. The book ends with the opening words of this harangue: "This guy didn't want nothing for himself. . . ."

The strength of proletarian fiction is in that note, of comrades who want nothing for themselves alone—who sink their personal interest in that of the whole tribe of underdogs.

Thus Steinbeck had already broken ground in the earlier novel for the subject matter he was to handle so magisterially in The Grapes of Wrath. But In Dubious Battle is a hole-in-the-corner thing in comparison with the later work. In the intervening years the subject had been growing in his mind and imagination. He had written up for a San Francisco newspaper his observations on seasonal labor and life in the bunkhouses. He had visited the Oklahoma dustbowl which sent so many homeless families to California, and had made the trek West along with them. He had seen the uprooting of men in its epic proportions. He had reflected on the broad social problems underlying the special predicament of the California orchards. And so, taking his departure naturally from what he had seen in his native valley, from the men and women of his own acquaintance in Monterey County, he had let his thought widen out and deepen down until he was ready to make of his story the vehicle of comprehensive and significant attitudes on the major topics of social philosophy. He had things to say of large scope on the home, the family, the community of those who live in one place, on motherhood and fatherhood, as well as on such political and economic topics as the function of police, property in land, the nature of capitalistic enterprise, the balance of power between labor and management, and the strike as a weapon of the class struggle.

The story of The Grapes of Wrath is simple and uncomplicated. A family of tenant farmers in Oklahoma, the Joads. The great dust storms ruin their crops, and then they are forced to give up their land. It is to be worked on a large scale by the bankers' syndicate. The huge tractors plow up the land for miles on end and topple over the poor shacks of the farmers as they shave their foundations. There is only one thing to do. They will go to California, where the handbills promise employment for thousands in the orchards. The Joads get themselves a rickety second-hand Hudson six and turn it into a sort of covered wagon. They slaughter pigs for food on the journey and load their truck with such of their possessions as are indispensable for the long overland trek. And then they pile in—grampa and grandma, ma and pa, six children, a son-in-law, Uncle John, and the preacher Casy.

They are self-respecting people of old American stock, who have never had more than enough to fill their bellies. Their ways and speech are crude; but there is in them a sound root of wisdom and generosity, of courage and persistence. The eldest son Tom has just been paroled from the penitentiary. He is a good sort, a reliable member of the tribe; but he had killed a man who stuck a knife in him in a drunken brawl. It is dangerous for him to leave the state, breaking parole, but he cannot abandon the family by staying behind. He will try to keep his temper down henceforth so as not to get back in the clutches of the law. Casy is the thinker of the group. He has been a preacher of the Holiness persuasion, a great exhorter, and much of a sinner where the women are concerned. He has lost his faith in religion, but is earnestly seeking to find the way of truth and right in human affairs. The strongest character of all is Ma. She is a tower of strength in all that concerns the family welfare and the great mission of keeping them together and intact. She is dreaming of the little farm and the little white house among the orange trees where they will live together in peace when they have once found a place to work and save. But it is her misfortune to see them fall away one by one under the terrible stress of their misfortunes.

The journey is a long one, since they do not dare to push their old jallopy more than a certain speed. It is a desperate race against time; they are determined to get to the promised land before their money and supplies give out. Every night they camp beside the road in some place where there is water. They give help to other desperate pilgrims and receive help in turn. The hardships of the trip are great, and both Grampa and Grandma die on the way. In the promised land they find they are unwelcome and despised. They are called by the insulting name of Okies and regarded as scarcely human. They are pushed around by the police. They get employment gathering peaches; but they cannot make enough to meet the prices charged for food at the company store; and when the wage is cut in two, they move on to the cotton fields. Both Casy and Tom get involved in strikes; Casy is killed by the strike-breakers, and Tom becomes a fugitive and leaves the family so as not to bring trouble on them. He disappears into the anonymous band of those who give their lives to the cause of organized labor. Misfortunes pour down upon them. Rosasharn's husband deserts, and her baby is born dead in a box-car camp during the autumn floods. The last scene shows father and mother and the three remaining children taking refuge in a barn. Here they come on a boy and his father, the father dying of starvation; and Rosasharn nurses him back to life with the milk that nature intended for her child.

This final episode is symbolic in its way of what is, I should say, the leading theme of the book. It is a type of the life-instinct, the vital persistence of the common people who are represented by the Joads. Their sufferings and humiliations are overwhelming; but these people are never entirely overwhelmed. They have something in them that is more than stoical endurance. It is the will to live, and the faith in life. The one who gives voice to this is Ma. When they are driven out of their Hooverville and Tom is with difficulty restrained from violent words and acts against the deputies, it is Ma who explains to him what we might call the philosophy of the proletariat.

> "Easy," she said. "You got to have patience. Why, Tom—us people will go on livin' when all them people is gone. Why, Tom, we're the people that live. They ain't gonna wipe us out. Why, we're the people—we go on."
> "We take a beatin' all the time."
> "I know," Ma chuckled. "Maybe that makes us tough. Rich fellas come up an' they die, an' their kids ain't no good, an' they die out. But, Tom, we keep a comin'. Don' you fret none, Tom. A different time's comin'."
> "How do you know?"
> "I don' know how."

That is, you will recognize, the philosophy of Sandburg in *The People, Yes*—the mystical faith of the poet in the persistence and the final triumph of the plain people. Sandburg knows no better than Ma how he knows. He feels it in his bones. And that feeling is, I suppose, with Ma the very mark of the will to live.

Rosasharn's gesture in the barn is not the only symbol of this will to live. Very early in the book the author devotes a whole chapter—a short one—to the picture of a turtle crossing the highway. It is an act of heroic obstinacy and persistence against heavy odds. This is a gem of minute description, of natural history close-up, such as would delight the reader of Thoreau or John Burroughs. There are things like this in Thomas Hardy's Wessex novels. And as in Hardy, so here—it is not a mere piece of gratuitous realism. It may be enjoyed as such. But it inevitably carries the mind by suggestion to the kindred heroisms of men and women. It sets the note for the story that is to follow.

This chapter is an instance of a technical device by which the author gives his narrative a wider reference and representative character. The story of the Joads is faithfully told as a series of particular incidents in their stirring adventure. We hang with concern and suspense over each turn of their fortunes. But the author is not content with that. He wishes to give us a sense of the hordes of mortals who are involved with the Joads in the epic events of the migration; and along with the material events he wishes to see the social forces at play and the sure and steady weaving of new social patterns for a people and a nation. And so, to every chapter dealing with the Joads, he adds a shorter, more general, but often not less powerful chapter on the general situation.

There is, to begin with, an account of the dust storm over the gray lands and the red lands of Oklahoma—a formidable example of exact and poetic description matched by few things in fiction. Like Hardy with Egdon Heath, Steinbeck begins with physical nature and comes by slow degrees to humanity. The chapter ends with an account of the reactions of the men, women and children in the face of this catastrophe. The conception is large and noble. Humanity has been stripped of all that is adventitious and accidental, leaving the naked will and thought of man. Under the stress of desperate calamity the children watch their elders to see if they will break. The women watch the men to see if this time they will fail. It is a question of going soft or going hard; and when the men go hard the others know that all is not lost. The corn is lost, but something more important remains. And we are left with the picture of the men on whom they all depend. It is man reduced to the simplest terms—man pitted against the brute forces of nature—man with the enduring will that gives him power to use his brains for the conquering of nature. Man's thinking is an extension of his powers of action—he thinks with his hands. And so we read: "The men sat in the doorways of their houses; their hands were busy with sticks and little rocks. The men sat still—thinking—figuring." It is a kind of parable, summing up the theme of the book in its widest, most general form.

Most of these intercalary chapters have more particular themes. There is the theme of buying cheap and selling dear—the wonderful chapter of the second-hand automobile dealers. There is the theme of social forms coming into being as occasion requires. In the roadside camps the separate families are quickly assembled into one community; and community spontaneously develops its own laws out of its own obvious needs. There is the theme of large-scale production for economy and profit—the land syndicates in California who ruin the small owners. There is the theme of spring in California—its beauty, the scent of fruit, with the cherries and prunes and pears and grapes rotting on the ground to keep up the price. There are hungry men come for miles to take the superfluous oranges; but men with hoses squirt kerosene on the fruit. "A million people hungry, needing the fruit—and kerosene sprayed over the golden mountains." And there is the theme of the blindness of property in its anonymous forms.

> And the companies, the banks worked at their own doom and they did not know it. The fields were fruitful, and starving men moved on the roads. The granaries were full and the children of the poor grew up rachitic, and the pustules of pellagra swelled on their sides. The great companies did not know that the line between hunger and anger is a thin line. And money that might have gone to wages went for gas, for guns, for agents and spies, for blacklists, for drilling. On the highways the people moved like ants and searched for work, for food. And the anger began to ferment.

There is the theme of a common interest as opposed to a private and exclusive. "Not my land, but ours." "All work together for our own thing—all farm our own lan'." And finally we have the theme of man who has lost his soul and finds it again in devotion to the common cause.

Some of these themes are expressed in the spontaneous utterance of the Okies; some of them in the more abstract and theoretical language of the author. In general we may say that he is most effective when he puts his views in the mouths of the characters. For this is fiction; and fiction has small tolerance for the abstractions of an author. Still, there are cases where the theme is too broad and too complicated to find adequate expression in the words of a single man on a particular occasion. This is a great challenge to the ingenuity of a writer, and Steinbeck has found a number of ingenious and effective means of dramatizing the thought of a whole group of people faced with a difficult problem in economics. There is one remarkable chapter in which he shows us the debate between the tenant farmers and the agents of the banking syndicates come to put them off the land. It is a debate which recurs over and over again with each unfortunate family; and Steinbeck has presented it in a form that is at the same time generalized and yet not too abstract and theoretical. We are shown the farmers squatting on their heels while the owner men sit in their cars and explain the peculiar nature of the institution which they represent. It is a kind of impersonal monster that does not live on side-meat like men, but on profits. It has to have profits all the time, and ever more profits or it will die. And now that the land is poor, the banks cannot afford to leave it in the hands of men who cannot even pay their taxes.

And at last the owner men came to the point. The tenant system won't work any more. One man on a tractor can take the place of twelve or fourteen families. Pay him a wage and take all the crop. We have to do it. We don't like to do it. But the monster's sick. Something's happened to the monster.

But you'll kill the land with cotton.

We know. We've got to take cotton quick before the land dies. Then we'll sell the land. Lots of families in the East would like to own a piece of land.

The tenant men looked up alarmed. But what'll happen to us? How'll we eat?

You'll have to get off the land. The plow'll go through the dooryard.

And now the squatting men stood up angrily. Grampa took up the land, and he had to kill the Indians and drive them away. And Pa was born here, and he killed weeds and snakes. Then a bad year came and he had to borrow a little money. An' we was born here. There in the door—our children born here. An' Pa had to borrow money. The bank owned the land then, but we stayed and we got a little bit of what we raised.

We know that—all that. It's not us, it's the bank. A bank isn't like a man. Or an owner with fifty thousand acres, he isn't like a man either. That's the monster.

Sure, cried the tenant men, but it's our land. We measured it and broke it up. We were born on it, and we got killed on it, died on it. Even if it's no good, it's still ours. That's what makes it ours—being born on it, working it, dying on it. That makes ownership, not a paper with numbers on it.

We're sorry. It's not us. It's the monster. The bank isn't like a man.

Yes, but the bank is only made of men.

No, you're wrong there—quite wrong there. The bank is something else than men. It happens that every man in a bank hates what the bank does, and yet the bank does it. The bank is something more than men, I tell you. It's the monster. Men made it, but they can't control it.

Thus, in a kind of parable, with allegorical figures, and with Biblical simplifications, our author has managed to give in summary, in essence, what must have gone on a million times all over the world, when the two groups were confronted—two groups that represent two opposed and natural interests, and both of them caught in an intricate web of forces so great and so automatic in their working that they are helpless to combat them or even to understand them. This is not an individual scene of drama; but many of the remarks must have been made a thousand times in individual cases. It is not an economic treatise; but the substance of many such a treatise is presented in simplified form suited to the apprehensions of the men who speak. There is enough local color to make it appropriate to this story of the Okies; and sufficient differentiation of the manner of the two groups to give it a properly fictional cast. The apologetic tone of the one party, their patience and firmness; the bewilderment and indignation of the other party; the reasonableness on both sides—are admirably rendered. In each case the speaker is like a chorus in ancient tragedy, embodying the collective sentiments of a large group. Anyone who has tried to write will understand the number of difficulties which have been overcome in the application of this literary device. Anyone, at least, who has tried to write fiction, and who has tried in fiction to present a general view of things without cutting loose from the concrete and particular. This is but one of many instances in *The Grapes of Wrath* of Steinbeck's resourcefulness in meeting his main problem—to reconcile the interests of theory with those of imaginative art—to render the abstractions of thought in the concrete terms of fiction.

It would take long to list the technical variations and combinations which Steinbeck brings to the solution of this problem. Often he is more direct and less dramatic than in the passage quoted above. He will give a generalized account of some development among the migrants, as where, with the eye of a sociologist, he describes the spontaneous evolution of social codes and governmental agencies among these people in the camps and on the roads.

> And as the worlds moved westward, rules became laws, although no one told the families. It is unlawful to foul near the camp; it is unlawful in any way to foul the drinking water; it is unlawful to eat good rich food near one who is hungry, unless he is asked to share. . . . There grew up government in the worlds, with leaders, elders. A man who was wise found that his wisdom was needed in every camp; a man who was a fool could not change his folly with his world. . . . Thus they changed their social life—changed as in the whole universe only man can change. They were not farm men any more, but migrant men. And the thought, the planning, the long staring silence that had gone out to the fields, went now to the roads, to the distance, to the West.

He tells in general terms, in a passage earlier cited, how the companies and banks worked at their own doom without knowing it, while the anger of the hungry began to ferment. Here he is the social philosopher, commenting on a phase of economic psychology.

Such passages are just frequent enough to offend some readers having cut-and-dried notions of fictional technique, who make it a principle that no philosophy may show its head in fiction, and whose nose for propaganda is so keen that they are distressed at any hint of an idea. As a matter of fact, these general and theorizing passages are fairly rare and generally very short. They are interspersed with concrete instances and vivid images. And the style is so pithy and picturesque that it gives the whole an effect as different as possible from that of prosing science.

More often what we have is not generalized narrative but a composite of many short incidents and dialogues, racy and individual, but building up a general picture of some phase of the migrant life: people discovering common acquaintances back in the home county, small boys exchanging audacities, a man strumming his guitar while the people sing the old songs in the evening. Such is the bulk of the seventeenth chapter, from which I have quoted sociological observations, and of the twelfth, with its diversified picture of life on Highway 66. The most famous instance is Chapter Seven, with its dizzy riot of sales talk, frightened farmers, old tires, wheezy motors, glinting headlights, bargains, profits and overreaching. It is developed thematically like a tone poem by Roy Harris, and renders as nothing else could the sense of frenzied movement, confusion and anxiety which accompanies so much of our daily living, and particularly that of men caught like straws in the whirlwind of loss and misfortune.

The narrative method in these chapters is thus an extremely flexible medium, in which many different modes of statement are composed in a consistent whole diversified in coloring as a Persian carpet. What really needs stressing is the virtuosity of the performance, a virtuosity fully as great as—say—Thornton Wilder's, though it is likely to be passed over because of the homeliness of the subject matter, because Steinbeck is supposed to be simply rendering the plain reactions of plain people. And so he is, and much concerned not to introduce any foreign element of preciousness or affectation. But he is rendering them, the reactions of plain people, with tenderness, insight, and artistic detachment, and with the power of modulating freely round the dominant key. He is like an actor capable of doing things with his voice, varying his tone with the changing role and emotion. He has more than usual of the storyteller's ventriloquism.

He is one who feels strongly on the subject of man's essential dignity of spirit and his unexhausted possibilities for modification and improvement. It is natural that at times he should slip into a prophetic tone not unlike that of our midwestern poet.

> For man, unlike any other thing organic or inorganic in the universe, grows beyond his work, walks up the stairs of his concepts, emerges ahead of his accomplishments. . . . Having stepped forward, he may slip back, but only half a step, never the full step back. This you may say and know it and know it. . . . And this you can know—fear the time when Manself will not suffer and die for a concept, for this one quality is the foundation of Manself, and this one quality is man, distinctive in the universe.

Here let me lay my cards on the table. About such a passage as this I have a divided feeling, as I do about some of the quietly eloquent sayings of Tom to his mother when he leaves her to take up the cause of labor. These statements of Tom about his mission, these statements of Steinbeck about Manself, do not seem to me among the best things in the book, considered as literary art; and yet I do not see how we could dispense with them. I would not wish them away. For they are important clues to the author's feeling—to his hope and faith in humanity. But they do not seem to me altogether successful as imaginative shapings of the stuff of life in keeping with the most rigorous demands of fictional art.

The passage about Manself and dying for a concept is considerably longer than what I have quoted. It is in substance highly creditable to the author's feeling about man's nature and destiny. But there is something a trifle stiff about it, a trifle abstract, "talky," and magniloquent. It is as if at this point Steinbeck's art, generally so flexible and sure, had weakened—as if he was hurried or tired, and had for the moment allowed mere words to take the place of images or the dramatic evocations which are his most effective medium. In the case of Tom's remarks to his mother when he is setting out on his career as a labor organizer (Chapter Twenty-eight), they are cast, like all the dialogue, in the familiar language of the Okie, the untutored man of the people. Perhaps for that very reason, however, there is something just a bit questionable in the high seriousness, the wistful Christlikeness, of the sentiments he expresses. One does not so much question his harboring these sentiments, along with others less exalted in tone; what one questions is whether he could have brought himself to utter just these sentiments in just this tone. One asks whether the author has not a little too obviously manipulated his material here in order to point the moral of his tale.

And this reminds me of a statement of Farrell's about Steinbeck which is worth considering, and which involves a crucial problem in criticism. In an article dealing with the 1930's in American literature, Farrell comments on the work of younger writers who have come from the bottom or near the bottom of American society and have duly exploited the order of life with which they are acquainted. "Some of it is serious," he says, "in the sense that Matthew Arnold would have used that word in relation to literature. But this tendency has also created a new type of popular fiction, the hard-boiled novel. This type of novel relies on expressive language; it lacks any underlying structure, but does fit a Hollywood pattern of action; it is swift; it has all the mannerism, and none of the substance of genuine realistic writing. . . . These books stand in a sort of intermediate position between genuinely serious works of realistic writing, and merely fictional entertainment." As examples of this sort of writing he cites Jerome Weidman, James Cain, and Steinbeck in *Of Mice and Men.*

This is an extremely interesting utterance, whatever we may think of it; and it would be too simple to suppose that Farrell is jealous of Steinbeck's skill and popularity and unwilling to give him credit for what he has done. There is, I believe, a serious opposition of temper underlying this criticism, and a serious divergence in literary theory.

Steinbeck does not ignore the function of literature as entertainment, or at least its function of refreshing man's spirit. He writes in one place of this attribute of some literature, and the book he names as an example of this refreshment is none other than the immortal story of *Alice in Wonderland.* Farrell can afford to like Alice's adventures because they are so frankly adventures in Wonderland. What he does not like is making a sugar-candy wonderland of real life, as Stark Young does in *So Red the Rose*—that is the example that Farrell gives.

What he has in mind in Steinbeck's tale is, I suppose, a certain theatricality in his treatment of his theme. You remember that *Of Mice and Men* was cut to the model of a play. The situation is greatly simplified and so are the people. They are pointed up and colored so as to emphasize the characteristic—their decency where they are decent, their meanness where they are mean. The superhuman strength of the moron, his absolute devotion to his friend, the circumstances that lead to his death, make of him a character as picturesque and stagey as Hugo's hunchback of Notre Dame. Everything about the story is arranged so as to give it an effectiveness seldom found in actual life.

I don't know what Farrell thinks of *The Grapes of Wrath*; but I fancy that he would feel much the same way about that book. He would naturally be sympathetic to the sort of propaganda which it represents. But he would probably complain that it is more propaganda than literature. He would complain that both Casy and Tom are idealized for the sake of the social doctrine Steinbeck wishes to convey. Perhaps he would say the same of Ma, and of the final scene in which Rosasharn gives her breast to the starving man. He would say that, while much of the book is a faithful transcription of such reality as Steinbeck has observed, much of it is an invention for carrying the attitudes which he wishes to convey. And I have confessed that for myself some of the more idealistic passages do not ring quite true—that there is a slight suspicion here and there of a sentimental forcing of the note. But this is for me a question merely of an occasional slip in phrasing, and not of a radical fault in the conception of the book.

If I have rightly interpreted Farrell's position, I would say, in general, that I respect his view, and I believe that what he has in mind is a real danger to serious writing. But I doubt whether Steinbeck is a good example of the vice in question. Perhaps Farrell has too narrow and exclusive a notion of what makes good literature. Naturalism is one great school of fiction, and I have not the slightest disposition to question this way of writing when it is done well. But naturalism does not cover the whole ground, and taken by itself it does not fully satisfy the needs of the human imagination and the human spirit.

The life of the imagination has two poles—that of the real and that of the ideal. One of our strongest and most normal passions is the passion for the truth. Our intellectual nature and our moral nature alike drive us to the finding and the publishing of the truth. But there is another pole to the imagination which is just as valid and important as the realistic pole. Whatever the cold facts of life as they are, they derive all their meaning for us from our idea of what can be made of them. We believe that men have the faculty of fixing goals and striving for their attainment. We believe that such striving is itself a fact of life —the most important of all, since it is the means by which the will of man is given effect in the world of reality. We believe that certain goals are more worth while than others, since they represent our most persistent notions of human well-being. Such goals we call *ideals*. They have their origin in our moral sense, our vision of better and worse; and it is by reference to them that we organize our most serious activities.

Now, the ideal may be most faintly and imperfectly represented in the daily course of human life. But it is certainly present. And without some indication of its presence, we hardly know how to orient ourselves, how to read directions. One reason why Steinbeck is more widely read than Farrell at the present moment is that, while the element of reality is very largely present in his books, there is also a sufficient indication of ideal directions toward which the human compass points. The moral appeal is not merely negative, through revulsion from the ugly. It is also in some measure positive. We respond to the good qualities and impulses in Casy and Tom and Ma and in many of the minor characters. And we do not feel so lost and helpless in this world of positive directions as many readers feel in the world of Studs Lonigan.

A similar difference may be stated in esthetic terms. We are more aware in Steinbeck of the principle of selection for effect. This is a prime esthetic merit in all the arts, making for definition and appeal. Farrell piles up details in the same key without diversification of effect, with the result that a certain monotony is felt. This has long been noted as a characteristic weakness of naturalistic fiction, as in the novels of Zola and Dreiser.

On the whole we must say that Steinbeck is a more versatile and skillful craftsman, a more natural craftsman, than Farrell. This is not saying that he will turn out to be the greater writer of the two in the judgment of critical posterity. There are other things that may come in to determine a different verdict. Farrell is more obviously dealing with things which he knows down to the ground from personal experience. There is an unmistakable sincerity and a passion of earnestness in him which may tell in the long run. His monotony is one phase of his earnestness and substance. His record of social fact may prove to be the more profound and reliable. I will not undertake to say which of these two men is more likely to take his place in the hall of the immortals. The chances are good for both of them. And certainly they both have much to say to us of this generation.

If I were asked to say just exactly what are the economic theories of John Steinbeck, and how he proposes to apply them in terms of political action, I should have to answer: I do not know. The book offers no specific answer to these questions. It reminds us of what we all do know: that our system of production and finance involves innumerable instances of cruel hardship and injustice; that it needs constant adjustment and control by the conscience and authority of the sovereign people. This author is concerned with what has been called the forgotten man; it is clear that he holds the community responsible for the man without work, home, or food. He seems to intimate that what cannot be cured by individual effort must needs be met by collective measures. It is highly important that our people should be made aware of the social problems which remain to be solved within the system which is so good to so many of us. And there is no more effective way of bringing this about than to have actual instances presented vividly to our imaginations by means of fiction. For this reason I regard *The Grapes of Wrath* as a social document of great educational value.

Considering it simply as literary art, I would say that it gains greatly by dealing with social problems so urgent that they cannot be ignored. It gains thereby in emotional power. But it is a notable work of fiction by virtue of the fact that all social problems are so effectively dramatized in individual situations and characters—racy, colorful, pitiful, farcical, disorderly, well meaning, shrewd, brave, ignorant, loyal, anxious, obstinate, insuppressible, cockeyed . . . mortals. I have never lived among these Okies nor heard them talk. But I would swear that this is their language, these their thoughts, and these the very hardships and dangers which they encountered. They represent a level, material and social, on which the reader has never existed even for a day. They have lived for generations completely deprived of luxuries and refinements which in the life he has known are taken for granted as primary conditions of civilization.

And yet they are not savages. They are self-respecting men and women with a traditional set of standards and proprieties and rules of conduct which they never think of violating. Beset with innumerable difficulties, cut off from their familiar moorings, they are confronted with situations of great delicacy, with nice problems in ethics and family policy to be resolved. Decisions are taken after informal discussion in the family council organized on ancient tribal lines. Grampa was a rather flighty and childish old fellow. He was still the titular head of the tribe, but his position was honorary and a matter of custom. He had the right of first comment; but actual decision was made by the strong and wise, by Pa and Tom, and above all by Ma. Pa was the representative of practical prudence; Ma the voice of right feeling and generous impulse and the traditional code of decent conduct. It was she who decided that they should take Casy with them although they were already overcrowded. And she delivered the decision of the court in language pithy and judicial. Pa wanted to know, "Kin we, Ma?"

> Ma cleared her throat. "It ain't kin we? It's will we?" she said firmly. "As far as 'kin', we can't do nothin', not go to California or nothin'; but as far as 'will', why, we'll do what we will. An' as far as 'will'—it's a long time our folks been here and east before, an' I never heerd tell of no Joads or no Hazletts, neither, ever refusin' food an' shelter or a lift on the road to anybody who asked. They's been mean Joads, but never that mean."

And so the Joads and the Okies take their place with Don Quixote, with Dr. Faustus, with Galsworthy's Forsytes and Lewis' Babbitt, in the world's gallery of symbolic characters, the representative tapestry of the creative imagination. Will the colors hold? That is a large question, which only time can answer. It depends on whether the dyes are synthetic aniline or the true vegetable product. And who at the present moment can make sure of that?

I will put the question in another way. Is the subject too special for this book to have continuing artistic appeal? Are the issues fundamental enough in human nature to give it what is called universality? Perhaps the best theme is a combination of a particular and local subject with one more general and lasting. The particular subject here is the Oklahoma farmer and an oversupply of labor in the California orchards. The general subject is hunger; the general subject is man pitted against the forces of nature. There is much to remind one of Robinson Crusoe. Steinbeck will certainly do well if he can last as long and be as widely read as Daniel Defoe.

Martin Staples Shockley

CHRISTIAN SYMBOLISM
IN *THE GRAPES OF WRATH*

IN THEIR recent study of the Christ-symbol in modern fiction, novelist Alan Paton and theologian Liston Pope dismiss Jim Casy because their reaction to him "is essentially one of pathos rather than of awe."[1] I hesitate to disagree with two such eminent Christians; but I do. I propose an interpretation of *The Grapes of Wrath* in which Casy represents a contemporary adaptation of the Christ image and in which the meaning of the book is revealed through a sequence of Christian symbols.

Before and after *The Grapes of Wrath* Steinbeck has used symbolism and allegory; throughout his works he has considered a wide range of Christian or neo-Christian ideas; in relation to the context of his fiction as a whole, Christian symbolism is common. His use of Biblical names, for instance, is an inviting topic yet to be investigated. *The Pearl* is an obvious allegory on the evil of worldly treasure. The Pirate in *Tortilla Flat* exemplifies a Steinbeck character, pure in heart, simple in mind, rejected of men, clearly of the kingdom of heaven. More pertinent perhaps, the title of *The Grapes of Wrath* is itself a direct Christian allusion, suggesting the glory of the coming of the Lord, revealing that the story exists in Christian context, indicating that we should expect to find some Christian meaning.

It has, indeed, been found before. Professor F. I. Carpenter has pointed out the relationship of the Joad philosophy to the Unitarian transcendentalism of Emerson and Whitman.[2] I would not deny that Casy preaches the gospel according to Saint Walt; but I find further, stronger, more direct relations to the Bible.

Consider first the language of the novel. Major characters speak a language that has been associated with debased Piedmont culture. It is, I suggest, easy to find in vocabulary, rhythm, imagery, and tone

THIS ESSAY, "Christian Symbolism in The Grapes of Wrath," is to appear in a forthcoming issue of College English, and is reprinted here by permission of Martin Shockley and of Frederick L. Gwynn, editor of College English. Shockley's "The Reception of The Grapes of Wrath in Oklahoma" appears in the present book.

pronounced similarities to the language of the King James Bible. These similarities, to be seen in qualities of simplicity, purity, strength, vigor, earnestness, are easy to illustrate. The novel contains passages of moving tendeness and prophetic power, not alone in dialogue, but even in descriptive and expository passages.

Like the Israelites, the Joads are a homeless and persecuted people. They too flee from oppression, wander through a wilderness of hardships, seeking their own Promised Land. Unlike the Israelites, however, the Joads never find it. But, more specifically, let us examine the Christ-Casy relationship.

Jesus began his mission after a period of withdrawal into the wilderness for meditation and consecration; Preacher Casy comes into the book after a similar retreat. He tells Tom, "I went off alone, an' I sat and figured." Later when Casy and Tom meet in the strikers' tent, Casy says he has "been a-goin' into the wilderness like Jesus to try to find out sumpin." Certainly Steinbeck is conscious of the parallel.

Much has been made of Jim Conklin's name as a key to his identification in the symbolism of *The Red Badge of Courage*. Whether Steinbeck copied Crane is immaterial; Jim Casy is by the same initials identified with Jesus Christ.

Like Jesus, Jim has rejected an old religion and is in process of replacing it with a new gospel. In the introductory scene with Tom Joad, Tom and Jim recall the old days when Casy preached the old religion, expounded the old concept of sin and guilt. Now, however, Casy explains his rejection of a religion through which he saw himself as wicked and depraved because of the satisfaction of natural human desires. The old Adam of the fall is about to be exorcised through the new dispensation.

It should not be necessary to point out that Jim Casy's religion is innocent of Paulism, of Catholicism, of Puritanism. He is identified simply and directly with Christ, and his words paraphrase the words of Jesus, who said, "God is love," and "A new commandment give I unto you: that ye love one another."

Casy says, "What's this call, this sperit? . . . It's love. I love people so much I'm fit to bust sometimes." This is the truth Casy has found in his wilderness, the gospel he brings back to the people he loves.

Beyond this simple, central doctrine, identical and cardinal to Jesus and to Jim, there is the Emerson-Whitman-Unitarian-pantheism which Professor Carpenter notes. Jim elaborates: "There ain't no sin and there ain't no virtue. There's just stuff people do. It's all part of the same thing."

I would avoid theological subtleties; I see Jim Casy as a simple and direct copy of Jesus Christ. Yet Casy's doctrine, "all that lives is holy," comes close to the doctrine of one of the most distinguished Christian theologians of our time, whose famous and familiar phrasing of the same concept was known to us as "reverence for life" even before impresario Hutchins presented Albert Schweitzer among the groves of Aspen, Colorado.

The third article of Casy's faith is a related one: " 'Maybe,' I figgered, 'Maybe it's all men and women we love; maybe that's the Holy Sperit— the human sperit—the whole shebang. Maybe all men got one big soul ever'body's a part of.' Now I sat there thinking it, an' all of a suddent— I knew it. I knew it so deep down that it was true and I still know it." Casy's knowledge of the oversoul is derived from the same source as Emerson's and Whitman's, from within himself, or if you prefer, from God speaking within him.

Jim realizes, as did Jesus, that organized religion will reject his new teaching. Tom points this out: "You can't hold no church with idears like that," he said. "People would drive you out of the country with idears like that." In both cases, people did.

I should like to go on from this formulation of a creed to the expression of doctrine through deeds, to the unfolding of the incidents of the plot in which Jim Casy reveals himself through significant, symbolic acts.

First, he feels a compulsion to minister, to serve, to offer himself. When the Joads are preparing to leave for California, he tells them: "I got to go . . . I can't stay here no more. I got to go where the folks is goin'."

Not long afterward, Casy offers himself as the sacrifice to save his people. When Tom is about to be arrested, Casy tells the police that he is the guilty one. "It was me, all right . . . I'll go 'thout no trouble." So the Joads escape the consequences of their transgressions. "Between his guards Casy sat proudly, his head up and the stringy muscles of his neck prominent. On his lips there was a faint smile and on his face a curious look of conquest." Jim Casy had taken upon himself the sins of others.

Casy's death symbolically occurs in the middle of a stream to represent the "crossing over Jordan" Christian motif. Particularly significant, however, are Casy's last words directed to the man who murders him, "Listen," he said, "You fellas don' know what you're doin'." And again just before the heavy man swings the pick handle Casy repeats, "You don' know what you're a-doin'." Jesus said, as they crucified Him, "Father forgive them; they know not what they do."

One of the major emotional climaxes of the novel is the scene in which Tom tells Ma goodbye and explains why he must leave. He has told Ma about Casy who, "Spouted out some Scripture once, an' it didn' soun' like no hell-fire Scripture." He goes on to repeat what Casy told him about two being better than one. He rehearses Casy's teaching about the individual and the collective soul, recalling that Casy went into the wilderness to find his soul, then found, "His little piece of a soul wasn't no good 'less it was with the rest, an' was whole." He explains to Ma Casy's theory of Christian Socialism. " 'Tom,' Ma repeated, 'What you gonna do?'

" 'What Casy done,' he said."

At this point Tom becomes Casy's disciple. He has learned from his master, and now he takes up his master's work. Two of Jesus' disciples were named Thomas. Most of those chosen by Him to found the religion we profess were called from among people like the Joads.

Tom's answer to Ma's worry lest he lose his life is the answer he has learned from Casy. "Then it don' matter. Then I'll be all aroun' in the dark. I'll be ever'where—wherever you look. Wherever they's a fight so hungry people can eat, I'll be there. Wherever they's a cop beatin' up a guy, I'll be there. If Casy knowed, why, I'll be in the way kids laugh when they're hungry an' they know supper's ready. An' when our folks eat the stuff they raise an' live in the houses they build—why I'll be there. See? God, I'm talkin' like Casy." The One that Casy talked like said, "Lo, I am with you always."

These evidences of a Christ-Casy relationship mean more to me than they do to Mr. Paton and Dean Pope. I would not argue that Mr. Steinbeck's interpretation of the relationship of pathos and awe in the Christian tradition is identical with the interpretation of Mr. Paton and Dean Pope, nor that his interpretation is more or less correct than theirs. Nevertheless, I find in the novel what seems to me to be adequate evidence to establish the author's intention of creating in Jim Casy a character who would be understood in terms of the Christ symbol.

Beyond this personal identification, I find further use of Christian symbols. The conclusion of *The Grapes of Wrath* has been said to be extreme, sensational, overwrought. The Joads have reached at last a condition of utter desolation. Rosasharn, her baby born dead, is rain-drenched, weak, her breasts heavy with milk. In the barn they come upon a boy and a starving old man, too weak to eat the bread his son had stolen for him. Ma knows what must be done, but the decision is Rosasharn's: "Ma's eyes passed Rose of Sharon's eyes, and then came back to them. And the two women looked deep into each other. The girl's breath came short and gasping.

"She said, 'Yes.' "

In this, her Gethsemane, Rosasharn says, in effect, "Not my will, but Thine be done."

The meaning of this incident, Steinbeck's final paragraph, is clear in terms of Christian symbolism. And this is the supreme symbol of the Christian religion, commemorated by Protestants in the Communion, by Catholics in the Mass. Rosasharn gives what Christ gave, what we receive in memory of Him. The ultimate mystery of the Christian religion is realized as Rosasharn "Looked up and across the barn, and her lips came together and smiled mysteriously." She smiles mysteriously because what has been mystery is now knowledge. *This is my body*, says Rosasharn, and becomes the Resurrection and the Life. Rose of Sharon, the life-giver, symbolizes the resurrective aspect of Christ, common in Christian tradition and literature, used by Mr. Eliot in his "multifoliate rose" image. In her, death and life are one, and through her, life triumphs over death.

Cited incidents occur at points of major importance in plot and action, accompany major emotional crises, relate to the major and most familiar examples of Christian symbolism. Other less obvious examples might be brought in, such as the incident at the roadside cafe where the waitress lets the migrant have a loaf of bread and is immediately rewarded by large and unexpected tips from the two truck drivers: she had cast her bread upon the waters. In a recent issue of the *Colorado Quarterly* Professor Bernard Bowron notes Noah's wandering off down the stream as possibly "a biblical association."[3] I would not, however, try to press my point; major examples are enough.

Certain of these symbols may be identified as pre-Christian. The motif of crossing water in death is, of course, widespread in folklore; and the Freudian, totemistic interpretation of the miracle of transubstantiation lies in the background. It is not within the scope of this paper to explore these labyrinthine shadows. Suffice it to say that we recognize in Christianity elements of older religions.

Further, it is easy to identify elements of Steinbeck's ideology with other religions. For example, the principle of reverence for life, or "all that lives is holy," has been believed and practiced for centuries by Buddhists. Such, however, I regard as incidental quibbling. In *The Grapes of Wrath* the major intended meaning is neither Buddhist nor Freudian nor Marxist; it is, I believe, essentially and thoroughly Christian. In my interpretation, Jim Casy unmistakably and significantly equates with Jesus Christ.

I find in *The Grapes of Wrath* a sequence of familiar Christian symbols, appearing at structural crises of the plot, dominating the narrative, determining the characterization, revealing the theme as conscious and consistent Christian allegory.

1. "The Novelist and Christ," *The Saturday Review of Literature*, XXXVII, 59 (December 4, 1954).
2. "The Philosophical Joads," *College English*, II, 315-25 (January, 1941). [See page 241, above.]
3. "*The Grapes of Wrath*: A 'Wagons West' Romance," III (Summer, 1954) 90.

V. THE LATER WORK

Antonia Seixas

JOHN STEINBECK AND
THE NON-TELEOLOGICAL BUS

THE MISUNDERSTOOD WRITER is as ubiquitous and inevitable as the misunderstood spouse—and far worse off. Most of us must accept being misunderstood as one of the concomitants—or by-products—of life. But the writer's chief business is to be understood; he paces the floor in the agony of choosing, out of twenty possibilities, the exact single word which will delicately and precisely convey his meaning. He struggles murderously—if he is a serious artist—to create a set of characters and situations, conflicts and climaxes. He struggles to communicate through these elements a vision of life, a truth, or a philosophy—his total meaning.

Nevertheless, if this vision, this "pattern of reality," is stated too explicitly his work becomes not art but propaganda. His vital communication must be implicit; it must be the "soul" of his work, infusing its body, but not obtrusive. And so we put our own interpretations on his work; we project, to whatever extent we possess them, our own visions of truth—or our own propagandas. But in so doing, we are "misunderstanding" the writer.

Furthermore, we are happy only when we can put things safely in

---

ANTONIA SEIXAS (Toni Ricketts), long a California resident, was for a time Mr. Steinbeck's secretary. She was also the wife of Ed Ricketts, Steinbeck's close friend and his collaborator in Sea of Cortez, where Steinbeck explicitly stated his scientific, non-metaphysical attitude.

"John Steinbeck and the Non-teleological Bus" was written for What's Doing on the Monterey Peninsula, the author having been a staff member of that periodical. The essay is copyrighted by Game and Gossip (successor to What's Doing on the Monterey Peninsula) and is reprinted here from the Vol. I, No. 12 issue of that magazine, March, 1947, by permission of its managing editor, Lee G. Harbick.

Permission to reprint has also been obtained from the author, Antonia Seixas, who now lives and teaches in Israel and who revised the whole essay for its present appearance. She writes that she would like to do a more complete essay on "Steinbeck's symbolism and non-teleology—and his hatred of the middle class, the real clue to his writing."

pigeon-holes. If we can classify a writer as vulgar (or earthy), Communist (or progressive), we need make no further effort at understanding. Wrongly classified and thus misunderstood, misunderstood and thus wrongly classified, in an automatically circular process, the unhappy writer can only writhe in rage, frustration, or despair. Occasionally he relieves himself in violent forewords, á la Henry James or James Cain.

Steinbeck and his work illustrate this circular process, possibly because he is such an excellent story-teller that readers can't see the woods for the trees. They pegged him as a Communist after *The Grapes of Wrath* because he portrayed so movingly the plight of the dispossessed Okies—losing sight of the deeper symbolism embodied in the turtle slowly, blindly crossing the road.

The reviewers chortled over the humor, quaintness, and charm of *Cannery Row*, while the critics, who must take things seriously, handed Steinbeck everything from a slap on the wrist for sentimentalizing bums and loafers, to a poke in the nose for abdicating his role as reformer and pretending that life isn't terribly, terribly earnest. A single critic, Malcom Cowley, puzzled by an underlying sense of violence in the book, read it again more carefully and concluded that if *Cannery Row* was a cream-puff, it was a "very poisoned cream-puff." If Cowley had read it yet again, said Steinbeck, he would have found how very poisoned it was.

For Steinbeck consciously writes on several levels. A look at *Of Mice and Men* will illustrate. Three levels are apparent to the careful reader: the obvious story-level, with its tragic and, to many, inexplicable ending; a "social protest" level—and to this the great mass of readers was particularly susceptible—on which the tragedy of the rootless and helpless was portrayed with great economy and compassion by Steinbeck the reformer; and a third level, apparent to the more thoughtful or imaginative—or those more inclined to read their own visions of truth into a work of art. This is the symbolic level, on which the characters can be extended to any dimension. Lennie represents the great, blind mass-humanity, destroying out of sheer clumsiness the things it loves; George represents the quick-witted, alertly shrewd shepherd and manipulator-leader. Or Lennie represents the psychological unconscious; George, the conscious. And so on. The interpretations are limited only by the ingenuity of the interpreters.

But there is a fourth level. The clue to it, perhaps the only clue, could have been found in the book's originally-intended title: "Something that Happened." Without this clue, only those who know Steinbeck and knew the discussions out of which the book arose could have seen the work in terms of its particular, and intended, underlying philosophy.

However, this philosophy, this "pattern of reality," is stated explicitly, simply, and often in *Sea of Cortez*. And since it may provide the clue to a fuller understanding, not only of *Of Mice and Men* but of *The Wayward Bus* as well, it seems worthwhile to describe briefly the philosophical idea on which *Of Mice and Men* was based, and which is central to *Sea of Cortez*. It is conveyed by the phrase "non-teleological thinking"—a phrase which embraces not only a philosophical notion but a *modus operandi* and, above all, an attitude toward reality—one of the many possible "patterns of reality." According to *Sea of Cortez*, this attitude "considers events as outgrowths and expressions rather than as results" of specific causes. It concerns itself "not with what could be, or should be, or might be, but rather with what actually 'is'—attempting at most to answer the already sufficiently difficult questions *what* or *how*, instead of *why*." "To most men," wrote Steinbeck, "the most hateful statement possible is A THING IS BECAUSE IT IS . . ." for they feel that such a statement leaves out hope—a belief in the purposiveness of events by which all things occur to some "good" end.

(Seen in this light, Steinbeck's achievement in *Of Mice and Men* is even more impressive: the hardest task a writer can set himself is to tell the story of "something that happened" without explaining "why" —and make it convincing and moving. And in this light, the death of Lennie is necessary; not so much tragic or brutal, as simply part of a pattern of events.)

With this philosophical attitude in mind (while remembering that we cannot divorce ourselves from our own projections—and "we" includes this reviewer) let's look at *The Wayward Bus*.

This latest work belongs on the shelf between *Of Mice and Men* and *Grapes of Wrath*, from the standpoint of length and of breadth, or scope of canvas. As for its comparative depth, that will depend entirely on the reader and *his* "pattern of reality." Many will find *The Wayward Bus* cold, cynical, and lacking in "answers," and so will condemn it as lacking in depth.

The reader's emotions of pity, sympathy, and identification with the characters are not stirred in this work to the extent that they are in Steinbeck's previous books. It seems that the author did not feel much warmth or love for the passengers of his bus. He delineates them with the objectivity of a man viewing little animals through a microscope. He describes them meticulously. An apprentice writer would do well to study the way, for example, in which the character and past life of

Juan Chicoy is conveyed through Steinbeck's inventory of his clothes, his scars, the contents of his pockets, the way he handles a wrench. And though Steinbeck devotes pages to marvelously selective descriptions of his main characters, he doesn't tell you how they got that way, or why.

It isn't necessary. For they are all "type specimens"—not merely "products," but components of our civilizations. Elliot Pritchard is the type-specimen business man; his wife, Bernice, is the type-specimen "Lady," sweet, gentle, and terrifyingly powerful, with the unconscious craftiness of the weak and lazy who must live by rules and force those rules on all around them. There is Horton, the traveling salesman, whose best-selling item is the "Little Wonder Artificial Sore Foot." There are the adolescents, Pimples Carson, apprentice mechanic, and Norma, the homely, pathetic waitress.

The three characters most honest, most nearly in contact with their realities are Mildred Pritchard, the college girl, Camille Oaks, the blond stripper, and Juan Chicoy, of whom George, in *Of Mice and Men* was a prototype. The two girls, each in her own way aware and accepting, seem to be opposite sides of the same coin. These three are the precipitants of what action there is. Curiously, each of them has some physical defect: Juan has an amputated finger; Camille has ugly forceps scars on her jaw; and Mildred is almost blind without her glasses. But even the two girls are slightly "flat," as the typical always is. Only Juan, the god of the machine, and his wife Alice, are more nearly round.

The framework of the story is that of an assortment of people isolated and in a spot. They all want to get to San Juan de la Cruz. (They don't *have* to get there; it's just a matter of convenience. This is worth bearing in mind, if one wishes to regard the journey as an allegory.) The river is in flood and the bridge is out. They can go back to Rebel Corners and make other plans, or they can take an old road, unused for years, which may have been washed out in the storm. They decide on the old road, though as Pritchard observes, "You've got two gambles and one sure thing and the sure thing don't get you through either." The bus gets stuck, through Juan's unconscious design, and the passengers are marooned on a bare hillside with caves for shelter and a crate of Mother Mahoney's Home Baked Pies for food.

The tensions, mostly sexual, which have been building up among them since the day before, come to a head. In explosions of varying intensity the characters define their relationships to each other; each of them is confronted with a reality within himself or in his world. And Alice Chicoy, at Rebel Corners, tries to escape the traps life has set for her by going on one of the most graphically described benders in literature.

At the end, nothing is resolved, nothing is very much changed for most of them. Only Norma's future has been affected, for Camille has showed her how to make up her face, and has given her a bit of her own hard honesty when she says ". . . everybody's a tramp some time or other. Everybody. And the worst tramps of all are the ones that call it something else."

And when at last the lights of San Juan come into view, "lost and lonely in the night, remote and cold and winking, strung on chains," the reader who is looking for symbols, who has chosen to interpret the book on the allegorical level, may feel that this is a description of the people in the story—or even of all members of our civilization—lost and lonely in the night, "strung on chains" but essentially remote from each other.

The first impression is of a book curiously cool and hard, tempting those who expect warmth, humor, and compassion to reject it. But it is for that reason, perhaps, curiously powerful and insistent. And Steinbeck is always a magnificent story teller. In a remarkably clear and economical style, which achieves its effect through significant and telling detail, he invests his people and scenes with a living, pictorial reality. Those who like to turn a work of art inside out and examine the seams will be delighted at the architecture of the book, the rise and fall of climaxes and the way an important chapter, the close of a "movement," ends with a sigh—with a "little wind blowing in over the fields, bringing the smell of lupine . . ." or timid mice scurrying in the straw.

On a second level, The Wayward Bus is biting social commentary. These are not bums, migrant workers, Okies; these are people we see around us every day, caught as we all are caught in traps of our own making—our hypocritical beliefs, our shallow dreams drawn from movies, magazine ads, and success stories. Here we are, in our various ways taking refuge in our dream worlds.

The author seems to be saying, "Here is a typical group of homo Americanus. See, this is how they look, this is how they act." And though he seems to be more charmed by certain of his specimens than by others, he is like an entomologist describing the antics of a group of insects; he neither praises nor blames. He understands them, as specimens; perhaps he even loves them in a way, but he would doubtless be horrified to find any but one or two of them in his bed.

Those who are so inclined will find the symbolic or analogical level more clearly visible than in any of his other books. Confronted with a swirling flood over which we have no control, our only crossing the skimpily built bridges—skimpy because of the dishonesties in our civilization and the stupidities and short-sightedness which prevent us from making proper use of our "funds"—the "sure thing" is the back road, the old road, the long way round. And even that isn't a sure thing. Our time-dented bus, brave in its aluminum paint, gets stuck and, deserted by our tough, unsentimental realists, we're helpless.

We are not deserted; the Juans walk back and dig us out, and the battered old bus lumbers on. But though we go forward, it is only to more of the same. For the non-teleological position is opposed to the teleological notion of "progress." That is, it is in opposition to the idea of a predetermined design or purpose in Nature by which any phenomena can be explained. But at the same time, this "non-causal" viewpoint is a "non-blaming" viewpoint, since according to this, everything is simply part of a pattern. The Pritchards, Horton, Pimples—they are all part of the pattern of our culture, which is, in turn, part of some larger pattern which cannot be encompassed by the finite mind because the finite mind is but a part of the pattern.

If the symbolic-cum-philosophic analysis be carried farther, it must be remembered that the bus is bound for San Juan de la Cruz—which is also the name of a mystic poet. But it must not be thought that there is any "answer" in these symbolisms, that any solutions are suggested. The bus is wayward; its passengers "are the way they are" and as members of society, they cannot be blamed. If we look to The Wayward Bus for "why's," we will be disappointed, perhaps repelled; and we will misunderstand the author yet again. If we regard it as an account, "not of what could be or should be, or might be, but rather of what actually is," the games we can play with its symbolism are endless.

Peter Lisca

THE WAYWARD BUS—
A MODERN PILGRIMAGE

STEINBECK'S NOVELS have always dismayed reviewers, and *The Wayward Bus* was more dismaying than most. "As narrative," wrote Bernard De Voto, "it is superb—a fine craftsman working at his most expert—as comedy it is excellent; as novel it is satisfying and no more."[1] While Mr. De Voto's qualification, like that of many other reviewers, was a reaction to the novel's preoccupation with sex, other commentators brought up the old bogie of Steinbeck's "animality," which has plagued Steinbeck criticism since Edmund Wilson's essay on Steinbeck in 1940. Freeman Champney, for example, found the characters of *The Wayward Bus* "animated by the simpler forms of protoplasmic irritability."[2] Even Joseph Henry Jackson, long a supporter of Steinbeck, was forced to conclude that ". . . now he appears to look at human beings almost as animals."[3] One reviewer tried to cope with the book by resorting to a critical strategy of the thirties—". . . each of Steinbeck's characters may be dimly identified with a stock role in a leftist parable."[4] To complete the general confusion, at least one reviewer found *The Wayward Bus* "clearly superior" to everything since *The Grapes of Wrath* "because his choice of characters and his emphasis on healthy positive values may point to a revival of his interest in the serious and significant themes of American life."[5]

The most perceptive reviewer of the book was Carlos Baker, who was taken by its "richness of texture" as well as by a "solidity of structure" which he found superior even to that of *In Dubious Battle*. Where other critics saw the book as a complete surrender to scientific naturalism, Baker remarked that only a sense of humor kept Steinbeck from "savage indignation." Unfortunately, the confines of a book review did not permit Mr. Baker to elucidate these observations.[6]

PETER LISCA based "The Wayward Bus—A Modern Pilgrimage" on a section of his doctoral dissertation, The Art of John Steinbeck: An Analysis and Interpretation of Its Development *(University of Wisconsin, 1955). This essay was prepared especially for its appearance here and has not been published previously. Lisca's biography of Steinbeck opens the first section of this volume, and his essay on* The Pearl *follows the present selection.*

The Wayward Bus may be taken with the other two books Steinbeck published after the war (*Cannery Row* and *The Pearl*) as forming a triptych which, while varying widely in materials and techniques, is dedicated to one purpose—an inquiry into the assumptions underlying modern civilization. *Cannery Row* had dealt with this civilization's "no-goods and blots-on-the-town and bums"—actually "the Virtues, the Graces, the Beauties," if seen through "another peephole." *The Pearl*, like the chapter on the gopher in *Cannery Row*, depicted the individual struggling between two worlds. *The Wayward Bus* is a pitiless examination of that world which Mack and the boys deny, the world to which the gopher succumbs, and the world over which Kino and Juana gain a tragic victory. This is the most obvious meaning of the book.

But the novel has another, more complex, level of meaning which is a part of the structure and technique. In a letter to Pascal Covici, Steinbeck remarked that the driver of the wayward bus, Juan Chicoy, was to be "all the god the fathers you ever saw driving a six cylinder, broken down battered world through time and space." After *The Wayward Bus* was published, Steinbeck told one interviewer that the book contained "an indefinite number of echoes" of "Chaucer,[7] the *Heptameron* and Boccaccio's *Decameron*." He might also have added the *Divine Comedy;* for like Dante's journey, the frame story of the wayward bus taking its assorted passengers cross-country from one main highway to another, coming to washed-out bridges, traveling the forgotten back road, and finally arriving at San Juan de la Cruz becomes itself a part of the meaning of the novel. There are two main "plots": the gathering of the characters and their interactions with each other; and the actual journey of the allegorical bus.

On the level of character the plot is held together by a play of tensions among the various personalities on the bus. These tensions are mostly sexual and are resolved in a series of incidents during the space of a few hours when Juan Chicoy temporarily abandons his passengers in a deep rut of the muddy back road to San Juan de la Cruz. In each of these incidents one of the characters is made to face some inner reality he had successfully suppressed in himself. Responsible for most of these clashes, directly or indirectly, is a blond stripper who calls herself Camille Oaks. She is introduced in a separate action on another bus, and by the time she joins the main group at Rebel Corners her future role as *femme fatale* is clear and the individuals of the main group have been defined by a series of little actions among themselves.

Because *The Wayward Bus*, unlike most of Steinbeck's novels, is more concerned with action on the level of character than on the physical level of events, it is necessary here to sketch in some detail the main personalities. They seem to be arranged into three main groups: the damned, those in purgatory, and the saved or elect. The damned are Mr. Pritchard, Mrs. Pritchard, Alice Chicoy, Louie (the first bus driver), Norma, and Van Brunt.

Mr. Pritchard is a variation on Sinclair Lewis's business man, and his description seems to come right out of *Babbitt*. "He was never alone. His business was conducted by groups of men who worked alike, thought alike, and even looked alike. His lunches were with men like himself who joined together in clubs so that no foreign element or idea could enter. . . . One night a week he played poker with men so exactly like himself that the game was fairly even." This similarity to Babbitt extends even to a youthful indiscretion: "He had once voted for Eugene Debs, but that had been a long time ago." Mr. Pritchard's role as a business unit is paralleled by his attitude toward sex. At the age of twenty he had made one drunken visit to a parlor house. He now goes to occasional stags, "but five hundred Mr. Pritchards were there with him." (pp. 40-41.)[8] During the course of the novel he suffers two quick shocks which force him to become aware of himself both in his business activities and his sexual adjustment.

Mr. Pritchard's wife, Bernice, is also a recognizable type.

> She was feminine and dainty and she dressed always with a hint of a passed period. . . . She met the ideas of other people with a quiet smile, almost as though she forgave them for having ideas. . . . Women of lusty appetites she spoke of as 'that kind of woman,' and she was a little sorry for them as she was for dope fiends and alcoholics. Her husband's beginning libido she had accepted and then gradually by faint but constant reluctance had first molded and then gradually strangled. . . . (pp. 61-63.)

In addition to this negative sexual power over her husband, Mrs. Pritchard resorts to sudden attacks of migraine headaches which may be brought on as the occasion requires.

While Mr. and Mrs. Pritchard are damned for being hypocritical and prudish, Juan Chicoy's wife, Alice, though she has lusty appetites, is also among the damned. "All relations and all situations to Alice were person-to-person things in which she and the other were huge and all others were removed from the world. There was no shading." (p. 35.) "Alice was not very aware of things or people if they did not in some way either augment or take away from her immediate life." (p. 88.) Her lack of ecological orientation is aptly and grotesquely symbolized by her attitude toward the common housefly, which she regards as a trespasser in her private world. There are several incidents illustrating this. The most amusing occurs during her prodigious drunk in the closed lunchroom after Juan has driven off with the passengers, when, while trying to kill a fly, she reduces the world of the lunchroom to a shambles.

Norma, the Chicoys' hired waitress, is another of the damned. Her spiritual flaw is a combination of the weak qualities exemplified by the elder Pritchards and Alice Chicoy. Her soul is an odd combination of sexual frustration and illusion. "The actual love-making in her life had been a series of wrestling matches, the aim of which was to keep her clothes on in the back seat of a car. So far she had won by simple concentration." (p. 10.) She writes long, intimate letters to Clark Gable, with whom she is in love, and is waiting for the day when he will walk into the lunchroom, recognize "this was his woman," and take her away from it all. She keeps his picture on her dresser and at night wears a gold wedding ring to bed. The rest of her soul is concocted of clichés about personal appearance—" . . . you could always find some little bit of beauty even on the wash dresses." (p. 11.) She brushes her hair "ten strokes on one side and ten on the other. And while she brushed she raised and flexed the muscles of one leg and then the other to develop the calves." (p. 49.)

While not involved in the central action of the book, Louie, the bus driver who brings Camille to Rebel Corners, is an important character because he clarifies the sexual attitudes of Juan Chicoy, Ernest Horton, and Camille Oaks. He is not a prude, but his attitude is cheap and vulgar. His masculinity is false and sterile. "Nearly all his waking hours Louie thought about girls. He liked to outrage them. He liked to have them fall in love with him and then walk away. He called them pigs. 'I'll get a pig,' he would say, 'and you get a pig, and we'll go out on the town' " (p. 99.) Camille Oaks sees through Louie's cheapness; her parrying of his "slick" advances provides some of the book's finest comedy.

The saved characters, the elect, are Juan Chicoy, Ernest Horton, and Camille Oaks. Juan Chicoy has all the characteristics of a Steinbeck hero. He is a skilled mechanic. He is self-reliant and self-contained. In contrast to Mr. Pritchard, who is always toying with a nail clipper, "His movements were sure even when he was not doing anything that required sureness. . . . His hands moved with speed and precision and never fiddled with matches or nails." (p. 15.) Unlike his wife Alice, in his dealings with other people he can "look at each thing in relation to the other. . . . He could see and judge and consider and enjoy."

(p. 35.) His relations with women are particularly successful because his sexuality is open and honest.

Like Juan, Ernest Horton is able to accept people as they are, is self-sufficient and honest. He immediately sees through Norma's dream world; but, unlike Alice, he does not make fun of her. Instead he plays along, even volunteering to deliver a letter to Clark Gable, and he tries to protect Norma when she has her final quarrel with Alice. Although Ernest Horton makes a living by selling comical gadgets (artificial sore toes, a shot glass in the shape of a toilet bowl), unlike Mr. Pritchard he is not taken in by his own salesmanship. His sexual desires are as honest and straight-forward as Juan's, and, like Juan, he too finds the trip successful in this respect.

Finally, there is Camille Oaks, the blond stripper. "She knew she was different from other girls, but she didn't quite know how. . . . Men couldn't keep their hands off her. . . . All men wanted the same thing from her." Like Juan and Ernest Horton, she has the eco-logical view. ". . . That was just the way it was. She took it for granted and it was true." (pp. 108-109.) Camille cannot help having this effect on men. For a time she had tried to counteract it. "She tried wearing severe clothes, but that didn't help much. She couldn't keep an or-dinary job. She learned to type, but offices went to pieces when she was hired." (p. 110.) Although she would like nothing better than "a nice house in a nice town, two children, and a stairway to stand on," she accepts the fact that this is impossible for her. "She didn't under-stand stags or what satisfaction the men got out of them, but there they were, and she made fifty dollars for taking off her clothes and that was better than having them torn off in an office." (pp. 109-110.)

These saved characters, no matter how different their surface lives seem, have four important traits in common: honesty with themselves and others, an ecological view of things, ability in their respective fields, and sexual attractiveness. They are also set apart from the damned by a common physical characteristic. Each has on his or her body some scar or mark caused by the world. Juan Chicoy has one joint missing from the third finger on his left hand, a scar alongside his nose, and a scar on his lip. Camille Oaks has deep forceps marks along her jaws. Ernest Horton's scars are not visible, but they are indicated by the purple heart ribbon which he wears in his lapel.

There are only two other passengers who have physical disfigure-ments—Pimples (suffering from acne) and Mildred Pritchard (almost blind without her glasses). Unlike the scars of the saved characters, both these disfigurements are natural, not caused by the world. Pimples and Mildred are purgatorial souls who progress upward several circles during the bus trip.

Mildred is a sexually attractive though slightly masculine woman of twenty-one who is slowly but successfully overcoming the effects of her home environment. In this struggle she has been helped by a college education and certain "dangerous companions," as her father calls them, "professors and certain people considered Red. Before the war she had picketed a scrap-iron ship bound for Japan. . . ." (p. 41.) She is approaching sexual maturity and already "had experienced two consummated love affairs which gave her great satisfaction and a steady longing for a relationship that would be constant." (p. 66.) She is immediately attracted to Juan Chicoy, but has not progressed to the cardinal virtues shared by the saved characters. There are definite indications, however, that she is well on the road. One doctor has told her that her weak eyes "had to do with puberty" and that she may get her eyesight back when she has her first baby.

Pimples Carson, like Mildred Pritchard, is in a state of Becoming. Like Norma, the elder Pritchards, and Louie, a good part of his soul is made up of advertising slogans and clichés of the "You too can be successful" type. He eats prodigious amounts of sweets because they are " 'rich in food energy. . . . Fellow's going to work, he needs food energy. Take about three o'clock in the afternoon when you get a letdown. Why, you need something rich in food energy.' " (p. 29.) He is planning to take a course in radar engineering, by mail, and believes that one gets valuable experience traveling. Like Mildred, however, Pimples has possibilities. His skin condition will clear up after adolescence. He has a genuine interest in mechanical things and, under Juan's tutorship, is actually a good apprentice. Juan trusts him to make preparations for the trip. Only Pimples knows enough about driving to realize that Juan stuck the bus on purpose, and when Juan abandons it he leaves Pimples in charge.

The last member of the group of passengers is Mr. Van Brunt, an old man of over sixty who does not clearly belong in any of the three categories. He may be intended to suggest the ultimate stage of the damned. His physical disfigurements are not caused by the world, but neither are they, like those of Pimples and Mildred, the temporary ones of youth. They are the ills of an old and decaying body. "He had his head bent permanently forward on the arthritic stalk of his neck so that the tip of his nose pointed straight at the ground. . . . His long, deeply channeled upper lip was raised over his teeth like the little trunk of a tapir. The point over his teeth seemed to be almost prehensile." (p. 77.) His twisted body is the sign of a twisted soul. His self-righteousness masks an essentially malicious and dirty mind, as Mildred points out. "Physical hatred of everyone around him crowded in his throat." (p. 293.)

These are the passengers of Steinbeck's allegorical bus. No one actually changes during the trip, but in a chain reaction of events culminating during Juan's temporary desertion of his six-cylinder world each of the damned and purgatorial souls is made to face some inner reality.

Under the Socratic examination of Ernest Horton, Mr. Pritchard is made to realize the fact that his business ethics and ideal of "service" are really "high-class blackmail." When Camille begins to tire of his persistent "fatherly" interest in getting her a job in his office, she tells him what his real motives are by revealing herself as the stripper he had ogled during a stag for business men in Chicago.

Mrs. Pritchard's illusion that her family is far removed from the vulgarity of other people is shattered when her daughter deserts her and runs after the Mexican-Irish Juan Chicoy. A short time later her husband, smarting under the two quick blows given him by Ernest Horton and Camille, assaults Mrs. Pritchard on the dirt floor of the cave and commits conjugal rape. When he leaves, Mrs. Pritchard gouges her cheeks and throat with her nails, bites her lips, and rubs dirt over her face.

Van Brunt tries to make Mildred Pritchard uncomfortable by pointing out that her slip is showing and then prolonging the conversation— "I don't care to hear about your underwear. . . . I don't want you to think I had any other motive. . . . Too many girls get self-conscious of their legs. They think everybody is looking at them." Remembering that Van Brunt had "never missed any show of legs," Mildred looks deliberately at him and says, "You see, there are two straps on each shoulder. One is for the slip and the other supports the brassière and the brassière holds the breasts up firmly. There isn't anything below that until the panties, if I wore panties, which I don't." (p. 193.) Van Brunt is uncomfortable for the rest of the trip.

For a while, under Camille's sympathetic interest, Norma seems to be becoming eligible for a place in purgatory along with Pimples and Mildred. But the reader, as well as the tutor, soon becomes aware that Norma has merely exchanged one immature illusion for another even more immature and compounded of still more clichés from movies and magazine ads. Her attitude toward sex is still that "Mr. Gable not only would not do things like that, but wouldn't like them if he heard about them." (p. 11.) She is brought up short when her expression of sympathy for Pimples results in his crude attempt to seduce her.

Mildred becomes disgusted with her parents and deserts them. She finds Juan in an old abandoned barn and is forced to admit to him, "I don't want you to think it's you. It's me. I know what I want. I don't even like you." She is even forced to make the advances. "You don't give me any pride. You don't give me any violence to fall back on later." (pp. 267-268.)

While these tensions are working themselves out among the passengers, the bus itself is engaged in an adventure which becomes a part of this vision of humanity. Although the journey from Rebel Corners to San Juan de la Cruz is described in realistic terms, the entire geography and toponymy of the book are fictitious, and there is an underlying suggestiveness in almost every detail. That *The Wayward Bus* is intended as more than a realistic narrative is also pointed out by its epigraph.

> I pray you all gyve audyence,
> And here this mater with reverence,
> By fygure a morall playe;
> The somonynge of Everyman called it is,
> That of our lyves and endynge shewes
> How transytory we be all daye.
>
> —EVERYMAN.

Juan Chicoy (whose initials, like those of Jim Casy in *The Grapes of Wrath*, are significant) has inherited his bus from a previous owner. One of the changes he has made in his "six cylinder . . . world" is painting out its previous inscription, which is "still barely readable"— *el gran Poder de Jesus*. "Now the simple word 'sweetheart' was boldly lettered on front and rear bumpers." (p. 21.) At various stages of the journey the pilgrims see such signs as REPENT and JESUS SAVES painted on rocks and cliffs and interspersed with advertisements for patent medicines.

Although Juan carries on the bus's dashboard "a small metal Virgin of Guadalupe painted in brilliant colors," its powers are not entirely trusted and there are false gods before it: "Hanging from the top of the windshield were the penates: a baby's shoe—that's for protection, for the stumbling feet of a baby require constant caution and aid of God; and a tiny boxing glove—and that's for power. . . . There also hung on the windshield a little plastic kewpie doll with a cerise and green ostrich-feather headdress and a provocative sarong. And this was for the pleasures of the flesh. . . ." (pp. 19-20.) Juan Chicoy, not "a believer in an orthodox sense, now he was fifty," keeps the Guadalupana only because he would have been "uneasy" without it. The penates and the Virgin are supported by a revolver, a roll of bandage, a bottle of iodine, smelling salts, and a pint of whiskey. "His religion was practical." (p. 21.)

Juan Chicoy's role as conductor of this six cylinder world is paralleled by the old man Van Brunt in his capacity as prophet. He foresees and tells of the raging San Ysidro river, the washed-out bridge, and the impassable back road; but his efforts are bent toward frustrating any positive action in the face of these difficulties. In this sense, as incarnating the everlasting nay, he is the Satan of this world on wheels. As Juan Chicoy is always in the driver's seat, so Van Brunt is always seen in the last seat back, watching the passengers with a baleful eye. Van Brunt is, however, a prophet without honor, for Juan Chicoy (in his capacity as "all the god the fathers") does not finally desert the "battered broken down world."

The events of the journey are also allegorical. The first adventure which is encountered after the bus leaves the crossroads significantly called Rebel Corners is the problem of crossing the San Ysidro river. This river, named after a patron saint of agriculture, is in flood and is destroying the farmers' property—tearing down fences, washing away topsoil, and drowning livestock. The bridge over this river is unsafe because it has been built by a crooked politician. It may be passable, but the passengers fear death by water. The only other alternatives are going back to Rebel Corners or leaving the paved highway and taking the old dirt road which had been used by the stagecoaches of their pioneer ancestors. Juan offers to let the passengers decide upon the course of action, and this they seem willing to do until Van Brunt points out that by making a decision they are shifting responsibility from Juan Chicoy onto themselves. When Juan chooses the long way around, the old back road, Van Brunt is the first to object, though he is also against the only two other possibilities—crossing the bridge and going back.

When Juan abandons the bus and walks off in the rain, it becomes clear that the passengers are unable to provide for themselves in any way and they must resort to caves for shelter and to a crate of MOTHER MAHONEY'S HOME-BAKED PIES for food. As Ernest Horton forces Mr. Pritchard to admit, the successful and enterprising business man knows nothing about gasoline engines, cannot keep from getting pneumonia under the circumstances, and cannot even " 'kill a cow . . . . cut it up and cook it.' " (p. 276.)

While the passengers are quarreling among themselves, Juan and Mildred have found each other and are consummating their love affair in an old barn. When they return to the bus, Juan digs it out of the mud and continues to drive it along the old back road to St. John of the Cross: "Far ahead and little to the left a cluster of lights came into view—little lights winking with distance, lost and lonely in the night, remote and cold and winking, strung on chains. Juan looked at them and called, 'That's San Juan up ahead.' " (p. 312.)

The novel ends on this positive note. The allegorical bus is on a wayward pilgrimage, but it does arrive at Saint John of the Cross. The prophet Van Brunt has not really foreseen all. Steinbeck seems to be saying that in that world in which el gran poder de Jesus is barely visible, where both the Virgin of Guadalupe and pagan idols must be backed up by a roll of bandage and a revolver, a world populated by artificial and dishonest Pritchards, deluded Normas, cynical Van Brunts, self-centered Alices, and vulgar Louies, there are also realistic and objective people like Juan Chicoy, without whom the world would founder, who always return to dig it out of the mud, people like Camille Oaks and Ernest Horton, who are capable of tenderness and affection toward their fellow passengers.

The energy of the novel derives from this constant tension between the plot on the level of character and the plot on the level of journey. The action of the novel can be graphed as an ascending spiral, the characters providing its circular and the journey its vertical motion. The parallel to the Divine Comedy is not accidental.

1. Bernard De Voto, "John Steinbeck's Bus Ride into the Hills." New York Herald Tribune Weekly Book Review, February 16, 1947, p. 2.
2. Freeman Champney, "John Steinbeck, Californian," Antioch Review, 7 (Fall, 1947), p. 359.
3. Joseph Henry Jackson, a book review in This World (San Francisco Chronicle), February 16, 1947, p. 17.
4. Anon., "Repent," Time, 49 (February 24, 1947), p. 119.
5. See Chicago Sun Book Week, February 16, 1947, p. 3.
6. Carlos Baker, "Mr. Steinbeck's Cross-Section," New York Times Book Review, February 16, 1947, pp. 1, 31.
7. [An excellent review by Henry Seidel Canby, written for the Book-of-the-Month Club News (February, 1947), stresses the parallels with Chaucer. E. W. T., JR. AND C. V. W.]
8. This and all further references to The Wayward Bus are to the first edition, published in New York by The Viking Press, 1947.

Peter Lisca

STEINBECK'S
FABLE OF THE PEARL

A S IS EVIDENT in such works as *The Red Pony, Of Mice and Men, Burning Bright,* some of the stories in *The Long Valley,* and certain chapters in *The Grapes of Wrath,* one of the distinguishing marks of Steinbeck's genius is his ability to fuse the realistic and the lyric into a fable-like texture and structure. Perhaps his greatest success with this strategy is *The Pearl* (1947), first published in 1945 as a short story called "The Pearl of the World."

Before attempting an analysis of *The Pearl,* it is instructive to note that its essential story first appeared in *Sea of Cortez* (1941) as Steinbeck's re-telling of an event "which happened at La Paz in recent years."

> An Indian boy by accident found a pearl of great size, an unbelievable pearl. He knew its value was so great that he need never work again. . . . In his great pearl lay salvation, for he could in advance purchase masses sufficient to pop him out of Purgatory like a squeezed watermelon seed. . . . He took his pearl to a broker and was offered so little that he grew angry, for he knew he was cheated. Then he carried his pearl to another broker and was offered the same amount. After a few more visits he came to know that the brokers were only the many hands of one head and that he could not sell his pearl for more. He took it to the beach and hid it under a stone, and that night he was clubbed into unconsciousness and his clothing was searched. The next night he slept at the house of a friend and his friend and he were injured and bound and the whole house searched. Then he went inland to lose his pursuers and he was waylaid and tortured. But he was very angry now and he knew what he must do. Hurt as he was he crept back to La Paz in the night and he skulked like a hunted fox to the beach and took out his pearl from under the stone. Then he cursed it and threw it as far as he could into the channel. He was a free man again with his soul in

---

PETER LISCA has prepared "Steinbeck's Fable of The Pearl," as one of three essays for the present volume, where it appears in print for the first time. Like the essay on The Wayward Bus, *which precedes it, it is based on Mr. Lisca's doctoral dissertation.*

danger and his food and shelter insecure. And he laughed a great deal about it.

Steinbeck kept this basic pattern when he returned to the story four years later—the discovery of the pearl, the persecution, the flight, and the renunciation. But in addition to fleshing out this pattern with a human context, he also introduced certain important changes. The Indian boy becomes the man Kino, husband of Juana and father to Coyotito. The pearl is to provide not "the ability to be drunk as long as he wished," but an education for Coyotito, who will then be able to liberate his people from the bondage of ignorance. The pearl is returned to the sea, but not before it has caused strife between husband and wife, destroyed their home, and resulted in the violent death of their child. Steinbeck also added several minor figures—a greedy doctor, a kind and understanding brother.

These changes were intended to amplify and make more complex those qualities of parable which Steinbeck perceived in the original.

> This seems to be a true story, but it is so much like a parable that it almost can't be. This Indian boy is too heroic, too wise. He knows too much and acts on his knowledge. In every way, he goes contrary to human direction. The story is probably true, but we don't believe it; it is far too reasonable to be true.

Similarly, in his introductory remarks to *The Pearl* Steinbeck wrote, "And because the story has been told so often, it has taken root in every man's mind. And, as with all retold tales that are in people's hearts, there are only good and bad things and black and white things . . . and no in-between anywhere." Five years later he said of the novelette, "I tried to write it as folklore, to give it that set-aside, raised-up feeling that all folk stories have."

Part of Steinbeck's success in creating this feeling in *The Pearl* lies in the theme itself. The action is simple, but, as in all parables, suggestive of underlying planes of meaning. The surface story of the finding of the pearl, the attempt to sell it for a fair price, and the final resignation in which there is also a tragic triumph is told in a manner which urges the reader to look beyond these physical events into their spiritual significance. As Alex Comfort has remarked (*The Novel and Our Time*, p. 59), "With the advent of an intelligent insight into symbolism, realism as we knew it before the new psychology must be reconsidered, because we now know that any imaginative narration exists both as a direct statement of events and as a reflection of conscious forces dictating the imagery in which it is presented." All of Steinbeck's statements about *The Pearl* point in this direction. "If this story is a parable," the author wrote in his introduction, "perhaps everyone takes his own meaning from it and reads his own life into it."

In the story itself there are several details which suggest the symbolic nature of this pattern of events. When Kino first finds the pearl it is described as "the greatest pearl in the world," and two pages later as "the Pearl of the World." After the first attack on Kino by unknown assailants, his wife Juana says of the pearl, "This thing is evil. This pearl is like sin! It will destroy us. Throw it away, Kino. Let us break it between stones. Let us bury it and forget the place. Let us throw it back in the sea. It has brought evil. Kino, my husband, it will destroy us." But Kino's face is set. The pearl has "cozened his brain with its beauty." The people of the village are suspicious. " 'That good wife Juana,' " they said, " 'and the beautiful baby Coyotito, and the others to come. What a pity it would be if the pearl should destroy them all.' " After Kino has insulted the agents who told him the pearl was of no great value, his brother Juan Tomás says to him, "You have defied not the pearl buyers, but the whole structure, the whole way of life, and I am afraid for you." After the second attack, Kino still refuses to give up the pearl and says, "This pearl has become my soul. If I give it up I shall lose my soul."

This aura of suggestion extends not only to the pearl itself, but to the characters and setting as well. Kino's assailants come at night and are never actually seen except as vague shadows. After the first attack Kino answers his wife's cries with, "I am all right. The thing has gone." After their hut has been ransacked and burned down, Kino asks Juana, "Who?" and she replies, "I don't know. The dark ones." The two Indians, "people from the inland," who guide the vague "dark man" on horseback in the pursuit of Kino and his family are described in animal terms. They "whined a little, like excited dogs on a warming trail," and are referred to only as "the dark trackers." Kino is named after a late seventeenth century Jesuit, Eusebius Kino, who was a missionary in the Gulf region and a great explorer, the first to prove that lower California was a peninsula, not an island. The name of Kino's wife, Juana, means simply "woman." The doctor and the pearl buyers are obviously symbols of greed.

The setting of *The Pearl* is just as suggestive as the theme, characters, and the pearl itself.

> The uncertain air that magnified some things and blotted out others hung over the whole Gulf so that all sights were unreal and vision could not be trusted; so that sea and land had the sharp clarities and

the vagueness of a dream. Thus it might be that the people of the Gulf trust things of the spirit and things of the imagination, but they do not trust their eyes to show them distance or clear outline or any optical exactness. . . . Part of the far shore disappeared into a shimmer that looked like water. There was no certainty in seeing, no proof that what you saw was there or was not there. And the people of the Gulf expected all places were that way, and it was not strange to them.

When Kino and Juana escape from their coastal village, they "go out into the world." At one point in their flight, the landscape, though realistically described, has that same symbolic suggestiveness that the landscape has in "Flight" and "The Great Mountains."

> The land was waterless, furred with the cacti which could store water and with the great-rooted brush which could reach deep into the earth for a little moisture and get along on very little. And underfoot was not soil but broken rock, split into cubes, great slabs, but none of it water-rounded. Little tufts of sad dry grass grew between the stones, grass that had sprouted with a single rain and headed, dropped its seed, and died. Horned toads watched the family go by and turned their little pivoting dragon heads. . . . The singing heat lay over this desert country, and ahead the stone mountains looked cool and welcoming.

This is but one of many passages in which the symbolic effect of the theme and setting is supported by some of Steinbeck's best prose, a prose curiously remote and yet intimate, like a medieval tapestry. The symbolic suggestiveness is vital because the book's theme is imbedded in a rich texture of the actual and specific. The materials are concrete before they are universal; the characters are humans before they are qualities. Even the way Kino wears his hat has relevance to a particular place and situation. "Kino put on his large straw hat and felt it with his hand to see that it was properly placed, not on the back or side of his head, like a rash, unmarried, irresponsible man, and not flat as an elder would wear it, but tilted a little forward to show aggressiveness and seriousness and vigor." This kind of prose fused the author's description with the very process of the character's thinking.

To balance those passages of description which carry symbolic weight, Steinbeck often renders physical objects and events in terms of pure realistic detail, whether it be a scorpion ("the scorpion moved delicately down the rope toward the box. . . . It stopped, and its tail rose over its back in little jerks and the curved thorn on the tail's end glistened") or Kino's pursuers as he sees them through a narrow opening in a tree branch.

Kino could see only their legs and only the legs of the horse from under the fallen branch. He saw the dark horny feet of the men and their ragged white clothes, and he heard the creak of leather of the saddle and the clink of spurs. The trackers stopped at the swept place and studied it, and the horseman stopped. The horse flung his head up against the bit and the bit-roller clicked under his tongue and the horse snorted. Then the dark trackers turned and studied the horse and watched his ears.

The more panoramic descriptions have this same reality and authenticity, which serve to create a firm foundation for the abstract pattern.

The beach was yellow sand, but at the water's edge a rubble of shell and algae took its place. Fiddler crabs bubbled and sputtered in their holes in the sand, and in the shallows little lobsters popped in and out of their tiny homes in the rubble and sand. The sea bottom was rich with crawling and swimming and growing things. The brown algae waved in the gentle currents and the green eel grass swayed and little sea horses clung to its stems. Spotted botete, the poison fish, lay on the bottom in the eel-grass beds, and the bright-colored swimming crabs scampered over them.

It is probably such passages as these that cause Maxwell Geismar to bring up again (in his review of the book) that old bogie of Steinbeck's animalism. "And what one notices again is how much more interested Steinbeck really is in the natural scene, and in animal life, than in the people or the human emotions of his narrative." In *The Pearl*, as in most of his novels and short stories, Steinbeck stays outside of his characters, using the technique of the objective narrator. This is probably the reason why so many critics have placed disproportionate and misguided emphasis on Steinbeck's descriptions of nature and animal life. These passages are well done and they do seem to stand out in his works. But it must be kept in mind that the technique which renders them so effective is in part the same technique he applies to his characters. Steinbeck's work, especially his best, often verges on the sentimental, and it is saved only by this stern control, this unwillingness to become, as author, subjectively entangled in the emotions of his characters.

It is this reticence which keeps such works as *Of Mice and Men* and *The Grapes of Wrath*, as well as *The Pearl*, from sinking into bathos. Like Hemingway, Steinbeck reveals his characters' emotions and states of mind only through what an objective observer can see and hear; but unlike Hemingway, he does not give the effect of suppressed sentiment by keeping a stiffer upper lip than is necessary. Steinbeck's attitude toward his characters is like that of Doc toward the other inhabitants of Cannery Row. "There is no ego in my work," Steinbeck once wrote, "and consequently there is no danger for me in it. . . . If it once became introverted I wouldn't last twenty-four hours."

In *The Pearl*, as in his other works, Steinbeck makes use of various strategies to convey his characters' states of mind. Sometimes the technique is almost that of the objective correlative. In the office of the pearl buyers, for example, the agent's agitation while he is waiting for Kino to walk up the street is conveyed by the description of a nervous tic which is at the same time an adequate symbol of his *leger de main* activities as a pearl buyer.

> He rolled a coin back and forth over his knuckles and made it appear and disappear, made it spin and sparkle. The coin winked into sight and as quickly slipped out of sight, and the man did not even watch his own performance. The fingers did it all mechanically, precisely, while the man hummed to himself and peered out the door. Then he heard the tramp of feet of the approaching crowd, and the fingers of his right hand worked faster and faster until, as the figure of Kino filled the doorway, the coin flashed and disappeared.

As Kino talks to him about his pearl, the agent's fingers "worked furiously with the coin." When Kino places the magnificent pearl on the velvet pad, he quickly glances up at the agent's face. "But there was no sign, no movement, the face did not change, but the secret hand behind the desk missed in its precision. The coin stumbled over a knuckle and slipped silently into the dealer's lap."

Sometimes this revelation of a character's state of mind is partly subjective, as with Steinbeck's use of musical motifs.

> And as he filled his basket the song was in Kino, and the beat of the song was his pounding heart as it ate the oxygen from his held breath, and the melody of the song was the gray-green water and the little scuttling animals and the clouds of fish that flitted by and were gone. But in the song there was a secret little song, hardly perceptible, but always there, sweet and secret and clinging, almost hiding in the counter-melody, and this was the Song of the Pearl That Might Be, for every shell thrown in the basket might contain a pearl.

There are similar passages which depict Kino's love, hate, anger, and fear. They would never do to describe the inner feelings of a Jamesian character, but they are adequate for the simple materials and parable structure of *The Pearl*.

Steinbeck had used this same device in *Cannery Row* to depict Doc's emotional states of mind, but it should be noted that the technique is modified to suit the more sophisticated character. Thus when Doc sees the drowned girl:

> Music sounded in Doc's ears, a high thin piercingly sweet flute carrying a melody he could never remember, and against this a pounding surf-like wood-wind section. The flute went up into regions beyond the hearing range and even there it carried its unbelievable melody . . . . the flute climbed again and plucked cellos sounded below and the sea crept in and in toward the beach.

This device is not a retreat before the problems of a writer, but an experiment in attempting to render complex and partly subliminal emotions in terms of an objective correlative.

More often the characters' states of mind are revealed in a symbolic action the effectiveness of which depends on close reader-participation rather than author-participation in the emotions. After Coyotito is killed, Kino and Juana come back to their village and walk wordlessly through the crowded streets. "The sun was behind them and their long shadows stalked ahead, and they seemed to carry two towers of darkness with them." They do not pause until they come to the shore.

> And then Kino laid the rifle down, and he dug among his clothes, and then he held the great pearl in his hand. . . . Kino's hand shook a little, and he turned slowly to Juana and held the pearl out to her. She stood beside him, still holding her dead bundle over her shoulder. She looked at the pearl in his hand for a moment and then she looked into Kino's eyes and said softly, "No, you."
> And Kino drew back his arm and flung the pearl with all his might. Kino and Juana watched it go, winking and glimmering under the setting sun. They saw the little splash in the distance, and they stood side by side watching the place for a long time.

This is all there is, but for the reader who has been following the story these bare details are rich with meaning. He knows that when Kino first offers the pearl to Juana he is admitting that she had been right about the evil of the pearl, and he, the leader of the family, wrong. The reader recalls how Kino struck Juana brutally when she had once tried to throw the pearl into the sea and knows that they are both remembering the incident. The reader also understands that in Kino's simple gesture Juana recognizes her triumph and the humility of her man. By her refusal to throw the pearl she gives dignity and pride once more to her husband, whose position it is to do such final things. And all this is understood by Kino as he accepts again his position and throws the pearl into the sea.

The Pearl brings together many of Steinbeck's techniques and pre-occupations as a writer. His tendency to think of groups as unit animals comes up in his description of the "nerve lines" and "units" of a small town. His non-teleological thinking and his unwillingness to assign absolute blame and create "villains" is evident here as in In Dubious Battle, The Grapes of Wrath, The Moon Is Down, and Sea of Cortez. The pearl buyers' motives in attempting to cheat Kino are understood. Like the "owners" of In Dubious Battle and The Grapes of Wrath, they are but part of a system.

> And although these men would not profit beyond their salaries, there was excitement among the pearl buyers, for there was excitement in the hunt, and if it be a man's function to break down a price, then he must take joy and satisfaction in breaking it as far down as possible. For every man in the world functions to the best of his ability, and no one does less than his best, no matter what he may think about it. Quite apart from any reward they might get, from any word of praise, from any promotion, a pearl buyer was a pearl buyer, and the best and happiest pearl buyer was he who bought for the lowest prices.

Another of Steinbeck's strategies found in The Pearl is his technique of interrupting the action to insert a passage illustrating predatory nature as an implicit comment on that action. After the doctor has learned of Kino's great pearl and has come on a professional visit he had previously refused to make, there occurs the following paragraph:

> Out in the estuary a tight woven school of small fishes glittered and broke water to escape a school of great fishes that drove in to eat them. And in the houses the people could hear the swish of the small ones and the bounding splash of the great ones as the slaughter went on. . . . And the night mice crept about the ground and the little night hawks hunted them silently.

This and similar passages serve not to suggest that Nature is evil, but to remind us of man's biological heritage and to reveal the predatory drive beneath his civilized mask. Aesthetically they stem from the same impulse which led Steinbeck to intersperse Tortilla Flat, The Grapes of Wrath, and Cannery Row with little "inner chapters."

But the most interesting feature of The Pearl is that already discussed in part earlier in this essay—the parable or "pattern" tendency of Steinbeck's writing. Although this "pattern" seems just as evident in The Pearl as in Of Mice and Men, it has not received the critical com-

ment accorded to it in the earlier novel. The only extended discussion
of this quality, and the most interesting, is in a review of the book by
Thomas Sugrue.

From the gnostic fragment known as the "Acts of Judas Thomas"
Mr. Sugrue quotes a passage variously called "The Song of the Pearl"
and "Hymn of the Soul": "If thou goest down into Egypt, and bringest
the one pearl, which is in the midst of the sea, hard by the loud breathing serpent, then shalt thou put on thy toga, which is laid over it, and
with thy brother, our next in rank, thou shalt be heir in our kingdom."
Using this passage as a point of departure, Mr. Sugrue pieces out the
allegory of *The Pearl* as follows:

> The biting of the child [Coyotito] by the scorpion, or scarab, signifies
> the entrance of the divine nature into the mind; the pearl of great price,
> the knowledge of spiritual growth, must then be found so that even-
> tually the divine nature can be set free [Kino wishes to use part of the
> money from the pearl for his son's education] . . . . in the black and
> white of folklore Juana, or woman, is the emotion nature [she sucks
> out the scorpion's poison] . . . . The horseman is easy to identify as
> the Spaniard who conquered the Indian, though horsemen represent-
> ing desires of the lower mind normally in folklore pursue the ego in
> quest of the soul. Kino, refusing the adventure of the spirit, renounc-
> ing his opportunity for realization and understanding and identity,
> returns to the rim of unconsciousness, the primitive state wherein
> responsibility resides in nature and wherein man nurses, like a tree, at
> the breast of earth.

Attractive as this allegory may be, there are several difficulties. The
first of these difficulties lies in Mr. Sugrue's assumption that the Indians
of the Gulf have retained "somehow" this "symbology of the pearl."
Even if works like *The Golden Bough* and Joseph Campbell's *The
Hero With a Thousand Faces* suggest that such symbology could appear among the Indians independently of outside influence, the proposed allegory fails to meet the facts of the "pattern" created in *The
Pearl*. If in *Sea of Cortez* Steinbeck reported the tale substantially as
he heard it, and there is no reason to doubt that he did, several objections become evident. First, the story is not an old folk tale, but seems
to be of recent origin, "in recent years," as the author says. Secondly,
several vital details of the allegory are missing in this original: There
is no horseman, no one is bitten by a scorpion, there is no woman, and
the boy does not take the pearl with him in his flight. In the context
of the final form of the story in *The Pearl*, Mr. Sugrue's contention
that Kino refuses "the adventure of the spirit" is out of joint because

Kino returns only after the death of Coyotito, who was the one bitten by the scorpion. Finally, of the apocryphal fragment known as "Hymn to the Soul" only those few lines quoted above have any reference to *The Pearl*.

It is entirely possible, however, that Steinbeck was familiar with the apocryphal fragment. His interest in oriental and apocryphal Christian literature goes back as far as *To A God Unknown*, which takes its title, the name of a character (Rama), and its theme from the Vedic Hymns. While he was working on *The Pearl* he wrote to Pascal Covici about the *Arabian Nights*, "strange how you can find the roots of practically all western stories there." In his letters and fiction there are occasional references to the *Bhagavat-gita*, Buddhism, and oriental concepts of Being. Doc of *Cannery Row* quotes from "Black Marigolds." If Steinbeck put together a sentence from "Hymn of the Soul" and a folk tale he heard in Mexico to suggest a pattern of man's search for his soul, he also gave this union a more materialistic and practical meaning, a meaning related to his own concepts of non-teleological thinking and ecology. It has its roots in the same attitude which produced *Tortilla Flat* and, in the same year as *The Pearl*, *Cannery Row*.

As his brother, Juan Tomás, points out, Kino is not engaged in a private struggle and he is not defying just the pearl buyers, "but the whole structure, the whole way of life." Also, Kino is not the first one who has attempted to redeem his pearl for a greater price. All those who had tried in the past had never been heard of again, and the local priest takes this for a text at least once a year. As Kino sums up the sermon,

> "The loss of the pearl was a punishment visited on those who tried to leave their station. And the father made it clear that each man and woman is like a soldier sent by God to guard some part of the castle of the universe. And some are in the ramparts and some far deep in the darkness of the walls. But each one must remain faithful to his post and must not go running about, else the castle is in danger from the assaults of Hell."

In *Tortilla Flat*, Steinbeck had treated with tongue in cheek a withdrawal from social competition, and in *Cannery Row* he had written of the Virtues, Graces, and Beauties with humorous though serious approval of their acceptance of the position assigned them in "the castle of the universe."

> Our Father who art in nature, who has given the gift of survival to the coyote, the common brown rat, the English sparrow, the house fly and

the moth, must have a great and overwhelming love for no-goods and blots-on-the-town and bums, and Mack and the boys. Virtues and graces and laziness and zest. Our Father who art in nature.

The retreat from competition in these books is an accomplished fact. Both Danny and his paisanos and Mack and the boys have thrown the pearl back into the sea before their stories begin. In *The Pearl* Steinbeck shows one man's struggles against what in *Cannery Row* he had called the "blind jackals" (pearl buyers), the "strictured bulls" (doctor), and the "tigers with ulcers" (pursuing horseman). His great accomplishment in *The Pearl* is that he has been able to give this materialistic level of meaning an archetypal reference, making of this simple story a parable of man's constant spiritual struggle to adjust himself to an essentially materialistic world.

Steinbeck's work shows a persistent interest not only in man's biological heritage, but also in his mythopoeic heritage, as seen in *To A God Unknown, Of Mice and Men, The Grapes of Wrath, The Moon Is Down, The Pearl, Burning Bright,* and *East of Eden.* Taking note of this latter aspect, Harry Slochower groups Steinbeck with Heinrich Mann, Anna Seghers, Mikail Sholokoff, André Malraux, and Thomas Mann, and he says of their work:

. . . [It] acknowledges the power of circumstances, those from above and those from below. And they look back to history and myth for the prototypes of human fate. But they reach back not out of love for the dark night, as is the case with anti-intellectualism, but because with Freud and Marx, they seek the categories which on a higher level chart a liberating future . . . . they are for these men the promises of continuity and recurrence. Their work reclaims our faith in the rationality of man's natural history. It is a kind of moral-esthetic counterpoint to the physical disorder of our day. Their art is the contemporary secular equivalent of man's divinity. In this sense the idea of universal man is not opposed to reason. The archetypal forms remain the same, but the process, meaning and direction depend on the impact of the individual will and of the imagination on the force of circumstances. In short, man can *define* the process of his microcosmic history. To that extent he can mold his fate.

Slochower's reading of Steinbeck is brilliant in its insight, coming as it did before *The Pearl, Burning Bright,* and *East of Eden.* But it had a sound basis in Steinbeck's fiction up through *Cannery Row,* and Steinbeck had said about *Sea of Cortez* that it was a "careful statement of the thesis of work to be done in the future."

Joseph Wood Krutch

JOHN STEINBECK'S
DRAMATIC TALE
OF THREE GENERATIONS

M R. STEINBECK'S new novel is described as his most ambitious effort since "The Grapes of Wrath." That is inevitable, but it is also entirely inadequate because "East of Eden" is a novel planned on the grandest possible scale. In some of his recent books the author may have seemed to be letting himself off easy, but in this he spares nothing. Here is one of those occasions when a writer has aimed high and then summoned every ounce of energy, talent, seriousness and passion of which he was capable. The most unfriendly critic could hardly fail to grant that "East of Eden" is the best as well as the most ambitious book Mr. Steinbeck could write at this moment.

The scene is mostly the Salinas valley in California; the action mostly events in the lives of three generations of two families. In each generation two brothers in one of the families play the leading roles and in each case there is some sort of Cain-Abel relationship between them. Obviously the action is intended to be significant on three levels. In addition to being the story of certain individuals it is a story supposed to illustrate and typify certain phases in the cultural development of America. But that is not all or even the most important intention. Besides being individuals first and types second the characters are also something else—they are also symbols.

Here, so we are being told, is not only the story of certain families and the story of a frontier, but also the story of mankind. Mr. Steinbeck

JOSEPH WOOD KRUTCH now lives in Tucson, Arizona. There, after an eminent career in the East as teacher, scholar, biographer, and critic, he is fashioning a new and equally distinguished career as naturalist while continuing literary work. His recent books include The Voice of the Desert: A Naturalist's Interpretation *and* The Desert Year. *Among earlier volumes were* The Measure of Man, The Best of Two Worlds, Henry David Thoreau, *and* Samuel Johnson. *The review of* East of Eden *is reprinted here from* The New York Herald Tribune Book Review, *September 21, 1955, by permission of the treasurer of* The New York Herald Tribune *and of Mr. Krutch.*

is not, either as man or writer, very much like Thomas Mann, but one thinks of "The Magic Mountain" as the most obvious example of another modern novel which operates upon the same three levels. And like Thomas Mann, Mr. Steinbeck employs almost the whole repertory of novelistic devices. Besides highly dramatized scenes there are panoramic descriptions, philosophic dialogues and interpolated disquisitions in which the author, speaking in his own person, discourses ironically upon such subjects as the whore house as a social institution or what goes on when women meet at the village dressmaker's.

Leaving aside for a moment the question of symbolic meaning, the first thing to be said is that the whole ramifying narrative holds the attention to an extraordinary degree throughout the six hundred long pages. Quiet, almost idyllic, passages alternate with scenes of extravagant violence. There are sadistic beatings, a rape, murders and even worse horrors almost too numerous to count. But considered at least as separate self-contained episodes they nearly always come off because Mr. Steinbeck's talents seem to be under that disciplined, self-critical control too often absent in his lesser works, which often degenerated into sentimental melodrama. The violent scenes are, moreover, thrown into high relief by the consequences of the fact that Mr. Steinbeck seems to know when, as narrator, to participate in the hysteria of the scene, when to withdraw into the detached, faintly ironical spectator. Never, I think, not even in "The Grapes of Wrath," has he exhibited such a grip upon himself and upon his material. If one has sometimes been tempted to dismiss him as merely a routine manipulator of the more obvious tricks of the tough-tender, hardboiled-softboiled school, he cannot be so dismissed here. There is seriousness as well as violence; passion rather than sentimentality. He is also, when the occasion requires, master of a quietly and humorously deft little phrase of description or comment which strikes precisely that note of serenity necessary to highlight the violence. When a wet year came to the Salinas valley "the land would shout with grass." Samuel Hamilton's Irish wife was "a tight hard little woman humorless as a chicken."

What is most likely to disturb a reader, at least during the first third of the book, is the tendency of the characters to turn suddenly at certain moments into obviously symbolic figures as abstract almost as the dramatis personae in a morality play. This awkwardness—and awkward it certainly is—becomes less and less noticeable as the story proceeds. Whether that is because Mr. Steinbeck learns better how to fuse the individual and the symbol or because the reader comes to accept his method I am not quite sure. But in any event it is not because the symbolic intention becomes any less clear or important. In each generation the Abel-Cain relationship is symbolized by a childish gift offered by each brother to the father and always in one case seemingly rejected. And in each generation one of the pair carries a scar on his forehead. Indeed, Mr. Steinbeck states explicitly as one of his theses: "The greatest terror a child can have is that he is not loved, and rejection is the hell he fears. I think everyone in the world to a large or small extent has felt rejection. And with rejection comes anger, and with anger some kind of revenge for rejection, and with the crime, guilt—and there is the story of mankind." Furthermore, the central character in the whole story, a son in the second generation, is named Adam despite the fact that he is also Abel, and his wife (intended perhaps as Lilith) is a figure of pure evil outside the reach of all good human impulses. She was a whore and murderess before she married Adam and she leaves him to become both again.

Mr. Steinbeck does not stop with this attempt to embody a meaningful myth in the chronicle history of a modern family. He goes on to draw a further moral and to pronounce a further thesis. Stated in the barest and most abstract terms this thesis is, first, that Good and Evil are absolute not relative things and, second, that in making a choice between them man is a free agent, not the victim of his heredity, his environment, or of anything else.

This thesis is first announced parenthetically, casually, and without any hint of its importance on page twelve, where it is remarked in passing that the first settlers survived their trials because they were more self-reliant than most people seem to be today, "because they trusted themselves and respected themselves as individuals, because they knew beyond doubt that they were valuable and potentially moral units." Nearly three hundred pages later it receives its most explicit discussion in a dialogue between two of the characters concerning the meaning of a phrase in the Cain-Abel story which refers, apparently, to "sin."

In the King James version the phrase reads "and thou shalt rule over him"; in the American Standard Bible it appears as "Do thou rule over him." But according at least to one of Mr. Steinbeck's characters, the crucial Hebrew word is *timshel* and it means "thou mayest." "Don't you see?" he cried. "The American Standard translation *orders* men to triumph over sin, and you can call sin ignorance. The King James translation makes a promise in 'Thou shalt,' meaning that men will surely triumph over sin. But the Hebrew word, the word *timshel*—'Thou mayest'—that gives a choice. It might be the most important word in the world." And lest we might possibly fail to see that upon this point the whole meaning of the book is intended to depend, its last sentences are: "Adam looked up with sick weariness.—His whispered word seemed to hang in the air: *Timshel!* His eyes closed and he slept."

Moral relativism and some sort of deterministic philosophy have commonly seemed to be implied in the writings of that school of hard-boiled realists with which Mr. Steinbeck has sometimes been loosely associated. It is difficult to imagine how any novel could more explicitly reject both than they are rejected in "East of Eden." The author, who was acclaimed as a social critic in "The Grapes of Wrath" and sometimes abused as a mere writer of sensational melodrama in some subsequent books, plainly announces here that it is as a moralist that he wants to be taken.

The merits of so ambitious and absorbing a book are sure to be widely and hotly debated. The final verdict will not, I think, depend upon the validity of the thesis which is part of a debate almost as old as human thought or upon any possible doubt concerning the vividness of Mr. Steinbeck's storytelling. On the highest level the question is this: Does the fable really carry the thesis; is the moral implicit in or merely imposed upon the story; has the author recreated a myth or merely moralized a tale? There is no question that Mr. Steinbeck has written an intensely interesting and impressive book.

A POSTSCRIPT FROM STEINBECK

December 7, 1956

Dear Mr. Dickey:

I have read with very much interest the book, Steinbeck and His Critics, particularly since I have not seen most of the material before. It is always astonishing to read a critique of one's work. In my own case, it didn't come out that way but emerged little by little, staggering and struggling, each part alone and separated from the others. And then, after the fact—long after—a pattern is discernible, a clear and fairly consistent pattern, even in the failures. It gives me the pleased but uneasy feeling of reading my own epitaph.

So many of the judgments and arguments in this book of opinions seem to me to be true. I only wonder why I didn't think of them myself. I guess I was so lost in the books I couldn't see the long structure. Of course, in this river of opinion there are special pleaders—men who were backing their own particular horses—but also there seem to me to be many accuracies.

It is interesting to me that so many critics, instead of making observations, are led to bring charges. It is not observed that I find it valid to understand man as an animal before I am prepared to know him as man. It is charged that I have somehow outraged members of my species by considering them part of a species at all. And how often the special pleaders use my work as a distorted echo chamber for their own ideas!

I am pleased and grateful for the enormous research and work that has gone into this book. What a huge amount of reading must have

JOHN STEINBECK was sent a set of page proofs for the present book just before printing with a letter from the University of New Mexico Press inviting him to comment. Mr. Steinbeck's warm letter of response and the short article, "Rationale," which he enclosed, are reproduced here. A telegram asking permission to publish the two pieces and inquiring about his forthcoming Viking Press book, obtained this reply, dated December 12, 1956: CERTAINLY YOU MAY USE LETTER AND RATIONALE. NEW BOOK IS AN ATTEMPT AT SATIRE, CALLED THE SHORT REIGN OF PEPPIN THE FOURTH. REGARDS. JOHN STEINBECK.

been done. This cannot fail to be flattering to me and I love compliments.

This book does make me aware of how long I have been at it. Good God, I must have been writing for hundreds of years. But I must assure you that it fails to make me feel old or finished or fixed. Perhaps my new book falls into the pattern, and perhaps the two books in process will drift in the inevitable stream—but to me they are new and unique in the world and I am as scared and boastful and humble about them as I was a thousand years ago when I began the first one. And it is just as hard and I am just as excited as I was. The approach to a horizon makes the horizon leap away. And the more one learns about writing, the more unbelievably difficult it becomes. I wish to God I knew as much about my craft, or whatever it is, as I did when I was 19 years old. But with every new attempt, frightening though it may be, is the wonder and the hope and the delight. As the angels said in Petracca, " 'Che luce è questa e qual nova beltate?' "

Perhaps you will be interested in a "Rationale" prepared some time ago. Anyway, I include it.

Yours sincerely,

John Steinbeck

John Steinbeck

RATIONALE

RECENTLY I was asked by a University for a Rationale of the corpus of my work. I didn't know the word.

The Oxford Dictionary defines a "Rationale" as: 1. A reasoned exposition of principles, an explanation or statement of reasons, a set of reasoned rules or directions; and 2. The fundamental reason, the logical or rational basis for anything. Or in simpler words—what did you write and why did you write it?

There may be writers who before the fact of writing may have been able to do this. In my own case, I fear that a *rationale* might well be a rationalization, undertaken after the fact—a critic's rather than a writer's approach. It is like asking a prisoner, "Why did you commit murder?" His reply might be, "Let me think. I guess I didn't like the guy, and— well I was mad." He can work out why he did it but he can't really remember the emotional pressure which drifted his hand toward the knife.

So in my work I can say, "It must have been this way or this"—but I am not at all sure that I remember. I can say of one book, "I suppose I saw things which made me angry." Of another, "It was just an idea which amused me and I wrote it." Of another, "It is possible that I was trying to explain something—something that was not clear to me. I may have felt that writing it would make me understand it better."

My basic rationale might be that I like to write. I feel good when I am doing it—better than when I am not. I find joy in the texture and tone and rhythms of words and sentences, and when these happily combine in a "thing" that has texture and tone and emotion and design and architecture, there comes a fine feeling—a satisfaction like that which follows good and shared love. If there have been difficulties and failures overcome, these may even add to the satisfaction.

As for my "reasoned exposition of principles," I suspect that they are no different from those of any man living out his life. Like everyone, I want to be good and strong and virtuous and wise and loved. I think that writing may be simply a method or technique for communication with other individuals; and its stimulus, the loneliness we are born to. In writing, perhaps we hope to achieve companionship. What some people find in religion, a writer may find in his craft or whatever it is,—absorption of the small and frightened and lonely into the whole and complete, a kind of breaking through to glory.

A lady of my acquaintance was asked by her young daughters where babies came from, and after making certain that they really wanted to know, she told them. They listened solemnly and at the end, the mother asked, "Now are you sure you understand?"

The oldest girl said, "Yes, we understand what you do—but why do you do it?"

The mother thought for a moment and then replied, "Because it's fun!"

And that could well be my rationale. My work is and has been fun. Within myself, I find no hunger to inquire further.

❲

A CHECKLIST
OF STEINBECK'S BOOKS

1929 The Cup of Gold
1932 The Pastures of Heaven
1933 To a God Unknown
1935 Tortilla Flat
1936 In Dubious Battle
   Saint Katy the Virgin
   (included in The Long Valley)
1937 Of Mice and Men (play)
   Of Mice and Men (novel)
   The Red Pony
   (also later included in The Long Valley)
1938 Their Blood Is Strong
   (a reprint of articles that had appeared in 1936
   in The San Francisco News)
   The Long Valley
1939 The Grapes of Wrath
1941 The Forgotten Village
   (script for a documentary filmed in Mexico)
   Sea of Cortez (with Ed Ricketts)
1942 The Moon Is Down (play)
   The Moon Is Down (novel)
   Bombs Away
1943 The Portable Steinbeck
   (Revised edition issued January, 1946, with
   introduction by Lewis Gannett
   and additional material)
1945 Cannery Row
   The Pearl of the World
   (serialized in The Woman's Home Companion)
1947 The Wayward Bus
   The Pearl
   A Russian Journal
1950 Burning Bright
   The Log from Sea of Cortez
1952 East of Eden
1954 Sweet Thursday